SEE DAD COOK

SEE DAD
COOK

The Only Book a Guy Needs
to Feed Family and Friends
(and Himself)

WAYNE HARLEY BRACHMAN

Clarkson Potter/Publishers
New York

ALSO BY WAYNE HARLEY BRACHMAN

American Desserts

Retro Desserts

Cakes and Cowpokes

Copyright © 2006 by Wayne Harley Brachman
Illustrations copyright © 2006 by Nigel Holmes

Published in the United States by Clarkson Potter/Publishers, an imprint of the
Crown Publishing Group, a division of Random House, Inc., New York.
www.crownpublishing.com
www.clarksonpotter.com

Clarkson N. Potter is a trademark and Potter and colophon are registered trademarks
of Random House, Inc.

Library of Congress Cataloging-in-Publication Data
Brachman, Wayne Harley.
    See Dad cook: the only book a guy needs to feed family and friends (and himself)
/ Wayne Harley Brachman.
    Includes index.
1. Cookery, American.   I. Title
TX715.B79375   2006
641.5973—dc22   2005024242

ISBN 13: 978-1-4000-8187-5
ISBN 10: 1-4000-8187-4

Printed in the United States of America

Design by Jane Treuhaft

10   9   8   7   6   5   4   3   2   1

First Edition

JUL

2006

FOR MY DAUGHTERS, VIOLET AND ISABELLA,

and their great-grandma Bessie,
who taught me how to cook

CONTENTS→

INTRODUCTION

You wake 'em up, dress 'em, make 'em breakfast, and pack their lunches (doesn't anybody like the same thing?). You referee the first battle in front of the television. Then, it's brush their teeth, fix their hair, and get 'em to pee (not necessarily in that order). They're going to be late for school again. Finally at the door—wait!—is everything in their backpacks?

If this sounds like your kind of morning, then **YOU MUST BE A . . . DADDY!**

Today, Dad has to work, clean, take the kids to ballet class, and, more often than not, cook. Sure, you can order takeout or haul the family off to some restaurant, but just about anything you make at home will be cheaper and healthier and—once you've got your kitchen skills going—will taste a whole lot better than the artificially flavored, chemically enhanced, precooked, portion-controlled sludge that they dole out at those fast-food franchises and restaurant chains. Another important benefit of cooking is that you get to sit down at the dinner table, as a family, in your own home. After all, the communal ceremony of cooking and eating together is one of the oldest and most unifying of human, tribal rituals, dating back to the time of Fred Flintstone.

If you are reading this book, then you already know that today's dad has to be lean, has to be mean, and, even more important, has to have a pot roast working in the oven. So, what do you do if you've never filled a pot with water, let alone boiled any? Well, if you want to take up golf, you go to a pro and take lessons, right? If you want some cooking skills, you need some guidance also. Well, lucky for you, I happen to be a professional chef and can teach you the ins and outs of slicing and dicing, sautéing and roasting, mixing and baking. But I'm also a dad, so I know how to cook in the real world—in a home kitchen, where you've got limited time and space and a family full of finicky eaters driving you wacko. This cookbook, full of battlefield-tested, family-functional recipes, will teach you how to make delicious, home-style food for your family, your friends, and yourself. Once you get started, you'll find that cooking can be a lot of fun and infinitely less frustrating than, say, chasing a little ball around a golf course. In a relatively short time, preparing the family's meals could be almost as easy as turning on the TV and falling asleep on the couch.

FEEDING KIDS: YOUR DINING ROOM TABLE AS BATTLEFIELD

Feeding kids can be a unique experience, very much like feeding cats, dogs, or other animals—wild animals—on a rampage. Their palates are different than ours and so are their eating quirks. Some of them will go ballistic if a single pea touches a single carrot. They can also change radically from day to day. Last week they loved the mac and cheese; tonight it's "yucky." On Monday, they eat like birds; on Tuesday, they're pterodactyls. As you probably know by now, growing up is a mysterious and unpredictable process. Never assume that your kids have been miraculously cured of some finicky habit or, conversely, that they will never outgrow it. Don't get upset; they just may not be ready for asparagus or eggplant. Then again, they could also have a culinary epiphany when you least expect it. Aim to have them try just one bite of new food, and always keep in mind that when they get picky and hard to please, it probably has nothing to do with your cooking. They are just being kids. Chill out and go with the flow.

Your constant goal should be to have them eat a variety of healthy foods. Even if you serve something as low-down as chicken-fried steak, pair it with string beans and fresh corn. Meals should look completely balanced, like those school charts with all of the food groups.

Peace, love,
AND EATING LIKE AN ADULT EVERY NOW AND THEN

If you are entertaining another family, you may want to serve two different meals: one for the kiddies and something more sophisticated for the adults. Feeding the youngsters in a separate shift allows you to give them all of your attention and a meal that they will enjoy. You can then stick them in front of a movie while you and your guests enjoy dinner in peace, grown-up style— remember that?

Like many other skills, getting your children to eat without incident can be a matter of having a few tricks up your sleeve and the right attitude. Try to pick plates, cups, and utensils that match exactly. This will prevent the battle over who gets the ducky and who gets the dinosaur. Kids need to do things by themselves but may not have the motor skills or know-how to do so. They will pour a quart of ketchup on their French fries, and then complain that there's too much. To minimize spillage and other potential disasters, put sauces and condiments in little bowls and containers (kids love little containers). I like to use little squeeze bottles, which are available at kitchen supply shops and, believe it or not, beauty supply shops.

HOW TO COOK WITH THE KIDS

Cooking is fun, but letting your children join in and help you cook is a truly rewarding experience for all concerned. Everything will take five times longer than normal and you'll have to clean half of the ingredients up from the floor, but big deal. Chores and assignments need to be age appropriate. It's a thrill for even the tiniest tots to just push the button on the blender (with your supervision, of course). Then they can claim that they helped to make the salad dressing (and they're more likely to eat that salad). Let young children measure and add ingredients like bread crumbs or milk, peel vegetables, and count ingredients. Bigger kids can crack eggs, open cans, or grate cheese. All kids love to mix just about anything. Most teenagers don't want to be told what to do. Give them a part of a recipe to execute and some casual advice, but don't freak out if they make a mistake; that's how they learn. Make sure that all children wash their hands before and after cooking, especially if they have touched raw meat or eggs.

TOOLS

As with so many other things, the sky can be the limit when it comes to outfitting a kitchen with equipment. But you really don't need all that much to get started. A knife or two, a few basic pots, pans, and utensils, and you're on your way. In the vast majority of circumstances, you get what you pay for. My brother-in-law got me a wrench at the 99-cent store that is actually useful, but I wouldn't go back there to stock my workshop. If you want to look good, you spring for a nice suit. If you want to cook good, you might want to splurge on a couple of quality knives and pans. Here's what to look for.

Knives (and a cutting board)

It's better to have two good knives than an arsenal of junk. Knives fused from one piece of stainless steel will have the best balance. The softer the steel the easier it will be to sharpen, but avoid carbon steel, which stains, wears down too easily, and requires frequent sharpening. Look for stainless steel,

the type used for many German and Japanese knives. For best balance, the steel blade should run all the way through the handle.

You can accomplish most kitchen tasks with **a four-inch paring knife and either an eight-inch chef's knife or a seven-inch santoku,** a Japanese-style knife. Also useful would be **a serrated bread knife.** If you really get into cooking, you may want an eight-inch slicer and a six-inch utility knife and maybe a boner. Choose European or Asian designs (see illustrations below). You will also need some kind of **sharpening device.** For daily sharpening and fine-tuning, a steel is the best choice. Whip out a steel and your blade—everyone will know that you mean business. Pick one that matches your knife set, so it will have the correct Rockwell hardness rating. When you need to redo your edge, use a stone or a reputable sharpening device. You can also take your knife to a pro sharpener.

The only place to do knife work is on a cutting board. Choose a polypropylene board that can go right into the dishwasher. Never slice food

in the pan. You will destroy the surface of the pan and the edge of the knife.

Once you've purchased some knives and a cutting board, you'll want to learn a few moves.

➡ **To hold a knife,** grab the top of the blade on opposite sides with your thumb and index finger right next to where it meets the handle. (This is the actual fulcrum of the knife.) Curl your remaining three fingers around the handle as if you're holding a bat or a golf club. This grip will give you the most control and balance for cutting.

➡ **To slice, say, a carrot,** lay it down on a cutting board so the part that you want to cut first is facing to the right. (Lefties will have to reverse these directions.) Curl the fingers of your left hand on the top of the carrot with your nails digging in slightly to hold it down. Now, look straight down: you should not be able to see your fingernails. Tuck your left thumb behind your fingers and use it to push the food. Using your curled fingers as a guide for the knife, slice straight down.

➡️ **To slice an onion,** cut it in half through the root end. Peel it. Lay one half down with the root pointing to the left, then hold your hands as above. Using your curled fingers as a guide, slice.

➡️ **To chop an onion,** cut it in half through the root end. Peel it. Lay one half down with the root on your left. Pointing the knife tip toward the root, cut vertical slices, leaving the root intact so the onion doesn't 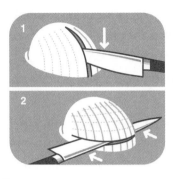  fall apart. Starting at the bottom, cut a few horizontal slices. Finally, slice the onion in downward slices. It will fall into diced pieces.

➡️ **To mince an onion,** first chop it with the above method, then finely mince it with the two-handed chop, below.

➡️ **For two-handed chopping and mincing,** grab the top of the blade with one hand at each end. Hold the point end down with your left hand to create a fulcrum and chop with a rocking motion. Use the blade to rake the ingredients back into a pile, and chop some more.

Pots and Pans

If you want to grow a petunia, you need a pot. If you want to cook . . . same deal, except you will need more of a variety. Pots and pans should be made of material that conducts heat well and should have a nonreactive surface. The most practical choices are pots made of thick anodized aluminum or aluminum pots with stainless-steel interiors. Nonstick surfaces are easy to clean and require less oil when cooking, but the nonstick surface eventually wears away (and may be dangerous if brought to too high a temperature over direct heat). Stainless steel with a laminated aluminum or copper bottom is another very good choice. Just make sure the bottom is thick and heavy and not just for show. Enameled iron is a great choice for a Dutch oven.

Get at least one **saucepan** that has a capacity of two quarts or more. These are great for everything from cooking rice to reheating pasta sauce. Speaking of pasta, you'll also need a big pot for cooking noodles and making soup.

Pros call a slope-sided fry pan a sauté pan. They use it for everything from frying eggs to pan-roasting meat. If you go into a store and ask for a sauté pan, you'll probably get a chicken fryer (which the pros call a *sauteuse*). For simplicity's sake, we will call all pans of the frying ilk "skillets" and the best choice for a **skillet** is a slope-sided one. Ideally you should have an eight-inch, a ten-inch, and a twelve-inch, but, for starters, you can accomplish most tasks with a ten-inch.

Beyond these bare essentials, I also recommend a heavy, lidded braising pan or Dutch oven for pot roasts and stews; a heavy ten by sixteen-inch aluminum roasting pan for the roasting of chickens, potatoes, and meat loaves; and a three-quart ceramic, enamel, or nonreactive metal baking pan for macaroni and cheese and other casserole-type dishes. If you want to bake some cookies, you'll need a nonstick cookie sheet. (It can also function as a cover for large pots and pans if you don't have a big enough lid for them.) A nonstick muffin pan and a loaf pan are also good to have if you want to do some baking.

Utensils, Gadgets, and Other Equipment

It's easy to go insane with kitchen utensils. Calm down; you don't need too many, and there are an awful lot of silly, useless gadgets out there. Here are some of the tools that are most essential. Keep in mind that if you use non-stick or anodized aluminum pots and pans, you should only use nylon or wooden tools on them. Check the manufacturer's recommendations.

To start, you'll need some **basic, basic tools:**

➡ A few mixing bowls

➡ A colander for draining pasta, among other things

➡ Professional spring-loaded stainless-steel tongs

➡ A couple of spatulas—a soft rubber one for folding and a stiff one for flipping and turning hot foods in a skillet—and assorted spoons

➡ A peeler. Try to find one that is shaped like a wishbone. It will be ergonomically easier to use.

➡ A ten-inch wire whisk for making sauces, gravy, and dressing. Look for a slightly tapered shape with thin wires.

➡ A box grater (one of those rectangular graters with different sizes of grates and shredders on each side) for shredding cabbage to make coleslaw or for grating. If you like to grate fresh cheese onto pasta, opt for an individual cheese grater with a handle, so you can take it to the dinner table.

Down the road, you may want some **more advanced equipment:**

➡ A food blender and/or processor for assorted chopping and blending chores like making dressings or finely mincing

➡ If you get serious about baking, you will want an electric mixer. A stand mixer, like the one made by KitchenAid, makes doughs and batters a cinch.

➡ For more accurate frying, you may want to have a candy or deep-frying thermometer that will tell you the exact temperature of your oil. Get one with a clip, so it can hook onto the side of the pan.

➡ You can make do with paper towels, but a salad spinner will thoroughly and easily dry lettuce without bruising it.

➡ Quality plastic or glass storage containers with tight-sealing lids will prolong the life of leftovers and sauces. You can wash and reuse plastic take-out containers for this purpose, but always check to make sure that they are microwave safe before popping them into the microwave.

INGREDIENTS

Now that you have the tools, it's time to hit the market.

Meat

You can go to a good butcher shop and get prime steaks, chops, and poultry, but there are also plenty of quality selections at the supermarket. It's all about knowing how to choose wisely. Start out by checking the "sell by" date on the label to make sure that the meat is fresh. Red meat should look bright red; pork and veal should be pink. Avoid buying meat with brown discoloration. It may just be caused by minor oxidation, but this is not a good starting point for your family's dinner. (If it turns brown in your home refrigerator, it may still be okay. All meat and poultry should be able to pass the "stink test." Pick it up and give it a good whiff. There should be virtually no odor at all.) Designer labels usually indicate quality. The livestock have been better selected and cared for and raised on more wholesome diets, and are usually free of additives. This translates into better flavor. Ditto for products that have been labeled as organic, grain-fed, or free-range. To save time and labor, buy meat and poultry that is cut exactly the way you will need it. Fat is an integral part of any steak, chop, or burger. In the right place and amount, it plainly translates into good flavor, so make sure there is a moderate amount, evenly marbled through the meat. Excess fat around the outer edges should be trimmed away, leaving a layer no thicker than one eighth inch. Unless you plan on braising the meat (as in pot roast), avoid cuts that have thick lines of gristle or tendon running through them. To find out more about specific cuts of meat, refer to the individual recipes.

Fish and Shellfish

Unless it is purchased canned or frozen, seafood must be absolutely fresh. Buy your fish from a place that looks like it has a brisk turnover. Seafood should smell like the ocean and never "fishy" or ammoniated. When you buy fish at a seafood shop, you can inspect the whole fish and have the monger fillet it. It should have clear eyes and red gills and be coated in a very thin, shiny layer of natural slime. At the supermarket, read the "sell by" date on packages of fillets and steaks. Store seafood in the lowest part of your refrigerator (which is probably the coldest) and use it as soon as possible, preferably the same day you buy it. Many grocers are now carrying high-quality frozen fish, which is an excellent alternative to fresh. Defrost overnight in the refrigerator before cooking. For more information on shrimp, see page 103.

Seafood, especially larger fish, may contain mercury. Children and pregnant women should not have more than one six-ounce serving of tuna, swordfish, mako, mahi-mahi, or any other large fish per week.

Dairy

As with other foods, the best dairy products should be free of chemicals and other industrial-strength means of production. Look for products that are labeled as such. Milk, especially for kids, should be free of antibiotics and growth hormones. The most important thing to check on dairy products is the "sell by" date. Make sure that it will give you a reasonable amount of time to use it up after purchase.

Large eggs are the standard size for recipes in this book (and most other cookbooks). The healthiest and best-tasting eggs will be from chickens that are grain-fed, free-range, and antibiotic-free.

Pro chefs always reach for unsalted butter. Salt is added to butter to extend shelf life, but it also inhibits the development of the enzymes that give butter flavor. Salted butter ends up tasting like salt and oil, while unsalted butter tastes like . . . butter. Unsalted butter is the only kind that should be used for baking. Whether you believe they are butter or not, there are lots of quality butter substitutes on the market. Feel free to use them instead of real butter, especially if you need to control fat, calorie, or cholesterol intake. You may also want to use products that are low in, or do not contain, partially hydrogenated oils (a.k.a. trans fat).

Produce

Today, you can find just about any fruit or vegetable at any time of the year. A lot of this produce is grown to look good after long-distance travel and may not have the best flavor or nutritional value. Fruits and vegetables are best when they are in season. Get your peaches in the summer and your pears in the fall. For even finer tuning of your selection, try to purchase produce that has been locally grown without too much help from chemicals. Shop at farmer's markets or quality grocers and check out old-fashioned or heirloom varieties for best flavor.

For purchasing tips on individual fruits and vegetables, refer to specific recipes. There are, however, two important vegetables that you will be handling regularly: onions and garlic.

Spanish onions are the big, yellow ones that are in between a softball and a baseball in size. A large yellow onion will be around the size of a cue ball. Both kinds are inexpensive and the most flavorful onions for cooking. You can use them interchangeably. Either one should be nice and firm, with no signs of gray mold under the skin or outer layer. Of course there are plenty of other onions around, like Vidalias or red, but they are better eaten raw. Refer to the section on knife skills for how to cut onions (page 15).

Garlic should feel firm and have a little heft to it (pick up a few heads and compare). Make sure that there is no gray mold lurking under the first layer of skin. When you cut a clove open, it should be creamy white, with no green stripe running down the center. To peel garlic, first tear away the dry outer skin, and then break the cloves off the head. Lay a clove flat and place the flat side of a wide knife on top of it. With the butt of your hand, forcefully press the blade down until the skin cracks. The skin should slip off easily.

Dry Goods and Other Pantry Staples

Many of the ingredients that you will be cooking with will come right off the supermarket shelf and need little introduction. Others may need a bit of explanation. As you get further into meal planning, you will know better about just which staples you will need to keep on hand for your family. (In the meantime, the following list is a good place to start.)

There are times when you may be itching to cook, but don't have enough time to make everything from scratch. It's a good strategy to have a "spare meal" or two tucked away. Keep a stash of frozen, breaded chicken or fish fillets in the freezer. You can serve them with a fresh vegetable or, conversely, keep frozen peas and corn around as a quick accompaniment for burgers or steaks. Always be prepared to get a good meal out fast and not a bad meal out half fast.

Since you don't want to be running to the supermarket for every ingredient, you should keep Old Papa Hubbard's cupboard stocked with staples like pasta, rice, flour, and mayonnaise. As you progress and develop a repertoire of recipes, you will get a better handle on just what backups you need to keep on hand.

Here's a list of groceries that you will want to have on hand.

Vegetable oil
   (preferably canola)
Extra-virgin olive oil
Nonstick vegetable oil
   spray
Red wine vinegar
   and/or balsamic
   vinegar
Salt
Pepper
Chicken bouillon
Chili powder
Ground cumin
Rice
Pasta
Bread crumbs
   (preferably
   Japanese panko)
Ketchup

Mustard
Mayonnaise
Milk
Eggs
Butter
Parmesan or Pecorino
   Romano cheese
Onions
Garlic
Carrots
Celery
Lemons or limes
Frozen peas
Frozen corn
Frozen French fries
Frozen fish fillets
Frozen breaded
   chicken cutlets
Ice cream

All-purpose flour
Baking powder
Baking soda
Sugar
Light brown sugar
Dark brown sugar
Confectioners' sugar
Maple syrup
Bread
Dry cereal
Crackers
Chips or other snacks
Juice
(And don't forget the
   beer!)

OIL

Throughout this book you will see recommendations for canola oil. (No, I don't own a canola oil well and I don't get kickbacks from the canola squeezers' syndicate.) Almost all chefs genuinely swear by the stuff because it has a very high smoking point, so it doesn't burn easily and is relatively flavorless. It also has no trans fat and is extremely low in saturated fat, two qualities that make it extremely heart-friendly.

Quality olive oil is a great investment, but don't go hog wild and buy too much. It starts to lose its flavor soon after the lid gets popped. Buy as much as you can use up within two or three months.

At room temperature, extra-virgin olive oil has an incomparably rich and fruity flavor. Just a little bit of the stuff can turn a humdrum salad into a masterpiece. But cooking with it is like trying to putt with a TaylorMade driver. Sure it's top of the line, but it burns at a very low temperature, making it the wrong oil for cooking. Mixing canola and olive oils together will give you a blend that can withstand the heat of a sauté pan but has a rich olive flavor. (This concept also applies to butter, which should also be mixed with canola oil when heated to high temperatures.)

FLOUR

All-purpose flour is the only kind that you will need for most recipes. If you get serious about baking you might want to hunt down some cake flour. Because of its low protein content, it will make lighter, fluffier cakes and biscuits. Don't use self-rising flour, which has leavening agents added to it and can screw up your recipe. Unbleached flour will be less processed than bleached.

SUGAR

Granulated sugar is not just for desserts. Use it in everything from pancakes (see page 30) to carrots (page 173). Brown sugar is granulated sugar that has had the molasses (originally removed during processing) replaced. Confectioners' sugar is milled to a fine powder and has a small amount of starch in it to prevent clumping. It is good for whipped cream and for dusting on baked goods.

DRY SPICES

Dry spices tend to get stale relatively quickly, so buy them in small amounts that you know you can use up. You won't save a buck by buying that eight-pound bargain jug of Egyptian fenugreek. A good place to purchase spices is at specialty or health food stores that sell them in bulk but let you pack them yourself. This way you can get a small amount at a reasonable price. Make sure to store your spices in airtight containers and get rid of them when they go stale. In general, spices start to lose their potency a couple of months after they are opened.

Pepper tastes best if it is freshly ground. If you don't have a pepper mill you should buy ground pepper in small amounts. Black pepper has a nicer flavor than white pepper, which can taste slightly sour or tart. Chefs use white pepper when they don't want it to be seen, like in a white sauce, mashed potatoes, or macaroni and cheese.

SALT

Is all that salt the same? Pro chefs hardly ever use common, iodized table salt. It has a weird flavor and the crystals are way too small. It is hard to feel them between your fingers, so you can't get an accurate read on how much you are sprinkling. Sea salt and kosher salt taste much better and have larger crystals. (There is an exception to all of this. The large crystals in kosher and coarse sea salt will actually cut the albumen in egg whites, inhibiting cakes from rising. For baking, use table salt or fine-crystal sea salt.)

BOUILLON CUBES

When I first started out as a line cook, we used a great cheap-shot trick that, if done properly, would give everything, from sauces to vegetables, a real flavor boost. We would substitute something called "base" (essentially powdered bouillon cube) for some of the salt in our sauces, a little chicken base in a chicken sauce, beef base in a beef sauce, and so on. Today, most chefs chortle and guffaw when I tell them about this, but at least one superstar chef (whose name will not be revealed) still very successfully uses this ploy. Throughout this book, you will see bouillon cubes being used as a substitute

You know the expiration date that's printed on the label of a bottle of water? It was put there as a marketing ploy. Expired water is an oxymoron. What's it gonna do, turn into H₃O? Maybe the plastic bottle will one day deteriorate, but the oceans have been around for a gazillion years and, unless the seal is opened and bacteria get in, the water in the bottle will last for a gazillion more.

for "base." When used conservatively, they can add an amazing amount of flavor distance to your cooking drive in everything from gravy to broccoli.

WATER

Yes, water is an ingredient, and you should give it a little attention. If a recipe calls for hot water, don't use the stuff from the faucet. It tastes like tin can and could contain all sorts of junk, maybe even lead. Put filtered, bottled, or cold tap water in a saucepan and heat it up. Unless your local water is grade "A" and flavorless, use filtered or bottled water for all culinary purposes.

A FEW TIPS BEFORE YOU START

The secret to successful cooking lies in the difference between how amateurs cook and how pros cook. The home cook often attacks a recipe in its entirety, mixing the chopping and prepping and the actual cooking into one big Texas cage match. They start heating the oil, then chop up the garlic. While the garlic is cooking, they trim and slice the broccoli . . . oops, the garlic just burned. With this free-for-all approach there is little room to roll with the punches but plenty of latitude for panic. Professionals, on the other hand, completely separate the prep phase from the cooking. They wash, trim, and otherwise prepare every ingredient before anything goes into a hot pan. It's a process called setting the *mise en place,* or getting everything ready and in its place. The pro would mince his garlic, trim and slice the broccoli, and measure out every other ingredient that he will need. Then, and only then, would he start to cook. This is how restaurant cooks can crank out hundreds of meals, one after another, without a hitch.

The first thing to do when you look at a recipe is actually read it. Go through the ingredient list and the directions, and then figure out what you will need. If you have to go shopping, write out a grocery list. Pull out the pans, chop the onions, mince the garlic, measure the cream, whatever. You want to be first and ten, instead of fourth and scrambling for a play.

Most recipes can be broken down into very simple, doable steps, and the more you cook, the smoother it will get.

THE TWO WORLDS OF
BREAKFAST

Pancakes
French Toast
Scrambled Eggs
Fried Eggs
Huevos Rancheros
Breakfast Burrito
Bacon
Grilled Ham
Oatmeal

"It's the most important meal of the day." Well, it is according to those PBS puppets. But you don't have to take Grover or Big Bird's word for it. You know from experience that getting your family off to a good start in the morning can make a huge difference in how they handle their day. Here are the basics for the breakfasts kids love.

ON WEEKENDS IT'S EASY to supervise everything and make sure the whole clan is starting the day out right. Dad can casually take the kitchen over as his own personal domain, get a groove on, and flip some flapjacks. DURING THE WEEK IS ANOTHER STORY ENTIRELY, when it becomes a berserk scramble to get a wholesome meal down their gullets and pack 'em off to school. What makes that weekday breakfast so difficult is that you have an enormous check list to get through: comb their hair, brush their teeth, pack their lunches, and look for that last page of math homework (it's behind the couch), other sock (under the pillow), and lunchbox (full of worms in the backyard). If Saturday and Sunday are like feeding the sea lions at the zoo, Monday turns into live alligator wrestling.

All of these breakfast recipes are meant to stick to your kids' ribs and fuel the furnace for a while, but it's still a good idea to serve fresh fruit on the side. If you are pressed for time, frozen waffles, dry cereal, toast, muffins, or other breakfast pastries can be brought in as pinch hitters, but then you absolutely need that fresh fruit to balance things out and give them a jolt of vitamins and nutrients.

PANCAKES

Assembling the batter for these big, fluffy pancakes is almost as easy as opening up a box of the instant stuff. It can be quickly thrown together for Sunday morning with the family and, if you need to feed a whole bunch of hungry breakfasters, the recipe can be doubled or tripled. If you are making pancakes for a crowd, you will need a game plan. Some people like to stash the first few panfuls in a slow oven (275°F) or put them on a plate and cover with foil. This will keep them warm while the rest of the batter gets cooked off, but they get kinda steamed up. Another approach is to just stay in the kitchen and keep on cooking until everyone has a plateful. This way everyone gets perfect pancakes, hot off the griddle. Knock off the last batch for yourself. You can then call it quits and relax with your own breakfast. There are some other benefits to this method. After a display of self-sacrifice like this, you will probably be excused from any other family chores or duty for a while.

Cook your flapjacks in a skillet or on a griddle. Don't bother serving butter with these flapjacks. Just put some extra butter in the pan to give them a great, crisp exterior and a blast of buttery flavor.

Monday morning might be rough, but you can at least get breakfast covered. If you make some extra pancake batter on Sunday, it will keep, covered, in the refrigerator for 24 hours.

2 tablespoons unsalted butter, plus more for cooking the pancakes

1 cup all-purpose flour

1 tablespoon sugar

$3/4$ teaspoon baking powder

$1/4$ teaspoon baking soda

$1/4$ teaspoon salt

1 large egg

1 cup buttermilk

Vegetable oil (preferably canola), for cooking the pancakes

Maple syrup and berries, for serving

1. In a large skillet, melt 2 tablespoons of butter over low heat. Do this in the pan that you are going to make the pancakes in. Set aside.

2. Put the flour, sugar, baking powder, baking soda, and salt in a large bowl and mix together. Make a well in the center and add the egg and buttermilk. Stir it all together with a spoon until the big lumps are gone. Add the melted butter and stir until just barely combined. (The batter should still have small lumps.) Let sit for 5 minutes.

3. Heat the skillet over medium heat for 1 minute. Add $1\frac{1}{2}$ teaspoons butter and $1\frac{1}{2}$ teaspoons oil and heat to sizzling, about 1 minute more.

4. Working in batches, pour $\frac{1}{3}$ cup batter for each pancake into the skillet. They will spread, so leave room. Cook until the bubbles that appear on the surface start to pop and the undersides of the pancakes are golden brown, about 3 minutes. Flip the pancakes over and cook until golden brown on the second side, 1 to 2 minutes more. Continue with the rest of the batter, adding more butter and oil when needed.

5. Serve with syrup and fresh berries.

DO IT LIKE THE PROS

Do not overmix! Overworked pancakes will have a dense and rubbery texture. Mix the ingredients just enough so they come together. Your batter should look lumpy but should not have any dry patches of flour.

BLUEBERRY, RASPBERRY, OR BANANA PANCAKES
Sprinkle 1 to 3 tablespoons of berries or 4 or 5 slices of banana over the batter for each pancake just after you spoon it into the pan. Cook as above.

CHOCOLATE CHIP PANCAKES
Mix $\frac{1}{2}$ cup chocolate chips into the batter. Cook as above.

SPRINKLE PANCAKES
Sprinkle 1 teaspoon rainbow sprinkles or jimmies over the batter for each pancake just after you spoon it into the pan. Cook as above. Serve bottom side up.

FRENCH TOAST

Makes 6 to 8 pieces

White bread, whole wheat, baguette, or whatever's available, even stale bread will work. That's what makes horse racing and also makes French toast. The trick to making French toast that's crisp on the outside and custardy (but not soggy) on the inside is in the dunking—a little less for light, fresh bread and a little more for dense stuff that's been around for a while. If you are cooking for younger children, slice their French toast into sticks. It might turn out to be the little trick that gets them to sit still and finish without a fuss.

3 large eggs
1 cup milk
Vegetable oil (preferably canola), for cooking
Unsalted butter, for cooking
6 to 8 slices brioche, challah, white or wheat bread, or
   12 $^3/_4$-inch diagonal slices French or Italian bread
Maple syrup and berries or jam, for serving

1. Put the eggs and milk in a large bowl and whisk together.

2. Heat a large skillet over medium heat for 1 minute. Add 1 tablespoon oil and 1 tablespoon butter and heat to sizzling, about 1 minute more.

3. One at a time, dunk the bread slices into the eggy milk mixture for 3 to 8 seconds on each side to soak up some of the liquid (white bread will just take 3 seconds, baguette about 8), then place as many slices of bread as will comfortably fit in the pan in a single layer. Cook until golden brown on the bottom, about 4 minutes. Flip the toast over and cook the other side until brown, about 4 minutes more. Continue with the rest of the batch, adding more oil and butter, when needed.

4. Serve with maple syrup and berries or jam.

CINNAMON FRENCH TOAST

Add 1 teaspoon cinnamon and 1 tablespoon sugar to the egg and milk mixture.

VANILLA FRENCH TOAST

Add ½ teaspoon vanilla extract and 1 tablespoon sugar to the egg and milk mixture.

SCRAMBLED EGGS

Serves 2

Whisking a little milk into your eggs before cooking them will make them fluffy and moist. Just be careful not to let your pan get too hot. If the eggs cook too fast they can end up dense and rubbery. This may be okay for food-fight ammo, but let's get them to eat breakfast first.

4 large eggs
2 tablespoons milk
Salt and pepper
1 teaspoon unsalted butter
1 teaspoon vegetable oil (preferably canola)

1. Crack the eggs into a bowl. Whisk in the milk and salt and pepper to taste.

2. Heat a skillet over medium heat for 1 minute. Add the butter and oil and heat until sizzling, about 1 minute more.

3. Pour the eggs into the pan, let cook for 1 minute, and then stir lightly with a spatula, scraping the bottom of the pan, until the eggs are set, about 2 minutes more.

FRIED EGGS

Serves 2

Sunny-side-ups and over-easies may sound like the easiest things in the world, but making them still requires a bit of skill. First off, until you get good, don't crack the eggs straight into a pan. Believe me. You don't want to be picking shells out of your breakfast. Play it safe and crack the eggs into a small bowl, then slide them into the pan. Also, unless you have some really cool moves down, use a spatula to flip your eggs. Don't try to flip more than two eggs at a time . . . and do it gently so you don't break the yolks. You want everything to land back in the pan, not on the floor . . . or ceiling.

1 teaspoon unsalted butter
1 teaspoon vegetable oil (preferably canola)
4 large eggs

1. Heat a skillet over medium heat for 1 minute. Add the butter and oil and heat until sizzling, about 1 minute more.

2. Gently add the eggs to the pan. For sunny side up, cook until the whites are nice and set, $3\frac{1}{2}$ minutes, then slide a spatula under the eggs to loosen them and lift 'em out. For over-easy, cook for 3 minutes. Slide a spatula under one or two of the eggs to loosen them, then gently flip them over. Cook for 30 more seconds. For over-hard, flip them and cook for another 1 to 2 minutes.

THE SHORTCUT CLUB

A less risky method for over-easy is to just cover the pan with a lid from the start. Let cook for 4 minutes. While the bottom fries, the top will just barely set.

HUEVOS RANCHEROS

Serves 2

Having your huevos "ranch" style is a treat that is usually reserved for brunch in a restaurant, but these are actually easy to whip up at home. This is especially true if you do a little think-ahead meal planning and stash some extra Jole Mole Sauce (page 150) away in the fridge or freezer. You can also use salsa. Huevos Rancheros also make a quick-fix, last-minute dinner.

4 large eggs
2 tablespoons milk
Salt and pepper
1 teaspoon unsalted butter
1 teaspoon vegetable oil (preferably canola)
$1/4$ cup Jole Mole Sauce (page 150)
1 ounce ($1/4$ cup) grated Monterey Jack, Cheddar,
    or Mexican mix cheese
Tortilla chips, for serving
Sour cream, for serving (optional)

1. Crack the eggs into a bowl. Whisk in the milk and season with salt and pepper.

2. Heat a skillet over medium heat for 1 minute. Add the butter and oil and heat until sizzling, about 1 minute more.

3. Pour the eggs into the pan and let cook for 1 minute. While lightly stirring with a spatula or fork, and scraping the eggs from the bottom of the pan, cook until just starting to set, about 1 minute more. Turn the heat down to low.

4. Spoon the mole sauce on top of the eggs, and then sprinkle the cheese on top. Cover the skillet and cook for 2 to 3 more minutes, until the cheese is melted and the sauce is heated through.

5. Serve on top of tortilla chips, with some sour cream on the side.

THE SHORTCUT CLUB

If you don't have time to make Jole Mole Sauce, try Salsa (page 96) or store-bought salsa.

SLOPPY JOSÉ'S HUEVOS RANCHEROS

Beef up your huevos by substituting Sloppy José's taco filling (see page 128) for the Jole Mole Sauce.

BREAKFAST BURRITO

Serves 2

Take something as simple as scrambled eggs, a little cheese, maybe some bacon or ham, and wrap it all up in a tortilla . . . Boom! You just knocked breakfast right out of the park. These burritos are easy to handle, making them great for a road trip. Hand them out to the kids and they can finish them off in the backseat, eliminating that first overprocessed, high-cholesterol pit stop at the fast-food franchise.

Four 8- or 9-inch flour tortillas
4 large eggs
2 tablespoons milk
Salt and pepper
1 teaspoon unsalted butter
1 teaspoon vegetable oil (preferably canola)
1^1/$_2$ ounces (^{1}/$_3$ cup) grated Monterey Jack, Cheddar, or Mexican mix cheese

1. Warm each tortilla in an ungreased skillet over medium heat for 10 seconds on each side. Otherwise, wrap a stack of tortillas in aluminum foil and pop them into a 325°F oven until they are soft and pliable, about 4 minutes. Alternatively, you can microwave the tortillas, 6 at a time: wrap the stack in a clean kitchen towel and heat for 30 to 60 seconds. Keep covered under foil or a clean kitchen towel.

2. Crack the eggs into a bowl. Whisk in the milk and season with salt and pepper.

3. Heat a skillet over medium heat for 1 minute. Add the butter and oil and heat until sizzling, about 1 minute more.

Like shirts, hats, and underpants, tortillas come in a variety of sizes. Also like shirts, hats, and underpants, the "SM" can be huge and the "XL" can be "who-can-fit-into-something-this-small?" Sizes do change from brand to brand, but for most brands, fajita or quesadilla-size tortillas are 7 inches, soft taco–size are 8 inches, and burrito-size are 9 inches.

4. Pour the eggs into the pan and let cook for 1 minute, and then stir lightly with a spatula, scraping the bottom of the pan, until barely set, about 1 minute more.

5. Turn the heat down to low. Sprinkle the cheese over the eggs and cover the pan. Cook for 2 minutes more, until the cheese is all nice and melted.

6. Divide the eggs among the tortillas in a stripe going down the middle. If you want, top with additions (see box). Fold up the bottom half inch of the tortilla, and then roll the rest of the tortilla into a tube. For an illustration of how to fold a burrito, see page 138.

Every guy knows that when it comes to burritos, more is more. Here are some additions to doll things up a bit.

Crumbled cooked bacon (see page 40)
Grilled Ham (page 41)
Jole Mole Sauce (page 139), **Salsa** (page 96), **or store-bought salsa**
Sloppy José's taco filling (see page 128)
Black Beans (page 197)

BACON

There's no real trick to makin' bacon. You just have to choose your pan and start cooking. If you have a square griddle pan or a griddle built into your stovetop, then you will have virtually no geometry or layout problems. If you use a round skillet, then you may have to tweak the Pythagorean theorem and maneuver the bacon strips to fit into a circle in the skillet.

Lay the bacon out in a single layer in a large skillet. Cook over medium heat, turning the strips over so they cook evenly, for 8 to 10 minutes, until crisp and brown. To microwave bacon, put the bacon on a microwavable dish and microwave on high for 1 minute per slice. Drain on a plate lined with paper towels.

DO IT LIKE THE PROS

To cook a whole bunch of bacon at once, restaurant cooks lay the bacon out on rimmed baking sheets called sheet pans and put them in a 350°F oven for 12 minutes. You will still have to turn the strips over for even cooking and drain on paper towels. Since bacon fat gets very hot, and the sheet pan may be difficult to balance, it's best to wait until everything cools down before getting rid of the excess fat. Discard with care. It can easily spill down your leg . . . or worse!

GRILLED HAM

Talk about a two-minute drill! Grilling ham in a skillet takes exactly that long, making it a nice and easy alternative to bacon. Of course, it isn't actually grilled, but ham takes on a whole new crusty dimension when it's heated up in a skillet or on a griddle. If you buy your ham at the deli counter (where it will probably be of better quality than the packaged stuff), have them slice it fairly thick. If you use a nonstick pan, you can skip the nonstick vegetable oil spray.

Nonstick vegetable oil spray
4 ounces thick-sliced ham

1. Heat a skillet over medium heat for 1 minute. Lightly coat the pan with nonstick vegetable oil spray.

2. Lay as many slices of ham in the skillet as will fit in a single layer. Cook for 1 minute, until the ham is starting to color on the bottom. Flip the ham over and cook the other side for 1 minute. Cook the remaining ham in the same way.

OATMEAL

Remember that blonde who trashed the bears' place, mooched their porridge, and nodded out in their bed? What was her name? The names of a whole bunch of tabloid pseudo-stars come to mind, but no, it was Goldilocks.

Oatmeal (or porridge, as some of Grizzly Adams's buddies like to call it) makes for a quick and wholesome breakfast. Just don't be fooled by the oversimplified instructions on the container. They don't turn out the best porridge in the cottage. With some milk and a little food styling, you'll have a creamy bowl of porridge that will prepare your baby bears for a day of house wrecking.

1^1/$_2$ cups water
^{1}/$_2$ cup milk, plus more for serving
Pinch of salt
1 cup quick or old-fashioned rolled oats
Light or dark brown sugar, for serving

1. In a medium saucepan, bring the water, milk, and salt to a boil. Stir in the oats, and then turn the heat down until the porridge barely simmers. Cook, occasionally stirring and scraping the bottom of the pot, for 3 to 4 minutes for quick oats and 4 to 5 minutes for old-fashioned. The oatmeal is ready when it looks all creamy and luscious.

2. Spoon the oatmeal into bowls. Sprinkle some brown sugar on top and let it melt. Pour a little milk around the inner rim of the bowl before serving.

If you have a house full of serial cereal eaters, try making porridge with Farina, Irish oatmeal, or any other hot cereal. Follow the cooking instructions on the package, then garnish according to the instructions in step 2, right.

CINNAMON–RAISIN OATMEAL

Add $\frac{1}{4}$ cup raisins along with the oats.
Continue with the rest of the recipe.
Sprinkle a little ground cinnamon on
top before serving.

LUNCHTIME
THE FAST AND THE FURIOUS

```
Chicken      →  Egg Salad   →  Tuna Salad  →  Fruit       →  Tossed
Salad                                          Salad          Green Salad
                                                                  ↓
Mozzarella   ←  Russian     ←  Blue Cheese ←  Italian     ←  Vinaigrette
and Tomato      Dressing       Dressing       Dressing       or
Salad                                                         Fancy French
  ↓                                                           Dressing
Semi-Cobb    →  Macaroni    →  Pasta Salad →  Potato      →  Coleslaw
Salad           Salad          Primavera      Salad
                                                                  ↓
Split Pea    ←  Philly      ←  Reuben      ←  Grilled     ←  Tuna Melt
and             Cheese         Sandwich       Cheese
Carrot Soup     Steak                         Sandwich
  ↓
Chicken      →  Queso       →  Corn        →  Reuben      →  Chicken       →
Soup            Quesadillas    Quesadillas    Quesadillas    Quesadillas
```

You may not have to plan lunchtime seven days a week. Your kids may buy lunch at school and you may eat out at work, but there are plenty of occasions, like the weekends and holidays, when lunch is a full-fledged meal at home. When those times come, you have to **BE FAST** and you have to **BE EFFICIENT.** Everybody has places to go and things to do, especially you. You have to know all about salads, soups, and the nuts and bolts of making a great sandwich. Of course lunch can be as simple as some salami slapped between two slices of bread, but it's even better to turn lunches into balanced meals by serving veggies or fruit along with that sandwich. Garnish your plate with carrot sticks, slices of cucumber, wedges of apple, or other fresh produce and get the kids into all kinds of salads. (For more suggestions, see recipes for veggies, starting on page 164, or Fruit Salad, page 52.) Incidentally, those same veggies can be put into a plastic bag and packed off to school in your child's lunch box.

CHICKEN SALAD

Makes 2 cups, enough for 4 sandwiches

DO IT LIKE THE PROS

Add one of the following to turn your basic bird salad into a real barn burner.

1 clove garlic, peeled, minced and sautéed with 2 tablespoons olive oil and 1 tablespoon chopped fresh rosemary leaves for 2 minutes over medium heat

$1/2$ medium onion, peeled, minced, and fried in 1 tablespoon canola oil over high heat until golden brown, 5 to 7 minutes

1 tablespoon dark, Asian-style sesame oil and 2 chopped scallions, white and green parts

1 teaspoon curry powder or 2 teaspoons chili powder

Chicken salad is great stuff, but it seems like a bit too much work to cook an entire chicken just to make salad. If you need a few scraps for shims or supports, you just pick them out of the odds and ends bin, right? Now I'm not saying you should make chicken salad with leftovers from the lumberyard, but chicken salad is the kind of thing that should be made with leftover chicken. If you don't have any leftover chicken from, say, a soup or a roast chicken, you can easily pick up a roast chicken (half of a roast chicken is all you need) from the supermarket or deli.

2 cups cooked, cubed chicken (about $1/2$-inch chunks are ideal)
$1/4$ cup mayonnaise
$1/4$ chicken bouillon cube dissolved in 1 tablespoon hot water
1 stalk celery, chopped (optional)
Salt and pepper

In a large bowl, combine the chicken, mayonnaise, bouillon mixture, and celery. Season with salt and pepper. Serve immediately or refrigerate for up to 48 hours.

EGG SALAD

Makes 2 cups, enough for 4 sandwiches

Lately there has been all sorts of controversy about the health bene-fits (or lack thereof) of eggs. One week they're bad for you and the next week they're manna from heaven. Who knows which side of the scales of culinary justice the incredible, edible you-know-what will tip tomorrow. There is one fact that can't be denied: egg salad is homey and delicious and makes a great, refreshing lunchtime sand-wich or salad plate.

6 hard-boiled large eggs (recipe follows), peeled and quartered
3 tablespoons mayonnaise
1/2 stalk celery, finely chopped
2 tablespoons peeled and finely minced red onion, scallion,
    or shallot
Salt and pepper

In a medium bowl, mash the eggs with a fork. Mix in mayonnaise, celery, onion, and salt and pepper to taste. Serve immediately or refrigerate for up to 48 hours.

EGG SALAD WITH SMOKED SALMON

Heat a skillet over medium heat for 1 minute. Lightly coat the pan with nonstick vegetable oil spray. Add 2 ounces (2 to 3 slices) smoked salmon and cook for 30 seconds on each side, until just heated through. Remove the salmon from the heat and set aside to cool. Shred the salmon and mix it into the egg salad. You may also want to add 2 tablespoons finely minced red onion.

HARD-BOILED EGGS

Hard-boiled eggs are good straight up, or in a variety of recipes. Cooking them perfectly is a matter of timing so get a timer, and use it. Now, what about getting those shells off? The easy deal for an easy peel is to cool the eggs down fast and rip the shells off immediately.

1. Put 2 to 8 eggs in a large saucepan and add enough cold water to cover them by 1 inch. Bring to a boil over medium-high heat. Turn the heat down to low and let the eggs simmer gently for 11 minutes.

2. Drain and immediately run the eggs under cold water. As soon as they are cool enough to handle, peel.

Both the egg, and the salad that you make of it, can stand alone, but it's also fun to mix in a culinary hook or two. Try adding any of the following to the basic egg salad recipe:

Cooked and crumbled bacon (page 40)
Chunks of salami, roast beef, pastrami, turkey, ham or
    precooked sausage or kielbasa
2 tablespoons minced red onion or scallion
2 tablespoons salmon roe, paddlefish roe, or American caviar
    plus 2 tablespoons minced red onion or scallion
1/2 teaspoon curry powder

TUNA SALAD

Makes 2 cups, enough for 4 to 6 sandwiches

Tuna salad. It sounds simple enough, but you may still have to run a few plays to get it past more than one kid. Add scallions and one kid blocks. Mix in celery and another intercepts. In the end, you have to size up your options and pick a combination of ingredients that will please everyone. Incidentally, there are some cooks (and I use the phrase very loosely) who use pickle relish in their tuna salad. Pickle relish? There's a flag down on that play.

Two 6-ounce cans tuna (see The Mercury is Rising, opposite)
1/3 cup mayonnaise
Juice of 1/2 lemon or lime (about 1 tablespoon)
Salt and pepper
1 stalk celery, finely chopped (optional)
2 scallions, white and green parts, peeled and minced, or 3
**   tablespoons peeled and finely minced red onion (optional)**

Drain the tuna, pressing the tops of the open cans against the tuna to get out all of the extra liquid. Put the tuna, mayonnaise, and lemon juice in a medium bowl and season with salt and pepper. With the back of a fork, completely mash it all up until the tuna is broken into very small pieces. Mix in the celery, scallion, or red onion, if using. Serve immediately or refrigerate for up to 48 hours.

The Mercury Is Rising . . .
AND NOT JUST FROM GLOBAL WARMING

And, speaking of punt or play: the big question among devotees of canned tuna is dark or white, a query that, until recently, aficionados never even considered: solid white was always the Charlie of choice. But, alas, mercury, that slipperiest of elements, is turning up in high amounts in larger fish and has completely changed the picture (see page 19). You and I, and most of the guys we know, may have been functioning on soggy brain cells for years, but mercury is too toxic a substance to expose kids to. Dark tuna (usually called "light") has considerably less mercury than solid white albacore, but its "fishy" flavor might be a turn-off for many kids. With this in mind, you may want to try a combo of the "light" and white. At any rate, it is recommended that children have no more than one small serving per week. Any women in your life who are, or may become, pregnant should have no more than six ounces of tuna or any other mercury-risky fish per week. As for the other big question—packed in water or oil—you can chip or pitch-and-run. There seems to be little difference and it's strictly a matter of personal preference.

FRUIT SALAD

Of course fruit salad makes a nutritious dessert, but try to pull that one on a bunch of kids and get ready for World War Three. They will feel absolutely and justifiably ripped off. This is not to say that kids don't like fruit salad, because they do. Serve it as a snack, at breakfast, as a side dish, or as a main course at lunch. Just don't act like it's there to replace ice cream or cake.

While some fruits are available year-round, many run seasonally, so you have to pick and choose from what's available at your market. Oranges are great in the late winter, peaches in the summer. If your starting five aren't working, go to the bench to mix and match an altogether new lineup. Quite often, the fruits that are on sale or featured are also at their peak.

Assemble a mélange of bite-size chunks from the following fruits. You will need 1 to 1½ cups of fruit per person.

WATERMELON Look for seedless watermelons; they will make your life a heck of a lot easier. Slice into wedges, cut off the green rinds, and cut the red flesh into chunks.

CANTALOUPE, HONEYDEW, and other melons Ripe melons will have a little "give" when pressed at the stem end. Cut in half, and then scoop out the seeds. Slice the rind away with a sharp knife. Make sure there is no green left (except for honeydew, which is all green to start with). Cut the flesh into bite-size pieces.

APPLES AND PEARS Core and cut into wedges. Mix together 1 part lemon juice to 1 part water and sprinkle over the fruits to keep them from going brown.

BANANAS Peel and add to the salad just before serving; otherwise they will turn brown.

BERRIES Rinse, drain, and dry on paper towels.

GRAPES Just pluck 'em off the vine. Cut them in half lengthwise if little ones are going to be eating them.

KIWI Ripe kiwis have the slightest give when pressed. Peel with a small knife and slice.

ORANGES Choose seedless oranges. Navel oranges are a sweet choice. Peel, then separate into sections or cut into chunks.

PEACHES, PLUMS, NECTARINES, or any other stone fruits Cut around the equator, twist into halves, and pry out the pit. Cut the fruit into chunks.

PINEAPPLE With a big, sharp knife, cut off the top and bottom of the pineapple. Cut lengthwise into four quarters. Slice off the tough core from each piece. Cut under and around each quarter to free the flesh from the skin. Remove any "eyes" that may remain. Slice into $1/3$-inch-thick wedges.

ADULTS ONLY

Spike your fruit salad with a sprinkle of orange liqueur, flavored vodka, or coconut rum.

TOSSED GREEN SALAD

Serves 4 to 6

Be careful: small children may have trouble chewing and swallowing leafy greens.

Think of an empty salad bowl as a blank canvas, except you're going to put lettuce into it (and if you hang it on the wall, all of the tomatoes and cucumbers and stuff are going to fall out on the floor). What I mean is that you can toss just about any type of lettuce or tender, leafy green into a salad; the artistic part is how you dress it up.

Buy bags of precut stuff or purchase whole heads and rip 'em up yourself. A great choice is a mix called *mesclun.* It's an assortment of flavorful little leaves of specialty lettuce and is available in most supermarkets. Choose crisp, fresh greens that show no signs of slime, wilting, or browning around the edges. Spice up your salad with a little variety. Add cucumber slices, bell pepper strips, cherry tomatoes, grape tomatoes, tomato wedges, shredded carrots, shredded red cabbage, or sprouts. Store greens in the refrigerator, in a plastic bag with a damp paper towel to retain moisture.

1 head of green leaf, red leaf, Boston, Bibb, radicchio, iceberg, or Romaine lettuce, or 6 cups bagged, preshredded lettuce
Salad dressing from pages 56–59

1. Pull the whole lettuce apart and toss out the core. Pick through and discard any wilted leaves or pieces. Wash and dry well, even if the lettuce comes in a bag and looks clean (see Do It Like the Pros, opposite).

2. Use a knife to cut up crisper varieties of lettuce, like iceberg or Romaine. Tear more delicate lettuce, like red leaf or Bibb, into bite-size pieces with your hands. Put the greens in a large bowl.

3. When you are ready to serve, toss the greens with just enough dressing to coat the leaves. Do not drown the salad and do not dress it too far ahead of time. Lettuce can turn into slimy muck when it sits in dressing for too long.

DO IT LIKE THE PROS

All lettuce should be washed before serving. This does not mean dangling each leaf under the faucet like you're rinsing out delicate lingerie. Fill the biggest bowl you have with water or wash out the sink, plug it up, and fill it up. Dunk the lettuce leaves into the water and agitate them around. Pull the leaves out of the water. Rinse out the bowl or sink and repeat the procedure until there is absolutely no sand left. Dry the leaves in a salad spinner or colander. If they are still wet, lay them out on towels and pat dry.

VINAIGRETTE OR FANCY FRENCH DRESSING

Makes about 1 cup

French dressing is called *American dressing* in Japan and in France it doesn't even exist. What the French like to do is to whip up a simple, zippy dressing called *vinaigrette*. It's fresh and full of the tangy flavors of its two main ingredients, vinegar and olive oil. It will taste best if you use high-quality stuff. It seems intricate but it couldn't be simpler, especially if you use a blender. If you don't have a blender, finely chop the shallot, then proceed as below, using a wire whisk and a medium bowl. For the olive oil, pick one that has been pressed from Italian olives and is classified as extra-virgin. For the vinegar, pick balsamic, sherry, or a good wine vinegar. The mustard, which helps to emulsify the dressing, should have a pedigree also. Dijon or other strong imported mustards will taste best.

THE SHORTCUT CLUB

Just put all of the ingredients in a jar and shake vigorously before serving.

1 shallot, peeled and coarsely chopped (see Note)
3 tablespoons balsamic, red wine, or sherry vinegar
1 teaspoon Dijon mustard
³/₄ cup extra-virgin olive oil
Salt and pepper

1. Put the shallot, vinegar, and mustard in a blender or mini processor. Pulse for 10 seconds, or until the shallot is finely chopped.

2. While the blender is running, slowly drizzle in the oil. Season with salt and pepper. Use immediately or refrigerate for up to 3 days.

NOTE: Shallots are one of the magical substances that make French food so great. They are in between a garlic and an onion in both flavor and size. Deal with them just as you would an onion (see page 15). If you can't find them, you can substitute the white parts of 2 scallions.

ITALIAN DRESSING

Makes about 1 cup

THE SHORTCUT CLUB

Just put all of the ingredients in a jar and shake vigorously before serving.

This is a tangy garlic-and-herb version of Vinaigrette (opposite).

$^3/_4$ cup extra-virgin olive oil

1 clove garlic, peeled and chopped

3 tablespoons red wine vinegar

1 teaspoon Dijon mustard

1 teaspoon dried oregano and/or 2 tablespoons minced fresh
   basil leaves

2 tablespoons grated Parmesan or Pecorino Romano cheese

Salt and pepper

1. In a small saucepan, heat $^1/_4$ cup of the olive oil and the garlic over medium-high heat for 2 minutes, or until the garlic bubbles for 15 seconds. Remove the pan from the heat and set aside to cool. Stir in the rest of the olive oil.

2. Put the vinegar, mustard, and herbs in a blender or mini processor and process for 10 seconds, or until finely minced and blended.

3. While the blender is running, slowly drizzle in the oil. Add the grated cheese and season with salt and pepper. Use immediately or refrigerate for up to 3 days.

BLUE CHEESE DRESSING

Makes 1¹/₂ cups

Thick, creamy, and tangy, this dressing has a much looser consistency than the Blue Cheese Dip on page 92, making it perfect to plop on a salad. Just about any blue cheese will work here. You can pick up a package of precrumbled stuff or do your own demolition on a chunk of Roquefort, Gorgonzola, Maytag, Danablu, or other blue.

1 cup buttermilk
¹/₂ cup crumbled blue cheese
¹/₄ teaspoon pepper

Put all of the ingredients in a bowl and mix them together. Use immediately or refrigerate for up to 3 days.

RUSSIAN DRESSING

Makes 1$^{1}/_{2}$ cups

You could call Russian dressing a cross-dresser. It's very good on top of a crisp salad of cucumbers, Romaine or iceberg lettuce, and tomatoes. It's spectacular shmeared on a corned beef, pastrami, or Reuben sandwich.

1 cup mayonnaise
$^{1}/_{4}$ cup ketchup or chili sauce
$^{1}/_{2}$ sour pickle, chopped, or $^{1}/_{4}$ cup pickle relish
1 clove garlic, peeled and minced

Put all of the ingredients in a bowl and mix them together. Use immediately or refrigerate for up to 5 days.

MOZZARELLA AND TOMATO SALAD

Serves 4 to 6

This simple-to-assemble summer salad always looks chic and continental . . . no matter how slobby and bad you look. If you need a pitch to sell this to the kids, call it "pizza salad." Tomatoes should be bright red or yellow and give a little when gently squeezed. The true test of a tomato is to pick it up, hold it right under your nose, and snort. It should have a pronounced smell of—you guessed it— tomato. Look for heirloom varieties, which vary in color but are usually spectacular in flavor. If you can only find tomatoes that are hard, let them sit out, at room temperature, for a day or two to soften up a bit. Serve this salad with Italian bread or a French baguette.

2 large tomatoes
1 pound mozzarella, preferably fresh
1 small bunch of fresh basil, leaves only
$1/4$ cup extra-virgin olive oil
$1/4$ cup balsamic vinegar
Salt and pepper

1. With a paring knife or "shark" (see Note), cut the little stem end out of each tomato. With a serrated knife, cut the tomatoes into $1/3$-inch-thick slices.

2. Slice the mozzarella about $1/4$ inch thick.

3. Alternate slices of tomato with slices of mozzarella and basil leaves, fanned out like playing cards on individual plates. Drizzle the olive oil and vinegar over the top and season with salt and pepper.

NOTE: There's a little gadget called a "tomato shark." It looks like a melon baller with teeth and works great for cutting out tomato stems.

MOZZARELLA AND TOMATO SALAD WITH OREGANO

Substitute fresh oregano for the basil. Coarsely chop the leaves and scatter over the tomatoes and mozzarella.

CHEESE AND TOMATO SALAD

As we now know, the Yankees aren't the only team that can win the World Series and mozzarella isn't the only cheese that you can pair with tomatoes in a salad. Try substituting crumbled feta, thinly sliced or chunked Havarti, small cubes of ricotta salata (Italian sheep's milk cheese), *manouri* (a mild and creamy Greek sheep's milk cheese), or Pecorino Romano or Parmesan cheese, shaved with a vegetable peeler.

THE SHORTCUT CLUB

Specialty food shops usually carry little balls of fresh mozzarella called "bocconcini." They are, very often, already marinating in a dressing. (If they are packed in water or whey, drain and rinse before using.) Just mix bocconcini with some cherry or grape tomatoes, which in winter, the off season for tomatoes, will very likely taste better than the large, slicing varieties.

SEMI-COBB SALAD

Serves 6

In between a chef's salad and a Cobb salad, this is a full meal, chopped salad style. It's easy to assemble and, basically, just requires a trip to the deli to pick up your favorite turkey, ham, roast beef, or luncheon meat. The classic Cobb salad was invented in the 1920s by the manager of the Brown Derby in Los Angeles (whose name, coincidently, happened to be Bob Cobb).

Feel free to make as many substitutions as you want. After all, it's your salad. This especially applies to the selection of meats and salad dressing.

1 head romaine lettuce
2 half-inch-thick slices roast turkey breast
2 half-inch-thick slices ham
2 half-inch-thick slices roast beef
6 slices cooked and crumbled bacon (page 40)
3 hard-boiled eggs, peeled and cut in half (page 49)
1 large tomato, cut into 6 wedges
Blue Cheese Dressing (page 58)

1. Wash and dry the lettuce (see Do It Like the Pros, page 55). Chop into 1-inch pieces.

2. Cut the turkey, ham, and roast beef into $1/2$-inch cubes.

3. Divide the lettuce among 6 plates. Arrange the turkey, ham, roast beef, bacon, eggs, and tomato wedges on top of the lettuce. Serve with Blue Cheese Dressing.

MACARONI SALAD

Serves 6 to 8

DO IT LIKE THE PROS

If you use pasta shells or spiral pasta (fusilli), the same ol' macaroni salad will look twice as expensive. Just cook the pasta according to the package directions.

For all of you traditionalists, here's a classic deli-style macaroni salad.

2 cups (half of a 1-pound box) elbow macaroni
Salt
1 teaspoon vegetable oil (preferably canola)
$1/2$ cup mayonnaise
$1/4$ cup red wine vinegar
1 teaspoon sugar
1 large carrot, peeled and shredded
1 cup ($1/2$ box) frozen peas, thawed (optional)
Pepper

1. In a large pot, bring 3 quarts of water to a rolling boil. Stir in the pasta, $1/2$ teaspoon salt, and the vegetable oil. After the water returns to a boil, cook according to package directions (about 7 minutes for most macaroni brands). Put the pasta in a colander and rinse under cold water until cooled down. Drain well.

2. In a large bowl, combine the mayonnaise, vinegar, sugar, carrot, and peas. Mix in the pasta and season with salt and pepper. Serve immediately or refrigerate for up to 48 hours.

PASTA SALAD PRIMAVERA

Serves 4 to 6

Kids will eat pasta in just about any form, and pasta salad is no exception. Here's a pasta side dish that covers all the bases. It's chock-full of vegetables, Italian seasonings, and tons of flavor, making it an adult favorite, too.

2 cups (half of a 1-pound box) pasta shells or fusilli (spirals)
Salt
1 teaspoon vegetable oil (preferably canola)
1 cup broccoli florets
2 tablespoons olive oil
2 cloves garlic, peeled and chopped
$^1/_2$ cup mayonnaise
3 tablespoons red wine vinegar
$^1/_2$ teaspoon sugar
$^3/_4$ teaspoon dried oregano
1 medium carrot, peeled and shredded or thinly sliced
$^3/_4$ cup frozen peas, thawed
Pepper

1. In a large pot, bring 3 quarts of water to a rolling boil over high heat. Stir in the pasta, $^1/_2$ teaspoon salt, and the vegetable oil. After the water returns to a boil, cook according to package directions (about 12 minutes for most brands of shells or fusilli, but read the next sentence now). One minute before the pasta is ready, drop in the broccoli. Cook for that last minute, then drain the pasta and broccoli in a colander and rinse under cold water until cooled down. Drain well.

2. Meanwhile, in a small pan or skillet, heat the olive oil and garlic over medium-high heat for 2 minutes, or until the garlic bubbles for 15 seconds. Remove the pan from the heat and set aside to cool.

3. In a large bowl, combine the mayonnaise, vinegar, sugar, oregano, garlic, oil, carrot, and peas. Mix in the pasta and season with salt and pepper. Serve immediately or refrigerate for up to 48 hours.

POTATO SALAD

Serves 4 to 6

Potato salad: it's the comfort food of the salad world. It's also a great make-ahead carbohydrate course for summer meals. If you use red-skinned potatoes, don't bother to peel the potatoes (unless it freaks the kids out). It will give your potato salad more flavor and a rustic, gourmet look.

1½ pounds large red-skinned or Yukon Gold potatoes
Salt
¼ cup olive oil or vegetable oil (preferably canola)
3 tablespoons red wine vinegar
1 tablespoon Dijon or whole-grain mustard
Pepper
¼ medium red onion, peeled and finely chopped
½ cup mayonnaise
1 carrot, peeled and shredded, and/or 1 stalk celery,
    finely diced

1. Peel the potatoes and cut them into ¾-inch chunks. Put them in a large saucepan and add enough cold water to cover them by 1 inch. Add ½ teaspoon salt and bring to a boil. Cook over medium heat until just tender, 18 to 20 minutes. Drain.

2. Meanwhile, in a large bowl, mix together the oil, vinegar, mustard, salt, pepper, and onion. While still warm, fold in the potatoes. Set aside or refrigerate until cool.

3. Fold in the mayonnaise, carrot, and celery. Serve immediately or refrigerate for up to 48 hours.

Try adding any of the following to your potato salad.

2 hard-boiled eggs (see page 49)**, coarsely chopped**

Cooked and crumbled bacon (see page 40)

Chunks of salami, pastrami, turkey, or ham or precooked sausage or kielbasa

Cut-up bits of smoked salmon

Cooked shrimp (page 102), cut into chunks

Canned tuna, drained

1 cup thawed frozen peas

1 cup cooked fresh corn (see Corn off the Cobb, page 179) or thawed frozen corn

COLESLAW

Good coleslaw is crisp and refreshing like a salad, but also cool and creamy like a comfort food. The key to creating slaw in this perfect and blissful state is to let the coleslaw help to make itself. Give it time to sit and the cabbage will releases its own juices, generating a crunchy, unctuous slaw, almost on its own.

We all know that two heads are occasionally better than one, but there are also times, despite what your wife says, when half of a head can come in handy. Finding half a head of cabbage can be the big dilemma of coleslaw production. If your market doesn't carry them, you may have to bite the bullet and make a double batch of slaw. Hey, things could be a lot worse. At any rate, look for heads that feel heavy for their size and are free of gray bruise marks. Discard the outer leaves before you play "Jason" on the cabbage head.

$1/2$ **medium head of cabbage ($1^1/4$ to $1^1/2$ pounds), loose outer leaves removed**
1 medium carrot, peeled
$1^1/2$ teaspoons celery seeds
3 tablespoons cider, white, or wine vinegar
1 tablespoon plus 1 teaspoon sugar
$1/2$ teaspoon salt
$1/4$ teaspoon pepper
$3/4$ cup mayonnaise

1. Cut the thick core out of the cabbage. In a food processor fitted with the shredding disk, on the large holes of a box grater, or just with a sharp knife, shred the cabbage. While you're at it, shred the carrot.

2. In a large bowl, combine the cabbage, carrot, celery seeds, vinegar, sugar, salt, and pepper. Let it all sit for 20 to 30 minutes, until the cabbage starts to release some liquid.

3. Mix in the mayonnaise, then refrigerate, covered, for at least 2 hours, or overnight, occasionally stirring, until nice and creamy.

DO IT LIKE THE PROS

For an interesting change in color or texture, try red cabbage or Savoy cabbage (it looks wrinkled and tender) for your slaw.

TUNA MELT

In New York City, an old-school coffee shop called Eisenberg's has always served the best tuna melts in town. The insides are oozing with melted cheese and the outsides are crisp, with incredibly crunchy edges. The only problem was that for years you had to tolerate the guy who made them. He looked like an old biker except he wore tons of jewelry—and not biker jewelry, I'm talking *jewelry* jewelry. He drove everyone there nuts. Workers quit because of him, customers walked out, but man, could he make a tuna melt. As soon as my girls were old enough to prop themselves up on a stool at the counter, I took them there to watch the master at work while they chomped away at the greatest tuna melt on earth.

1/2 cup Tuna Salad (page 50)
2 slices bread
1 slice American, Cheddar, Swiss, or Monterey Jack cheese
2 teaspoons unsalted butter
2 teaspoons vegetable oil (preferably canola)

1. Spread the tuna salad onto a slice of bread. Cover with the cheese and top with the remaining slice of bread.

2. Heat a skillet over medium heat for 1 minute. Add 1 teaspoon of the butter and 1 teaspoon of the oil and heat until the butter sizzles. Put the sandwich into the pan. As it cooks, occasionally press it down with a wide spatula. When the bottom is golden brown and toasty, about 3 minutes, lift the sandwich with the spatula and add the remaining teaspoon of butter and remaining teaspoon of oil to the pan. Flip the sandwich over, back into the pan, and cook until the second side is brown and the cheese is all melty, about 2 minutes more.

Lunch Box

Now that you have become a brilliant chef, Junior may not be so turned on by the gruel that gets doled out at the school cafeteria. This means that you are on deck for yet another chore: packing the lunch box. Plan your cooking week so you will have leftovers to work with. Pot Roast (page 120), Chicken Schnitzels (page 134), and fried fish (pages 160 and 162) make great sandwiches, so make a little extra. Always include some kind of raw fruit or vegetable in the lunch box but also tuck a small treat in there (as long as your kids are responsible enough to have it after they finish the rest of their lunch). Pack some juice or other healthy beverage. If there is rush-hour gridlock in your house, wrap up as much as possible the night before and get things as close to ready as you can, so all you have to do in the morning is assemble sandwiches. Supplies like resealable plastic bags and portion cups with snap-on lids will make both packing and eating go a lot more smoothly.

GRILLED CHEESE SANDWICH

Makes 1 sandwich

Take a plain old cheese sandwich, flip it on the griddle, and you end up with something really spectacular. To make great grilled sandwiches, restaurants are equipped with sandwich presses, but you can griddle with the best of them by making grilled cheese in a pan and simply pressing your sandwich down with a nice wide spatula. You can also replicate a sandwich press at home. Lightly coat the bottom of a clean pan with nonstick vegetable oil spray and put it on top of the sandwich while it is cooking. If you need to make more than one sandwich, just fit several in one big pan or make them in several batches.

2 slices American, Cheddar, Swiss, or Monterey Jack cheese
2 slices bread
2 teaspoons unsalted butter
2 teaspoons vegetable oil (preferably canola)

1. Put the cheese between the slices of bread.

2. Heat a skillet over medium heat for 1 minute. Add 1 teaspoon of the butter and 1 teaspoon of the oil and heat until the butter sizzles. Put the sandwich into the pan. As it cooks, occasionally press it down with a wide spatula. When the bottom is golden brown and toasty, about 3 minutes, lift the sandwich with the spatula and add the remaining teaspoon of butter and remaining teaspoon of oil to the pan. Flip the sandwich over, back into the pan, and cook until the second side is brown and the cheese is all melty, about 2 minutes more.

GRILLED CHEESE WITH HAM

Put a slice of ham between the cheese in each sandwich before cooking.

GRILLED CHEESE WITH BACON

Put 2 slices of cooked bacon between the cheese in each sandwich before cooking.

GRILLED CHEESE WITH TOMATO

Put a nice, thick slice of beefsteak tomato between the cheese in each sandwich before cooking.

REUBEN SANDWICH

Like the roots of a lot of other great classics, the origin of the Reuben sandwich is shrouded in mystery. From New York to Omaha, guys named Reuben have claimed to have invented it. At any rate it's a phenomenal combination of ingredients, stuffed together to make a superstar sandwich. Good corned beef is the main attraction of this sandwich, but please don't neglect the cheese. Imported Swiss cheese will generally be much more flavorful than domestic, and Swiss that is actually imported from Switzerland (as opposed to Finland, Argentina, or Ireland) will be top of the line. If you need to make more than one sandwich, you can just fit several in one big pan or make them in several batches. You can also make a pretty tasty Reuben with pastrami.

2 slices Swiss cheese
2 slices rye bread
3 ounces sliced corned beef
1/4 cup Sauerkraut (page 191)
3 teaspoons vegetable oil (preferably canola)
Russian Dressing (page 59)

1. Put one slice of cheese on a slice of bread. Pile on half of the corned beef, and then spread Sauerkraut on top. Pile on the rest of the corned beef and place the other slice of cheese on it. Top with the last slice of bread.

2. Heat a skillet over medium heat for 1 minute. Add 2 teaspoons of the oil and heat for 30 seconds. Put the sandwich into the pan. As it cooks, occasionally press it down with a wide spatula. When the bottom is golden brown and toasty, about 3 minutes, lift the sandwich

with the spatula and add the remaining teaspoon of oil to the pan. Flip the sandwich over and back into the pan, and cook until the second side is brown and the cheese is all melty, about 2 minutes more.

3. Serve with Russian Dressing for dipping.

How to Pack a Sandwich
NEW YORK DELI STYLE

If you've ever eaten in a kosher-style New York deli, you know how humongous the sandwiches can be. At places like Katz's or the Carnegie, a pastrami on rye can weigh in at over a pound. On top of that they are "packed," a method that makes them appear even bigger. Just getting them into your mouth poses a serious engineering problem. To replicate this architectural marvel, pick up at least 1/4 pound of sliced meat and clump it into a loose mound right in the center of a piece of bread. Top with coleslaw, sliced tomato, or whatever, schmear mustard on a second slice of bread, and put that on top. Place your knife in the ready position at the middle of the sandwich. Bridge the thumb and fingers of your left hand over the blade. As you slice, press down on the ends of the bread with these fingers. The sandwich should separate into two gigantic wedges.

PHILLY CHEESE STEAK

Makes 4 sandwiches

To make a genuine Philly cheese steak, you really need a professional-quality meat slicer and, technically, the sandwich should be fabricated within the city limits of Philadelphia, grinder capital of the universe. But, not to worry, you can still make this great sandwich without a slicing machine or having to take the family to see the Liberty Bell. It does require going to the deli and buying some thinly sliced roast beef, the rarer the better. This recipe is for a sandwich smothered in fried onions, or a "cheese steak with."

2 tablespoons vegetable oil (preferably canola)
1 medium onion, peeled and thinly sliced
12 ounces thinly sliced roast beef
4 ounces sliced Cheddar, Provolone, Monterey Jack, or American cheese
1 large loaf of Italian bread or French baguette

1. In a skillet, heat the oil over medium-high heat for 1 minute. Add the onion and sauté, stirring once in a while, for 7 minutes, or until lightly browned.

2. Mix in the roast beef. Top with the cheese and cover the pan. Cook for 2 to 3 minutes, until the cheese has melted.

3. Meanwhile, cut the bread into 4 portions and slice each piece in half lengthwise to open up. Pile on the meat and cheese.

SPLIT PEA AND CARROT SOUP

Makes about 8 cups, or 6 to 8 servings

Pea soup needs to be thick, the kind of soup you could almost eat with a fork. This one is just that kind of stick-to-your-ribs soup. Pea soup takes a while to cook and if the bottom scorches, there's little you can do to correct the situation. To prevent that, set a timer to remind you to check on it and stir up the bottom regularly.

1 pound (2 cups) split peas
1 large Spanish onion, peeled and finely chopped
1 1/2 pounds smoked ham hocks or shanks
8 cups water
3 medium carrots
4 ounces thick-sliced ham or turkey
Salt and pepper

1. Put the peas, onion, ham hocks, and water in a large pot and bring to a boil. Turn the heat down to low and let simmer for 1 1/2 hours, occasionally stirring so the bottom doesn't burn.

2. Meanwhile, peel the carrots and slice 1/4 inch thick. Add to the soup. Cook for 30 minutes more, or until the peas are mushy and soft.

3. Cut the ham or turkey into little chunks and stir it into the soup. Add salt and pepper to taste and cook for 5 minutes more. Remove the hocks before serving.

CHICKEN SOUP

Makes 2$\frac{1}{2}$ to 3 quarts, or 8 to 12 servings

Chicken soup has magical properties that will cure just about anything. Think of it as the "Matrix" of comfort foods; only a boiled
chicken is a much better actor than Keanu Reeves. You can make this
with a whole chicken or you can buy packages of precut chicken
parts. There is almost always something on sale at the supermarket.
The more chicken you use, the richer the flavor. To intensify that flavor, pros like to first brown their chicken in the oven. You can just
sear the chicken in the stockpot to achieve that same golden color
and roasted chicken flavor.

One 3- to 4-pound chicken, cut up, or 3 pounds chicken pieces
3 large carrots
1 large Spanish onion, peeled and cut in half
$\frac{1}{2}$ head of garlic, cut in half and broken into cloves (you may
    leave the skin on)
6 whole peppercorns
Salt

Since there will be a lot of chicken meat left over, you don't have to put it all in the soup. Use it for Chicken Salad (page 47) or Chicken Que-sadillas (page 84).

1. Rinse the chicken under cold running water. If using a whole
chicken, remove the bag of giblets. You may use the neck, gizzard,
and heart in the soup, but do not put the liver in.

2. Heat a large pot over high heat for 2 minutes. Sear the meat on all
sides until the skin is golden, about 3 minutes per side. (You may
have to do this in batches. If so, remove finished pieces to a platter
while you sear the rest.)

3. Return all of the chicken to the pot. Add the carrots, onion, garlic,
and peppercorns. Add enough water to cover by 1 to 2 inches (3 to
3$\frac{1}{2}$ quarts) and bring to a boil. Turn the heat down to low and let it
all simmer for 1$\frac{1}{2}$ to 2 hours. Occasionally skim any gray scum off
the top.

4. Add salt to taste. With tongs, pick the chicken and vegetables out of the soup. Let any liquid drain back into the pot. Strain the soup into a large bowl or clean pot. If you're not serving it right away, refrigerate for 4 hours or overnight. When the soup is cool, skim the fat off the top. The broth will keep, covered in the refrigerator, for 3 days, or in the freezer for 3 months.

5. Meanwhile, when the chicken is cool enough to handle, peel off the skin and discard. Pull the meat from the bones, and then cut into bite-size pieces. Refrigerate until needed, or up to 3 days.

6. To serve, add the chicken meat to the broth and cook over medium heat for 10 minutes, until the broth simmers and the meat is heated through.

CHICKEN NOODLE SOUP

Use spaghetti, broken into pieces; egg noodles; or any other pasta. Cook according to the package directions, adding 3 more minutes to the directed time. Drain and add to the hot soup. Let simmer for 7 minutes.

CHICKEN RICE SOUP

Cook White or Brown Rice, following the recipes on pages 188 or 190, but omit the butter. Add to the hot soup and simmer for 10 minutes.

THE SHORTCUT CLUB

Chicken and Vegetable Soup

Drop frozen peas, corn, and/or carrots into the soup. Let them simmer for just a minute or two to heat through before serving.

QUESO QUESADILLAS (THAT MEANS JUST "PLAIN CHEESE", GRINGO)

Makes 4 quesadillas, enough for 4 main courses
or 8 appetizers

A few tortillas and some cheese and you've got the ersatz Mexican
grilled cheese sandwiches that make lunch a tap-in. Small kids can
devour mountains of these. Teenagers (who can devour mountains of
just about anything, anyhow) will eat entire continents. Quesadillas
can be served plain or with all sorts of accompaniments, depending
on your crowd.

8 ounces (2 cups) grated Monterey Jack or Mexican mix cheese
Eight 7-inch flour tortillas
Nonstick vegetable oil spray

Should you buy a chunk of cheese or get one of those bags of pregrated stuff? Well, it's six of one and yadda, yadda, yadda. You'll have to grate the chunk on the coarse side of a grater but, depending on what you buy, the quality could be better and it will probably cost you less. The grated cheese in the zipper bag is, of course, a whole lot easier to use, but the quality may be a little compromised.

1. Sprinkle ½ cup of the grated cheese on a tortilla. Firmly press
another tortilla on top. Assemble the rest of the quesadillas in the
same manner. (You can do this while the first quesadilla is cooking.)

2. Heat a large skillet over medium heat for 1 to 2 minutes. Lightly
coat with nonstick vegetable oil spray. Put a quesadilla in the pan
and press it down with a wide spatula. Cook for 2 minutes, or until
the bottom is a spotty golden brown. With the spatula, carefully flip

the quesadilla over. Continue to cook for another 2 minutes, or until the cheese is all nice and melty.

3. Transfer the quesadilla to a cutting board. Cut into 6 wedges. Repeat with the remaining quesadillas.

Serve your quesadillas with any, or all, of the following accompaniments:

Jole Mole Sauce (page 139)
Black Beans (page 197)
Guacamole (page 94)
Salsa (page 96 or store-bought), **hot sauce, and/or sour cream**
Chopped fresh cilantro leaves

CORN QUESADILLAS

Makes 4 quesadillas, enough for 4 main courses or 8 appetizers

THE SHORTCUT CLUB

Substitute 1 cup thawed frozen corn for the fresh.

Adding a little fresh (or even frozen) corn to a simple quesadilla gives it a lot of texture and flavor. It also makes this fun food much more nutritious.

2 ears fresh corn
1 teaspoon vegetable oil (preferably canola)
8 ounces (2 cups) grated Monterey Jack or Mexican mix cheese
Eight 7-inch flour tortillas
Nonstick vegetable oil spray

1. Cut the corn from the cob (see Corn off the Cob, page 179).

2. In a medium saucepan, heat the oil over medium heat for 30 seconds. Add the corn and cook for 3 minutes.

3. Sprinkle $\frac{1}{4}$ cup of the grated cheese on a tortilla. Top with about $\frac{1}{4}$ cup corn, then cover with another $\frac{1}{4}$ cup of the cheese. Firmly press another tortilla on top. Assemble the rest of the quesadillas in the same manner. (You can do this while the first quesadilla is cooking.)

4. Heat a large skillet over medium heat for 1 to 2 minutes. Lightly coat with nonstick vegetable oil spray. Put 1 quesadilla in the pan and press it down with a wide spatula. Cook for 2 minutes, or until the bottom is a spotty golden brown. With the spatula, carefully flip the quesadilla over. Continue to cook for another 2 minutes, or until the cheese is all nice and melty.

5. Transfer the quesadilla to a cutting board. Cut into 6 wedges. Repeat with the remaining quesadillas.

REUBEN QUESADILLAS

Makes 4 quesadillas, enough for 4 main courses
or 8 appetizers

The Reuben Sandwich (page 74) is an all-star, but turning it into a quesadilla really knocks it out of the park. The crisp tortillas give it a great crunchy texture and, since there isn't as much bread, the flavors of the corned beef and sauerkraut really shine through. You may want to put some hot sauce in your Russian Dressing for this one.

12 ounces sliced Swiss cheese
Eight 7-inch flour tortillas
1 pound sliced corned beef
1 cup Sauerkraut (page 191)
Nonstick vegetable oil spray
Russian Dressing (page 59)

1. Lay 1 to $1\frac{1}{2}$ slices Swiss cheese in a single layer on a tortilla. Place a layer of corned beef over the cheese. Spread $\frac{1}{4}$ cup Sauerkraut on top. Add another layer of corned beef, then a final layer of Swiss cheese. Firmly press a tortilla on top. Assemble the rest of the quesadillas in the same manner. (You can do this while the first quesadilla is cooking.)

2. Heat a large skillet over medium heat for 1 to 2 minutes. Lightly coat with nonstick vegetable oil spray. Put a quesadilla in the pan and press it down with a wide spatula. Cook for 2 minutes, or until the bottom is a spotty golden brown. With the spatula, carefully flip the quesadilla over. Continue to cook for another 2 minutes, or until the cheese is all nice and melty.

3. Transfer the quesadilla to a cutting board. Cut into 6 wedges. Repeat with the remaining quesadillas.

4. Serve with Russian Dressing.

CHICKEN QUESADILLAS

Makes 4 quesadillas, enough for 4 main courses or 8 appetizers

Now here's a quesadilla that becomes a full-fledged meal, especially if you serve it with some salsa and beans or other et ceteras (see page 81). Make these with leftover or store-bought roast chicken.

1 teaspoon vegetable oil (preferably canola)
$^1/_2$ small onion, peeled and minced
$1^1/_2$ cups shredded, cooked chicken meat
2 teaspoons chili powder
6 ounces ($1^1/_2$ cups) grated Monterey Jack or Mexican mix cheese
Eight 7-inch flour tortillas
Nonstick vegetable oil spray

1. In a medium skillet, heat the oil over medium heat for 30 seconds. Add the onion and cook for 4 minutes, or until golden. Remove from the heat and stir in the chicken and chili powder.

2. Sprinkle approximately 3 tablespoons of the grated cheese on a tortilla. Top with $^1/_3$ cup of the chicken mixture, then cover with another 3 tablespoons of the cheese. Firmly press another tortilla on top. Assemble the rest of the quesadillas in the same manner. (You can do this while the first quesadilla is cooking.)

3. Heat a large skillet over medium heat for 1 to 2 minutes. Lightly coat with nonstick vegetable oil spray. Put 1 quesadilla in the pan and press it down with a wide spatula. Cook for 2 minutes, until the bottom is spotty golden brown. With the spatula, carefully flip the quesadilla over. Continue to cook for another 2 minutes until the cheese is all nice and melty.

ADULTS ONLY

Spice up any of your quesadillas by putting some hot sauce on top or some minced jalapeño inside. Coarsely chopped cilantro leaves (pick them off the stems first) make a flavorific, sophisticated addition to the fillings.

4. Transfer the quesadilla to a cutting board. Cut into 6 wedges. Repeat with the remaining quesadillas.

CHICKEN AND CORN QUESADILLAS

While you're at it, add some corn to the Chicken Quesadillas (see Corn Quesadillas, page 82).

Quesadillas
THE CROWD-PLEASERS

Quesadillas are perfect for mass feedings. While you are set up to make one quesadilla, it's a simple switch of gears to make any of the others. A good plan for a party is to make plain Queso (cheese) or Corn Quesadillas (pages 80 and 82) for the kids and fancier versions, like Reubens (see page 83), for the grown-ups. If you are feeding a moderate-size group, you should have some time to set up batch number two while the first one's cooking. If you're working a big party, you may want to assemble your quesadillas in advance.

SNACKS
AND STARTERS

```
                 ┌──────────────────┐
                 │     Veggies      │
                 │ for Dipping ...  │──┐
                 │       or         │  │
                 │ Just for Eating  │  ▼
                 └──────────────────┘  ┌──────────────────┐
                                       │      Blue        │──┐
                                       │  Cheese Dip      │  │
                                       └──────────────────┘  ▼
                                                          ┌──────────────────┐
                                                          │   Chili Dip      │
                                                          └──────────────────┘
```

Veggies for Dipping . . . or Just for Eating → Blue Cheese Dip → Chili Dip

Chili Popcorn ← Salsa ← Guacamole

(Chili Dip → Guacamole)

(Chili Popcorn → Garlic Buttered Popcorn)

Garlic Buttered Popcorn → Naked Nachos → Kitchen Sink Nachos

Kitchen Sink Nachos → Shrimp Cocktail → Cocktail Sauce →

Whether it's an after-school snack, a quick bite during a break at the playground, or a nosh in front of the tube, snacks are an important energy booster for growing children. Kids can have the metabolism of a hummingbird, the stomach capacity of an ant, and the attention span of . . . of a kid. You have to keep packing little nibbles into them all day long. These can be as simple as an apple or as big a production as a platter of nachos. The important thing is to keep things in the relatively healthy column, at least most of the time. Snacks don't have to be junk food or empty calories. **EVEN NACHOS CAN BE DRESSED UP** with salsa, guacamole, beans, and vegetables to provide vitamins, fiber, and other nutrients (see Kitchen Sink Nachos, page 100). Snack time is a great opportunity for cutting a deal, so always have fruits and vegetables available. If they want those cookies, they'd better eat that orange or that carrot. There are times when snacks are important for you also. How else could you keep up your energy level until halftime?

In restaurants, appetizers are a strategic tool. They can be put out quickly to calm down diners while the main course (which usually takes much longer to cook) is prepared. With families it works in a similar fashion. Sometimes you need to buy some time to tide the kids over until dinner is on the table, and a starter can both calm them down and warm them up before the main event is ready. Also, if you have guests over and are planning on eating after you feed the kids, you may want to give the adults a little something to nibble on.

VEGGIES FOR DIPPING... OR JUST FOR EATING

If you want an easy way to get vitamins, roughage, and all sorts of other nutrients down your family's gullets, all you really have to do is hack up some fresh veggies. You should always have some on hand. They are good straight up or, if your family needs a little enticement, served with a nice dip. They're perfect for everything from an after-school snack to lunch-box side dish to a back-of-the-car pick-me-up.

A good general rule to follow is to always look for crisp, firm veggies with uniform colors and no blemishes or soft spots. Always wash fresh vegetables under cold running water. Here is a list of snackable vegetables and how to handle them.

STRING BEANS Make sure they are firm, deep green, and have no rust-colored spots. Trim off the ends.

BROCCOLI Pick firm, dark green, evenly colored broccoli. Cut the head into bite-size florets.

CARROTS Any size will do, from those great big ones to the medium-size ones that come in plastic bags. Make sure that they are hard and there are no little hairs growing from them. Trim off the ends. Peel, then cut them into 3-inch pieces. Cut the pieces lengthwise into sticks. If you are pressed for time, buy a bag of mini carrots.

CELERY Look for firm celery. Cut off the bottom knob to separate the stalks. Cut off the leaves. Slice into sticks or just serve whole stalks.

CUCUMBERS Check that they are firm and have no soft spots. The best are those long, green, seedless types, sometimes called "English" or "burpless" cucumbers. They just need to be rinsed and sliced. Plain cucumbers should be peeled. Cut cucumbers into 1/4-inch disks.

SNOW PEAS AND SUGAR SNAP PEAS Choose firm, evenly colored pods. Break or cut off the stem end and pull off the "string" that runs along the inner curve. If there is a string running along the outer curve, pull this off also.

BELL PEPPERS Look for very firm peppers with no soft spots. Usually, a deep red or yellow color indicates sweetness, while deep green will indicate tartness. Cut the tops off the peppers and pull out the cores and seeds. Cut out and discard all of the inner white membrane. Cut the flesh into thick strips.

BEAN SPROUTS Kids like to nosh on plain old sprouts. Just wash them very well.

CHERRY OR GRAPE TOMATOES These tiny, flavorful tomatoes just need to be rinsed and served. If you have young children, cut the tomatoes in half lengthwise.

DO IT LIKE THE PROS

Well, pros don't really do this, but fancy-pants amateurs do, and it always looks very nice. Use a vegetable peeler to strip away the skin of a cucumber but leave a few "stripes" of skin intact, and then slice.

BLUE CHEESE DIP

Makes about 1 cup

Little kids may not go for anything as intensely flavored as a Blue Cheese Dip, but older kids might take the bait. After all, there are an awful lot of Buffalo wings getting eaten out there. Most important, even if your kids are way too young, this dip will get Dad to eat his vegetables. Use any kind of blue cheese that you like, from the generic, precrumbled stuff to ritzy Roquefort, Gorgonzola, or Maytag. Serve with chips or veggies.

¹/₂ cup sour cream
¹/₂ cup crumbled blue cheese
Pepper

In a small bowl, stir the sour cream and blue cheese together. Season to taste with pepper.

CHILI DIP

Makes 1 cup

This is a cool dip that goes great with tortilla chips . . . and also vegetables, of course.

1 cup sour cream
2 tablespoons chili powder
1 tablespoon ground cumin

In a small bowl, stir all of the ingredients together. Serve with chips or veggies.

ADULTS ONLY

Add 1 teaspoon hot sauce. If you want a real flame thrower, keep going.

GUACAMOLE

Makes about 1½ cups

If you are not serving your guacamole right away, press some plastic wrap tightly against it. This will help keep it from turning brown, at least for a little while.

Mashing up guacamole is exactly the kind of fun kitchen chore that kids love to do, so invite them to join in and don't worry if it doesn't turn out completely smooth. Some lumps in your guacamole will give it character. No matter how hard you beat on an unripe avocado, it just won't mash. Avocados are one of the few fruits and vegetables that continue to ripen after they have been picked, so if yours are a bit on the hard side, let them sit out for a day or so, until they give a little when you press them.

There are two types of avocado. For guacamole, you want to get the black, pebbly-skinned Hass variety. Don't try this recipe with those green, leathery Caribbean ones (they are sometimes called alligator pears). They have a watery texture and are better reserved for salads. Serve your guac with tortilla chips and veggies (see page 90).

2 ripe Hass avocados
2 scallions (white and green parts), peeled and thinly sliced, or
    ½ small red onion, peeled and minced
Juice of 1 lime (a tiny bit more than 2 tablespoons)
Pepper

1. Lay the avocados on a flat surface and cut each in half. (Your knife blade will stop when it hits the pit.) Twist to separate the two halves. Strike the pit with a knife as if you are chopping wood, and then twist the knife to pull out the pit. With a spoon, scoop out the flesh. Put it in a medium bowl.

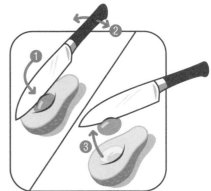

2. Add the scallions and lime juice to the bowl. With an avocado masher, a potato masher, or a fork, mash everything together. Season with pepper.

ADULTS ONLY

A tangy, mild guacamole may be very tasty, but putting around a miniature golf course might not be what you really had in mind. You can add a little hot sauce, but if you want authentic heat in your guac, then you've got to pull out Big Bertha—and nothing drives farther than the fiery rush of fresh jalapeño or serrano chiles. Be cautious when handling chiles. It's a good idea to wear plastic gloves (use the thin food-service type) or use plastic wrap to hold that jalapeño down. Wash your hands thoroughly after handling, and keep your fingers away from your eyes. Chile peppers can vary in heat, so add them in increments and taste your guacamole as you go.

Split a jalapeño or serrano chile lengthwise and cut off the stem end. Scoop out and discard the seeds and white pulp. Mince the dark green flesh and add to the guacamole.

SALSA

Salsa is supposedly more popular in the United States than ketchup these days. Now, the average kid could probably knock off about a quart of ketchup just on one burger with fries. If you do the math, that means we must consume an amount of salsa equivalent to, say, the combined weight and volume of Mount Rushmore and the Republic of Mongolia. Make your own Dad's-brand salsa to use as a dip or to doll up nachos, quesadillas, and tacos.

3 plum tomatoes, seeded and diced (about 1 cup)
1 1/2 cups canned crushed tomatoes (about half of a
    28-ounce can)
1 medium red onion, peeled and minced
2 jalapeño chiles, minced (see page 95)
1 teaspoon ground cumin
1/2 cup chopped fresh cilantro leaves
Juice of 1 lime (about 2 tablespoons)

In a medium bowl, combine all of the ingredients. The salsa will keep for 4 days in the refrigerator.

CHILI POPCORN

Makes 3 quarts—enough for 1 quarter or 2 innings

Whether plain or flavored, popcorn is a nutritious snack that can easily be thrown together for after-school playdates. Most packages of popcorn come complete with instructions and will produce a very lovely snack, but why settle for a plain brown wrapper when you can have the cover of *Sports Illustrated* . . . swimsuit edition? Tossing your popcorn in a chili mixture gives it that addictive can't-stop-eating-it flavor.

3 tablespoons vegetable oil (preferably canola)
1/2 cup popping corn
2 tablespoons chili powder
1 teaspoon ground cumin
1 tablespoon sugar
1 tablespoon salt

1. Mix the oil and popping corn in a big, heavy-bottomed pot and turn the heat up to medium high. Cover so the lid is just slightly ajar.

2. Meanwhile, in a small bowl, mix together the chili powder, cumin, sugar, and salt.

3. As the corn pops, give it a few shakes to move the "old maids" down to the bottom. When the popping stops, remove from the heat. Transfer the popcorn to a large bowl and stir in the chili mixture.

THE SHORTCUT CLUB

Yes, you can also use one of those premeasured bags of popcorn or the prepacked units designed for popping in a microwave. Just follow the instructions on the bag, and then mix in the spices. You can also use one of those popcorn popper machines, but . . . why?

GARLIC BUTTERED POPCORN

Makes approximately 3 quarts

Remember buttered popcorn? They haven't used real butter on popcorn at the movies for ages. For that matter, they rarely use fresh popcorn. The machines are there literally for "show and smell." Most theaters pop a few batches for the aroma but the stuff that they sell comes from giant bags of already popped commercial stuff. Real buttered popcorn is fantastic, but garlic butter is just over-the-top incredible. Use it on plain or Chili Popcorn (see page 97).

FOR THE GARLIC BUTTER
1/4 cup vegetable oil (preferably canola)
4 tablespoons (1/2 stick) butter
4 cloves garlic, peeled and chopped

FOR THE POPCORN
3 tablespoons vegetable oil (preferably canola)
1/2 cup popping corn
Salt

1. Make the Garlic Butter: In a small saucepan, heat the oil and butter over medium heat for a minute or two until bubbling. Add the garlic and cook for $1\frac{1}{2}$ minutes, or until it barely starts to color. Remove from the heat.

2. Make the Popcorn: Mix the oil and popping corn in a big, heavy-bottomed pot and turn the heat up to medium high. Cover so the lid is just slightly ajar. As the corn pops, give it a few shakes to move the "old maids" down to the bottom. When the popping stops, remove from the heat.

3. Put the popcorn in a large bowl, season with salt, and drizzle the garlic butter on top.

NAKED NACHOS

Served in their simplest form, nachos are just tortilla chips smothered in melted cheese. Kids love them like this, and the cornmeal in the tortilla chips is a good source of roughage, making this a relatively healthy snack. You can also turn Naked Nachos into a great lunch. Just serve them with some cucumber slices, carrot sticks, or other raw veggies.

Many chain restaurants pump liquefied cheese-food product over some corn chips, plop a couple of canned jalapeños on top, and call it nachos. . . . Yeah, maybe nachos for the Toxic Avenger. Making real nachos is a heck of a lot better and even easier than ordering them at one of those chain clip joints. Choose nice, big chips; they will be easier to handle. To minimize cleanup, coat your baking sheet with aluminum foil or nonstick vegetable spray. If your baking sheet isn't big enough, you may have to bake your nachos in several batches, but your kids will probably want more, no matter how much you make.

Aluminum foil or nonstick vegetable oil spray
Approximately 9 ounces tortilla chips (bags vary by brand, but the 9-ounce size is fairly common)
8 ounces (2 cups) grated Monterey Jack, Mexican mix, or Cheddar cheese

1. Set a rack in the middle of the oven and preheat the oven to 350°F. Line a large baking sheet with aluminum foil or lightly coat it with nonstick vegetable spray.

2. Spread as many tortilla chips as will fit in one layer on the baking sheet. Sprinkle cheese on top. Bake until the cheese is all melty, about 5 minutes. If needed, repeat with the rest of the chips and cheese.

KITCHEN SINK NACHOS

Serves 6 to 8

As you've probably figured out, no two members of your family like anything the same way. Why should it be any different with nachos? As a matter of fact, it's probably going to be more so with nachos because . . . well, because it can be. The official rule book says that nachos should be made by plopping beans, chiles, and assorted other stuff onto chips and then sprinkling the whole kit and caboodle with cheese. But playing by the rules and getting the job done are two very, very different matters. To make everyone happy, bake the chips and cheese à la Naked Nachos (page 99), then let everybody put whatever they want on top . . . like it's a Mexican smorgasbord.

YOUR CHOICE OF ANY OF THE FOLLOWING
1 or 2 fresh jalapeños, minced (see page 95)
¹/₂ cup canned sliced jalapeños, drained
Guacamole (page 94)
Salsa (page 96)
Black Beans (page 197)
Jole Mole Sauce (page 139)
Sloppy José's taco filling (see page 128)
Sour cream
Hot sauce

Naked Nachos (page 99)

1. Have ready any of the condiments from the ingredient list. Make sure everything is in easy-to-access containers or bowls and that each bowl has a serving spoon or two.

2. Prepare Naked Nachos, then go to town, letting everyone dig in and set up their nachos the way they want to.

FRENCH FRIED NACHOS

Instead of using tortilla chips, use French fries. Bake frozen French fries according to the directions on the bag. Sprinkle on the cheese and bake for 5 more minutes. Set them up and serve the same way as Naked or Kitchen Sink Nachos.

SHRIMP COCKTAIL

Serves 6

DO IT LIKE THE PROS

For extra flavor, pros like to cook shrimp in a seasoned concoction called court bouillon. Make a simple version of it by adding 2 bay leaves, 2 stalks celery, and a few peppercorns to your pot of water. Let this boil for 5 minutes and then add your shrimp and follow the directions in the above recipe.

Playing the stock market, investing in real estate, and boiling shrimp —they're all about timing. You don't want to be kicking yourself and saying that you shoulda pulled out sooner. Overcooked shrimp can have the texture of rubber, while undercooked aren't exactly what you're looking for, either. The best strategy is to hedge your bets and pull your little shrimps out early. Even if it seems a bit premature, the residual heat will probably finish cooking them. And, you can always throw them back into the pot for another round if they need it. If you have little kids, completely remove the tail. Although it makes a convenient handle, you don't want them swallowing and gagging on a chunk of shell.

1 pound medium (26 to 30 count or larger) shrimp, in the shell
1/2 teaspoon salt
Cocktail Sauce (recipe follows)

1. With your fingers, pull the soft shells off the shrimp. (You may leave the tail on as a decorative little handle.) With the tip of a small knife, make a shallow cut down the shrimp's back. Scrape out and discard any dark gunk (euphemistically called the "vein"). Rinse under cold running water.

2. In a large pot, bring 3 quarts of water and the salt to a boil. Drop in the shrimp and turn the heat down to medium. Simmer for 3 minutes. Turn the heat off and let the shrimp sit for 2 more minutes. Drain in a colander and run under cold water until cooled down. Refrigerate until chilled.

3. Serve the shrimp with Cocktail Sauce.

COCKTAIL SAUCE

Makes about 1 cup

$^3/_4$ cup ketchup
2 to 3 tablespoons prepared horseradish
2 tablespoons lemon juice
$^1/_2$ teaspoon hot sauce (optional)

In a small bowl, stir together the ketchup, horseradish, lemon juice, and hot sauce, if using.

Buying Shrimp

Just about any shrimp that you buy were, at some point, frozen. They usually arrive at fish stores and restaurants in big, icy blocks. Freshness is actually determined by how long it has been since they were thawed. Buy shrimp from a shop that looks like it is doing a brisk business so you know you're getting fresh stuff. The shrimp should feel wet but not slimy and have no ammonia odor.

Not all shrimp are created equally puny. Commercial shrimp are graded according to size, and yes—size matters. For cocktails choose 26 to 30 count. This means 26 to 30 shrimp make 1 pound. You can also use larger shrimp, say 21 to 25 count. The lower the count number, the bigger the shrimp.

DINNER'S
ON THE TABLE

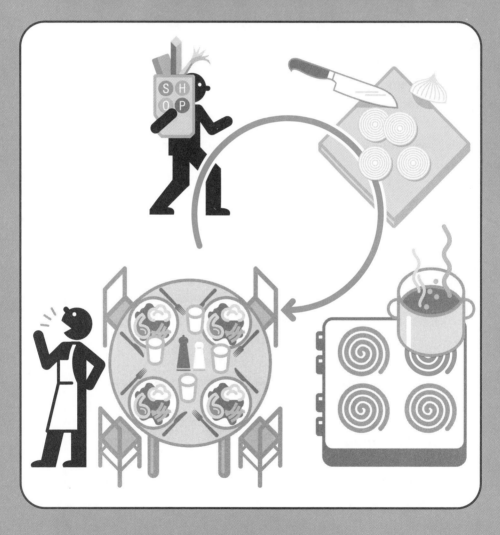

Perfect Pasta → Pizza Noodles → Bolognese Meat Sauce → Pasta with Fresh Tomatoes → Creamy Macaroni and Cheese

Red-Eye Gravy ← Chicken-Fried Steak with Red-Eye Gravy ← Pot Roast with Pan Gravy ← Perfect Steak ← Baked Macaroni and Cheese

Great Burgers → Horseradish Sauce → Sloppy José's Soft Tacos → Meat Loaf → Baked and Roasted (Broasted) Chicken

Roast Chicken ← Jole Mole Sauce ← Monterey Jack Chicken ← Chicken Parmigiana ← Chicken Schnitzels

Chicken Gravy → Grilled Chicken Breast → Barbecue Sauce → Chicken Marsala → Boneless Fried Chicken

Shrimp Oreganata ← Shrimp on the Barbie ← Sausages and Peppers ← Pork Chops ← Chicken Stir-Fry

Batter-Fried Fish → Tartar Sauce → Crumb-Fried Fish →

➡ **I SAID, DINNER'S ON THE TABLE!!** Once upon a time, families gathered in a nightly ritual around the dinner table. They talked about their day and dug into platters of Mom's home-style cooking. It was a time-honored tradition that went back to the days when we lived in caves. "Okay, no one gets any frozen mammoth until they finish their spinachadactyl leaves. They're delicious. Let's talk about what you hunted and gathered in school today." Times sure have changed. Nowadays, parents and kids often eat in shifts, between soccer practice, piano lessons, play-dates, and homework. And it's rare to find one meal that everyone can agree on to eat together. As far as conversation is concerned, who can hear each other when the TV is turned up so loud?

You may not be able to change their schedules around, but you can serve a meal that could get them all to sit down, turn the TV off, and maybe even have a discussion. Nothing seems to work better at dinnertime than those basic, classic recipes that are commonly referred to as comfort food. There's a perfectly logical reason for it. When given an option, almost every animal will hunt down, forage, or scavenge for the most delicious food it can find—all animals, that is, except humans. We often try to defy the "natural" choice and pick whatever is currently considered "healthy," no matter how bad it tastes. Children have not been spoiled by the intellectual or social implications of eating certain foods. To them it's a purely visceral choice of whatever has the best flavor. Most dads agree, and when you take over KP duty, you get to choose what's for dinner. Now, this is in no way an endorsement for feeding your family mountains of fried junk and candy. On the contrary, all food, especially rich comfort foods, should be served as part of a balanced menu. Remember those charts when you were in school, the ones with all the food groups? They should be your goal.

In this chapter you'll find the meat—and fish and other main courses—of this book. Turn to the next chapter for veggies and sides to serve with these to even things out. One night can be meat loaf with string beans and corn and the next grilled chicken with broccoli and French fries. Too many heavy components, no matter how yummy, can result in culinary overkill; but cook an intelligently planned meal and you will have a well-fed, happy, and harmonious brood.

PERFECT PASTA

Serves 4

Pasta cries out for grated cheese. You can buy pregrated stuff, but the fresh flavor, and the ceremony of picking up a chunk of cheese and grating it on top of that spaghetti, can't be beat. Parmigiano is very good, but a personal favorite is Pecorino Romano. It has a robust but mellow flavor and costs a good deal less than Parmigiano. If you have a kid with a steady enough hand, let him be the grating monitor.

There are two rules for perfect pasta. First, don't crowd everything. Use a big pot, filled with lots of water. For one pound of pasta, you should use six quarts of water. (If you are really strapped, you can get away with four quarts.) Second, use a timer or watch the time carefully. The package directions should tell you exactly how long your noodles have to cook. Pasta tastes best "al dente" or slightly chewy, but you know how your family likes it, so adjust the time accordingly. Serve with Bolognese Meat Sauce (page 110) or Marinara Tomato Sauce (page 111).

1 pound pasta

1 teaspoon salt

1 tablespoon vegetable oil (preferably canola)

1. In a BIG pot, bring 6 quarts of water to a boil.

2. Add the pasta and salt and stir in the oil. Start the clock when the water returns to a boil. Cook according to the timing on the package directions, stirring occasionally.

3. Thoroughly drain in a colander.

Cooking times for different brands may vary, but here are some general timings and guidelines:

Spaghetti—9 to 10 minutes

Elbow macaroni—6 to 8 minutes

Fusilli, farfalle (bowties), penne—12 minutes

Large shells—13 minutes

Small shells, fettuccine—11 minutes

PIZZA NOODLES

Serves 6 to 8

Lasagna needs to be constructed. That doesn't mean you need blue-prints or permits, but it is a whole production. Pizza Noodles are like a sloppy lasagna. You can throw everything together, practically blindfolded. And what kid can resist the name?

1 pound ziti, rigatoni, or shells
1 tablespoon olive oil
3 cups Bolognese Meat Sauce (page 110), Marinara Tomato Sauce
**   (page 111), or store-bought pasta sauce**
1 pound ricotta cheese
1 pound mozzarella, coarsely shredded or thinly sliced
Grated Pecorino Romano or Parmesan cheese, for serving

1. Cook the pasta according to the package directions (see oppo-site). Drain thoroughly.

2. Preheat the oven to 400°F. Spread the oil around the bottom and sides of a 3-quart baking dish.

3. In a large bowl (or the pot you cooked the pasta in), mix together the pasta and sauce. Gently fold in the ricotta cheese. (You just want it to be partially and unevenly blended in.)

4. Put the pasta mixture into the baking dish. Cover with mozzarella and bake for 25 minutes, or until the cheese is all melty and spotty brown. Serve with grated cheese.

BOLOGNESE MEAT SAUCE

Makes 2½ quarts

Here's the perfect, everyday spaghetti sauce. It will always beat the factory-made stuff in a jar, hands down. This recipe intentionally makes too big a batch. You can serve some tonight and freeze the rest like a pack rat, because when you're in the bottom of the ninth, it's nice to be able to pull this one out of the bull pen. You can even double the batch size. Let it cool, and then pack it in pint-size containers. It will keep in the freezer for 3 months.

2 tablespoons vegetable oil (preferably canola)
2 tablespoons olive oil
1 medium onion, peeled and minced
1 pound ground beef chuck, round, or sirloin
4 large cloves garlic, peeled and minced
One 28-ounce can peeled Italian tomatoes
One 28-ounce can crushed tomatoes
½ teaspoon fennel seeds
2 teaspoons dried oregano
Salt and pepper

1. In a large, heavy-bottomed pot, heat both of the oils over medium heat for 1 minute. Add the onion and cook, stirring occasionally, until softened and just starting to color, about 8 minutes.

2. Add the ground beef and garlic. As the meat cooks, break it up with a spoon. It is done when it is no longer pink, about 8 minutes.

3. With a small knife, break the peeled tomatoes into large chunks. (You can do this right in the can.) Add both cans of tomatoes and bring to a simmer. Turn the heat down to very low and cook for 1 hour, occasionally scraping the bottom to prevent scorching. Add the fennel seeds, oregano, salt, and pepper and simmer for 15 minutes more.

MARINARA TOMATO SAUCE

Marinara Sauce is the vegetarian version of Bolognese. Now, for the name: Remember that song "la Bamba?" Some guy sings about being a big shot captain and not some twerp marinero. I always thought this meant that he didn't like living in a jar like a tomato, or something. As it turns out, a marinero is a sailor. (Okay, it's Spanish but it's close enough.) An Italian sailor's wife is a marinara. So what does this have to do with tomato sauce? Apparently, when the ships were sighted, she had to run home, from whatever she was up to, and cook up a sauce for her returning husband, pronto. This marinara sauce would fit the bill perfectly.

Omit the meat from the Bolognese Meat Sauce. Simmer the sauce for just 30 minutes before adding the herbs and seasonings and continuing with the recipe. Makes a little less than 2 quarts.

PASTA WITH FRESH TOMATOES

Serves 4 to 6

If you have a bunch of pasta eaters who won't eat their vegetables, or a tweenie vegan—or if you're just up for a dinner that's a little lower on the food chain—try this light, summery dish.

Most tomatoes are best during the summer, but plum tomatoes may have an extended season. Look for plum tomatoes that are brightly colored and have a distinct tomato aroma.

1 pound pasta
$1/4$ cup olive oil
4 cloves garlic, peeled and minced
$1^1/_2$ pounds fresh plum tomatoes, cored and quartered
    lengthwise
2 tablespoons fresh oregano leaves, minced,
    or $1^1/_2$ teaspoons dried
Salt and pepper
Grated Pecorino Romano or Parmesan cheese, for serving

1. Cook the pasta according to the package directions (see page 108).

2. In a large skillet, heat the oil over medium-high heat for 1 minute. Add the garlic and cook for $1^1/_2$ minutes, or until it just starts to color. Add the tomatoes and oregano. Season with salt and pepper. Cook until the tomatoes are hot and juicy but still hold their shape, about 3 minutes.

3. Drain the pasta and toss with the tomatoes. Serve with grated cheese.

PASTA WITH FRESH TOMATOES AND BASIL

Substitute $\frac{1}{3}$ lightly packed cup of basil leaves sliced into thin ribbons for the oregano.

PASTA WITH FRESH TOMATOES AND OLIVES

Add $\frac{1}{2}$ cup pitted kalamata or other olives just when the tomatoes are done. (Kalamata are robustly flavored small, black Greek olives shaped like footballs.) Go easy on the salt; the olives will add enough on their own.

PASTA WITH TUNA, OLIVES, AND FRESH TOMATOES

When the tomatoes are done, mix in one 6-ounce can drained tuna and the juice of 1 lemon along with $\frac{1}{2}$ cup pitted kalamata or other olives. (Remember to go easy on the salt.)

CREAMY MACARONI AND CHEESE

Serves 6

Mac and cheese is the surefire hit that every kid loves. For generations, the big culinary family "secret" for mac-and-cheese recipes was to make it from a box, but to add extra cheese. Some secret! It's about as easy and a whole lot better to make your own.

One 1-pound box elbow macaroni
2 tablespoons unsalted butter
3 tablespoons all-purpose flour
2$\frac{1}{2}$ cups milk
4 ounces (6 slices) American cheese
8 ounces sharp Cheddar cheese, grated (2 cups)
$\frac{1}{4}$ cup grated Pecorino Romano or Parmesan cheese
Salt and pepper

1. Cook the macaroni according to the package directions (see page 108). Drain thoroughly.

2. In a medium saucepan, heat the butter for 1 minute, or until melted. Stir in the flour and cook over moderately high heat until the paste bubbles but doesn't brown, about 2 minutes. (It should look like wet, bubbling sand.) Gradually whisk in the milk and cook over moderate heat, whisking constantly, until the sauce is thickened and smooth, about 4 minutes. Remove the pan from the heat.

3. One by one, whisk the slices of American cheese into the sauce until melted. Gradually whisk in the Cheddar cheese.

4. In a large pot (you can use the one that you cooked the macaroni in), mix the macaroni and the cheese sauce together. Mix in the grated cheese. Season with salt and pepper.

5. Over low heat, while constantly stirring, cook the macaroni and cheese for a few minutes until heated through.

BAKED MACARONI AND CHEESE

Serves 8

It's extremely easy to make a fast and creamy macaroni and cheese that simply goes straight from the pot to the plate. You can also get a little fancy and bake the macaroni and cheese with a crisp crumb topping. It will still be easy. Pick one, but remember the rule: Never offer the kids or your wife a choice. It will only be an invitation to start a household civil war.

Nonstick vegetable oil spray
1 sleeve of saltine crackers with no-salt tops (40 crackers),
**   or 2 cups cracker crumbs**
2 tablespoons butter
2 tablespoons olive oil
Creamy Macaroni and Cheese (see opposite)

1. Set a rack in the middle of the oven and preheat the oven to 400°F. Lightly coat a 2-quart baking dish with nonstick vegetable oil spray.

2. If your crackers are not yet in crumb form, put them in a food processor fitted with the metal blade. Pulse until you have medium-size crumbs. If you don't have a food processor, put the crackers in a resealable plastic bag and viciously beat them into crumbs with a rolling pin, empty beer bottle, or your fists.

3. In a small saucepan, heat the butter and olive oil over low heat until the butter melts. Turn off the heat and stir in the cracker crumbs.

4. Put the cooked macaroni and cheese in the baking dish. Top with the cracker crumbs. Bake for 20 minutes, or until lightly browned on top.

If the crumbs are not browning but the casserole is all bubbly, you can flash it under a broiler for 15 seconds to crisp the crumbs. Set the casserole as far from the broiler flames as possible and watch it like a hawk. It can go from raw to disco inferno in a flash.

Serves 4

With all of the cuts that a cow has to offer, there are two that are a cut above the rest. Rib steak comes from the front ribs of the cow, between the chuck and the strip. It oozes with juiciness and has just enough bite to give it that perfect steak texture. It is costly, but worth every penny. Skirt steak is leaner, very tender, and a relative bargain. Both are just packed with great beefy flavor. They are especially magnificent after they have had a nice soaking in garlic oil. That's how they make steak Fiorentina (rib) in northern Italy and Romanian "tenderloin" (skirt) on New York's Lower East Side. Speaking of tenderloin, cuts like filet mignon or Chateaubriand are very tender, and sound fancy, but they are very expensive and have relatively little flavor, which is why they are usually served with some kind of sauce.

$1/2$ **cup vegetable oil (preferably canola)**
6 cloves garlic, peeled and chopped
Four $3/4$-inch rib-eye or bone-in rib steaks, or two 1-pound
     skirt steaks, each cut into two pieces
Salt and pepper

1. In a small saucepan, heat the oil over medium heat for 1 minute. Add the garlic and cook for $1\frac{1}{2}$ minutes, or until it barely starts to color. Remove from the heat and let cool.

2. In a large bowl or resealable plastic bag, combine the steaks and garlic oil. Cover and set in the refrigerator to marinate for 2 to 8 hours, turning occasionally. Take the steaks out of the refrigerator 30 minutes before you plan on grilling them.

You may also cook your steaks in a hot grill pan or skillet. Those clamshell-shaped indoor grilling machines happen to be very good.

3. Preheat a grill or broiler to high.

4. Drain the oil from the steaks and season with some salt and pepper. Place on the preheated grill or under the hot broiler. Cook on each side for the following times:

	RIB	SKIRT
rare	3 minutes per side	2 minutes per side
medium rare	4 minutes per side	3 minutes per side
medium	5 minutes per side	4 minutes per side
medium well	6 minutes per side	5 minutes per side

Taking Charge
OF THE GRILL

Dads and their backyard barbecue grill: it's an obsessive-compulsive relationship that dates back to the days (give or take a million years) when guys would fling a brontosaurus onto the campfire. It's a great humanoid tradition, but how many dads actually know what they're doing? Here are some simple rules and guidelines so you can grill like a pro instead of a schmo.

It is most important to have everything ready ahead of time: Take meat out of the fridge 20 minutes before you grill it. It will cook faster and more evenly than if it is completely cold. Preheat your grill—10 minutes for gas and 20 minutes for charcoal. Check that everything is ready and conveniently located. You don't want to be scrambling for a play while your steaks are on the fire. Tools should be handy and ingredients as prepared as possible. All side dishes should be ready to serve. Beverages should be ready, condiments should be out, and the table should be completely set.

Any grill will do—gas, charcoal, or even a grill pan, a broiler, or one of those clamshell grilling appliances—as long as you have high, intense heat in one part of the grill surface. If you are a purist, use a kettle grill with hardwood lump charcoal. If you use briquettes, let them burn until white hot for a good 10 minutes to get rid of some of that chemical taste.

Instead of one of those dumb-ass barbecue sets, save money and get a real man's tool. Go to a restaurant supply house or kitchenware store that stocks pro equipment and buy real chef's tongs. You can probably keep the silly brush and spatula if you get one of those sets as a gift. As for the fork, well it's very old school and, unless you learned to cook in the seventies, not in a good way.

To help prevent sticking, chefs like to oil their grills just before they put food on them. Dip a cloth or paper towel in vegetable oil. Pick it up with tongs and wipe the grill surface. Don't get smart and try to do this with vegetable spray; you could set your toupee, or maybe even something else, on fire.

Pros like to use the hottest part of the grill to sear meat for a minute or two per side to form a delicious crust. They then move it to a cooler part of the grill so slower cooking will keep the interior of the meat tender and juicy. When grilling, seriously hunt around and figure out which parts of the grill are hotter than others. A simple test is to just hold your hand 6 inches above the grill. If you can keep it there for 4 seconds, then it's medium. If you spontaneously say "YEEEEAH!," it's hot.

Those nifty-looking grill marks on your chicken are there for a reason. They are forensic evidence that the meat has been properly seared. To get them, don't do anything. Be patient and don't fiddle around with your meat. Once you put that steak on the grill, move it as little as possible, especially until a crust forms. Continually moving it around is the equivalent of double dribbling and will result in a culinary penalty. The meat can end up sticking to the grill surface and then ripping off. You'll lose flavor, moisture, and points for presentation. If you just let it be, it will sear all crusty on the outside and be luscious in the interior.

POT ROAST WITH PAN GRAVY

Serves 8

There are more ways to cook a goose and more places to make a pot roast than in the oven. You can also make it on top of the stove. Use the heaviest pot you have and cover it tightly. You may want to seal it with foil and then put the lid on. Sear the meat and onions on high heat, and then turn the heat down as low as it will go for the braising phase.

To reheat leftover pot roast, cut it into slices. In a nonstick or lightly oiled skillet, set over high heat, lightly sauté the slices until heated through, about 1 minute per side.

So, let me tell you about my brother Gerald, also known as the Duke of Meat. When you put Gerry in a kitchen with a hunk of raw meat, something magical always happens. For years, *le duc* has been espousing the merits of braising with very little liquid, and when it comes to matters carnivorous, you don't argue with *el duque.* Follow his advice and you will end up with a tender, juicy, and flavorful pot roast. You can find chuck or bottom round either tied up into one big roast or in thick slabs. Both will work just fine. You can even use chuck steaks.

Pot roast can't live without gravy, and the essential ingredient for knockout gravy is the gunk that sticks to the bottom of the roasting pan. To get it out, and capture its amazing flavor, it has to be dissolved in a process called deglazing. Pros actually put the roasting pan right on the stove and boil everything together, a method that you too can resort to if a simple mixing and scraping doesn't work. Serve with Mashed Potatoes (page 186) or boiled noodles.

FOR THE POT ROAST
One 5-pound boneless beef chuck or bottom round pot roast
Salt and pepper
1 tablespoon vegetable oil (preferably canola)
1 large Spanish onion or 2 large yellow onions, peeled and quartered
6 cloves garlic, peeled
One 12-ounce bottle of beer (the Duke prefers a rich pilsner)

FOR THE PAN GRAVY
1 beef or chicken bouillon cube
1/4 cup all-purpose flour

1. Set a rack toward the bottom of the oven and preheat the oven to 350°F. Season the meat with salt and pepper.

2. In a large, heavy-bottomed Dutch oven or braising pan, heat the oil over high heat for 2 minutes. Sear the meat on all sides until deep brown, about 3 minutes per side. Remove to a platter.

3. Add the onions to the pan and cook until lightly browned, about 5 minutes. Add the garlic and cook for 2 more minutes. Add the beer, scraping the bottom of the pan to loosen any of the delicious gunk that may be stuck there before returning the pot roast to the pan.

4. Cover the pan with a tight lid. Roast in the oven for 3 hours. Check every now and then to make sure the liquid hasn't evaporated completely and add a cup or so of water if needed to maintain about 2 cups of liquid in the pot. Turn the roast over after about $1\frac{1}{2}$ hours. It is done when it is completely tender and on the verge of falling apart when you prod it with a fork. Transfer to a platter.

5. Put a strainer over a large measuring cup or bowl. Strain the liquids from the pan into the cup. Using a small ladle or tablespoon, skim the fat off the top of the liquids and reserve the fat in a small bowl.

6. Measure the juices. You are going to need at least $2\frac{1}{2}$ cups of liquid (not including the fat). Add enough water to the pot to make up the difference and scrape up all the gunky stuff that is sticking to the sides. Strain and add the liquid in the measuring cup. Dissolve the bouillon cube in the $2\frac{1}{2}$ cups of juices.

7. Make the pan gravy: In a medium saucepan, heat 3 tablespoons of the reserved fat for 1 minute. Stir in the flour and cook over moderately high heat until the paste bubbles but doesn't brown, about 2 minutes. (It should look like wet, bubbling sand.) Gradually whisk in the $2\frac{1}{2}$ cups juices and cook over moderate heat, whisking constantly, until the sauce is thickened and smooth, about 4 minutes.

8. Carve the pot roast in $\frac{1}{3}$-inch-thick slices and serve with the gravy.

DO IT LIKE THE PROS

To prevent stringy, hard-to-chew meat, always carve against the grain—a task that is easier said than done. The grain most often goes in several different directions through one roast. Just pay attention and be open to adapting your slicing strategy to each particular piece of meat.

The easiest way to separate the fat from the liquid is by sticking it in the refrigerator after it has been strained. After about 2 hours, the fat will solidify and you can just scrape it off with a spoon.

Another trick is to use one of those pitcher contraptions with a spout coming out of the bottom. Although a pro would never even think of using one of these, they work well in a home kitchen.

CHICKEN-FRIED STEAK WITH RED-EYE GRAVY

Serves 4

Deep-fried steak in a crunchy cracker-crumb crust, smothered in bacon gravy. It sounds dangerous, but boy, it's a real three-pointer. The trick to eating anything as rich and heavy as this is to balance the act out, and not make it too regular a habit. There's nothing wrong with a little indulgence every now and then, especially when it's served with a light and simple vegetable accompaniment, say string beans, fresh corn, or just a salad . . . and plenty of gravy. Red-eye gravy tends to be a bit on the salty side, so it's preferable to use "no-salt top" crackers for the steak coating. If you don't have enough large bowls, put your crumbs in a baking pan or any other large vessel. The idea is to avoid getting flour, eggs, and smashed crackers all over the kitchen.

1 sleeve saltine crackers with no-salt tops (about 40 crackers), or 2 cups cracker meal or bread crumbs
$3/4$ cup all-purpose flour
1 large egg
$3/4$ cup milk
$1^1/4$ pounds cubed round or shoulder steaks (four 5-ounce steaks)
Vegetable oil (preferably canola), for frying (about 2 cups)
Red-Eye Gravy (page 124)

1. If your crackers are not yet in crumb form, put them in a food processor fitted with the metal blade. Pulse until you have medium-size crumbs. If you don't have a food processor, put the crackers in a resealable plastic bag and viciously beat them into crumbs with a rolling pin, empty beer bottle, or your fists.

2. Put the flour in a medium bowl. In a second medium (or larger) bowl, mix together the egg and milk. Put the cracker crumbs in a large bowl.

3. Dip a steak in the flour so it is completely coated on all sides, and then shake off the excess. Dip it into the egg mixture to coat, and then dredge in the cracker crumbs to coat, pressing the crumbs into the meat so they really stick. Put the meat on a large plate. Repeat with the other steaks. (See Chicken Schnitzels, page 134.)

4. In a large skillet, heat $\frac{1}{2}$ inch of oil over high heat until it starts to shimmer, about 5 minutes. (You may also use a deep fryer or candy thermometer to gauge the temperature: 365°F is perfect.) Turn the heat down to medium high.

5. Fry the steaks, two at a time, for 2 to 3 minutes on each side until golden brown and cooked through. Remove from the oil with tongs and drain on paper towels.

6. Serve with Red-Eye Gravy.

CHICKEN-FRIED CHICKEN

You can "chicken-fry" chicken breasts. Follow the instructions for Chicken Schnitzels (page 134), but substitute cracker crumbs for the bread crumbs.

@!-#%. . . .
THAT'S HOT!!!
Use caution and keep the kids away from the hot fryer!

RED-EYE GRAVY

Makes about 2 cups

Bacon gravy with coffee grounds has been poured over biscuits, ladled over fried steaks—and nursed hangovers—for generations. This version, however, is made without the traditional coffee grounds, an ingredient that you would hardly want to feed to kids.

3 slices bacon
$^1/_2$ medium onion, peeled and minced
3 tablespoons all-purpose flour
**$1^1/_2$ cups chicken broth or 1 chicken bouillon cube dissolved
    in 1 cup hot water**
Pepper

1. Cook the bacon, following the directions on page 40. Transfer the bacon to a plate lined with paper towels. Crumble the bacon into bits.

2. Pour off all but 2 tablespoons of the fat from the pan and set over medium-high heat for 1 minute. Add the onion and cook, stirring occasionally, for 5 minutes, or until softened.

3. Stir in the flour and cook until the paste bubbles but doesn't brown, about 2 minutes. (It should look like wet, bubbling sand.) Add the bacon bits. Gradually whisk in the liquid and cook over moderate heat, whisking constantly, until the sauce is thickened and smooth, about 4 minutes. Season with pepper.

ADULTS ONLY
For the official Heartbreaks-and-Hangovers-style red-eye gravy, add $^1/_4$ teaspoon fresh coffee grounds after you add the bacon bits.

GREAT BURGERS

Makes 4 burgers

Many ground-meat packages list their fat content, but beware. Just as a glass can be half full or half empty, a label that reads 76 percent fat free also means 24 percent pure fat!

I have to break down and confess. This burger has a secret ingredient that was all my wife's idea. If you mix a little finely chopped onion into the meat, it will absolutely flavor-charge the beef. For once, her backseat driving had some validity to it. Serve with ketchup or horseradish sauce (page 127).

1¹/₂ pounds ground chuck (see page 132)
¹/₂ small onion, peeled and minced
Salt and pepper

1. Mix the beef and onion together and season with salt and pepper. Form into 4 inch-thick patties.

Because of the threat of harmful bacteria in ground beef, the days of the rare burger are long gone. You should always serve burgers cooked at least to medium.

2. Preheat a grill or griddle, or set a skillet over high heat for 2 minutes. Put the burgers in and sear the meat for 3 minutes. Don't fiddle with them or you will mess up the seared surface. Flip and cook for 2 minutes on the other side. Turn the heat down to medium or move to a cooler part of the grill and cook for another 5 minutes for medium, 7 for medium well.

TURKEY BURGERS

Substitute ground turkey for the beef and cook for 8 to 9 minutes on each side, until completely cooked through. Turkey burgers must be cooked to well done.

CHEESEBURGERS

Two minutes before the burgers are done, place a slice of American, Cheddar, Swiss, or any other cheese on top of the meat. Cover and cook for 2 minutes, or until the cheese is melted.

RECIPE CONTINUES ➡

MUSHROOM BURGERS

Slice 4 ounces of cremini or white button mushrooms $1/4$ inch thick. After the burgers are done, remove them from the pan and add 2 tablespoons vegetable oil (preferably canola). Cook the mushrooms over high heat for 3 minutes, stirring occasionally for even cooking. (If you are making your burgers on the grill, you can put a medium sauté pan right on the grates of the grill.) Top the burgers with the mushrooms.

INSIDE-OUT CHEESEBURGERS

Here's a flipped-out way to make a burger. It is particularly good with blue cheese but will also work well with other cheeses.

Mix and form burgers as for Great Burgers (page 125), and then flatten each patty so it is $1/4$ inch thick. Divide 4 ounces blue cheese or 6 ounces cheddar, Swiss, or American cheese into 4 equal parts. Place the cheese in the center of each flattened burger. Fold up the edges so the cheese is completely encased in meat, making sure that there are no holes. Flatten a little so the burgers end up about $1 1/4$ inches thick. Grill as for Great Burgers.

HORSERADISH SAUCE

Makes 1 cup

Here's a nice strong horseradish sauce to use on a burger or roast beef sandwich. It also works well as a dip for chips or veggies.

$1/2$ cup sour cream
2 tablespoons mayonnaise
$1/2$ cup prepared white horseradish

In a small bowl, stir all of the ingredients together.

ADULTS ONLY

Mix in $1/2$ teaspoon wasabi powder or $1/2$ teaspoon dry mustard or 1 tablespoon hot mustard. Wasabi powder is that green, Japanese horseradish that is served with sushi. Be careful, the heat in the wasabi doesn't come out at first. It builds up, for around a half hour after it has been mixed in.

SLOPPY JOSÉ'S SOFT TACOS

Serves 4

Here's a great beef filling for tacos. It's sort of a beanless chili. You can either fold the tacos in half and eat them soft-taco style or, for easier handling, tuck the bottom ½ inch up and roll like a burrito.

2 tablespoons vegetable oil (preferably canola)
1 medium onion, peeled and chopped
2 cloves garlic, peeled and minced
1 pound ground chuck, round, or sirloin
One 8-ounce can tomato sauce
2 tablespoons chili powder
1 teaspoon ground cumin
Twelve 8-inch flour tortillas
³/₄ cup sour cream
4 ounces (1 cup) grated Monterey Jack, Cheddar,
    or Mexican mix cheese
1¹/₂ cups shredded lettuce leaves

1. In a large skillet, heat the oil over medium-high heat for 1 minute. Add the onion and cook, stirring occasionally, for 3 minutes, or until slightly softened.

2. Add the garlic and ground beef. As the meat cooks, break it up with a spoon. It is done when it is no longer pink, about 5 minutes.

3. Stir in the tomato sauce, chili powder, and cumin. Cook for 2 minutes more.

4. Warm each tortilla in an ungreased skillet over medium heat for 10 seconds on each side. Otherwise, wrap a stack of tortillas in aluminum foil and pop them into a 325°F oven until they are soft and pliable, about 4 minutes. Alternatively, you can microwave the

tortillas, 6 at a time. Wrap the stack in a clean kitchen towel and heat for 30 to 60 seconds. Keep covered under foil or a clean kitchen towel.

5. To assemble: Place a tortilla on a plate. Spread approximately 1 tablespoon of sour cream in a stripe down the middle. Spoon some beef filling on top of the sour cream. Sprinkle on some cheese and shredded lettuce. Fold the bottom $1/2$ inch of tortilla up, and then roll the rest of the tortilla into a tube (see page 138).

SLOPPY JOSÉ'S CORNY SOFT TACOS

Add the kernels of 2 ears of fresh corn (see Corn off the Cob, page 179) or $1^1/_2$ cups thawed, frozen corn to the filling just before adding the tomato sauce.

SLOPPY JOSÉ'S MEXICAN SPAGHETTI

Make the taco filling using a 15-ounce can of tomato sauce. Serve over spaghetti or any other pasta.

MEAT LOAF

There's a standard warning that's included with almost every meat loaf recipe: Do not overmix or the meat loaf will be dense. So, what's the matter with dense? We're talkin' about meat loaf and not a soufflé. You want to be able to sink your teeth into it, scarf down way too much, and then lay down on the couch to recover.

2 pounds ground chuck
1 medium onion, finely chopped
1 or 2 cloves garlic, peeled and minced
1 cup plain dry bread crumbs
2 large eggs
$1/2$ cup ketchup
1 tablespoon soy sauce
$1/2$ teaspoon dried oregano
$1/4$ teaspoon ground pepper

1. Preheat the oven to 400°F.

2. Combine all of the ingredients in a bowl. Form the mixture into a loaf about $4 1/2$ inches wide and 3 inches high. Place on a rimmed baking sheet or in a roasting pan.

3. Bake until the juices run clear when you poke the meat loaf with a knife and the meat loaf is completely cooked through, about 50 minutes.

4. Let rest for 5 minutes, and then cut into ¾-inch slices.

GOBBLER LOAF

Ground turkey makes a great meat loaf with a lower fat content. The sage gives it a flavor hint of stuffing. Follow the instructions for Meat Loaf, substituting ground turkey for the beef, 1 teaspoon dried sage for the oregano, and 1 chicken bouillon cube, dissolved in 2 tablespoons hot water, for the ketchup.

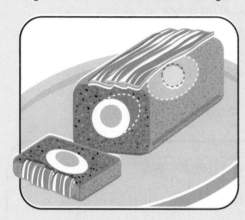

BACON AND EGG MEAT LOAF

Line up two peeled, hard-boiled eggs in the center of the loaf and encase completely in the meat. Before baking, drape 3 to 4 slices of bacon on top of the loaf and bake as for Meat Loaf.

RECIPE CONTINUES ➡

MEAT LOAF WITH ROASTED POTATOES

Meat loaf always gets teamed up with mashed potatoes and gravy, but it's even easier to roast potatoes with a meat loaf, and they taste just great.

After putting the meat loaf in the oven, toss $1\frac{1}{2}$ pounds Yukon Gold potatoes (cut large ones into 1-inch chunks; leave small ones whole) with 2 tablespoons vegetable oil (preferably canola). Bake the meat loaf for 20 minutes, and then place the potatoes around the meat loaf. Continue to bake for another 35 minutes, turning the potatoes every 10 minutes for even browning (check to make sure they don't burn on the bottom), until the meat loaf is completely cooked through and the potatoes are crunchy and golden brown.

Show Me the Beef

It's good to know just what part of the cow your beef was ground from. This often determines how fatty and flavorful it will be once cooked.

Ground beef usually has the highest percentage of fat but good flavor. It can, however, be from any part of the cow. If this factor concerns you, choose a ground beef with a pedigree.

Ground chuck is from the shoulder. It has excellent flavor and just the right amount of fat. It is the all-around best choice for burgers.

Ground round is from the hind quarter (the booty, the shelf, or the saddlebags of the thigh). It has good flavor and lower fat content.

Ground sirloin is from the rear of the cow's ribs. If you are after a healthier burger, this is for you. It has a very low fat content but tends to be a bit dry.

BAKED AND ROASTED (BROASTED) CHICKEN

Serves 6

Once upon a time some enterprising entrepreneur came up with the idea of a chicken that was half roasted and half baked. He called it "broasted." Diners and roadside eateries of all ilks put up big signs to declare that they had the ability to broast their birds. Cars would come to screeching stops because everyone had to try the stuff. The craze lasted maybe a week and a half. Truth is, cooks have been marinating, baking, and roasting chickens for ages and probably will be for ages to come. It's a classic way to prepare the bird and a favorite of just about everyone because the meat is moist and flavorful and the skin crisp. There will be a lot of delicious gunk left on the bottom of your roasting pan, so why not make gravy? Follow the instructions for Chicken Gravy (page 142).

2 tablespoons vegetable oil (preferably canola)
$^1/_2$ cup soy sauce
2 tablespoons vinegar (any kind will do)
1 tablespoon dried oregano
4 cloves garlic, peeled and chopped
3 pounds chicken parts (legs, breasts, drumsticks, thighs, wings)

1. In a large bowl, mix together the oil, soy sauce, vinegar, oregano, and garlic. Add the chicken and toss to coat. Cover and refrigerate for 2 to 6 hours, turning once during this time.

2. Preheat the oven to 400°F.

3. Take the chicken out of the marinade, discard the marinade, and put the chicken in a roasting pan in a single layer. Bake for 35 to 40 minutes, until the chicken is golden brown and cooked through and the juices run clear when the legs are pierced with a knife.

4. Serve with Barbecue Sauce (page 144) or Chicken Gravy (page 142).

Now, just what is the difference between roasting a chicken and baking it? Well, your guess is as good as any. They are sort of the same.

CHICKEN SCHNITZELS

Serves 4 to 6

Breaded, boneless chicken breast: it's the concept behind all of those chicken nuggets and fingers that kids go wild for. You can find them in any fast-food joint, where they have about as much to do with real chicken as the bodies of Hollywood stars have to do with . . . uh, real chicken. The fact of the matter is that when you make your own chicken cutlets, or "schnitzels," they are light-years ahead of those processed bird-nuggies, in both flavor and nutrition.

$1^1/_2$ **pounds skinless, boneless chicken breast halves**
$^3/_4$ **cup all-purpose flour**
1 large egg
$^3/_4$ **cup milk**
2 cups plain dry bread crumbs, preferably Japanese *panko*
    (see Do It Like the Pros, left)
Vegetable oil (preferably canola), for frying (about $2^1/_2$ cups)

1. Horizontally slice the breasts in half so they are about $^1/_2$ inch thick. (If you want genuine, super-thin schnitzel, put the breasts between two sheets of wax paper or plastic wrap and gently hammer them out until they are $^1/_3$ inch thick. You can use a meat mallet, an empty beer bottle, or a plain old hammer.)

2. Put the flour in a medium bowl. In a second medium (or larger) bowl, mix together the egg and milk. Put the bread crumbs in a large bowl. (If you don't have enough large bowls, put your crumbs in a baking pan or any other large vessel.)

3. One by one, dip the chicken in the flour to coat and shake off the excess. Dip into the egg mixture to coat, and then thoroughly coat with bread crumbs. Put on a large plate.

DO IT LIKE THE PROS

The best bread crumbs are *panko* from Japan. Go figure. *Panko* fry up super-crunchy and seem to absorb less oil. It's worth hunting them down at an Asian market, but your schnitzels will still be major-leaguers if you make them with plain old bread crumbs from the supermarket.

THE SHORTCUT CLUB

You'll pay a little more, but if you buy thin-cut chicken breast or chicken tenders, you will be able to skip slicing the chicken yourself.

 **A** FLOUR

 **B** EGG MIXTURE

 **C** CRUMBS

4. In a large skillet, heat ¾ inch of oil over high heat until it starts to shimmer, about 6 minutes. (You may also use a deep fryer or candy thermometer to gauge the temperature: 365°F is perfect.) Turn the heat down to medium high.

5. Working in small batches, fry the schnitzels for 4 minutes on each side, or until golden brown and cooked through. Remove from the oil with tongs and drain well on paper towels.

@!-#%. . . .
THAT'S HOT!!!
Use caution and keep the kids away from the hot fryer!

CHICKEN PARMIGIANA

Serves 4

Dinner is often a desperate scramble to get things on the table, but here's a great way to turn "stuck on your own 20" into "first and goal." While you are set up for chicken schnitzels, make a double batch and save half of them for the next night. You'll just have to put some cheese and sauce on them to make a great second dinner.

2 cups Bolognese Meat Sauce (page 110) or store-bought tomato sauce
Chicken Schnitzels (page 134)
8 ounces mozzarella cheese, shredded or thinly sliced

1. Preheat the oven to 400°F.

2. Spread the sauce in the bottom of a large baking dish. Place the schnitzels in as close as you can get to one layer over the sauce. Top with the cheese.

3. Bake until the sauce is hot and the cheese is melted and spotty brown, 10 to 12 minutes.

MONTEREY JACK CHICKEN

Serves 6 to 8

Authentic Mexican food can be absolutely delicious or it can be . . .
well, authentic. This unfortunately is the situation when chefs think
they need to educate as opposed to cook a good meal. The Jole Mole
Sauce for this chicken has absolutely no certificate of authenticity. It
is, however, packed with flavor and tastes absolutely great. It also is
fun to assemble.

**1¼ pounds skinless, boneless chicken (breasts, thighs,
   or a combination)**
2 tablespoons vegetable oil (preferably canola)
8 ounces (2 cups) grated Monterey Jack cheese
Twelve 8-inch flour tortillas
¾ cup sour cream
Jole Mole Sauce (page 139)

1. Cut the chicken into bite-size pieces.

2. In a large skillet, heat the oil over medium heat for 1 minute. Add
the chicken and sauté until browned on all sides and barely cooked
through, about 8 minutes.

3. Top the chicken with the cheese and cover the pan. Cook for 2 to
3 minutes, or until the cheese has melted.

4. Warm each tortilla in an ungreased skillet over medium heat for
10 seconds on each side. Otherwise, wrap a stack of tortillas in aluminum foil and pop them into a 325°F oven until they are soft and pliable, about 4 minutes. Alternatively, you can microwave the tortillas,
6 at a time: wrap the stack in a clean kitchen towel and heat for 30 to
60 seconds. Keep covered under foil or a clean kitchen towel.

RECIPE CONTINUES ➡

5. To assemble: Place a tortilla on a plate. Spread 1 tablespoon of sour cream in a stripe down the middle. Put a few pieces of chicken on top of the sour cream. Spoon 2 tablespoons of the Jole Mole Sauce over the chicken. Fold the bottom ½-inch of tortilla up, and then roll the rest of the tortilla into a tube.

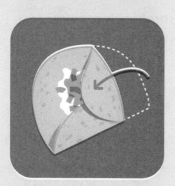

JOLE MOLE SAUCE

Makes 1¹/₂ cups

Real mole sauce, as made in the Mexican state of Puebla, often contains some chocolate and is fairly complicated to make. This is a much easier version, but just as effective in the flavor department. If you have any left over, freeze it for another meal.

1 tablespoon vegetable oil (preferably canola)
3 large cloves garlic, peeled and minced
One 15-ounce can tomato sauce
2 tablespoons chili powder
2 teaspoons ground cumin

1. In a medium saucepan, heat the oil over medium heat for 1 minute. Add the garlic and cook for 1¹/₂ minutes, or until it barely starts to color.

2. Turn the heat down to low and carefully add the tomato sauce. Bring to a boil and let simmer for 10 minutes. Stir in the chili powder and cumin and simmer for 5 minutes more.

ROAST CHICKEN

Serves 4 to 6

For a moist and crisp-skinned chicken, you must repeatedly and attentively baste your pullet. You can use a spoon or a brush for basting, but the easiest and most efficient way is to suck the juices up and hose the bird down with a bulb baster. Use pot holders to lift the pan out of the oven and place on the stovetop. Make sure that you close the oven door to retain the heat.

It is worth the effort to make yourself into a human rotisserie and repeatedly turn the bird. It will ensure even cooking and crisping of the skin. While you're at it, give the vegetables a couple of squirts before returning the pan to the oven. This will help to spread around the flavor.

One 4- to 5-pound roasting chicken
5 tablespoons vegetable oil (preferably canola)
Salt and pepper
1 large onion, peeled and quartered
4 cloves garlic, peeled
1¼ pounds red-skinned potatoes, washed and quartered
4 carrots, peeled and cut into 3-inch pieces
Chicken Gravy (page 142)

1. Set a rack toward the bottom of the oven and preheat the oven to 425°F. Remove the bag of giblets from the chicken's cavity and save to make gravy. Rinse the chicken, inside and out, under cold, running water. Pat completely dry with paper towels.

2. Put the chicken in a roasting pan, breast up, and rub with 1 tablespoon of the oil. Season liberally with salt and pepper. Roast for 25 minutes.

3. Toss the onion and garlic in 1 tablespoon of the oil and scatter around the roasting pan. Baste the chicken with the oil from the bottom of the pan. Roast for 20 more minutes.

4. Toss the potatoes in 2 tablespoons of the oil. Place around the chicken. Turn the chicken on one side. Baste the chicken with the oil from the bottom of the pan. Roast for 20 more minutes.

5. Toss the carrots in the remaining tablespoon of oil and place around the chicken. Turn the chicken on its other side. Stir up the potatoes for even browning. Baste the chicken with the oil from the bottom of the pan. Roast for 20 more minutes.

6. Turn the chicken breast side up. Stir the vegetables and baste again. Roast for 35 minutes more, or until cooked through. The juices that come out when the chicken legs are pierced should be clear or yellow, not pink, and a leg should move around in its socket when lightly twisted.

7. Remove the chicken and vegetables to a serving platter. Serve with Chicken Gravy.

CHICKEN GRAVY

Makes a little more than 2 cups

Use the bag of giblets from inside the chicken to make gravy, but please, do not boil the liver. Either fry it up as a snack or chuck it.

1 small onion, peeled and quartered
1 clove garlic, peeled
Neck, gizzard, and heart of the chicken
2$\frac{1}{2}$ cups water
1 chicken bouillon cube
$\frac{1}{4}$ cup all-purpose flour

1. While the chicken is roasting, put the onion, garlic, and neck, gizzard, and heart (but not the liver) in a saucepan with approximately 2$\frac{1}{2}$ cups water and place over medium heat. Let simmer for 30 minutes. Dissolve the bouillon cube in the liquid.

2. When the chicken is done and after you've transferred it to a platter, pour the liquid from the saucepan into the roasting pan and scrape up all the gunky good stuff that is sticking to the bottom of the pan. Strain into a glass measuring cup. Skim off as much fat as possible, reserving 3 tablespoons of the fat.

3. In a medium saucepan, heat the 3 tablespoons of chicken fat for 1 minute. Stir in the flour and cook over moderately high heat until the paste bubbles but doesn't brown, about 2 minutes. (It should look like wet, bubbling sand.) Gradually whisk in the liquid from the measuring cup and cook over moderate heat, whisking constantly, until the sauce is thickened and smooth, about 4 minutes.

GRILLED CHICKEN BREAST

Serves 4

Chicken—what's not to like? And when it's a cutlet marinated in garlic and soy sauce and then grilled, it's altogether a tap-in. This easy recipe can be made outside on the grill or inside, right under the broiler.

¼ cup vegetable oil (preferably canola), plus a little more
    for the grill
2 tablespoons soy sauce
2 tablespoons red wine vinegar
3 cloves garlic, peeled and chopped
Four 6- to 8-ounce skinless, boneless chicken breast halves
Salt and pepper
Barbecue Sauce (page 144) (optional)

No, you can't reuse that old marinade. Think of it like the oil in your car. Once you drain that crank case, it's got to get thrown out.

1. In a shallow bowl or baking dish, mix the oil, soy sauce, vinegar, and garlic. Add the chicken and turn to coat. Cover and refrigerate for 2 to 6 hours.

2. Preheat the grill to medium high. Lightly coat the grill rack with vegetable oil.

3. Shake any excess marinade off the chicken and grill until browned and completely cooked through, around 6 minutes per side. Season with salt and pepper to taste. Serve with Barbecue Sauce, if you like.

BARBECUE SAUCE

Makes 3 cups

Everyone from celebrity chefs to commercial food conglomerates to fast-food joints makes, hawks, and brags about their barbecue sauce. Now you can save some bucks and earn bragging rights to your own signature sauce. It's great with pork chops, chicken, steaks, or just about anything else that goes on a grill or under a broiler. This recipe intentionally makes a fairly big batch. If you don't need it all, put some in the freezer for another barbecue. For a chunkier barbecue sauce, mince the onion and garlic but don't strain the sauce.

2 tablespoons vegetable oil (preferably canola)
1 medium onion, peeled and chopped
2 cloves garlic, peeled and chopped
One 15-ounce can tomato sauce
1 cup cola
$1/2$ cup cider or white vinegar
$1/4$ cup dark brown sugar
1 tablespoon chili powder

1. In a medium saucepan, heat the oil over medium heat for 1 minute. Add the onion and cook, stirring occasionally, for 4 minutes, or until softened. Add the garlic and cook for $1\frac{1}{2}$ minutes, until it barely starts to color.

2. Carefully add the tomato sauce, cola, vinegar, and brown sugar. Bring to a boil, then turn the heat down to low and let simmer for 15 minutes, or until thickened. Stir in the chili powder and simmer for 5 minutes more. Strain.

SPICY BARBECUE SAUCE

Mix in 1 teaspoon to 2 tablespoons hot sauce. Even better, mix in $1/2$ to 1 teaspoon ground chipotle chile or finely chop and add 1 to 2 tablespoons canned chipotles in adobo sauce. Both are available in Mexican and specialty shops.

CHICKEN MARSALA

This recipe may seem sophisticated, but most kids really get into it. If yours don't, omit the Marsala and substitute $1/2$ cup chicken stock or another $1/2$ cup cream. Make sure that you use real, imported Marsala. Avoid the domestic stuff and really steer clear of the "cooking wine" that is sold in supermarkets. A bottle should run you under ten bucks, and you will just use about $1.25 worth for a full recipe. The bottle will last in the cupboard for six months. This recipe will also work with Madeira or a mild sherry. This is great over rice or pasta.

8 ounces mushrooms
**1$1/4$ pounds skinless, boneless chicken (breasts, thighs,
    or a combination)**
2 to 3 tablespoons vegetable oil (preferably canola)
1 tablespoon butter
1 shallot (see Note, page 56), peeled and minced
$1/2$ cup heavy cream
1 chicken bouillon cube
$1/2$ cup Marsala wine
1 cup frozen peas, thawed

1. Clean the mushrooms and trim off the stem bottoms (see Sautéed Mushrooms, page 177). Slice the caps $1/4$ inch thick.

2. Cut the chicken breasts on the diagonal into $3/4$-inch-thick strips. Pat completely dry with paper towels.

3. Heat a large skillet over medium-high heat for 2 minutes. Add 1 tablespoon of the oil and let it heat up for 30 seconds. Add as much chicken as will fit comfortably in one layer. Sauté until lightly browned and just cooked through, about 4 to 5 minutes per side. (You may have to do this in two batches. If so, you'll also have to add another tablespoon of oil before adding batch two.) Remove the chicken to a large plate and cover with foil to keep warm.

4. Still using the same pan, turn the heat up to high. Add the butter and the remaining tablespoon of canola oil to the pan and heat to sizzling, about 15 seconds. Add the shallot and sauté for 2 minutes. Add the mushrooms and sauté for 3 minutes more. Add the cream, bouillon cube, and Marsala. Cook until the sauce is thickened, about 4 minutes more.

5. Add the peas and return the chicken to the pan. Cook for 1 more minute, or until heated through.

BONELESS FRIED CHICKEN

Serves 4 to 6

Fried chicken usually means chicken-on-the-bone and chicken-in-the-box, but it's well worth it to defy both of these concepts and make your own. Customize your recipe to meet the demands of your crowd by buying packages of the exact chicken parts that you want. If everyone likes white meat, just buy breasts. If they like dark, you can buy boneless thighs. The most efficient way to coat the chicken is to put the flour in a container with a lid, add a piece or two of chicken, and shake it up, baby. You can also toss it together in a large resealable plastic bag.

$1^3/_4$ **pounds skinless, boneless chicken (breasts, thighs, or a combination)**
2 cups buttermilk
1 tablespoon plus 1 teaspoon salt
$^1/_4$ teaspoon cayenne pepper or $^1/_2$ teaspoon hot sauce (optional)
$1^1/_2$ cups all-purpose flour
$^1/_4$ teaspoon black pepper
Vegetable oil (preferably canola), for frying (about $2^1/_2$ cups)

1. Cut the breasts to separate into halves. Cut the thighs open so they lie flat.

2. In a large bowl, combine the buttermilk, 1 tablespoon of the salt, and the cayenne pepper, if using. Add the chicken pieces and turn them to coat in the liquid. Cover and refrigerate for at least 2 hours or overnight.

3. In a large container (use one with a lid) or plastic bag, mix together the flour, the remaining teaspoon salt, and the black pepper.

While you are set up . . . this is a great opportunity to make Onion Rings (page 181). Soak the onions in the same buttermilk that you used for the chicken and fry in the same oil.

4. One at a time, place the chicken pieces in the container and shake to coat. Put the coated pieces on a large plate.

5. In a large skillet, heat ¾ inch of oil over high heat until it starts to shimmer, about 6 minutes. (You may also use a deep fryer or candy thermometer to gauge the temperature: 365°F is perfect.) Turn the heat down to medium high.

6. Working in small batches, carefully fry the chicken for 10 minutes on each side, or until golden brown and completely cooked through. (Don't let the oil get too hot; if it looks like the chicken is browning too fast, turn down the heat.) Remove the chicken from the oil with tongs and drain well on paper towels.

OLD-FASHIONED FRIED CHICKEN ON THE BONE
Because big pieces of chicken take too long to cook through to the center, make sure to use parts from a small chicken: a 3- to -3½-pound bird is perfect. You will need 3 cups of oil and you should put it in a fairly deep pot to keep the splattering down to a minimum. Increase cooking time to about 12 minutes per side.

@!-#%. . . .
THAT'S HOT!!!
Use caution and keep the kids away from the hot fryer!

CHICKEN STIR-FRY

Serves 4

Stir-fry is the basic method that Chinese restaurant cooks use when they toss your dinner in those big woks. It's also the easiest way to put out a delicious one-pan meal with a minimum of effort. If you have a wok, by all means, use it, but stir-fry can be easily accomplished in a big skillet. Because everything cooks up so quickly, the trick to a successful stir-fry (even more than other cooking methods) is to have everything ready and cut into bite-sized pieces before you start. Serve the stir-fry over rice or noodles.

1 tablespoon soy sauce

$1/2$ cube chicken bouillon, dissolved in $1/2$ cup water

1 teaspoon cornstarch

2 tablespoons vegetable oil, preferably canola

1 pound skinless, boneless chicken (breasts, thighs, or a
combination), cut into $1/4$-inch strips

2 cloves garlic, peeled and minced

3 cups vegetables, such as a combination of broccoli florets;
trimmed string beans; carrots, cut into $1/4$-inch slices; mushrooms, sliced $1/4$ inch thick; and/or canned baby corn, drained

2 scallions, sliced

1 tablespoon dark sesame oil

Dark sesame oil is made from toasted sesame seeds and has a pungent aroma and nutty flavor. It is available in the Asian section of most supermarkets. Do not confuse it with light sesame oil, which is meant primarily for salad dressings.

1. In a small bowl, stir together the soy sauce, chicken bouillon, and cornstarch. Let sit for 1 minute, and then stir again until completely smooth.

2. Heat a large skillet over medium-high heat for 2 minutes. Add 1 tablespoon vegetable oil and let it heat up for 30 seconds. Add the chicken and sauté until browned on all sides and just cooked through, about 7 minutes. Remove to a large plate.

3. In the same skillet, heat the remaining tablespoon oil over medium-high heat for 1 minute. Add the garlic and cook for 1 minute. Add the vegetable combination and cook, occasionally stirring, until they are barely tender, about 5 minutes.

4. Stir in the soy sauce mixture and cook, stirring, for 1 minute, until the liquid turns clear. Add the chicken, scallions, and sesame oil. Cook for 2 minutes, until heated through.

PORK CHOPS

Here is an ideal method for cooking "the other white meat." It's called pan searing and it's a pro favorite. First, you sear the chops in a hot skillet, to form a crust that will flavor the meat, and then you slowly finish them off in the oven so the meat doesn't tighten up and stays nice and tender. If you have a skillet with a flame-proof handle, or a sturdy Dutch oven or roasting pan, you can use it on top of the stove and then stick it in the oven. There was a time when it was necessary to cook pork all the way through until it was gray, dry, and overdone, but notorious culprits like trichinosis are extremely rare, with most cases these days traced to undercooked bear or wild boar meat.

Four ³/₄-inch-thick loin or rib pork chops (about 10 ounces each)
Salt and pepper
2 teaspoons vegetable oil (preferably canola)
Barbecue Sauce (page 144), or store-bought, or store-bought
    applesauce (optional)

1. Set a rack toward the bottom of the oven and preheat the oven to 375°F.

2. Pat the pork chops dry with paper towels. Season with salt and pepper.

3. In a large skillet or Dutch oven, heat the oil over high heat for 2 minutes, until very hot. Carefully put as many pork chops in the pan as will fit in a single layer. If necessary, you can do this in batches. Sear until browned, 2 minutes per side. Don't fiddle with them as they brown or you will mess up the seared surface.

4. Cover the pan or, if you've been working in batches, transfer the chops to a covered roasting pan, and bake for 8 minutes. Uncover and bake for another 4 minutes, or until just cooked through.

5. Serve with Barbecue Sauce or applesauce if you want.

DRY-RUB PORK CHOPS

Dry rubs, a mixture of ground spices, add a crusty exterior and a completely new dimension of flavor to ribs, chicken, or anything else that you would put on a grill. That's why they are used in barbecue pits across the country. But the rub doesn't have to be limited to backyard cooking: it also works wonders on a pan-seared pork chop.

Mix together 2 tablespoons paprika, 1 tablespoon chili powder, 1 tablespoon garlic powder, 1 teaspoon ground cumin, and 1 teaspoon salt. Prepare pork chops through step 3. Dust the browned chops on all sides with the spice rub before transferring to the oven and finishing the recipe.

SAUSAGES AND PEPPERS

Serves 6

When I was a teenager, we used to go to street fairs in Little Italy and eat the most amazing sausage-and-peppers hero sandwiches. Today, street fairs are a dime a dozen and you see the same stands at every one of them. The sausages are as flavorless as sawdust. I take my kids to the "old neighborhood," which, although not "my old neighborhood," turns out to be exactly where we live now. We pick up incredible sausages at a butcher shop, stop at a vegetable stand for peppers and onions, and then run home to fry it all up. Lately, I've noticed that many supermarkets now carry very high-quality and inexpensive Italian sausages.

Congressmen may not be able to take the pork out of their legislation, but excellent sausages, stuffed with chicken, turkey, fish, and duck are now available in most supermarkets. American-made sausages have gone through a revolution in quality, variety, and availability. They are easy to cook and can be a new, easy, and—get this—healthy main course for you and your family. As good as these sausages are, many are geared toward specific tastes. You will probably have to try a few brands and varieties before you settle on your own personal winner.

2 tablespoons canola oil

1 tablespoon olive oil

1 large Spanish onion or 2 large yellow onions, peeled
   and sliced

$1^{1}/_{4}$ pounds sweet Italian sausages (about 7 links),
   cut into $^{3}/_{4}$-inch pieces

1 large red bell pepper, cut into strips (see page 91)

1 large green bell pepper, cut into strips (see page 91)

$^{1}/_{2}$ teaspoon dried oregano

Salt and pepper

1 pound penne, rigatoni, shells, or other pasta

Grated Pecorino Romano or Parmesan cheese

1. In a large skillet, heat both of the oils over medium-high heat for 1 minute. Add the onion and sauté, stirring occasionally, until softened, about 4 minutes.

2. Add the sausages and cook, occasionally turning, until browned and almost cooked through, about 8 minutes. Add the bell peppers and oregano. Cook, covered, for another 5 minutes. Season with salt and pepper to taste.

3. While the sausages are cooking, cook the pasta according to the package directions (see page 108).

4. Serve the sausages and peppers over the pasta and sprinkle with grated cheese.

SHRIMP ON THE BARBIE

Serves 4 to 6

Remember that line from *Crocodile Dundee?* No, not "You call that a knife? . . . *This* is a knife"—the one about "throwing some shrimp on the barbie." Well, even if Paul Hogan is a genuine Australian, there aren't too many other Aussies who act like him, wear silly hats like him, or cook anything called "shrimp on the barbie." Down Under they don't even call shrimp "shrimp." They are "prawns." Regardless, shrimp are great for grilling and provide an excellent relief from the usual burgers and dogs, even if you are "a few bangers short of a barbie." Putting bamboo skewers through the shrimp will make it easier to turn them and help them to sit flat on the grill. Soak the skewers in water before threading to help prevent them from burning.

Bamboo skewers
1 pound large shrimp (20 to 25 count; see Buying Shrimp, page 103), in the shell
2 tablespoons canola oil
2 tablespoons olive oil
2 tablespoons fresh lemon or lime juice
4 cloves garlic, peeled and minced
1 tablespoon soy sauce
1 lime or lemon, cut into wedges

1. Put the bamboo skewers in water to soak for 30 minutes.

2. With your fingers, pull the soft shells off the shrimp. With the tip of a small knife, make a shallow cut down each shrimp's back. Scrape out and discard any dark vein or gunk. Rinse under cold water, and then pat dry.

ADULTS ONLY
Add $1/4$ teaspoon cayenne or $1/2$ teaspoon hot sauce to the marinade.

3. Drain the skewers. Line up 2 or 3 shrimp so they lie flat, with the inside curve of the shrimp facing you. Pierce a skewer through the thick ends of the shrimp. Pierce another skewer, parallel to the first, through the tail ends.

4. In a large baking dish, combine the oils, lemon juice, garlic, and soy sauce. Coat the skewered shrimp with the marinade. Cover and refrigerate for 1 to 2 hours, turning once or twice to coat in the marinade.

5. Preheat a grill to medium high. Shake any excess marinade off the shrimp and discard. Grill until the shrimp are opaque and just cooked through, about 2 to 4 minutes per side.

6. Serve with lime or lemon wedges.

SHRIMP OREGANATA

Serves 4 to 6

Some kids like shrimp and others just plain don't, but there's enough garlic and tangy lemon-lime flavor in this shrimp dish to make some serious converts. Serve this over pasta with a sprinkling of grated Pecorino Romano or Parmesan cheese.

1 pound large shrimp (26 to 30 count; see Buying Shrimp, page 103)

1/4 cup all-purpose flour

1 to 2 tablespoons vegetable oil (preferably canola)

2 tablespoons olive oil

4 to 6 cloves garlic, peeled and minced

1/4 cup chicken broth or 1 chicken bouillon cube dissolved in 1/4 cup hot water

Juice of 1 lemon (2 tablespoons)

Juice of 1 lime (2 tablespoons)

2 tablespoons chopped fresh oregano leaves or 1 1/2 teaspoons dried

Salt and pepper

1. With your fingers, pull the soft shells off the shrimp. With the tip of a small knife, make a shallow cut down each shrimp's back. Scrape out and discard any dark vein or gunk. Rinse under cold water, and then pat dry.

2. Toss the shrimp in the flour just to lightly coat. Discard any excess flour.

3. Heat a large skillet over medium-high heat for 2 minutes. Add 1 tablespoon of the vegetable oil and let it heat up for 30 seconds. Add as much shrimp as will fit comfortably in one layer. Sauté for 1 to 2 minutes on each side until they curl up, turn pink, and are

barely cooked through. (You may have to do this in two batches. If so, you'll also have to add another tablespoon of oil before adding the second batch.) Remove the shrimp to a large plate.

4. In the same skillet, heat the olive oil over medium-high heat for 1 minute. Add the garlic and cook for $1\frac{1}{2}$ minutes, or until softened. Add the chicken broth, lemon and lime juices, and oregano. Cook together for 2 minutes, scraping up all the gunk from the bottom of the pan.

5. Add the shrimp and cook for 1 minute to heat through and coat with sauce. Season with salt and pepper.

SHRIMP OREGANATA WITH PLUM TOMATOES

Core and quarter 1 pound of plum tomatoes. Add along with the chicken broth. Cook for 3 minutes before returning the shrimp to the pan.

BATTER-FRIED FISH

Serves 4

Chip or pitch, punt or play, J. Lo or Elizabeth Hurley. These are the decisions that confront us daily, but, when reality finally checks in, the choice is really bread crumbs or batter. Both are wonderful and it's strictly a matter of taste.

This very simple batter wraps your fish fillets in a crisp, flavorful crust.

1 cup buttermilk
$1/2$ cup all-purpose flour
$1/4$ teaspoon baking powder
$1/2$ teaspoon salt
$1 1/4$ pounds sole, flounder, or other white fish fillets
Vegetable oil (preferably canola), for frying (about 2 cups)
1 lemon or lime cut into wedges, malt vinegar (see Note), and/or Tartar Sauce (see opposite)

1. Put the buttermilk in a medium bowl. In a large bowl, mix together the flour, baking powder, and salt.

2. One by one, dip the fish fillets in the flour mixture to coat and shake off the excess. Dip into the buttermilk to coat, and then coat again with the flour mixture.

3. In a large skillet, heat $1/2$ inch of oil over high heat until it starts to shimmer, about 6 minutes. (You may also use a deep fryer or candy thermometer to gauge the temperature: 365°F is perfect.) Turn the heat down to medium high.

@!-#%. . . .
THAT'S HOT!!!
Use caution and keep the kids away from the hot fryer!

4. Working in small batches, fry the fillets for 3 minutes on each side, or until golden brown and cooked through. Remove from the oil with tongs and drain well on paper towels. Serve with lemon wedges, malt vinegar, and/or tartar sauce.

NOTE: Malt vinegar is a sweet-tart vinegar, traditionally used at British fish-and-chips shops.

TARTAR SAUCE

Makes 1 cup

In America we sometimes take some of our freedom for granted. In particular, the free tartar sauce that you get when you order fried fish. In some countries, like England and Australia, customers have to pay extra for the stuff. How can you eat fried fish without tartar sauce? Lucky for us, four score and give-or-take a couple hundred years ago, our forefathers had the foresight to grant us the right to free tartar sauce. And a wedge of lemon.

$3/4$ **cup mayonnaise**
$1/4$ **cup pickle relish, finely minced scallion, or finely minced
    fresh chives**
Juice of $1/2$ lemon (1 tablespoon)
$1/4$ **teaspoon ground black pepper or pinch of cayenne pepper**

In a small bowl, stir all of the ingredients together.

CRUMB-FRIED FISH

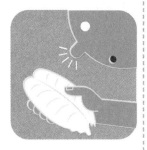

This is a schnitzel-like fried fish with a super-crunchy light coating. Always buy the freshest fish you can get and make sure it can pass the smell test. Fresh fish smells like the ocean and should not have any funky or "fishy" odor at all. Even if it is already filleted, run your fingers over the fish to check for any small bones.

1/2 cup all-purpose flour
1 large egg
1/2 cup milk
1 1/2 cups plain dry bread crumbs, preferably Japanese *panko*
    (see Do It Like the Pros, page 134)
1 1/4 pounds sole, flounder, or other white fish fillets
Vegetable oil (preferably canola), for frying (about 2 cups)
1 lemon or lime cut into wedges
Tartar Sauce (page 161) (optional)

1. Put the flour in a medium bowl. In a second medium (or larger) bowl, mix together the egg and milk. Put the bread crumbs in a large bowl. If you don't have enough large bowls, put your crumbs in a baking pan or any other large vessel.

2. One by one, dip the fish fillets in the flour to coat and shake off the excess. Dip into the egg mixture to coat, and then thoroughly coat with bread crumbs. Put on a large plate. See Chicken Schnitzels (page 134).

3. In a large skillet, heat 1/2 inch of oil over high heat until it starts to shimmer, about 6 minutes. (You may also use a deep fryer or candy ther-

@!-#%. . . .
THAT'S HOT!!!
Use caution and keep the kids away from the hot fryer!

mometer to gauge the temperature: 365°F is perfect.) Turn the heat down to medium high.

4. Working in small batches, fry the fillets for 3 minutes on each side, or until golden brown and cooked through. Remove from the oil with tongs and drain well on paper towels. Serve with lemon or lime wedges and Tartar Sauce.

FINISH YOUR
VEGETABLES
. . . AND SIDE DISHES

```
Garlicky            Zucchini  →      Asparagus  →     String
Broccoli     →                                        Beans
                                                        ↓
Sautéed             Braised          Peas        ←     Orange-
Mushrooms    ←      Kale       ←                        Glazed
  ↓                                                     Carrots

Corn on             Corn off         Corn on           Onion
the Cob      →      the Cob          the Grill         Rings
                                                        ↓
Mashed              Stuffed          Baked       ←     Roasted
Potatoes     ←      Double-    ←     Potatoes           Potatoes
  ↓                 Baked
                    Potatoes

French-Fried        White Rice  →    Brown Rice  →     Sauerkraut
Potatoes     →                                          ↓
  ↓
Black               Baked      ←     Garlic      ←      Un-Stuffing
Beans        ←      Beans            Bread
  ↓
```

→ Someone once said that the key to Southern, country-style cooking is that none of the vegetables taste like vegetables. This sounds like a concept that could really work. Most vegetables can be made so delicious that just about any kid can be converted to like them.

There are many ways and methods to cook vegetables, each with its own advantages and disadvantages. BOILING drains out vitamins, but in some cases, like potatoes, you don't have much of a choice. You can also use a MICROWAVE, which is fast, but that completely commits armed robbery on the nutrients. STEAMING them for a short time is best for retaining their nutrients and antioxidants but leaves most of them tasting bland. SAUTÉING them in a lot of butter or oil and/or garlic makes them taste real good, but adds fat and calories. With this in mind, here are some easy methods for injecting and preserving as much positively reinforced flavor into each vegetable, while still retaining their healthful benefits.

Now, some vegetables, like broccoli, asparagus, or kale, really need help. Reach for garlic, olive oil, chicken bouillon, or anything else that might boost the flavor. With others, like peas, corn, or string beans, it's best to serve them as simply as possible. Sure, you can put a sauce on them or make the recipe more complicated, but you risk hiding their positive flavor and adding a whole lot of pointless busywork. Pros call this kind of overkill "torturing the food." The most important thing is to just find a way that your family will discover vegetables to be one of the more delicious parts of the meal.

It's best to pick your vegetables when they are displayed unwrapped. This way you can really give 'em a good squeeze and thorough inspection. Many stores now stock packages of pre-trimmed and cut vegetables. They are more expensive and may lose some nutrients in the process of precutting, but they will still be pretty good. Convenience may make this option a worthwhile trade-off.

GARLICKY BROCCOLI

Serves 4

George Bush Senior was famous for saying "I do not like broccoli," supporting a popular belief that it is detested by both presidents and children alike. Regardless of your political leanings, the truth of the matter is that lots of kids absolutely love broccoli. Even more of them like it when you doll it up a bit, and a little garlic will turn it into one of the most kid-friendly vegetables you can put on the table. Since the bouillon already has salt in it, you should not have to add any more. Look for broccoli that's brightly colored, unblemished, and firm.

1 large bunch of broccoli (approximately 1¼ pounds)
2 tablespoons vegetable oil (preferably canola)
2 tablespoons olive oil
2 large cloves garlic, peeled and minced
½ cube chicken bouillon dissolved in 3 tablespoons hot water

1. Cut the stalks off the broccoli and peel off the tough outer skin. Diagonally slice the stalks into ½-inch pieces. Cut the florets into bite-size pieces.

2. In a large skillet, heat both of the oils over medium-high heat for 1 minute. Add the garlic and cook for 1½ minutes, or until it barely starts to color.

3. Add the chunks of stalk and then the chicken bouillon. Cook covered for 4 minutes. Add the florets and cook, covered, until the broccoli turns bright green, 5 minutes more.

4. Uncover and turn the heat up to high. Mix so all of the broccoli is basted in the liquid and cook for 3 to 4 more minutes, until the liquid is evaporated and some of the garlic gets the slightest bit of color.

ZUCCHINI

Zucchini are probably the easiest vegetables to prep for cooking; just trim off the ends and slice. Most cooks slice them into thin disks, but they are much easier to handle in the pan when they are cut into chunks. Buy zucchini that are firm, unblemished, and not too large.

1¼ pounds zucchini (about 3 medium)
1 tablespoon vegetable oil (preferably canola)
1 tablespoon olive oil
2 large cloves garlic, peeled and minced
½ cube chicken bouillon dissolved in 3 tablespoons hot water
½ teaspoon dried oregano
Pepper

1. Trim the ends off the zucchini. Slice them in quarters lengthwise, and then cut them into ¾-inch pieces.

2. In a large skillet, heat both of the oils over medium-high heat for 1 minute. Add the garlic and cook for 1½ minutes, or until it barely starts to color.

3. Add the chunks of zucchini and chicken bouillon and mix. Cook covered for 4 minutes. Uncover and cook for 4 more minutes, mixing so the zucchini is basted in the liquid, until the liquid evaporates. Stir in the oregano and season with pepper to taste.

ASPARAGUS

Serves 4

When I was a kid, my mom used to buy these slimy asparagus that came in a jar. Getting them down your gullet was like swallowing something from *Fear Factor*. Today, we know that the crisp bite of a tender, fresh asparagus spear is where it's at. There's another very important factor in the perfection of the asparagus: If you got 'em, peel 'em, especially if they are thick. If the girth of your stalks is any thicker than $\frac{1}{2}$ inch, peel away the outer skin from the bottom half with a vegetable peeler. If you find thin, or pencil, asparagus at the market, don't bother to peel them. Just trim an inch or so off their tough butts. For younger children, cut asparagus into bite-size pieces so they don't attempt to slurp whole spears down in one shot. Asparagus are a vegetable that really lend themselves to "Pop the Magician" (see Stupid Vegetable Tricks, opposite). Choose firm asparagus with intact tips. The stalks should never look wrinkled.

1 pound asparagus
1 tablespoon vegetable oil (preferably canola)
1 tablespoon olive oil
2 large cloves garlic, peeled and minced
$\frac{1}{4}$ cube chicken bouillon dissolved in 3 tablespoons hot water

1. Trim the tough butts off the stalks. If the stalks are more than $\frac{1}{2}$ inch thick, peel the outer skin off the bottom halves.

2. In a large skillet, heat both of the oils over medium-high heat for 1 minute. Add the garlic and cook for $1\frac{1}{2}$ minutes, or until it barely starts to color.

3. Add the asparagus and then the chicken bouillon. Cook covered for 4 minutes. Uncover and cook for another 4 minutes or until tender, mixing so all of the asparagus are basted and the liquid is evaporated.

Stupid Vegetable Tricks

The great sage Barney Rubble once said, "You can fool some of the people all of the time and the rest of 'em half of the time, or somethin." (Abe Lincoln said something like this also, but it had a lot more impact when Barney said it on *The Flintstones.*) The same rule applies to children and vegetables. You can feed some of the kids most of their vegetables and most of the kids some of their vegetables, but you just can't get every vegetable down every kid's gullet at every meal. Here are some ways to coax the younger ones into ingesting something green . . . that was grown on a farm.

 **Pop the Magician**—Standing with the kid in question behind you, show the rest of the family a string bean, or whatever, and announce that you are the Great Daddini. Now, put it behind your back so the kid can make it disappear in his mouth. Presto! Present your empty hands to all.

Pop-Star-Worship Vegetable Frenzy—Okay, everyone who likes (Barbie, SpongeBob, The Wiggles . . .), eat a piece of broccoli!

The Vegetable Thief—Close your eyes and talk about how much you are going to enjoy that piece of asparagus: pick it up on your fork, and pretend you are going to take a bite, saying "I hope no one else steals it and eats it." They should pick up on the cue. Play up the drama when it disappears.

The Cape Canaveral Forward Pass—This is a much more dramatic version of the old choo-choo train routine. Just start at one end of the room and act like it is monumentally important and extremely difficult to "catch" the approaching vegetable in one's mouth.

STRING BEANS

Serves 4

String beans are the layup of the fresh vegetable world. They're easy and accessible, and with close to no effort, you can prep and cook them in a matter of minutes. They're the kind of vegetable that you can rely on when the kids have been eating nothing but junk food for the past 48 hours. They also work well when prepared simply. Many kids will just eat them raw. A word of caution: little ones may literally bite off more than they can chew. Keep an eye on younger children when they eat raw, or even cooked, string beans. They are fibrous and, unless they are properly chewed, can present a choking hazard.

1 pound string beans
3/4 cup water
1 tablespoon unsalted butter
Salt

1. With a small knife, trim 1/4 inch off both ends of the beans. Rinse them in cold water.

2. In a large saucepan or pot, bring the water to a boil. Add the string beans, cover, and cook for 6 minutes, or until just tender. Drain off all of the water. Stir in the butter until melted and season with salt to taste.

DO IT LIKE THE PROS

Always check your progress. When you reach the 5-minute mark, take one bean out of the pot and taste it to see if it is done enough. Remember, residual heat will continue to cook the beans even after you've drained them.

ORANGE-GLAZED CARROTS

Serves 4 to 6

A little orange juice and a pinch of sugar will make plain old cooked carrots something really special. It's a prescription that seems to work on some of the most vegetable-resistant kids.

Both small and large carrots have good flavor. Just make sure that they are hard and have no little hairy roots growing out of them when you purchase them. Baby carrots, which are sold already peeled, make a user-friendly pinch hitter for standard-size carrots.

1 pound carrots
1/4 cup orange juice
1/2 cup water
1 teaspoon light brown or granulated sugar
2 tablespoons unsalted butter
Salt and pepper

1. Peel the carrots and cut into 1/2-inch slices.

2. In a medium saucepan, heat the orange juice, water, and sugar over medium heat until boiling. Add the carrots, cover, and cook for 5 minutes, or until they are just starting to become tender.

3. Turn the heat up to high, uncover, and cook, occasionally stirring, until most of the liquid has evaporated, about 4 minutes more.

4. Drain off all but 1 tablespoon of liquid. Stir in the butter until melted and season with salt and pepper to taste.

If your crew happens to go for plain cooked carrots, make them according to the directions for string beans. Just let them go for 9 to 10 minutes.

PEAS

Serves 4

A bag of frozen peas makes a very good ice pack for burns and bumps.

Whether they are fresh or frozen, peas are a real labor-saving vegetable—and when it comes to labor, less is good and none is even better. If you are using fresh peas, never, ever shuck them yourself. They are the perfect diversion to keep the kids busy. Just show them how to open the pods and pluck out the peas. Issue a stern, but tongue-in-cheek, warning that they had better not eat one single pea. They will probably down a pound of them before they even get to the dinner table. It's like winning the division in the preseason. Now, when the clock is really running out, it's time to whip out the good ol' frozen peas. You should always have a few boxes or bags on hand in the freezer. They are the nutritious squeeze play that will help get a balanced meal on the table, pronto.

1 pound fresh peas in the pod or one 10-ounce package frozen peas
¹/₂ cup water
1 tablespoon butter
Salt and pepper

1. If the peas are fresh, have the kids pluck them out of the pods.

2. In a saucepan, bring the water to a boil. Add the peas, cover, and cook until just heated through, about 4 to 5 minutes. Drain off the liquid.

3. Stir in the butter until melted and season with salt and pepper to taste.

THE SHORTCUT CLUB

For microwaved peas: Put peas in a microwavable container with 2 table-spoons water and microwave, on high, in the microwave, for 5 minutes. Drain off the liquid. Stir in the butter until melted and season with salt and pepper to taste. (Have you noticed that the word "microwave" can be a verb, a noun, or an adjective? Have you also noticed that this isn't any faster than cooking them in a pan, on top of the stove?)

BRAISED KALE

Serves 4

These deep, dark, "hearty greens" consistently pop up on lists of healthiest foods, but that's not all. They are as amazingly delicious as they are nutritious. The big question is if kids will eat them. More often than not, the surprising answer is yes. This recipe will work just as well with collard greens, mustard greens, beet greens, Swiss chard, or spinach. Look for unblemished leaves with a high ratio of leaf to stem.

2 pounds kale
3 strips bacon
2 tablespoons vegetable oil (preferably canola)
2 cloves garlic, peeled and minced
$^3/_4$ cup chicken broth or 1 chicken bouillon cube dissolved in $^3/_4$ cup hot water

1. Wash the kale by plunging it into a big bowl of cold water and mixing. Repeat with fresh water until there is no sand at the bottom of the bowl, and then drain. Trim the thick stems from the bottoms of the kale leaves and discard. Coarsely chop the leaves into 1-inch pieces.

2. In a large saucepan, cook the bacon until crisp (see page 40). Remove it from the pan, drain on paper towels, and then crumble into pieces. Discard all but 1 tablespoon of the bacon fat from the pan.

3. Set the pan over medium heat, and add the oil and garlic to the pan. Cook for $1^1/_2$ minutes, or until the garlic is just starting to color. Add the chicken broth and then the chopped kale. Cook, covered, stirring occasionally, until the greens are tender, about 12 minutes. Drain any excess liquid before serving.

SAUTÉED MUSHROOMS

Serves 4

With mushrooms, it's all about texture, and the way to get a great, toothy bite is to give them plenty of room. They should fit in the pan comfortably, in a single layer, so their surfaces can sear and they can release their liquids. If there is too much of a pileup, they will just steam up and get icky. If necessary, sauté them in two batches.

There's nothing that wrong with plain old white button mushrooms, but to kick your fungus up a notch, try cremini. They are, in actuality, baby portobellos and have a heck of a lot more flavor than the cultivated white variety. When buying either mushroom, always make sure that the gills (on the undersides of the caps) are completely closed up. This indicates freshness and also allows you to give them a quick rinse without turning them soggy.

8 ounces mushrooms
1 tablespoon vegetable oil (preferably canola)
1 tablespoon olive oil
1 shallot (see Note, page 56), peeled and minced
Salt and pepper

1. If the gills (on the underside of the caps) are completely closed up, quickly rinse the mushrooms under running water and dry on paper towels. If the gills are exposed, wipe any sand or dirt off the mushrooms with a damp paper towel. Trim off the stems so they are no longer than ¼ inch and discard the remainder. Slice the caps ¼ inch thick.

2. In a large skillet, heat both of the oils over medium-high heat for 1 minute. Add the shallot and cook for 1½ minutes, or until softened.

3. Turn the heat up to high. Add the mushrooms and sauté, occasionally turning, until browned, 10 to 12 minutes. Season with salt and pepper.

CORN ON THE COB

As soon as corn is picked off the stalk, a chemical process begins, in which the sugar in the corn is converted into starch. That's why the fresher it is, the sweeter the corn is gonna be. Fanatics will try to get theirs from farm stands, immediately after it's been picked. They also inspect every ear, but just what is it that they are looking for when they peel down the husks and examine the cob as if they're conducting some kind of strip search? They are checking that there is no mold or damage on the ears and that the kernels are plump, unblemished, and lined up in straight rows, which indicates even growing and distribution of flavor.

4 ears corn
Salt
Butter

1. Remove the husks and silk from the corn.

2. Add $\frac{1}{2}$ teaspoon salt to a big pot of water and bring to a boil. Add the corn and boil for 5 minutes, or until tender. With tongs, yank the cobs out of the water (or drain them into a colander). Serve with plenty of butter and some salt.

Always use the right tool for the job. When it comes to buttering corn, the right tool is a slice of bread. Spread butter on the bread, and then, using the bread like it's a washcloth, rub it on the corn. It's the easiest way to evenly butter up a cob. You also end up with this buttery, steamy bread that has the faintest flavor of corn.

CORN OFF THE COB

Serves 4

THE SHORTCUT CLUB

So what can you do when corn isn't in season or you just don't have time for the fresh stuff? Reach for a 10-ounce package of frozen corn and cook it off, following the directions for peas (see page 174).

Sure, corn on the cob is fun, but there are plenty of times (like when you've got a toothless six-year-old) that you need to surgically remove those kernels from the cob. See Corn on the Cob (opposite) for buying tips.

4 ears corn
¼ cup water
1 tablespoon butter
Salt and pepper

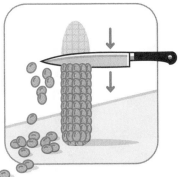

1. Remove the husks and silk from the corn. Stand one corn cob upright on a cutting board. With a thin, sharp knife, slice off the kernels. Repeat with the remaining cobs.

2. In a saucepan, bring the water to a boil. Add the corn, cover, and cook until just heated through, about 2 to 3 minutes. Drain off the liquid.

3. Stir in the butter until melted and season with salt and pepper to taste.

CORN ON THE GRILL

Grilling corn on the barbecue gives it an unstoppable, toasty flavor, but watch the cobs carefully. They can easily get too charred and burned.

4 ears corn
Butter
Salt

1. Preheat a grill to medium hot.

2. Remove the husks and silks from each ear of corn. Rinse the corn but do not dry; you want the corn a little wet when you add it to the grill.

3. Place the ears on the hot grill. Grill, covered, for 2 minutes on each side.

4. Serve with butter and salt.

OVEN-ROASTED CORN

You can replicate that great toasty, grilled flavor in the oven. Preheat the oven to 400°F. Pull the husks back to expose each ear. Remove the silks. Lightly pull the husks back over the ears. Soak the ears in water for 5 minutes, making sure that as much water as possible gets under the husks. Drain the ears. Roast the corn in the oven for 15 minutes. Remove the husks before serving.

ONION RINGS

Serves 4

They're not animal and they're not mineral, so that leaves one option. Yes, onion rings are a vegetable, probably even more so than ketchup. Choose a large onion that is firm throughout, without any signs of gray mold. These need a good, long soaking in buttermilk so the flour will stick, so plan accordingly.

1 large Spanish onion
1 cup buttermilk
3 teaspoons salt
Vegetable oil (preferably canola), for frying (about 2 cups)
1 cup all-purpose flour
$1/4$ teaspoon pepper

ADULTS ONLY
Add a teaspoon of hot sauce or $1/2$ teaspoon of cayenne pepper to the buttermilk.

1. Peel and slice the onion into $1/4$-inch-thick rings. Break the rings apart with your fingers.

2. In a large bowl, combine the buttermilk and 2 teaspoons of the salt. Add the onion rings and turn them to coat in the liquid. Cover and refrigerate for at least 2 hours or overnight.

3. In a large skillet, heat $1/2$ inch of oil over high heat until it starts to shimmer, about 5 minutes. (You may also use a deep fryer or candy thermometer to gauge the temperature: 365°F is perfect.) Turn the heat down to medium high.

**@!-#%. . . .
THAT'S HOT!!!**
Use caution and keep the kids away from the hot fryer!

4. In a large container (preferably one with a lid), a resealable plastic bag, or a bowl, mix together the flour, remaining teaspoon salt, and the pepper. Add the onion rings a few at a time, and shake to coat.

5. Working in batches that will comfortably fit in the pan, carefully fry the onion rings for 4 minutes on each side, or until golden brown. Remove from the oil with tongs and drain well on paper towels.

ROASTED POTATOES

Serves 4 to 6

This recipe is loosely adapted from one created by my brother Malcolm. My kids ask for it every time we visit him. Mal used to have a body like Brad Pitt: six-pack stomach, toned muscles, you know. He would also clear the dance floor every time he got out on it. It was like watching John Travolta in *Saturday Night Fever.* So, it's always an occasion when he shakes these potatoes up, 'cause in the process he also gets to shake his booty . . . only nowadays it's more like watching Gilbert Gottfried.

$1^1/_2$ **pounds Yukon Gold or red-skinned potatoes**
2 tablespoons vegetable oil (preferably canola)
1 teaspoon paprika
$^1/_2$ **teaspoon salt**
$^1/_4$ **teaspoon pepper**
1 medium onion, peeled and cut into chunks

1. Preheat the oven to 400°F. If you are using large potatoes, cut them into 1-inch chunks. If you are using small potatoes, cut them into halves or quarters.

2. Toss the potatoes in the oil, paprika, salt, and pepper or put everything in a resealable plastic bag and shake it all up. (White suit and platform shoes optional.)

3. Put the potatoes in a 2-quart baking dish. Bake for 10 minutes.

4. Mix in the onions and bake for about 20 more minutes, turning once or twice for even browning (check to make sure they don't burn on the bottom). The potatoes are done when they are crunchy and golden brown.

BAKED POTATOES

Serves 4 to 8

Baked potatoes may take a while to make, but you hardly have to do anything besides punch a few holes in them and pop 'em in the oven. This gives you plenty of time to start another project, watch some TV, and completely forget about what's going on in the kitchen. To prevent that panicked and ominous outburst of "Oh, no, the potatoes are still in the oven!," set a kitchen timer to remind you of their status. Don't waste your time with tricks like wrapping the potatoes in foil. Just stick 'em in the oven naked. They'll be perfect. For younger kids, serve half a potato per kid. Make sure your potatoes have few or no black bruise marks and absolutely no eyes, which indicates that they are over the hill. Potatoes should not be green in the interior.

4 large Russet or Idaho potatoes
Salt and pepper
2 tablespoons unsalted butter
Sour cream, minced scallions, and/or crumbled bacon
     (see page 40), for serving

1. Set a rack in the middle of the oven and preheat the oven to 400°F.

2. With a fork, pierce holes all around the potatoes; about 9 stabs per spud should be sufficient.

3. Place the potatoes right on the oven rack and bake until tender, about 1 hour.

4. Cut a deep slit lengthwise across the top of the potato. Sprinkle on salt and pepper to taste and top with a large pat of butter. Mash the butter into the flesh of the potato. Serve with sour cream, minced scallions, and/or crumbled bacon.

THE SHORTCUT CLUB

You can also bake the potatoes in a microwave on high until tender, about 10 minutes per side, turning once.

STUFFED DOUBLE-BAKED POTATOES

Serves 4

You take a potato and, bada-bing, bada-boom, it's a complete main dish. You might, however, run into one small problem. You have to hold your potatoes down while you work 'em over. If your potato is a little too hot to handle (and what spud that's done time in a 400°F oven isn't?), you have two options. First, you can use oven mitts, a towel, or tongs to hold it down. Second, and obviously more difficult, is that you can show a little patience and wait for it to cool down a little before grabbing it. A little bacon fat will give your filling great flavor, but it's strictly optional.

4 Baked Potatoes (page 183)
4 slices bacon
4 tablespoons ($^1/_2$ stick) unsalted butter
$^1/_4$ cup sour cream
Salt and pepper
3 ounces ($^3/_4$ cup) grated Cheddar or Swiss cheese

1. Preheat the oven to 400°F.

2. In a medium skillet, fry the bacon over medium heat until crisp and brown (see page 40). Transfer to paper towels to drain. Crumble the bacon into bits. Drain off all but 2 tablespoons of fat from the pan.

3. Cut off the top third of each potato. With a spoon, scoop the flesh out into a medium bowl, leaving a $^1/_4$-inch-thick potato shell. Mash the potato flesh with the butter, sour cream, salt, pepper, and 2 table-spoons reserved bacon fat, if desired. Mix half of the cheese and all of the bacon bits into the potatoes. Set the potato shells on a baking

pan. Heap the mixture into the potato skins and top with the remaining cheese.

4. Bake for 20 minutes, or until the potatoes are heated through and the cheese is all browned and melty.

MASHED POTATOES

Serves 4 to 6

Sometimes those great mashed potatoes that you get in restaurants can hardly be classified as vegetables. They're often made with tons of butter, cream, and milk but just a microscopic bit of potato to hold everything together. Here's a great recipe that maintains our favorite spud's integrity and more of its nutritional value.

DO IT LIKE THE PROS

For extra-smooth and creamy mashed potatoes, crank them through a food mill or push them through a strainer with a rubber spatula.

4 large Yukon Gold potatoes (about 2 pounds), peeled and
    quartered
4 tablespoons ($^1/_2$ stick) unsalted butter
$^1/_4$ teaspoon salt
$^1/_4$ teaspoon pepper
1 cup sour cream, half-and-half, milk, or a combination

1. Put the potatoes in a large pot of cold water (they should be completely submerged). Over medium heat, bring to a boil. Continue to cook for an additional 20 to 22 minutes, until tender when pierced with a knife.

2. Drain the potatoes, and then put them back in the pan. Mash them together with the butter, salt, and pepper. Mix in the sour cream, half-and-half, and/or milk.

3. If needed, warm them up over very low heat.

FRENCH-FRIED POTATOES

Serves 4 to 6

Put a plate of French fries in front of a kid on a hunger strike and she will eat them until she explodes. Fries just have that power. Authentic ones need to be fried twice: once as a primer and then again for a final crunchy finish. Of course, this is easy to do if you live in a diner and have a Frialator running all day. The rest of us need a more practical solution. The instructions on a package of frozen fries will probably tell you to just pop them in the oven, but the result will probably taste like cardboard. Actually frying them will, however, give them that double-fried flavor and crunchy texture. The oven may be a healthier option, but who eats fries because they're good for you?

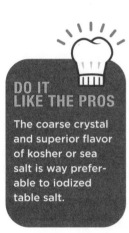

DO IT LIKE THE PROS

The coarse crystal and superior flavor of kosher or sea salt is way preferable to iodized table salt.

Vegetable oil (preferably canola), for frying (about 2 cups)
1 pound frozen French fries (that's half of a 2-pound bag,
**   for you numbers guys)**
Salt (preferably kosher or sea salt)

1. In a large skillet, heat $1/2$ inch of oil over high heat until it starts to shimmer, about 5 minutes. (You may also use a deep fryer or candy thermometer to gauge the temperature: 365°F is perfect.) Turn the heat down to medium high.

2. Working in batches that will comfortably fit in the pan, carefully fry the potatoes, turning occasionally, for 12 minutes, or until golden brown. Remove from the oil with tongs and drain well on paper towels.

3. Sprinkle with salt.

@!-#%. . . .
THAT'S HOT!!!
Use caution and keep the kids away from the hot fryer!

WHITE RICE

Cooking rice is an extremely simple task. Trust me; you don't need one of those hi-tech rice cookers. Measure right, set a timer, and you pretty much can't fail. Common long-grain rice is fine, but something a little more exotic could make a sweet change in your rice bowl. Try Japanese-style short-grain rice (there are some very good ones grown in California) or basmati rice, from India. They are both available in Asian markets and some health-food stores and supermarkets.

2 cups water
1/4 teaspoon salt
1 cup white rice
1 tablespoon unsalted butter

Like many other "hard-to-pick-up" foods, rice should be served to little kids with a spoon, or you may find yourself cleaning up with a chisel.

1. In a 2-quart saucepan, bring the water and salt to a boil.

2. Stir in the rice and butter. When the water returns to a boil, turn the heat down as low as it will go and cover the pot. Let simmer for 20 minutes (you may want to check it after 16 minutes). It is done when the water is evaporated and the rice is tender and studded with steam holes.

3. Remove it from the heat and let it stand, covered, for 5 more minutes. Fluff with a fork.

CORNY RICE

There probably isn't a kid around who doesn't like corn. Most of them like rice, also. Hence, this one-pan combo side dish will drive kids wild.

Stir 1 cup corn kernels, either from 1 ear (see Corn off the Cob, page 179) or thawed frozen corn, plus 1 extra tablespoon butter into White Rice (see opposite) or Brown Rice (page 190) about 5 minutes before they should be done.

BROWN RICE

Serves 4

Brown rice needs to go on one of those TV shows to get a makeover. It still has that hippy-dippy image. Yes, it is very good for you, but it also has a great, nutty flavor. Kids will generally prefer the processed, white version of rice, but cook your brown rice with a little butter, the way you would the white stuff, and it will have more than a fighting chance at the dinner table.

2¼ cups water
¼ teaspoon salt
1 cup brown rice
1 tablespoon unsalted butter

1. In a 2-quart saucepan, bring the water and salt to a boil.

2. Stir in the rice and butter. When the water returns to a boil, turn the heat down as low as it will go and cover the pot. Let simmer for 35 minutes (you may want to check it after 30 minutes). It is done when the water is evaporated and the rice is tender and studded with steam holes. Remove it from the heat and let it stand, covered, for 5 more minutes. Fluff with a fork.

SAUERKRAUT

Makes 2 cups

Sauerkraut is a neglected vegetable condiment. Most of the time it is barely heated and plopped on top of a hot dog. This, however, is not how great sauerkraut was meant to be served. Good kraut should be cooked, preferably Polish style, with onions, to give it a sweet, deep, and brilliant flavor dimension. This is the sauerkraut to try with your next hot dog, kielbasa, or Reuben Sandwich (see page 74). It's the kind of kraut you could easily eat a whole plate of. Sauerkraut may not be a favorite for little kids, but eventually, most of them grow up. When I had my deli, it was always a thrill to watch kids graduate from a hot dog with ketchup to a frank with mustard and kraut. You will usually find sauerkraut in your supermarket's refrigerated meat case.

1 tablespoon vegetable oil (preferably canola)
1 medium onion, peeled and cut into $1/4$-inch-thick slices
One 1-pound bag sauerkraut

1. In a large skillet, heat the oil over medium heat for 1 minute. Add the onions and cook, stirring occasionally, for 10 minutes, until completely browned.

2. Add the sauerkraut with all of its liquid. Continue to cook, stirring occasionally, until all of the liquid is evaporated and the sauerkraut is light golden brown.

UN-STUFFING

Just about everyone goes berserk for stuffing, but the best way to make it is outside the chicken. If you make it in the bird, the stuffing takes too long to cook. By the time the stuffing is done, the meat will be overcooked and dried out. Hence, the concept of un-stuffing, which is made on top of the stove or, in this case, separately in the oven. Stale bread chunks are the best for stuffing. Lay them out a day before you need them or dry them in the oven. While your stuffing bakes, check to make sure the bottom does not burn. If it looks like it is cooking too fast, slide a cookie sheet under the pan and turn the oven temperature down to 300°F.

One 1-pound loaf white, wheat, or just about any other bread
2 tablespoons vegetable oil (preferably canola), plus extra for
the baking dish
1 medium onion, peeled and chopped
2 cloves garlic, peeled and minced
1 teaspoon ground sage
1/4 teaspoon ground pepper
1 1/2 cups chicken broth or 2 chicken bouillon cubes dissolved in
1 1/2 cups hot water
2 tablespoons unsalted butter
2 large eggs, lightly beaten

1. Cut or rip the bread into 1-inch pieces. You should have about 7 cups. Put the bread chunks on a cookie sheet to dry out overnight or bake in a 300°F oven for 10 minutes, turning once.

2. Set a rack toward the top of the oven and preheat the oven to 350°F. Put the bread in a large bowl.

3. In a large skillet, heat the oil over medium heat for 30 seconds. Add the onion and cook, stirring occasionally, for 5 minutes, or until softened. Add the garlic, sage, and pepper and cook for 1 minute more. Stir in the broth and butter.

4. Thoroughly mix the liquid into the bread chunks. Mix in the eggs.

5. Lightly grease a 2-quart baking dish. Add the stuffing and cover with foil. Bake until heated through, about 12 minutes. Uncover and bake for 12 minutes more, until crusty on top.

GARLIC BREAD

The classic method for making garlic bread is to slice the loaf vertically, cutting hatches down to within $\frac{1}{2}$ inch of the bread base, and then sliding the butter and garlic between each crevice . . . huh? This is garlic bread, not an engineering project, so let's just dumb it down a bit, 'cause for incredibly good garlic bread, all you have to really do is slice the loaf in half and schmear.

$\frac{1}{4}$ **cup olive oil**
4 tablespoons ($\frac{1}{2}$ stick) butter
6 cloves garlic, peeled and minced
1 baguette (French bread) or 1 loaf of Italian bread

1. Set a rack in the middle of the oven and preheat to 425°F.

2. In a small saucepan, heat the oil and butter over medium-low heat for a minute or two until the butter melts. Add the garlic and cook for 1 minute. Remove from the heat and let sit for 10 minutes.

3. Slice the bread in half lengthwise then place it, cut side up, on a long sheet of aluminum foil. (If it doesn't fit, cut each piece in two and place each piece on its own sheet of aluminum foil.)

4. Spoon the garlic and butter over the bread. Sandwich the bread together and wrap loosely in the aluminum foil.

5. Bake for 12 minutes. Unwrap and turn the bread cut sides up. Bake for 8 more minutes, or until golden and crisp on top.

PARMESAN GARLIC BREAD

Sprinkle $1/2$ cup grated Parmesan or Pecorino Romano cheese on the buttered sides of the bread for the final, unwrapped stage of the baking.

CHILI GARLIC BREAD

Stir 2 or 3 tablespoons chili powder into the garlic butter before spooning it onto the bread.

BAKED BEANS

Making baked beans from scratch can take up to 24 hours, from soaking the dried beans to the long, slow cooking. With the help of a few simple, "secret" ingredients, this recipe takes less than 20 minutes to make. You will, however, need a very specialized piece of equipment called a can opener. Serve these beans out of a heavy old pot and everyone will assume that you made them with a recipe handed down from the Pilgrims.

1 teaspoon vegetable oil (preferably canola)
1 medium onion, peeled and minced
Two 15-ounce cans vegetarian baked beans
$1/4$ cup molasses
Pepper

1. In a medium saucepan, heat the oil over medium-high heat for 1 minute. Add the onion and cook, stirring occasionally, for 4 minutes, or until softened.

2. Add the beans and bring to a simmer. Turn the heat down to medium low and cook for 5 minutes. Add the molasses and cook for 8 minutes more, stirring occasionally. Season with pepper to taste.

BLACK BEANS

Serves 6

Here's another "gimme" bean recipe that just about any bunch of kids, or adults, will go for. Black beans are a standby side dish on pan-Latino menus. Try them with tacos (page 128), quesadillas (pages 80–84), nachos (pages 99–101), or Monterey Jack Chicken (page 137) or anything else Latino in a pan.

1 tablespoon vegetable oil (preferably canola)
1 medium onion, peeled and minced
1 clove garlic, peeled and minced
Two 15-ounce cans black beans, with their liquid
$1/2$ cup water
2 teaspoons chili powder

1. In a medium saucepan, heat the oil over medium-high heat for 1 minute. Add the onion and cook, stirring occasionally, for 4 minutes, or until softened. Add the garlic and cook for 1 minute more.

2. Add the beans and water. Bring to a simmer, and then turn the heat down to low and cook for 15 minutes. Mix in the chili powder and let cook, occasionally stirring, for 10 minutes more, or until the beans are broken up and goopy.

A GUY'S GUIDE TO BAKING AND
DESSERTS

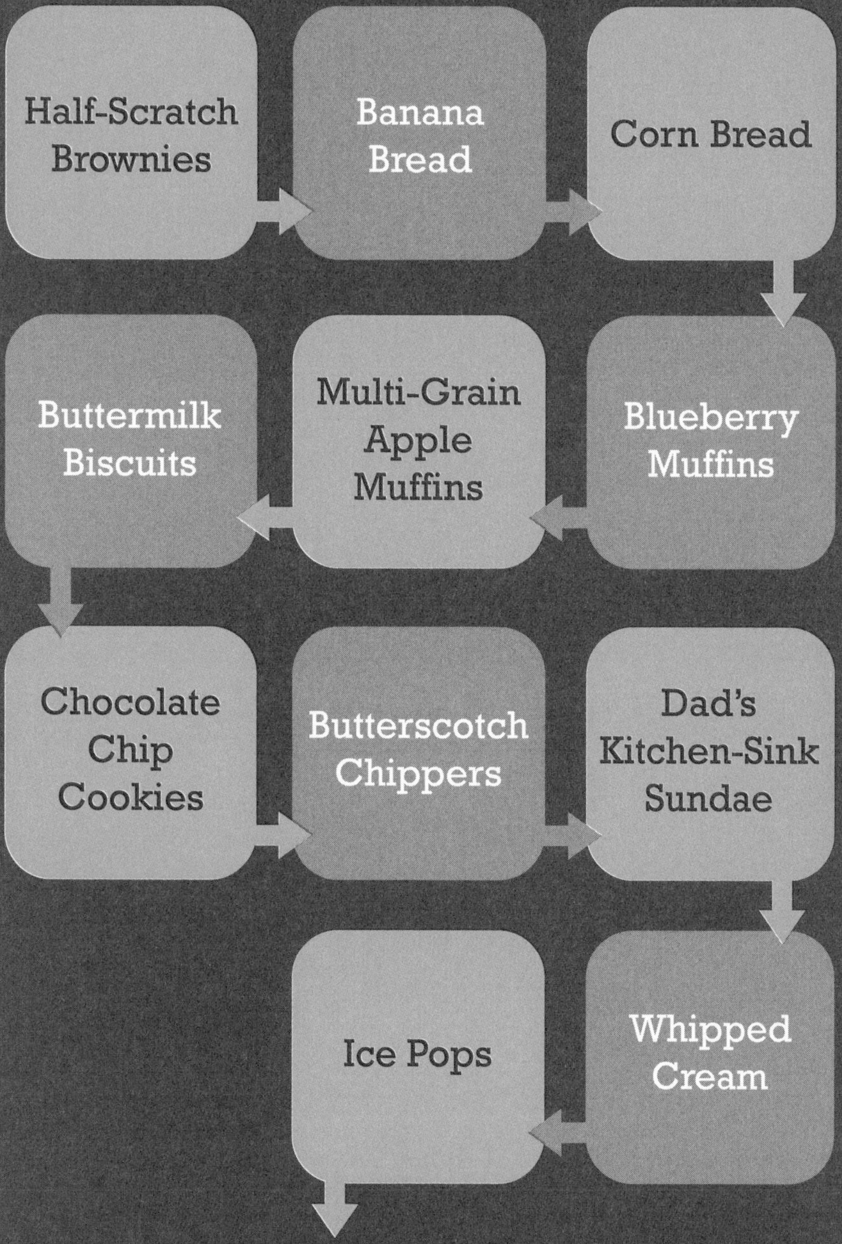

```
Half-Scratch          Banana            Corn Bread
Brownies      →       Bread      →

                                            ↓

Buttermilk      Multi-Grain      Blueberry
Biscuits    ←   Apple       ←    Muffins
                Muffins

   ↓

Chocolate                         Dad's
Chip        →   Butterscotch  →   Kitchen-Sink
Cookies         Chippers          Sundae

                                     ↓

                Ice Pops     ←    Whipped
                                  Cream

                   ↓
```

➡ **BAKING IS LIKE CARPENTRY.** First you figure out exactly what has to be done, then it's measure twice and cut once. There are no mulligans, so you have to be accurate and get it right the first time. Once that cake batter goes into the oven, the die has been cast. But as long as you follow the recipe carefully and pay attention to the details, you will easily make your point. Still, some guys are intimidated by baking and think that it is strictly the domain of women in the kitchen. Remember, Betty Crocker, the most famous female pastry chef of all time, was a fictitious character, made up by someone in an advertising agency. But the Pillsbury Dough Boy is, and always has been, a real, live person.

HALF-SCRATCH BROWNIES

Makes 16 brownies

Lately, there has been a lot of talk about semi-homemade food. Instead of making everything from scratch, you start out with a prepared food or store-bought mix and fix it up. It's a concept with some merit. After all, if you need a new window, you buy one that's pre-hung. Unfortunately, many of these semi-from-scratch recipes just taste semi-good. Here is a chocolaty, rich, and chewy brownie that is not only kid-tested but could probably fool most major-league pastry chefs.

Nonstick vegetable oil spray
3 ounces semisweet chocolate
$^1/_2$ cup unsalted butter
One 19.5- or 21-ounce package brownie mix
2 large eggs
$^1/_2$ cup water

1. Set a rack in the middle of the oven and preheat the oven to 350°F. Spray a $9 \times 13 \times 2$-inch baking pan with nonstick vegetable oil spray.

2. Put the chocolate and butter in a completely dry bowl or in the top of a double boiler and set it over barely simmering water. Stir occasionally, until melted. (You could also melt it in the microwave for 1 minute.)

3. In a large bowl, thoroughly mix together the brownie mix, eggs, and water. Mix in the chocolate and butter.

4. Spread the batter in the prepared pan. Bake for 30 minutes, or until just barely set but still moist in the center. Let cool for 30 minutes, and then cut into squares.

Brownie mix generally comes in two size groups. The 19.5- to 21-ounce size is made to fit in a 9×13-inch rectangular pan. The 15.5-ounce size is designed for an 8-inch square pan. If that is what you have in your cupboard, follow the instructions, but use only 1 egg, 6 tablespoons ($^3/_4$ stick) butter, and 2 ounces chocolate. It will make 9 to 12 brownies.

BANANA BREAD

Makes 1 loaf

There's no need to toss those soft old bananas. As long as they aren't brown or runny inside, they will make great banana bread. Try spreading some peanut butter or chocolate-hazelnut spread and fresh sliced banana between two slices of this bread for a great lunch-box sandwich.

Nonstick vegetable spray
$2^1/_2$ cups all-purpose flour
1 teaspoon baking soda
$^1/_4$ teaspoon baking powder
$^1/_4$ teaspoon salt
$^3/_4$ cup ($1^1/_2$ sticks) unsalted butter, at room temperature
$1^1/_4$ cups sugar
3 large eggs
3 large, ripe bananas
$^1/_2$ cup sour cream
1 teaspoon vanilla extract

1. Set a rack in the middle of the oven and preheat the oven to 350°F. Lightly coat a 6-cup loaf pan with nonstick vegetable oil spray.

2. In a medium bowl, mix together the flour, baking soda, baking powder, and salt.

3. In a large bowl, beat the butter and sugar together for 15 seconds, or until combined. (You may use an electric mixer or wooden spoon.) Add the eggs, one at a time, beating until each is incorporated. Continue beating until light and fluffy, about 6 minutes more.

4. In a medium bowl, mash the bananas with a fork until soupy. Stir in the sour cream and vanilla.

5. With the mixer on its lowest setting (or a wooden spoon), beat in half of the flour mixture. Beat in the banana mixture and then the remaining flour.

6. Spread the batter in the prepared pan and bake for 40 minutes, or until the center springs back when lightly pressed and a knife inserted into the center comes out clean. Set the pan on a rack to cool. Unmold and slice before serving.

CHOCOLATE CHIP BANANA BREAD

Mix ½ cup chocolate chips into the batter before baking.

NUTTY BANANA BREAD

Mix ½ cup lightly toasted walnuts or pecans (page 213) into the batter before baking.

CORN BREAD

Serves 8

Corn bread is a family-friendly quick bread that fits in with just about any meal. You can serve it with bacon and eggs for breakfast or fried chicken for dinner. Since it's made in one big pan, you can make a big batch in one simple shot. Although it is at its optimum when still warm from the oven, it can also be made several hours ahead of time. Yellow, white, or even blue cornmeal will all work equally well for this recipe.

Cupcake liners or nonstick vegetable oil spray

2 cups cornmeal

2 cups all-purpose flour

$1/4$ cup sugar

2 tablespoons baking powder

$1^1/2$ teaspoons salt

2 large eggs

$2^1/2$ cups buttermilk

1 cup (2 sticks) unsalted butter, melted

Yes, this recipe does have a bit of butter in it. If you want to cut it down, substitute $1/2$ cup vegetable oil, preferably canola, for $1/2$ cup (1 stick) of the butter.

1. Set a rack in the middle of the oven and preheat the oven to 375°F. Lightly coat a $13 \times 9 \times 2$-inch baking pan with nonstick vegetable oil spray.

2. In a medium bowl, stir together the cornmeal, flour, sugar, baking powder, and salt. Make a well in the center and stir in the eggs and buttermilk. Stir in the melted butter just until combined.

3. Transfer the batter to the pan. Bake for 25 minutes, or until completely set and a knife inserted into the center comes out dry. The corn bread should be lightly golden and crusty on top. Let cool for at least 10 minutes, and then slice into squares.

CORN AND JALAPEÑO CORN BREAD

Stir 1 minced fresh jalapeño or serrano chile; $\frac{1}{2}$ small onion, minced; the kernels from 1 ear fresh corn (see Corn off the Cob, page 179) or $\frac{3}{4}$ cup frozen corn into the batter.

Quick Breads

Muffins, banana breads, and corn bread are part of a culinary family called quick breads. They get their leavening from baking powder or baking soda, which react with liquid and heat almost instantaneously. Yeast-leavened breads, on the other hand, need to go through a much longer process of proofing, kneading, and fermenting in order to rise. It's a very simple job to assemble the batter for quick breads. Depending on the recipe and available equipment, quick beads can be mixed together in a variety of methods. An electric mixer is the easiest way to combine everything, but be careful when you add the flour. If the mixer is running too fast, you could end up wearing the stuff. You can also make them with a wooden spoon and a bowl.

BLUEBERRY MUFFINS

Makes a dozen muffins

Use fresh or frozen blueberries for these mellow, classic muffins, but if you use frozen, don't thaw them out. They will squish into the batter and turn your muffins all mushy. Mix them right in, hard and frozen. Always line your muffin pan with either paper or foil cupcake liners or coat the pan with nonstick vegetable oil spray. This will prevent the muffins from sticking to the pan and make cleanup much easier.

Cupcake liners or nonstick vegetable oil spray
2 cups all-purpose flour
2 teaspoons baking powder
$1/2$ teaspoon salt
$1/2$ cup (1 stick) unsalted butter, at room temperature
$3/4$ cup sugar
2 large eggs
$1/2$ cup milk
1 teaspoon vanilla extract
1 pint (2 cups) fresh or frozen blueberries

1. Set a rack in the middle of the oven and preheat the oven to 375°F. Line a 12-slot muffin tin with cupcake liners or coat with nonstick vegetable oil spray.

2. In a medium bowl, stir together the flour, baking powder, and salt. Set aside.

3. In a large bowl, beat the butter and sugar together for 15 seconds, or until blended. (You may use an electric mixer or wooden spoon.) One at a time, beat in the eggs until smooth and incorporated, about 15 seconds each.

4. Mix in half of the flour mixture, blending just to combine. Mix in the milk and vanilla and then the remaining flour mixture. Gently mix in the blueberries.

5. Fill the muffin cups three-quarters full of batter and bake for 30 minutes, or until light golden brown. The centers should spring back when lightly pressed and a toothpick inserted into the center should come out clean. Cool the muffins on a rack for 15 minutes, and then tap them out of the tin.

CRANBERRY MUFFINS

Cranberries add zing to your morning muffin. Once again, if your berries are frozen, do not let them thaw out before mixing them into the batter.

Substitute $\frac{1}{4}$ teaspoon orange oil or $\frac{1}{2}$ teaspoon orange extract for the vanilla and fresh or frozen cranberries for the blueberries.

MULTI-GRAIN APPLE MUFFINS

Makes a dozen muffins

"Healthy" isn't always synonymous with "tasty," but these muffins completely defy that old stereotype. They are full of fresh fruit and whole grains and are as delicious as they are wholesome. Most of the ingredients on your shopping list can easily be found at the super-market, but you may have to visit the local health food store to find the miller's bran (sometimes called wheat bran).

Cupcake liners or nonstick vegetable oil spray
1^1/$_2$ cups all-purpose flour
^{1}/$_2$ cup miller's bran (wheat bran)
^{1}/$_2$ cup old-fashioned rolled oats
^{1}/$_2$ cup wheat germ
1^1/$_2$ teaspoons baking powder
^{3}/$_4$ teaspoon baking soda
^{3}/$_4$ teaspoon ground cinnamon
^{3}/$_4$ cup firmly packed dark brown sugar
2 large eggs
^{1}/$_2$ cup vegetable oil (preferably canola)
^{1}/$_2$ cup frozen apple juice concentrate, thawed
1^1/$_4$ cups milk
2 Granny Smith apples, peeled, cored, and cut into ^{1}/$_2$-inch chunks

1. Set a rack in the middle of the oven and preheat the oven to 375°F. Line a 12 slot-muffin tin with cupcake liners or coat with nonstick vegetable oil spray.

2. In a medium bowl, stir together the flour, bran, oats, wheat germ, baking powder, baking soda, and cinnamon. Set aside.

3. In a large bowl, beat the brown sugar and eggs together with an electric mixer on high speed for 2 minutes, or until creamy. (You can also do this with a whisk and a lot of elbow grease.) Continue beating, slowly drizzling in the oil until well blended and emulsified.

4. With the mixer on its lowest setting, beat in half of the flour mixture, blending just to combine. Gradually beat in the apple juice and milk and then the remaining flour mixture. Gently mix in the apples. Do not overmix.

5. Fill the muffin cups three-quarters full of batter and bake for 30 minutes, or until light golden brown. The centers should spring back when lightly pressed and a toothpick inserted into the center should come out clean. Cool the muffins on a rack for 15 minutes, and then tap them out of the tin.

BUTTERMILK BISCUITS

Makes a dozen biscuits

Frank Perdue, the late chicken impresario, once said that it took a tough guy to make a tender chicken. To make tender biscuits, it just takes someone with the ability to follow a recipe. For the ultimate in flaky biscuits, use cake flour. Make sure you do not confuse cake flour with self-rising flour, a substance that you should avoid; the unspecified amount of leavening agents could radically throw a recipe off. Also, make sure that you don't overmix. The dough should look lumpy and barely come together. You can use butter, vegetable shortening, or a combination of the two. To cut and chill vegetable shortening, spread it on a piece of wax paper and score it into little pieces. Stick it in the freezer until you're ready to add it to the dough.

2 cups cake or all-purpose flour (do not use self-rising flour)
1 tablespoon baking powder
1/2 teaspoon baking soda
1/2 teaspoon salt
1 teaspoon sugar
3 tablespoons cold butter, cut into pea-size bits
2 tablespoons vegetable shortening, cut into small bits
1 cup buttermilk
Approximately 2 tablespoons butter, melted

1. Set a rack in the middle of the oven and preheat the oven to 400°F.

2. In a large bowl, stir together the flour, baking powder, baking soda, salt, and sugar. Using a pastry blender, the flat beater attachment of an electric mixer, or your fingertips, work in the butter and shortening until the mixture resembles coarse meal. Mix in the buttermilk to form a soft dough. On a lightly floured surface (such as a cutting board, plate, or cookie sheet), pat it out into a 1-inch-thick circle. Refrigerate for at least 1 hour, until firm.

3. Cut out 2-inch round biscuits and arrange them at 2-inch intervals on a nonstick or parchment-lined cookie sheet. If necessary, gently pat the scraps together and cut more biscuits to make a total of 12.

4. Bake for 16 to 18 minutes, until lightly tanned and springy when pressed. To serve, brush the warm tops with melted butter.

CORN BISCUITS

Mix 1 cup fresh corn (from 1 ear, see Corn off the Cob, page 179), 2 tablespoons minced onion, and ½ teaspoon dried sage into the dough along with the buttermilk.

CHEESE-TOP BISCUITS

Mix in ¼ cup grated Cheddar cheese and ¼ cup grated Parmesan or Pecorino Romano cheese along with the butter. Top each biscuit with a teaspoon of grated Cheddar before baking.

CHOCOLATE CHIP COOKIES

Makes 5 dozen cookies

Now that you've finally got the little nippers to eat their vegetables, it's time to treat 'em to some cookies, and the number-one favorite is the chocolate chip. Since you will have to bake these cookies in batches, it would be helpful to have two cookie sheets. If you only have one, let it cool down for 5 minutes before you remove the first batch and another 10 minutes before you set the next batch of cookies on it.

2$^1\!/_4$ cups all-purpose flour

1 teaspoon baking soda

$^1\!/_2$ teaspoon salt

1 cup (2 sticks) unsalted butter, at room temperature

$^1\!/_2$ cup granulated sugar

1 cup packed light brown sugar

2 large eggs

2 teaspoons vanilla extract

One 12-ounce bag semisweet chocolate chips

1$^1\!/_2$ cups walnut or pecan pieces, lightly toasted
    (see Do It Like the Pros, opposite) (optional)

1. Set two racks in the middle and top thirds of the oven and preheat the oven to 375°F.

2. In a medium bowl, stir together the flour, baking soda, and salt. Set aside.

3. In a large bowl, beat the butter and the granulated and brown sugars together for 15 seconds, or until blended. (You may use an electric mixer or wooden spoon.) One at a time, beat in the eggs until smooth, about 30 seconds more, and then beat in the vanilla.

With the mixer on its lowest setting (or with a wooden spoon), gradually add the flour mixture, blending just to combine. Mix in the chocolate chips and the nuts, if you are using them.

4. Drop tablespoons of dough onto nonstick or parchment-lined cookie sheets at 3-inch intervals. Dip your fingers in a little water, and then flatten and round the cookies out a little.

5. Bake for 12 minutes, turning the cookie sheet around midway through for even baking. The cookies are done when they are lightly and evenly browned around the edges. Set the cookie sheets on a rack to cool, and then lift the cookies off with a spatula.

DO IT LIKE THE PROS

Toasting nuts really brings out their flavor. To do it, spread them on a cookie sheet and bake at 325°F for 5 minutes, or until fragrant and very lightly browned. Remove from the oven and set aside to cool completely before mixing into doughs or batters.

BUTTERSCOTCH CHIPPERS

Makes 4 dozen cookies

Once upon a time, kids would brag that their dad was bigger than yours, or stronger than yours, or could play the cello better than yours. I took these Butterscotch Chippers into my seven-year-old's first-grade class. One of her classmates raised her hand and confessed that these cookies were even better than the ones her dad makes. Of course, my daughter was gloating with victory. Today, every dad needs a signature cookie he can call his own. This lil' chipper, basically a vanilla wafer loaded with butterscotch chips, is unique and unbeatable.

1¼ cups all-purpose flour
¼ cup cornstarch
1 teaspoon baking powder
½ teaspoon baking soda
¼ teaspoon salt
½ cup (1 stick) unsalted butter, at room temperature
1 cup sugar
1 large egg
2 teaspoons vanilla extract
One 12-ounce bag butterscotch chips

1. Set two racks in the middle and upper thirds of the oven and preheat the oven to 375°F.

2. In a medium bowl, stir together the flour, cornstarch, baking powder, baking soda, and salt. Set aside.

3. In a large bowl, beat the butter and sugar together for 15 seconds, or until blended. (You may use an electric mixer or wooden spoon.) Beat in the egg until smooth, about 30 seconds more, and then beat in the vanilla. With the mixer on its lowest setting (or with a wooden spoon), gradually add the flour mixture and half of the butterscotch chips, blending just to combine.

4. Drop tablespoons of dough onto nonstick or parchment-lined cookie sheets at 3-inch intervals. Press the remaining chips into the tops of the cookies. Dip your fingers in a little water, and then flatten and round the cookies out a little.

5. Bake for 8 minutes, turning the cookie sheet around midway through for even baking. The cookies are done when they are lightly tanned around their edges. Set the cookie sheets on a rack to cool, and then lift the cookies off with a spatula.

DAD'S KITCHEN-SINK SUNDAE

When I was a kid, Jahn's Ice Cream Parlor, in Queens, New York, was the place to go for a birthday celebration or when you won a big ball game. Their specialty was a humongous sundae called "The Kitchen Sink." It contained every topping imaginable and was big enough to feed an army. Predictably, half of us would end up with an ice-cream headache and at least one kid would send us all into hysterics when ice cream and/or soda came streaming out of his nose. This would be talked about for years. Try Jahn's winning concept by making one huge sundae and serving it family style. If you think that this might render the kids a bit out of control, just make individual sundaes instead.

Ice cream
Whipped Cream (opposite)
Chocolate sauce or syrup
Sprinkles (a.k.a. jimmies) (optional)
Any kind of nuts, lightly toasted (see Do It Like the Pros, opposite)
Any kind of berries and/or sliced banana

1. Set a large bowl in the freezer to chill.

2. Scoop ice cream into said bowl.

3. Plop on the whipped cream. Squirt on the chocolate sauce. Get creative and sprinkle on sprinkles, nuts, fruit, or anything else that the kids will like.

4. Gather 'round with spoons and plenty of napkins.

WHIPPED CREAM

DO IT LIKE THE PROS

Only use real vanilla extract. It is rumored that the imitation stuff is a by-product of the lumber industry. Urban legend or not, it tastes like a by-product of the cheap perfume industry.

Put a big glob of whipped cream on a scoop of ice cream, a slice of pie, or a dish of pudding and magically they turn into major desserts. Of course you can accomplish this by simply squirting some stuff out of a can, but you are now a major force in the kitchen, so that's no longer an option. You wouldn't serve peas or carrots out of a tin can, so why would you do it with something as important as whipped cream?

If you have a stand mixer, use the wire whisk attachment. It will be a cinch to make. If you have to use a hand whisk, get ready, Ahnold. This task takes a little muscle.

2 cups heavy or whipping cream
1/4 cup confectioners' sugar
1 teaspoon vanilla extract

In a large, chilled bowl, whip the cream (with an electric mixer or wire whisk) until slightly thickened. Add the sugar and then the vanilla. Whip to the consistency of shaving cream. This cream should hold up for 24 hours in the refrigerator. If it starts to collapse, just rewhip it.

THE SHORTCUT CLUB

If you choose to buy canned whipped cream, please buy the real stuff. Keep clear of anything labeled "whipped topping."

ICE POPS

Kids go wild over ice pops and, depending on which ones you buy, they can be a pretty wholesome treat. Too many of them, however, are made with artificial flavoring or artificial coloring, or come with artificially inflated prices. The healthy and economical alternative is to make your own. You will need an ice-pop set, which is sold in a variety of stores, from supermarkets to department stores. Look for the cleverly designed ones that have a rim to catch the drips and a plastic straw, so kids can suck the juice up as it melts. Just about any juice will do (well, maybe not tomato or clam). Even prune juice can be transformed into a treat (and if you're a dad, you know all about prune juice and that cranky little tyke).

Juice, lemonade, or fruit punch

Fill the ice-pop molds almost to the top. (Leave a little room for the ice to expand as it freezes.) Insert the sticks. Freeze until hard. The pops will usually pop right out. If you have any trouble, just wrap your hand around them for a few seconds to warm and loosen them up.

Acknowledgments

A special thank you to my wife, Jacqueline, who did a great job taking the photos for the illustrations. Particular recognition must be given to Nigel Holmes, the extremely clever and talented illustrator of this book. As always, thanks to my agent and longtime buddy, Jane Dystel. Thanks to my editor, Rica Allannic, her assistant Adrienne Jozwick, and book designer Jane Treuhaft.

Thanks to my food-biz colleagues for their advice, guidance, inspiration and information, Michael Lomonaco, Ernestine Sclafani, Terence Noonan, Rosemary Black, Cynthia Killian, Erica Marcus, Gael Greene, Michael Batterberry, Beverly Stephens, Danny Kowal, Neil Manackle, and Jesse Davis. Special thanks to Brian Maynard of KitchenAid and Chris Tracy of Calphalon for supplying so much of the equipment used in the development and testing of the recipes.

Thanks also to all the families and friends who gave their encouragement, comments, and appetites to the creation of this book. Extra-credit awards go to Julia and Dinah Bianchi, Anna and Jane Brooks; Manon and Soren Bushong; Marcus and Claudine Gabrielli; Kate, Benjamin, and Lucien Hicks; Ozzie and Nicky Hoffman; Lily and Georgia Hupfel; Harrison and Ian Rottman; and, of course, to Violet and Isabella Brachman, who helped to taste and make so many of the recipes.

INDEX

WAYNE HARLEY BRACHMAN is the author of *American Desserts, Retro Desserts,* and *Cakes & Cowpokes.* He has served as executive pastry chef at a number of well-known New York establishments, including Mesa Grill and Bolo, working alongside Bobby Flay for ten years. He is opening a family-friendly bakery/café in Manhattan's Greenwich Village in 2006. Brachman lives in New York City with his wife and two children.

Steck-Vaughn

English ASAP™

Connecting English to the Workplace

SCANS Consultant

Shirley Brod
Spring Institute for International Studies
Boulder, Colorado

Program Consultants

Judith Dean-Griffin
ESL Teacher
Windham Independent School District
Texas Department of Criminal Justice
Huntsville, Texas

Marilyn K. Spence
Workforce Education Coordinator
Orange Technical Education Centers
Mid-Florida Tech
Orlando, Florida

Brigitte Marshall
English Language Training
for Employment Participation
Albany, California

Dennis Terdy
Director, Community Education
Township High School District 214
Arlington Heights, Illinois

Christine Kay Williams
ESL Specialist
Towson University
Baltimore, Maryland

STECK-VAUGHN®
COMPANY

A Division of Harcourt Brace & Company

Acknowledgments

Executive Editor:	Ellen Northcutt
Supervising Editor:	Tim Collins
Assistant Art Director:	Richard Balsam
Interior Design:	Richard Balsam, Jill Klinger, Paul Durick
Electronic Production:	Jill Klinger, Stephanie Stewart, Alan Klemp, David Hanshaw
Assets Manager:	Margie Foster

Editorial Development: Course Crafters, Inc., Newburyport, Massachusetts

Photo Credits

Alhadeff–p.6, 15, 27, 34-35, 46-47, 51, 58-59, 63c, 75c, 75d, 94-95, 106-107, 111b, 114a, 118-119; Don Couch Photography–p.39a, 39c, 39d, 111c, 111d; Jack Demuth–3b, 3c, 13, 39b, 92a, 92b, 92c, 99b; Patrick Dunn–p.87a, 87b, 111a, 114b; Christine Galida–p.61, 63a, 63d, 75a, 87c, 107b; David Omer–p.22-23, 82-83; Sharon Seligman–p.75b, 87d; Park Street–p.3a, 3d, 10-11, 28, 53, 70-71, 99a, 99c, 99d, 101.

Additional photography: p. 63b ©Superstock.

Illustration Credits

Cover: Tim Dove, D Childress
Cindy Aarvig–p.30, 37, 64, 88, 97a; Richard Balsam–p.10-12, 14, 17-20, 22a, 23-25, 35, 55, 57-59, 62; Barbara Beck–p.70-72, 74, 76, 85; Antonio Castro (Represented by Cornell & McCarthy, LLC)–p.113; Chris Celusniak–p.29, 95; Rhonda Childress–p.4, 9; David Griffin–p.16 , 22b-d, 26, 33, 52, 68, 93; Dennis Harms–p.31, 34, 38; Chuck Joseph–p.77-79, 81-83, 85d, 86, 91, 94, 96, 106, 107a, 108, 109, 118-121; Linda Kelen–p.5; Michael Krone–p.40, 49, 65, 97b-d, 98, 112; John Scott–p.90, 105; Danielle Szabo–p.3, 15, 27, 36, 39, 41, 48, 49e, 50, 51, 56, 60, 63, 75, 87, 99, 111; Milburn Taylor–p.54, 66, 73, 89.

Contents

Units	SCANS Competencies	Workforce Skills
Communication	Communicate information Acquire and interpret information Work with cultural diversity Understand social systems	Introduce yourself Make introductions Complete forms for work
Your Workplace	Communicate information Acquire and interpret information Understand organizational systems Allocate time	Give directions to places at work Understand directions to places at work Name places at work Use a to-do list
Technology	Select, apply, maintain, and troubleshoot technology Teach others Interpret and communicate information	Listen to and follow instructions Set up and use a machine Read a diagram Explain how to use a machine
Time Management	Allocate time Organize, interpret, communicate, and maintain information Understand organizational systems	Read, write, and say times, days, and dates Interpret work schedules Ask to change your work hours Respond to schedule changes
Customer Service	Serve customers Negotiate Organize and maintain information Monitor and correct performance Understand social systems	Greet customers Give good customer service Understand commitments to customers Respond to customers' complaints
Culture of Work	Understand social systems Understand organizational systems Monitor and correct performance	Follow company rules Call in sick Use polite language Improve your performance
Finances	Allocate resources Understand organizational systems Work on teams Organize and communicate information	Count money Fill out a time card Make a deposit Understand a W-4 form
Health and Safety	Interpret and communicate information Understand organizational systems	Identify parts of the body Handle an emergency Describe an injury or illness Read safety signs Follow safety instructions
Working with People	Allocate human resources Work on teams Evaluate performance	Give and receive feedback Talk about job duties Evaluate your work Identify job skills
Career Development	Interpret and communicate information Acquire information Understand social systems	Describe your job skills Read help-wanted ads Figure out the best job for you Complete a job application

Each unit of *English ASAP* systematically presents one or more SCANS Competencies.
The SCANS Foundation Skills are integrated throughout the instruction.

Units	Grammar
Communication	Present tense of **be** (statements, contractions) Subject pronouns Possessive adjectives
Your Workplace	Present tense of **be** (**yes/no** questions, short answers) Prepositions of location Questions with **where** Imperatives
Technology	Present progressive tense (statements, negatives, **yes/no** questions, short answers) Possessive nouns Questions with **what** and **where**
Time Management	Expressions with **it** (statements, questions, negatives, short answers) Requests with **can**
Customer Service	Count/noncount distinction (**a, an/some**) Singular and plural nouns Questions with **how much** and **how many**
Culture of Work	Simple present tense (statements, negatives, questions, short answers) **This, that, these, those**
Finances	**There is/there are** Questions with **which**
Health and Safety	Questions with **how** Simple present of **have** and **feel**
Working with People	Contrast simple present/present progressive Adverbs of frequency (**always, usually, sometimes, never**)
Career Development	**Can/can't** (ability) Simple past tense of **be** Questions with **how long** and answers with **for/from...to**

Scope and Sequence

English ASAP is a complete, communicative, SCANS-based, four-skill ESL program for teaching adult and young adult learners the skills they need to succeed at work.

FEATURES

♦ *English ASAP* **is SCANS-based.** *English ASAP*'s SCANS-based syllabus teaches skills learners need to succeed in the workplace. The syllabus is correlated with the SCANS competencies, a taxonomy of work skills recognized by the U.S. Department of Labor as essential to every job. Additionally, the syllabus is compatible with the work skills and competencies in the Comprehensive Adult Student Assessment System (CASAS) Competencies, the Mainstream English Language Training Project (MELT), the National Institute for Literacy's Equipped for the Future Framework for Adult Literacy, and state curriculums for adult ESL from Texas and California.

 The *On Your Job* symbol appears on the Student Book page and corresponding page in the Teacher's Edition each time learners apply a SCANS-based skill to their jobs or career interests.

♦ *English ASAP* **is about the world of work.** All of the conversations, reading selections, listening activities, and realia are drawn from authentic workplace situations. *English ASAP* presents settings and workers from major career clusters, including transportation, health care, service occupations, office occupations, construction, hospitality, and industrial occupations.

♦ *English ASAP* **teaches the skills required in all job descriptions.** Learners gain valuable experience working in teams; teaching others; serving customers; organizing, evaluating, and communicating information; understanding and using technology; negotiating; allocating resources; and completing projects.

♦ *English ASAP* **is communicative.** Numerous conversational models and communicative activities in the Student Books and Teacher's Editions—including problem-solving activities, surveys, and cooperative learning projects—get learners talking from the start.

♦ **English ASAP is appropriate for adults and young adults.** The language and situations presented in *English ASAP* are ones adults and young adults are likely to encounter. The abundance of attractive, true-to-life photographs, illustrations, and realia will interest and motivate adult and young adult learners.

- *English ASAP* **addresses all four language skills.** Each level of *English ASAP* addresses listening, speaking, reading, and writing. Starting in Level 1, a two-page grammar spread in each Student Book unit plus corresponding Workbook reinforcement and supplementary grammar worksheets in the Teacher's Editions ensure that learners get appropriate grammar practice.

- *English ASAP* **starts at the true beginner level.** *English ASAP* begins at the Literacy Level, designed for learners who have no prior knowledge of English and have few or no literacy skills in their native language(s) or are literate in a language with a non-Roman alphabet. Learners master foundation literacy skills in tandem with listening and speaking skills. The next level, Level 1, is intended for learners with little or no prior knowledge of English. As learners continue through the program, they master progressively higher levels of language and work skills. The Placement Tests help teachers place learners in the appropriate level of the program. For information on placement, see page v of this Teacher's Edition.

- *English ASAP* **is appropriate for multilevel classes.** Because unit topics carry over from level to level with increasing sophistication, the series is ideal for use in multilevel classes. For example, a Literacy Level skill in the technology unit is naming machines. A Level 2 skill in the technology unit is completing machine maintenance reports. Units are situational and nonsequential, making *English ASAP* appropriate for open-entry/open-exit situations.

- *English ASAP* **meets the needs of individual workplaces and learners.** Because the demands of each workplace and each individual's job are unique, the abundance of *On Your Job* activities allows learners to relate their new skills to their workplaces and career interests. In addition, the Personal Dictionary feature in each unit lets learners focus only on the vocabulary they need to do their jobs. Finally, with Steck-Vaughn's *Workforce Writing Dictionary,* learners can create a complete custom dictionary of all the vocabulary they need to know to succeed.

COMPONENTS

English ASAP consists of:

♦ Student Books

♦ Workbooks starting at Level 1

♦ Teacher's Editions

♦ Audiocassettes

♦ Steck-Vaughn *Workforce Writing Dictionary*

♦ Placement Tests, Form A and Form B

Student Books

Each four-color Student Book consists of ten 12-page units, providing learners with ample time on task to acquire the target SCANS competencies and language.

♦ **The Student Books follow a consistent format for easy teaching and learning.** Each unit is consistently organized and can be taught in approximately eight to twelve classroom sessions.

♦ **Complete front matter offers valuable teaching suggestions.** Ideas on how to teach each type of activity in the Student Book units and suggested teaching techniques give teachers valuable information on how to use *English ASAP* with maximum success.

♦ **Clear directions and abundant examples ensure that learners always know exactly what to do.** Examples for each activity make tasks apparent to learners and teachers. Clear exercise titles and directions tell teachers and learners exactly what learners are to do.

♦ **Performance Check pages provide a complete evaluation program.** Teachers can use these pages to evaluate learners' progress and to track the program's learner verification needs. Success is built in because work skills are always checked in familiar formats.

Workbooks

The Workbooks contain ten eight-page units plus a complete Answer Key. Each Workbook unit always contains at least one exercise for each section of the Student Book. To allow for additional reinforcement of grammar, there are multiple exercises for the Grammar section. The exercises for each section of the Student Book are indicated on the corresponding page of the Teacher's Edition and in a chart at the front of each Workbook. Because the Answer Keys are removable, the Workbooks can be used both in the classroom and for self-study.

Teacher's Editions

The complete Teacher's Editions help both new and experienced teachers organize their teaching, motivate their learners, and successfully use a variety of individual, partner, and teamwork activities.

♦ **Unit Overviews provide valuable information on how to motivate learners and organize teaching.** Each opener contains a complete list of the SCANS and workplace skills in the unit to help teachers organize their teaching. The Unit Warm-Up on each unit opener page helps teachers build learners' interest and gets them ready for the unit. The openers also contain a list of materials—including pictures, flash cards, and realia—teachers can use to enliven instruction throughout the unit.

♦ **The Teacher's Editions contain complete suggested preparation and teaching procedures for each section of the Student Book.** Each section of a unit begins with a list of the workplace skills developed on the Student Book page(s). Teachers can use the list when planning lessons. The teaching notes give suggestions for a recommended three-part lesson format:

Preparation: Suggestions for preteaching the new language, SCANS skills, and concepts on the Student Book page(s) before learners open their books.

Presentation: Suggested procedures for working with the Student Book page(s) in class.

Follow-Up: An optional activity to provide reinforcement or to enrich and extend the new language and competencies. The Follow-Ups include a variety of interactive partner and team activities. Each activity has a suggested variant, marked with ♦ for use with learners who require activities at a slightly more sophisticated level. For teaching ease, the corresponding Workbook exercise(s) for each page or section of the Student Book are indicated on the Teacher's Edition page starting at Level 1.

♦ **The Teacher's Editions contain SCANS Notes, Teaching Notes, Culture Notes, and Language Notes.** Teachers can share this wealth of information with learners or use it in lesson planning.

♦ **Each Teacher's Edition unit contains an additional suggested Informal Workplace-Specific Assessment.** Teachers will find these suggestions invaluable in evaluating learners' success in relating their new skills to their workplaces or career interests. Designed to supplement the Performance Check pages in each unit of the Student

Books, these brief speaking activities include having learners state their workplace's customer service policies, their workplace's policies on lateness and absence, and the procedures they use at work to maintain equipment.

♦ **Blackline Masters.** In the Literacy Level, the Blackline Masters help teachers present or reinforce many basic literacy skills. Starting at Level 1, the Blackline Masters reinforce the grammar in each unit.

♦ **Additional features in the Teacher's Editions.** The Teacher's Editions contain Individual Competency Charts for each unit and a Class Cumulative Competency Chart for recording learners' progress and tracking the program's learner verification needs. A Certificate of Completion is included for teachers to copy and award to learners upon successful completion of that level of *English ASAP*. In addition, each unit of the Literacy Level Teacher's Edition contains an ASAP Project, an optional holistic cooperative learning project. Learners will find these to be valuable and stimulating culminating activities. Starting at Level 1, the ASAP Project appears directly on the Student Book pages.

Audiocassettes

 The audiocassettes contain all the dialogs and listening activities marked with this cassette symbol. The audiocassettes provide experience in listening to a variety of native speakers in the workplace. The Listening Transcript at the back of each Student Book and Teacher's Edition contains the scripts of all the listening selections not appearing directly on the pages of the Student Books.

Workforce Writing Dictionary

The Steck-Vaughn *Workforce Writing Dictionary* is a 96-page custom dictionary that lets learners create a personalized, alphabetical list of words and expressions related to their own workplaces and career interests. Each letter of the alphabet is allocated two to four pages and is illustrated with several workforce-related words. Learners can use the dictionary to record all of the relevant language they need to succeed on their jobs.

Placement Tests

The Placement Tests, Form A and Form B, help teachers place learners in the appropriate level of *English ASAP*. For more information see page v of this Teacher's Edition.

About SCANS

Each unit of *English ASAP* systematically presents one or more SCANS Competencies. The Foundation Skills are integrated through all the instruction.

WORKPLACE KNOW-HOW

The know-how identified by SCANS is made up of five competencies and a three-part foundation of skills and personal qualities needed for solid job performance. These include:

COMPETENCIES—effective workers can productively use:

- **Resources**—allocating time, money, materials, space, staff;

- **Interpersonal Skills**—working on teams, teaching others, serving customers, leading, negotiating, and working well with people from culturally diverse backgrounds;

- **Information**—acquiring and evaluating data, organizing and maintaining files, interpreting and communicating, and using computers to process information;

- **Systems**—understanding social, organizational, and technological systems, monitoring and correcting performance, and designing or improving systems;

- **Technology**—selecting equipment and tools, applying technology to specific tasks, and maintaining and troubleshooting technologies.

THE FOUNDATION—competence requires:

- **Basic Skills**—reading, writing, arithmetic and mathematics, speaking and listening;

- **Thinking Skills**—thinking creatively, making decisions, solving problems, seeing things in the mind's eye, knowing how to learn, and reasoning;

- **Personal Qualities**—individual responsibility, self-esteem, sociability, self-management, and integrity.

Reprinted from *What Work Requires of Schools—A SCANS Report for America 2000,* Secretary's Commission on Achieving Necessary Skills, U.S. Department of Labor.

For Additional Information

For more information on SCANS, CASAS, adult literacy, and the workforce, visit these websites.

For more information about Steck-Vaughn, visit our website.

www.steckvaughn.com

CASAS Information

www.casas.org

Center for Applied Linguistics

www.cal.org

Education Information

www.ed.gov

Literacy Link

www.pbs.org/learn/literacy

National Center for Adult Literacy

www.literacyonline.org/ncal/index.html

National Institute for Literacy

novel.nifl.gov

School-to-Work Information

www.stw.ed.gov

Workforce Information

www.doleta.gov

English ASAP

Steck-Vaughn

English ASAP ™

Connecting English to the Workplace

SCANS Consultant

Shirley Brod
Spring Institute for International Studies
Boulder, Colorado

Program Consultants

Judith Dean-Griffin
ESL Teacher
Windham Independent School District
Texas Department of Criminal Justice
Huntsville, Texas

Marilyn K. Spence
Workforce Education Coordinator
Orange Technical Education Centers
Mid-Florida Tech
Orlando, Florida

Brigitte Marshall
English Language Training
for Employment Participation
Albany, California

Dennis Terdy
Director, Community Education
Township High School District 214
Arlington Heights, Illinois

Christine Kay Williams
ESL Specialist
Towson University
Baltimore, Maryland

STECK-VAUGHN ®
C O M P A N Y

A Division of Harcourt Brace & Company

About SCANS, the Workforce, and *English ASAP: Connecting English to the Workplace*

SCANS and the Workforce

The Secretary's Commission on Achieving Necessary Skills (SCANS) was established by the U.S. Department of Labor in 1990. Its mission was to study the demands of workplace environments and determine whether people entering the workforce are capable of meeting those demands. The commission identified skills for employment, suggested ways for assessing proficiency, and devised strategies to implement the identified skills. The commission's first report, entitled *What Work Requires of Schools—SCANS Report for America 2000,* was published in June 1991. The report is designed for use by educators (curriculum developers, job counselors, training directors, and teachers) to prepare the modern workforce for the workplace with viable, up-to-date skills.

The report identified two types of skills: Competencies and Foundations. There are five SCANS Competencies: (1) Resources, (2) Interpersonal, (3) Information, (4) Systems, and (5) Technology. There are three parts contained in SCANS Foundations: (1) Basic Skills (including reading, writing, arithmetic, mathematics, listening, and speaking); (2) Thinking Skills (including creative thinking, decision making, problem solving, seeing things in the mind's eye, knowing how to learn, and reasoning); and (3) Personal Qualities (including responsibility, self-esteem, sociability, self-management, and integrity/honesty).

Steck-Vaughn's *English ASAP: Connecting English to the Workplace*

English ASAP is a complete SCANS-based, four-skills program for teaching ESL and SCANS skills to adults and young adults. *English ASAP* follows a work skills-based syllabus that is compatible with the CASAS and MELT competencies.

English ASAP is designed for learners enrolled in public or private schools, in corporate training environments, in learning centers, or in institutes, and for individuals working with tutors. *English ASAP* has these components:

Student Books

The Student Books are designed to allow from 125 to 235 hours of instruction. Each Student Book contains 10 units of SCANS-based instruction. A Listening Transcript of material appearing on the Audiocassettes and a Vocabulary list, organized by unit, of core workforce-based words and phrases appear at the back of each Student Book. Because unit topics carry over from level to level, *English ASAP* is ideal for multi-level classes.

The *On Your Job* symbol appears on the Student Book page each time learners apply a work skill to their own jobs or career interests.

An abundance of tips throughout each unit provides information and strategies that learners can use to be more effective workers and language learners.

Teacher's Editions

Teacher's Editions provide reduced Student Book pages with answers inserted and wrap-

wraparound teacher notes that give detailed suggestions on how to present each page of the Student Book in class. Teacher's Editions 1 and 2 also provide blackline masters to reinforce the grammar in each unit. The Literacy Level Teacher's Edition contains blackline masters that provide practice with many basic literacy skills. The complete Listening Transcript, Vocabulary, and charts for tracking individual and class success appear at the back of each Teacher's Edition.

Workbooks

The Workbooks, starting at Level 1, provide reinforcement for each section of the Student Books.

Audiocassettes

The Audiocassettes contain all the dialogs and listening activities in the Student Books.

This symbol appears on the Student Book page and corresponding Teacher's Edition page each time material for that page is recorded on the Audiocassettes. A Listening Transcript of all material recorded on the tapes but not appearing directly on the Student Book pages is at the back of each Student Book and Teacher's Edition.

Workforce Writing Dictionary

Steck-Vaughn's *Workforce Writing Dictionary,* is a 96-page custom dictionary that allows learners to create a personalized, alphabetical list of the key words and phrases they need to know for their jobs. Each letter of the alphabet is allocated two to four pages for learners to record the language they need. In addition, each letter is illustrated with several workforce-related words.

Placement Tests

The Placement Tests, Form A and Form B, can be used as entry and exit tests and to assist in placing learners in the appropriate level of *English ASAP.*

Placement

In addition to the Placement Tests, the following table indicates placement based on the CASAS and new MELT student performance level standards.

Placement

New MELT SPL	CASAS Achievement Score	English ASAP
0–1	179 or under	Literacy
2–3	180–200	Level 1
4–5	201–220	Level 2

About Student Book 1

Organization of a Unit

Each twelve-page unit contains these nine sections: Unit Opener, Getting Started, Talk About It, Keep Talking, Listening, Grammar, Reading and Writing, Extension, and Performance Check.

Unit Opener

Each Unit Opener includes photos and several related, work-focused questions. The photos and questions activate learners' prior knowledge by getting them to think and talk about the unit topic. The **Performance Preview**, which gives an overview of all the skills in the unit, helps teachers set goals and purposes for the unit. Optionally, teachers may want to examine the Performance Preview with learners before they begin the unit.

Getting Started

An initial **Team Work** activity presents key work skills, concepts, and language introduced in the unit. It consists of active critical thinking and peer teaching to activate the use of the new language and to preview the content of the unit. A **Partner Work** or **Practice the**

Dialog activity encourages learners to use the new language in communicative ways. A culminating class or group **Survey** encourages learners to relate the new language to themselves and their workplaces or career interests.

Talk About It

This page provides opportunities for spoken communication. **Practice the Dialog** provides a model for conversation. **Partner Work** presents a personalized **On Your Job** activity that allows learners to use the model in Practice the Dialog to talk about their own workplace experiences.

Useful Language | The **Useful Language** box contains related words, phrases, and expressions for learners to use as they complete Partner Work.

ASAP PROJECT | The **ASAP Project** is a long-term project learners complete over the course of the unit. Learners create items such as files of human resources forms, lists of interview questions, and work schedules that they can use outside of the classroom.

Keep Talking

The Keep Talking page contains additional conversation models and speaking tasks. It also includes the **Personal Dictionary** feature. This feature allows learners to record the language relevant to the unit topic that they need to do their jobs. Because each learner's job is different, this personalized resource enables learners to focus on the language that is most useful to them. In addition, learners can use this feature in conjunction with Steck-Vaughn's *Workforce Writing Dictionary* to create a completely customized lexicon of key words and phrases they need to know.

Listening

The Listening page develops SCANS-based listening skills. Tasks include listening for greetings, names of places, directions, instructions, and times.

All the activities develop the skill of **focused listening.** Learners learn to recognize the information they need and to listen selectively for only that information. They do not have to understand every word; rather, they have to filter out everything except the relevant information. This essential skill is used by native speakers of all languages.

Many of the activities involve **multi-task listening.** In these activities, called **Listen Again** and **Listen Once More**, learners listen to the same selection several times and complete a different task each time. First they might listen for the main idea. They might listen again for specific information. They might listen a third time in order to draw conclusions or make inferences.

Culminating discussion questions allow learners to relate the information they have heard to their own needs and interests.

A complete Listening Transcript for all dialogs recorded on the Audiocassettes but not appearing directly on the Student Book pages is at the back of the Student Book and Teacher's Edition. All the selections are recorded on the Audiocassettes.

Grammar

Grammar, a two-page spread, presents key grammatical structures that complement the unit competencies. Language boxes show the new language in a clear, simple format that allows learners to make generalizations about the new language. Oral and written exercises provide contextualized reinforcement relevant to the workplace.

Reading and Writing

Reading selections, such as excerpts from instruction manuals, job evaluations, and timecards, focus on items learners encounter at work. Exercises and discussion questions develop reading skills and help learners relate the content of the selections to their workplaces or career interests.

The writing tasks, often related to the reading selection, help learners develop writing skills, such as completing job applications, writing to-do lists, and writing schedules.

Extension

The Extension page enriches the previous instruction. As in other sections, realia is used extensively. Oral and written exercises help learners master the additional skills, language, and concepts, and relate them to their workplaces and career interests.

CultureNotes **Culture Notes**, a feature that appears on each Extension page, sparks lively, engaging discussion. Topics include asking for directions, using machines, using employee handbooks, and exchanging greetings.

Performance Check

The two-page Performance Check allows teachers and learners to track learners' progress and to meet the learner verification needs of schools, companies, or programs. All work skills are tested in the same manner they are presented in the units; so, formats are familiar and non-threatening, and success is built in. The **Performance Review** at the end of each test alerts teachers and learners to the work skills that are being evaluated. The check-off boxes allow learners to track their success and gain a sense of accomplishment and satisfaction. Finally, a culminating discussion allows learners to relate their new skills to their development as effective workers.

Teaching Techniques

Make Your Classroom Mirror the Workplace

Help learners develop workplace skills by setting up your classroom to mirror a workplace. Use any of these suggestions.

◆ Establish policies on lateness and absence similar to those a business might have.

◆ Provide learners with a daily agenda of the activities they will complete that day, including partner work and small group assignments. Go over the agenda with learners at the beginning and end of class.

◆ With learner input, establish a list of goals for the class. Goals can include speaking, reading, and writing English every day; using effective teamwork skills; or learning ten new vocabulary words each day. Go over the goals with learners at regular intervals.

◆ Assign students regular jobs and responsibilities, such as arranging the chairs in a circle, setting up the overhead projector, or making copies for the class.

Presenting a Unit Opener

The unit opener sets the stage for the unit. Use the photos and questions to encourage learners to:

◆ Speculate about what the unit might cover.

◆ Activate prior knowledge.

◆ Relate what they see in the photos to their own work environments.

Peer Teaching

Because each adult learner brings rich life experience to the classroom, *English ASAP* is designed to help you use each learner's expertise as a resource for peer teaching.

Here are some practical strategies for peer teaching:

◆ Have learners work in pairs/small groups to clarify new language concepts for each other.

◆ If a learner possesses a particular work skill, appoint that learner as "class consultant" in that area and have learners direct queries to that individual.

◆ Set up a reference area in a corner of your classroom. Include dictionaries, career books, and other books your learners will find useful.

Partner Work and Team Work

The abundance of Partner Work and Team Work activities in *English ASAP* serves the dual purposes of developing learners' communicative competence and providing learners with experience using key SCANS interpersonal skills, such as working in teams, teaching others, leading, negotiating, and working well with people from culturally diverse backgrounds. To take full advantage of these activities, follow these suggestions.

◆ Whenever students work in groups, appoint, or have students select, a leader.

◆ Use multiple groupings. Have learners work with different partners and teams, just as workers do in the workplace. For different activities, you might group learners according to language ability, skill, or learner interest.

◆ Make sure learners understand that everyone on the team is responsible for the team's work.

◆ At the end of each activity, have teams report the results to the class.

◆ Discuss with learners their teamwork skills and talk about ways teams can work together effectively. They can discuss how to clarify roles and responsibilities, resolve disagreements effectively, communicate openly, and make decisions together.

Purpose Statement

Each page after the unit opener begins with a brief purpose statement that summarizes the work skills presented on that page. When learners first begin working on a page, focus their attention on the purpose statement and help them read it. Ask them what the page will be about. Discuss with the class why the skill is important. Ask learners to talk about their prior knowledge of the skill. Finally, show learners how using the skill will help them become more effective on their jobs.

Survey

The **Survey** on each **Getting Started** page helps learners relate the new language and skills to their own lives. Before learners begin the activity, help them create questions they'll need to ask. Assist them in deciding how they'll record their answers. You may need to model taking notes, using tally marks, and other simple ways to record information. Assist learners in setting a time limit before they begin. Remember to allow learners to move about the room as they complete the activity.

Many Survey results can be summarized in a bar graph or pie chart.

◆ A bar graph uses bars to represent numbers. Bar graphs have two scales, a vertical scale and a horizontal scale. For example, to graph the number of learners who get paid by check versus those paid by direct deposit, the vertical scale can represent numbers of students, such as 2, 4, 6, 8, etc. The horizontal scale can consist of two bars. One bar represents the number of learners paid by check. The other bar represents the number of learners paid by direct deposit. The two bars can be different colors to set them apart. Bars should be the same width.

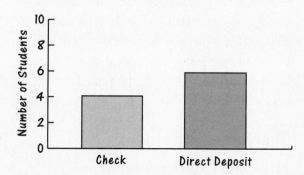

To the Teacher

- A pie chart shows the parts that make up a whole set of facts. Each part of the pie is a percentage of the whole. For example, a pie chart might show 40% of learners are paid by check and 60% are paid by direct deposit.

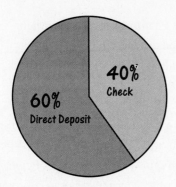

Presenting a Dialog

To present a dialog, follow these suggested steps:

- Play the tape or say the dialog aloud two or more times. Ask one or two simple questions to make sure learners understand.

- Say the dialog aloud line-by-line for learners to repeat chorally, by rows, and then individually.

- Have learners say or read the dialog together in pairs.

- Have several pairs say or read the dialog aloud for the class.

Presenting the Personal Dictionary

The Personal Dictionary enables learners to focus on the vocabulary in each unit that is relevant to their particular jobs. To use this feature, have learners work in teams to brainstorm vocabulary words they might put in their dictionaries. Have team reporters share their ideas with the class. Then allow learners a few minutes to add to their dictionaries. Remind students to continue adding words throughout the unit.

For further vocabulary development, learners can enter the words from their Personal Dictionary into their *Workforce Writing Dictionaries.*

To the Teacher

Presenting a Listening Activity

Use any of these suggestions:

- To activate learners' prior knowledge, have them look at the illustrations, if any, and say as much as they can about them. Encourage them to make inferences about the content of the listening selection.

- Have learners read the directions. To encourage them to focus their listening, have them read the questions before they listen so that they know exactly what to listen for.

- Play the tape or read the Listening Transcript aloud as learners complete the activity. Rewind the tape and play it again as necessary.

- Help learners check their work.

In multi-task listening, remind learners that they will listen to the same passage several times and answer different questions each time. After learners complete a section, have them check their own or each others' work before you rewind the tape and proceed to the next questions.

Presenting a Tip

Tip A variety of tips throughout each unit present valuable advice on how to be a successful employee and/or language learner. To present a tip, help learners read the tip. Discuss it with them. Ask them how it will help them. For certain tips, such as those in which learners make lists, you may want to allow learners time to start the activity.

Presenting a Discussion

English ASAP provides a variety of whole-class and team discussions. Always encourage students to state their ideas and respond appropriately to other learners' comments. At the end of each discussion, have team reporters summarize their team's ideas and/or help the class come to a consensus about the topic.

Prereading

To help learners read the selections with ease and success, establish a purpose for reading and call on learners' prior knowledge to make inferences about the reading. Use any of these techniques:

◆ Have learners look over and describe any photographs, realia, and/or illustrations. Ask them to use the illustrations to say what they think the selection might be about.

◆ Have learners read the title and any heads or sub-heads. Ask them what kind of information they think is in the selection and how it might be organized. Ask them where they might encounter such information outside of class and why they would want to read it.

◆ To help learners focus their reading, have them review the comprehension activities before they read the selection. Ask them what kind of information they think they will find out when they read. Restate their ideas and/or write them on the board in acceptable English.

◆ Remind learners that they do not have to know all the words in order to understand the selection.

Evaluation

To use the Performance Check pages successfully, follow these suggested procedures:
Before and during each evaluation, create a relaxed, affirming atmosphere. Chat with the learners for a few minutes and review the material. When you and the learners are ready, have learners read the directions and look over each exercise before they complete it. If at any time you sense that learners are becoming frustrated, stop to provide additional review. Resume when learners are ready. The evaluation formats follow two basic patterns:

1. **Speaking** competencies are checked in the format used to present them in the unit. Have learners read the instructions. Make sure learners know what to do. Then have learners complete the evaluation in one of these ways:

Self- and Peer Evaluation: Have learners complete the spoken activity in pairs. Learners in each pair evaluate themselves and/or each other and report the results to you.

Teacher/Pair Evaluation: Have pairs complete the activity as you observe and evaluate their work. Begin with the most proficient learners. As other learners who are ready to be evaluated wait, have them practice in pairs. Learners who complete the evaluation successfully can peer-teach those who are waiting or those who need additional review.

Teacher/Individual Evaluation: Have individuals complete the activity with you as their partner. Follow the procedures in Teacher/Pair Evaluation.

2. **Listening, reading,** and **writing** competencies are also all checked in the same format used to present them in the unit. When learners are ready to begin, have them read the instructions. Demonstrate the first item and have learners complete the activity. In Listening activities, play the tape or read the listening transcript aloud two or more times. Then have learners check their work. Provide any review needed, and have learners try the activity again.

When learners demonstrate mastery of a skill to your satisfaction, have them record their success by checking the appropriate box in the Performance Review. The Teacher's Edition also contains charts for you to reproduce to keep track of individual and class progress.

To the Teacher

Steck-Vaughn

English ASAP™

Connecting English to the Workplace

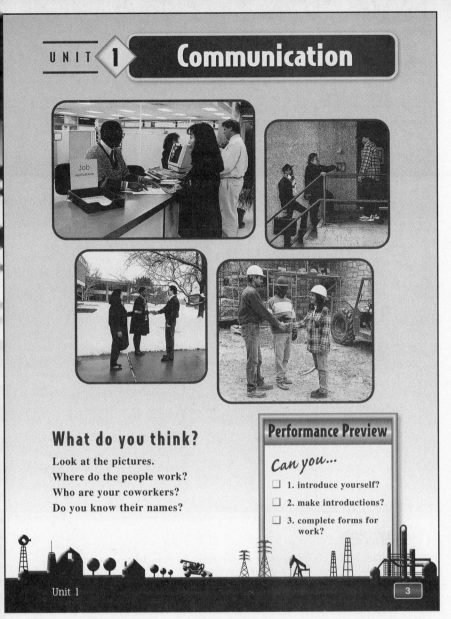

Unit 1 Overview
—SCANS Competencies—

★ Communicate information
★ Acquire and interpret information
★ Work with cultural diversity
★ Understand social systems

Workforce Skills

● Introduce yourself
● Make introductions
● Complete forms for work

Materials

● Picture cards of people in various jobs
● Large world map and map pins
● Blank slips of paper
● Samples of job applications and other simple forms
● Samples of driver's licenses, insurance cards, and Social Security cards
● Graph paper
● Telephone message pads

Unit Warm-Up

To stimulate discussion about the unit topic (giving and receiving personal information and completing forms), show pictures of people greeting one another. Ask learners to say words and phrases used to greet people in English.

★   ★   ★   ★   ★

WORKFORCE SKILLS (page 3)

● Introduce yourself
● Make introductions

★   ★   ★   ★   ★

Teaching Note

Make a point of greeting the class at the start of each lesson. A warm **Good morning** *or* **Hello** *will create a positive classroom environment and reinforce the content of the unit.*

PREPARATION

1. Introduce yourself to several learners. Have pairs of volunteers introduce themselves to each other. After a few pairs have made introductions, have the class stand up and walk around the room introducing themselves to as many people in the class as possible.

2. Help learners brainstorm a list of the words and phrases they used to introduce themselves to each other.

PRESENTATION

1. Focus attention on the photographs. Ask learners what the unit might be about. Write their ideas on the board and/or restate them in acceptable English.

2. Have learners talk about the photos. Ask them to describe what is going on in each picture and who is being introduced to whom. Help learners identify the body language associated with making introductions—shaking hands, making eye contact, and so on.

3. Help learners read the questions. Discuss the questions with the class.

4. You may want to use the Performance Preview to provide learners with an overview of the skills in the unit. Have learners read the list of skills and discuss what they will learn in this unit.

FOLLOW-UP

Discussing Differences: Have teams discuss different kinds of introductions. Write **supervisor, friend,** and **teacher** on the board. Ask learners to role-play each introduction. Talk about the differences between the introductions.

◆ Have each team role-play introductions at work and school. Ask learners to present their introductions to the class.

WORKBOOK

Unit 1, Exercises 1A–1B

WORKFORCE SKILLS (page 4)

Introduce yourself

Make introductions

★　　　★　　　★　　　★　　　★

Teaching Note

Use this page to introduce the new language in the unit. Whenever possible, encourage peer teaching. Supply any new language the learners need.

Culture Note

Encourage learners to make eye contact when greeting. Show them how to take your hand firmly when shaking it. Then have learners shake hands with each other.

Getting Started — Talking about yourself and your job

TEAM WORK

Look at the pictures. Write the name of the language each person speaks. Write his or her job title.

I'm from Puerto Rico.

I speak _____Spanish_____ and English.

I'm a _____mail clerk_____.

I'm from Russia.

I speak _____Russian_____ and English.

I'm a _____truck driver_____.

PRACTICE THE DIALOG

Student A chooses a picture. Student B talks about the person's country, language, and job.

A Where's she from?

B She's from Puerto Rico.

A What language does she speak?

B She speaks Spanish.

A What does she do?

B She's a mail clerk.

Now use the dialog to talk about yourself.

SURVEY

Talk to your classmates. Where are they from? Figure out what languages they speak. Do they use these languages at work? Compare information with the class.

4   Unit 1

PREPARATION

Introduce yourself to the class again. Tell learners your full name, your home country, and the languages you speak. Write your name on a slip of paper and pin it to the map in the appropriate place. Hold up one or two pictures of workers. Introduce the people in the pictures and give information about them: *Her name's Marta. She's from Mexico. She speaks English and Spanish. She's a waitress.* Pin the name *Marta* on Mexico on the map. Repeat for each picture.

PRESENTATION

1. Have learners read and discuss the Purpose Statement. For more information see "Purpose Statement" on page viii.

2. Focus attention on the illustrations. Encourage learners to say as much as they can about them. Write their ideas on the board and/or restate them in acceptable English.

3. Have teams read the Team Work instructions. Make sure each team knows what to do. Remind the teams that they are responsible for making sure that each member understands the new language. Then have teams complete the activity. Have team reporters share their answers with the class.

 4. Have partners read the Practice the Dialog instructions. Then present the dialog. See "Presenting a Dialog" on page ix. Have one or two partners present their dialogs to the class.

5. Have partners read the Survey instructions. Make sure everyone knows what to do. Then have the class complete the activity. Have several pairs of learners share their information with the class. For more information, see "Survey" on page viii.

FOLLOW-UP

Chart: Make a simple chart on the board. There should be columns labeled *Name, Language,* and *Country.* Have each learner write his or her name, country, and language on the chart.

♦ Help learners use the information in the chart to create a bar graph.

WORKBOOK

Unit 1, Exercises 2A–2C

Introduce yourself

★   ★   ★   ★   ★

Talk About It   Meeting a new coworker

 PRACTICE THE DIALOG

A   Hi, I'm the new machinist.

B   How are you? I'm Li Park.

A   My name's Rosa Morelos.

B   Did you say Rosa?

A   That's right.

B   Where are you from, Rosa?

A   I'm from El Salvador. What about you?

B   I'm from Korea.

A   It's nice to meet you, Li.

B   Nice to meet you, too, Rosa.

Useful Language

What languages do you speak?

I speak (Spanish) and English.

PARTNER WORK

Introduce yourself to a classmate. Tell your partner where you are from, what languages you speak, and what jobs you do. Use the dialog and Useful Language above.

ASAP
PROJECT

Make a chart with information about your class. Divide into three teams. Team 1 draws the chart and fills in the information. Team 2 asks for everyone's name and job. Team 3 asks for everyone's country and language. Look at the chart. Where do people in your class come from? Where do they work? Complete this project as you work through this unit.

Unit 1

5

Language Note

Talk about clarification strategies with learners. Explain that for English speakers, it is common for people to ask others to repeat or even to spell unfamiliar names to learn how to say or write them.

ASAP
PROJECT

Have learners read the instructions. Discuss the project and its purpose with learners. Make sure that everyone understands. Help learners assign themselves to teams depending upon their skills, knowledge, interests, or other personal strengths. Have each team select a leader. Throughout the rest of the unit, allow time for learners to work on the project. Have the teams agree on a deadline when the project will be finished. For more information see "ASAP Project" on page vi.

PREPARATION

1. Introduce yourself to someone in the class. Ask for the learner's name and use a clarification strategy to get them to repeat it: *Did you say ...?* Also be sure to model and clarify the introduction rejoinders *It's nice to meet you* and *Nice to meet you, too.*

2. Say the languages you speak, for example, *I speak English and Spanish.* Then ask several learners what languages they speak. Supply any language learners need.

PRESENTATION

1. Have learners read and discuss the Purpose Statement. For more information see "Purpose Statement" on page viii.

 2. Focus attention on the illustration. Encourage learners to say as much as they can about it. Have them focus on what the people are doing. Then present the dialog. See "Presenting a Dialog" on page ix.

3. Have partners read the Partner Work instructions. Focus attention on the Useful Language box. Help learners read the expressions. If necessary, model pronunciation. Then have learners complete the activity. Have learners switch partners and repeat the activity. Have one or two partners present their dialogs to the class.

FOLLOW-UP

Role-Play: Have groups of learners role-play meeting people the first day at work or school. Have groups present their dialogs to the class.

♦ Have pairs write out their dialogs and post them.

WORKBOOK

Unit 1, Exercise 3

WORKFORCE SKILLS (page 6)
Make introductions

★　　★　　★　　★　　★

Culture Note
Point out to learners that it is acceptable to gesture with the hand toward the person being introduced, but not to point with a finger.

 Personal Dictionary
Have learners add the words in their Personal Dictionary to their *Workforce Writing Dictionary*. For more information see "Workforce Writing Dictionary" on page v.

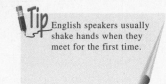 **Keep Talking** Making introductions

PRACTICE THE DIALOG

A Good morning, Leon.

B Good morning, Connie.

A Leon, I'd like you to meet Marty. Marty, this is Leon.

B It's nice to meet you, Marty.

C It's nice to meet you, too, Leon.

Tip English speakers usually shake hands when they meet for the first time.

TEAM WORK

Work with two other students. Take turns making introductions. Use the dialog above.

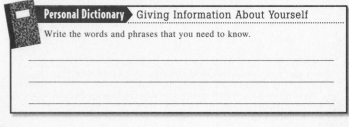 **Personal Dictionary** Giving Information About Yourself
Write the words and phrases that you need to know.

_____

_____

_____

6   Unit 1

PREPARATION
To preteach making introductions, introduce one learner to another. Encourage learners to use the rejoinders *It's nice to meet you* and *Nice to meet you, too.*

PRESENTATION
1. Have learners discuss the Purpose Statement. For more information see "Purpose Statement" on page viii.

2. Focus attention on the photograph. Encourage learners to say as much as they can about it. Have them speculate about the relationship of the people.

3. Have partners read the instructions for Practice the Dialog. Allow learners time to complete the activity, then change partners and repeat. Have several pairs present their dialogs to the class.

4. Have groups of three read the Team Work instructions. Make sure each team knows what to do. If necessary, model the dialog. Then have teams complete the activity. Have several groups present their dialogs to the class.

5. Have learners read the Personal Dictionary instructions. Then use the Personal Dictionary procedures on page ix. Remind learners to add words to their dictionaries throughout the unit.

Tip Have learners read the Tip independently. Have learners discuss how the advice will help them. For more information see "Presenting a Tip" on page ix.

FOLLOW-UP
I'd Like You to Meet.... Have learners work in groups of three. Give a slip of paper to each group with three job titles and names and brief instructions (Mr. Green, supervisor; Joe, new employee, Fred, coworker—Mr. Green introduces Joe to Fred.) Each learner role-plays a person. Ask them to make introductions. Have groups present their introductions to the class.

♦ Have students write their introductions. Pass them around the room.

WORKBOOK
Unit 1, Exercise 4

Introduce yourself

Make introductions

★　　★　　★　　★　　★

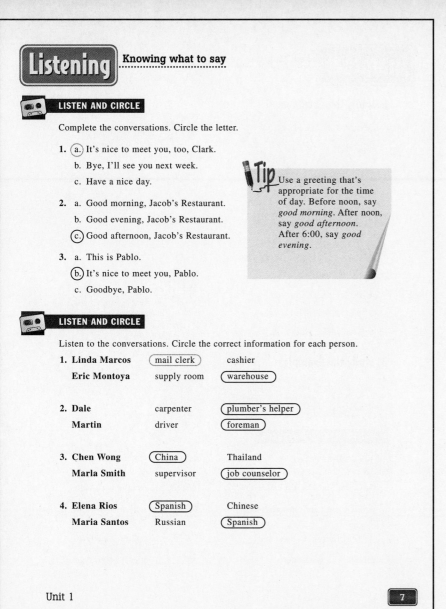

Listening　Knowing what to say

LISTEN AND CIRCLE

Complete the conversations. Circle the letter.

1. (a.) It's nice to meet you, too, Clark.
   b. Bye, I'll see you next week.
   c. Have a nice day.

2. a. Good morning, Jacob's Restaurant.
   b. Good evening, Jacob's Restaurant.
   (c.) Good afternoon, Jacob's Restaurant.

3. a. This is Pablo.
   (b.) It's nice to meet you, Pablo.
   c. Goodbye, Pablo.

> **Tip** Use a greeting that's appropriate for the time of day. Before noon, say *good morning*. After noon, say *good afternoon*. After 6:00, say *good evening*.

LISTEN AND CIRCLE

Listen to the conversations. Circle the correct information for each person.

1. **Linda Marcos**　(mail clerk)　cashier
   Eric Montoya　supply room　(warehouse)

2. **Dale**　carpenter　(plumber's helper)
   Martin　driver　(foreman)

3. **Chen Wong**　(China)　Thailand
   Marla Smith　supervisor　(job counselor)

4. **Elena Rios**　(Spanish)　Chinese
   Maria Santos　Russian　(Spanish)

Unit 1　　7

PREPARATION

Use the map to review the names of countries and languages. Have any learners who have not already done so pin their names to the map.

PRESENTATION

1. Have learners read and discuss the Purpose Statement. For more information see "Purpose Statement" on page viii.

2. Have learners read the Listen and Circle instructions. Then have them read the answer choices. Make sure that everyone understands the instructions. If necessary, model the first item. Then play the tape or read the Listening Transcript aloud two or more times as learners complete the activity. Check

learners' work. See "Presenting a Listening Activity" on page ix.

3. Have learners read the Listen and Circle instructions. Make sure that everyone understands the instructions. If necessary, model the first item. Then play the tape or read the Listening Transcript aloud two or more times as learners complete the activity. Check learners' work. See "Presenting a Listening Activity" on page ix.

> **Tip** Have learners read the Tip independently. Have learners discuss how the advice will help them. For more information see "Presenting a Tip" on page ix.

FOLLOW-UP

Listening and Responding: Say sentences used in greetings and introductions, such as *Hi, I'm Ed* or *I'm from China*. Ask learners what to say next.

♦ Have learners write what they'd say next. Ask several learners to say their answers aloud.

WORKBOOK

Unit 1, Exercise 5

Grammar Learning the language you need

A. Study the Examples

I	am	from Chicago.
He	is	
She		
It		
We	are	
You		
They		

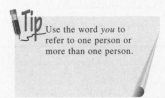

Tip Use the word *you* to refer to one person or more than one person.

COMPLETE THE SENTENCES

1. Anita _is_ a manager.

2. Carlos and Maria _are_ Mexican.

3. I _am_ from Korea.

4. Paolo _is_ Brazilian.

5. We _are_ sales assistants.

6. You _are_ from El Salvador.

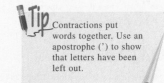

Tip Contractions put words together. Use an apostrophe (') to show that letters have been left out.

B. Study the Examples

I	+	am	=	I'm		We	+	are	=	We're
He	+	is	=	He's		You	+	are	=	You're
She	+	is	=	She's		They	+	are	=	They're

COMPLETE THE SENTENCES

1. I am the manager.   _I'm_ the manager of a clothing store.

2. Carlos and Maria are Mexican.   _They're_ from Mexico City.

3. Fred and I are sales assistants.   _We're_ sales assistants at Brand Store.

4. You are from El Salvador.   _You're_ Central American.

5. John is a mechanic.   _He's_ a mechanic at Auto Barn.

8

Unit 1

Teaching Note

Students from other cultures are often confused about first and last names in English. Point out that the order is for the given name to come first and the family name last. Sometimes there is a middle name.

PREPARATION

Review the language in the grammar boxes with learners before they open their books, if necessary. Follow the instructions in Preparation on pages 4 and 5.

PRESENTATION

1. Have learners read and discuss the Purpose Statement. For more information see "Purpose Statement" on page viii.

2. Have learners read the grammar box in A. Have learners use the language in the boxes to say as many sentences as possible. Tell learners that they can use the grammar boxes throughout the unit to review or check sentence structures.

3. Have learners read the instructions for Complete the Sentences. If necessary, model the first item. Allow learners to complete the activity. Have learners check each other's work in pairs. Ask several learners to read their completed sentences aloud while the rest of the class checks their work.

4. Focus attention on the grammar boxes in B. Follow the procedures in 2.

5. Have learners read the instructions for Complete the Sentences. If necessary, model the first item. Allow learners to complete the activity. Have learners check each other's work in pairs. Ask several learners to read their completed sentences aloud while the rest of the class checks their work.

Tip Have learners read the Tips independently. Provide any clarification needed. Ask learners to give a few examples for each one. For more information see "Presenting a Tip" on page ix.

 6. Have partners read the Partner Work instructions. Make sure each pair knows what to do. If necessary, model the activity. Have learners switch partners and repeat the activity. Ask several pairs to present their dialogs to the class.

7. Focus attention on the grammar box in C. Follow the procedure in 2.

8. Have learners read the instructions for Complete the Sentences. If necessary, model the first item. Then have learners complete the activity independently. Have a different learner read

PARTNER WORK

Talk about the people in your class or workplace.

A What does Rodolfo do?

B He's a bus driver.

A Where's he from?

B He's from Guatemala.

C. Study the Examples

I	my
he	his
she	her
it	its
we	our
you	your
they	their

My last name is Ramos.

COMPLETE THE SENTENCES

1. ___Their___ (Their, It's) last name is Lu.

2. ___Her___ (His, Her) address is 56 Stanley Street.

3. ___His___ (His, Her) middle name is Diego.

TEAM WORK

Work with a small group. Introduce yourself. Say everyone's name.

My name is Elena.
His name is Chris.
Her name is Sylvia.

Unit 1

9

---

each sentence aloud as the rest of the class checks their answers.

9. Have teams read the Team Work instructions. Make sure each team knows what to do. If necessary, model the activity. Then have teams complete the activity. Have learners change teams and repeat the activity.

FOLLOW-UP

Who Am I? Post the picture cards of people in various jobs from Preparation on page 4. Attach a name tag to each one. Have a learner stand in front of the class as that person: *I speak (language). I'm from (country). I'm a (job).* Have the rest of the class name the person.

♦ Have learners write out on slips of paper other statements they could use as clues. Have learners exchange papers, read the clues aloud, and name the person.

WORKBOOK

Unit 1, Exercises 6A–6D

BLACKLINE MASTERS

Blackline Master: Unit 1

★ ★ ★ ★ ★

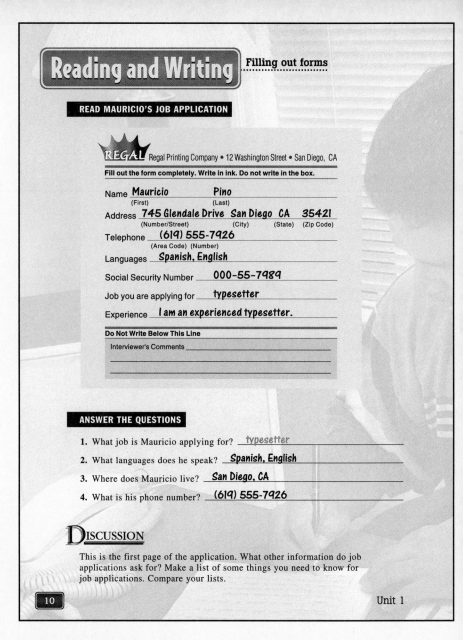

Reading and Writing   *Filling out forms*

READ MAURICIO'S JOB APPLICATION

REGAL Regal Printing Company • 12 Washington Street • San Diego, CA

Fill out the form completely. Write in ink. Do not write in the box.

Name **Mauricio**   **Pino**
            (First)   (Last)

Address **745 Glendale Drive San Diego CA   35421**
                (Number/Street)   (City)   (State)   (Zip Code)

Telephone **(619) 555-7926**
                (Area Code) (Number)

Languages **Spanish, English**

Social Security Number   **000-55-7989**

Job you are applying for ____ **typesetter**

Experience **I am an experienced typesetter.**

Do Not Write Below This Line

Interviewer's Comments _____

ANSWER THE QUESTIONS

1. What job is Mauricio applying for? ___ *typesetter* ___

2. What languages does he speak? ___ **Spanish, English** ___

3. Where does Mauricio live? **San Diego, CA**

4. What is his phone number? **(619) 555-7926**

DISCUSSION

This is the first page of the application. What other information do job applications ask for? Make a list of some things you need to know for job applications. Compare your lists.

10   Unit 1

SCANS Note

Tell learners that, when they fill out a job application or other form, they should ask for two copies so they can practice on one and have a friend or coworker check it for accuracy and completeness. Then they can copy a corrected version on the second copy.

PREPARATION

1. If necessary, talk about people in the class to review languages and countries: *(Name) is from China. She speaks Chinese.*

2. Preview the new vocabulary learners will see on the form. On the board, write a fictitious name, address, telephone number, Social Security number, languages spoken, job experience, and occupation. On the other side of the board write the words **name, address, telephone number, Social Security number, languages, experience** and **job.** In pairs, have learners match items from the two lists. Have a pair of learners present their ideas to the class. Provide any clarification needed.

PRESENTATION

1. Have learners read and discuss the Purpose Statement. For more information see "Purpose Statement" on page viii.

2. Have learners preview the application before they read. Encourage learners to say everything they can about the application. Ask them if they have ever seen or filled out a job application. Write their ideas on the board or restate them in acceptable English. Then have them read the application independently.

3. Have learners read the instructions for Answer the Questions. Make sure everyone knows what to do. Then have learners complete the activity independently. Have learners review each

other's work in pairs. Ask several learners to share their answers with the class while the rest of the class checks their work.

4. Have learners read the Discussion instructions. Make sure everyone knows what to do. Then have learners work in teams to come up with a list. Have team reporters share their lists with the rest of the class. Have the teams compare their lists.

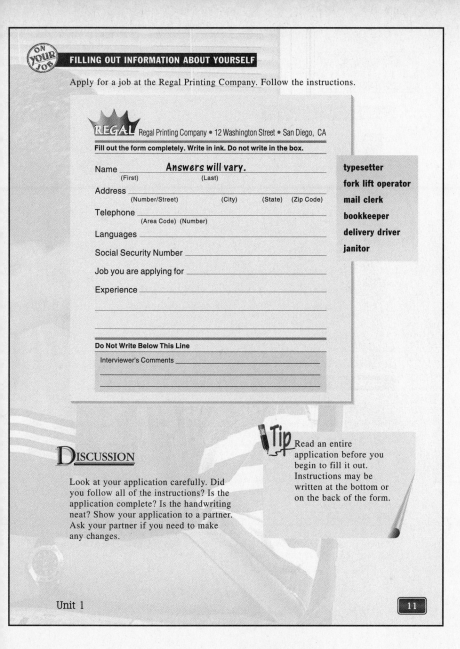

Apply for a job at the Regal Printing Company. Follow the instructions.

REGAL Regal Printing Company • 12 Washington Street • San Diego, CA

Fill out the form completely. Write in ink. Do not write in the box.

Name _____ Answers will vary. _____
     (First)   (Last)

Address _____
     (Number/Street)   (City)   (State)   (Zip Code)

Telephone _____
     (Area Code) (Number)

Languages _____

Social Security Number _____

Job you are applying for _____

Experience _____

_____

_____

_____

Do Not Write Below This Line

Interviewer's Comments _____

_____

_____

typesetter

fork lift operator

mail clerk

bookkeeper

delivery driver

janitor

DISCUSSION

Look at your application carefully. Did you follow all of the instructions? Is the application complete? Is the handwriting neat? Show your application to a partner. Ask your partner if you need to make any changes.

Tip Read an entire application before you begin to fill it out. Instructions may be written at the bottom or on the back of the form.

Unit 1   11

---

5. Have learners read the Filling Out Information About Yourself instructions. Make sure everyone knows what to do. If necessary, model the activity. Then have learners complete the activity independently. Have several learners share their applications with the class.

6. Have learners read the Discussion instructions. Model the activity if necessary. Then have learners work in pairs to complete the activity. Ask if anyone wrote below the line at the bottom of the form.

7. Have learners read the Tip independently. Discuss other reasons it is a good idea to read a form before filling it out. For more information see "Presenting a Tip" on page ix.

FOLLOW-UP

Design a Form: Divide the class into three or four groups. Assign each group a different type of form to design: a job application, a library card application, a magazine subscription form. Have each group prepare their form on blank paper. Have a member of each group present their form to the rest of the class.

♦ Have groups exchange forms. Have learners comment on the other groups' forms. Would they change anything? Why? Is the form easy or hard? Why?

WORKBOOK

Unit 1, Exercises 7A–7D

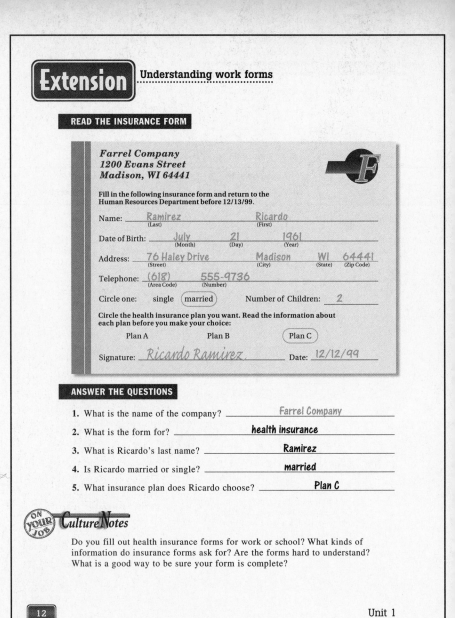

Extension — Understanding work forms

READ THE INSURANCE FORM

Farrel Company
1200 Evans Street
Madison, WI 64441

Fill in the following insurance form and return to the
Human Resources Department before 12/13/99.

Name: _____Ramirez_____ _____Ricardo_____
　　　　　(Last)　　　　　　　　(First)

Date of Birth: ___July___ ___21___ ___1961___
　　　　　　　　(Month)　(Day)　　(Year)

Address: __76 Haley Drive__ __Madison__ __WI__ __64441__
　　　　　　(Street)　　　　　(City)　　(State)　(Zip Code)

Telephone: __(618)__ ___555-9736___
　　　　　　(Area Code)　(Number)

Circle one:　single　(married)　　Number of Children: __2__

Circle the health insurance plan you want. Read the information about
each plan before you make your choice:

Plan A　　　　Plan B　　　　(Plan C)

Signature: _Ricardo Ramirez_　　　Date: _12/12/99_

ANSWER THE QUESTIONS

1. What is the name of the company? _____Farrel Company_____

2. What is the form for? _____health insurance_____

3. What is Ricardo's last name? _____Ramirez_____

4. Is Ricardo married or single? _____married_____

5. What insurance plan does Ricardo choose? _____Plan C_____

ON YOUR JOB — Culture Notes

Do you fill out health insurance forms for work or school? What kinds of
information do insurance forms ask for? Are the forms hard to understand?
What is a good way to be sure your form is complete?

12　　　　　　　　　　　　　　　　　　　　　　　　　Unit 1

PREPARATION

1. Talk about human resources departments with learners. Discuss with learners whether their company has a human resources department. Ask those learners to explain what a human resources department does.

2. Display the sample forms, licenses, and insurance cards to present or review **date of birth, single, married, insurance, date,** and **plan.**

PRESENTATION

1. Have learners discuss the Purpose Statement. For more information see "Purpose Statement" on page viii.

2. Have learners read the insurance form and say as much as they can about it. Write their ideas on the board or restate them in acceptable English.

3. Have learners answer the questions. Have learners review each other's work in pairs. Ask several learners to read their work aloud while the rest of the class checks their work.

 4. Have learners read Culture Notes and talk over their responses in teams. Have team reporters share their ideas with the class. Ask the teams to compare each other's ideas. For more information see "Culture Notes" on page vii.

FOLLOW-UP

Label: Make a simple form that does not include the names of the parts of the form. This can be done by masking out the names on an existing form and photocopying it. Pass the form out to groups of learners. Have learners label the parts of the form. Have the groups compare their final forms and discuss why they have chosen to put the labels where they have. Last, show them the original form. Have learners make any corrections they feel necessary.

♦ Make enough copies of each group's form to give one to each group member. Have them complete the form. Have group members compare their work. Have one or two students from each group share their completed forms with the class.

WORKBOOK

Unit 1, Exercise 8

Performance Check | How well can you use the skills in this unit?

Complete the activities. Go over your work with a partner or your teacher. Then complete the Performance Review on Page 14.

SKILL 1   INTRODUCE YOURSELF

Introduce yourself to a classmate. Tell your partner where you are from, what languages you speak, and where you work or what jobs you do. Shake hands when you meet.

SKILL 2   MAKE INTRODUCTIONS

Work with two other students. Introduce one student to another. Take turns.

Unit 1   13

PRESENTATION

Use any of the procedures in "Evaluation" on page x with pages 13 and 14. Record individuals' results on the Unit 1 Individual Competency Chart. Record the class results on the Class Cumulative Competency Chart.

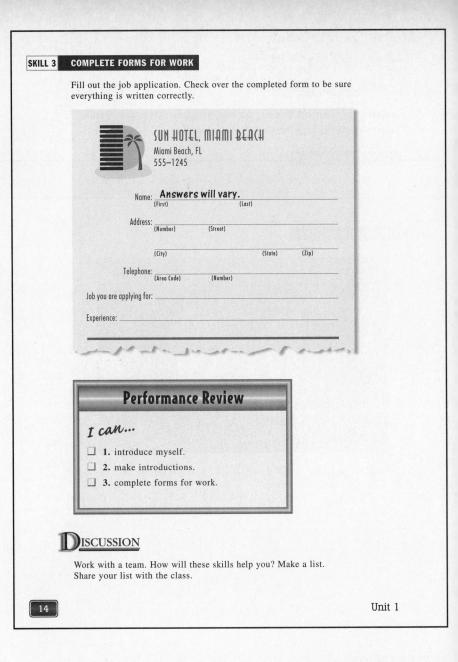

Fill out the job application. Check over the completed form to be sure everything is written correctly.

SUN HOTEL, MIAMI BEACH
Miami Beach, FL
555–1245

Name: **Answers will vary.**
            (First)   (Last)

Address: _____
          (Number)   (Street)

_____
(City)   (State) (Zip)

Telephone: _____
         (Area Code)   (Number)

Job you are applying for: _____

Experience: _____

Performance Review

I can...

☐ **1.** introduce myself.

☐ **2.** make introductions.

☐ **3.** complete forms for work.

DISCUSSION

Work with a team. How will these skills help you? Make a list. Share your list with the class.

Unit 1

PRESENTATION

Follow the instructions on page 13.

INFORMAL WORKPLACE-SPECIFIC ASSESSMENT

Have learners complete the personal information parts of a form related to their job or career interests. Provide feedback as needed.

WORKBOOK

Unit 1, Exercise 9

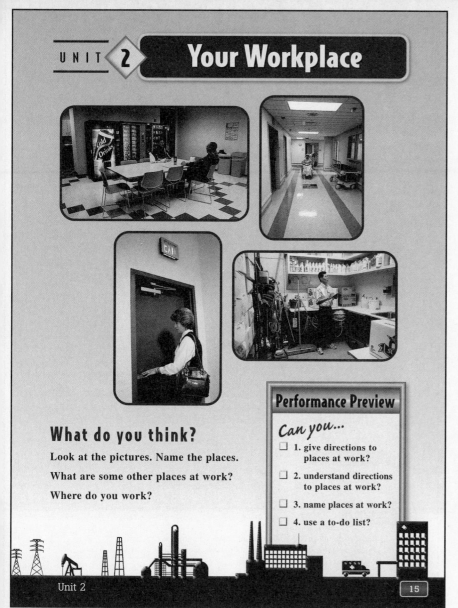

Your Workplace

What do you think?

Look at the pictures. Name the places.

What are some other places at work?

Where do you work?

Performance Preview

Can you...

☐ 1. give directions to places at work?

☐ 2. understand directions to places at work?

☐ 3. name places at work?

☐ 4. use a to-do list?

Unit 2   15

Unit 2 Overview
—SCANS Competencies—

★ Communicate information

★ Acquire and interpret information

★ Understand organizational systems

★ Allocate time

Workforce Skills

• Give directions to places at work

• Understand directions to places at work

• Name places at work

• Use a to-do list

Materials

• Picture cards or photographs of places in the unit and other places at learners' workplace(s) and/or school

• A large floor plan of the rooms near your classroom

• To-do lists

• Graph paper

Unit Warm-Up

To get learners thinking about the unit topic (asking for, giving, and understanding directions to places at work), act out feeling lost. Ask learners to figure out what is the matter. Encourage them to talk about times they need directions. What do they do to get help? Then write the unit title on the board. Ask learners what the unit might be about.

★   ★   ★   ★   ★

WORKFORCE SKILLS (page 15)

Name places at work

★   ★   ★   ★   ★

PREPARATION

1. Display the picture cards and the floor plan of rooms near your classroom. Have learners identify the rooms and locate your classroom and other places on the map. Encourage learners to use peer teaching to clarify any unfamiliar vocabulary.

2. Ask learners to name other places they need to go to at work and/or at school.

PRESENTATION

1. Focus attention on the photographs. Ask learners to speculate about what the unit might be about. Write their ideas on the board and/or restate them in acceptable English.

2. Have learners talk about the pictures. Have them identify the rooms, name the objects they see, and say what the people are doing. Help learners relate the rooms in the pictures to the places depicted on the picture cards and/or on the large map.

3. Help learners read the questions. Discuss the questions with the class.

4. You may want to use the Performance Preview to provide learners with an overview of the skills in the unit. Have learners read the list of skills and discuss what they will learn in this unit.

FOLLOW-UP

Same or Different: Have teams discuss ways that their school or workplace is the same as or different from the places in the photos. Have each group share its ideas with the class.

♦ Have teams write their ideas and post them.

WORKBOOK

Unit 2, Exercises 1A–1B

WORKFORCE SKILLS (page 16)

Name places at work

★   ★   ★   ★   ★

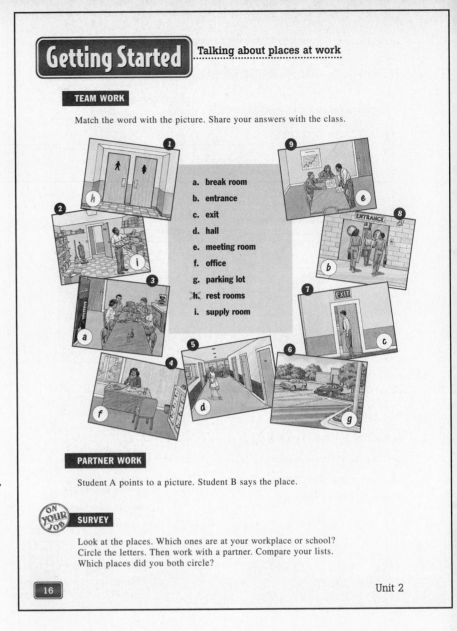

Teaching Note

Use this page to introduce the new language in the unit. Whenever possible, encourage peer teaching. Supply any new language the learners need.

PREPARATION

Ask teams to list as many places from work and/or school as they can. Have team reporters share their information with the class. As reporters name a place, have them indicate the picture card of the place.

PRESENTATION

1. Have learners read the Purpose Statement and briefly discuss what they will learn in this lesson. Use any of the Purpose Statement suggestions on page viii.

2. Focus attention on the illustrations. Encourage learners to say as much as they can about them. Write their ideas on the board and/or restate them in acceptable English.

3. Have teams read the Team Work instructions. Make sure each team knows what to do. If necessary, model the first item. Remind the teams that they are responsible for making sure that each member understands the new words. Then have teams complete the activity. Have teams share their answers with the class.

4. Have partners read the Partner Work instructions. Make sure each pair knows what to do. If necessary, model the activity. Then have pairs complete the activity. Have learners switch partners and repeat the activity. Have one or two partners perform their conversations for the class.

 5. Have partners read the Survey instructions. Make sure each pair knows what to do. Then have pairs complete the

activity. Have pairs share their answers with the class. For more information see "Survey" on page viii.

FOLLOW-UP

Table: Have the class work as a team to use the information from the Survey to create a table showing learners' names and the number of places each one circled. Have learners discuss the table.

♦ Help teams use the table to create bar graphs that show the number of places each learner circled. For more information on graphs see page viii. Discuss the bar graph with learners.

WORKBOOK

Unit 2, Exercises 2A–2B

Talk About It — Asking for and giving directions

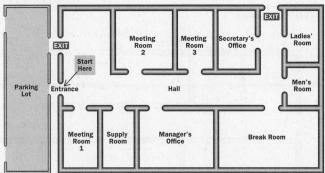

(Floor plan labels: Parking Lot, EXIT, Start Here, Entrance, Meeting Room 2, Meeting Room 3, Secretary's Office, EXIT, Ladies' Room, Hall, Men's Room, Meeting Room 1, Supply Room, Manager's Office, Break Room)

 PRACTICE THE DIALOG

A Please take this package to the supply room.

B Where's the supply room?

A Go down the hall. It's the second door on the right.

B Excuse me. Is it the first door on the right?

A No, it's the second door on the right. It's next to the manager's office.

B Thanks.

 PARTNER WORK

Ask your partner for directions. Use the map. Use the dialog and the Useful Language above.

Useful Language

Go down the hall.

Turn left/right.

It's the first/second/third/ fourth door on the right.

It's next to the supply room.

It's between the men's room and the exit.

It's across the hall from the supply room.

 ASAP
PROJECT

As a class, prepare a floor plan of your workplace or school. Divide into three teams. One team gets the information. Another team draws the floor plan. Another team writes questions about the floor plan for the class to answer.

Unit 2

17

WORKFORCE SKILLS (page 17)

Name places at work

Give directions to places at work

Understand directions to places at work

★   ★   ★   ★   ★

ASAP
PROJECT

Have learners read the instructions. Briefly discuss the project and its purpose with learners. Make sure that everyone understands. Help learners assign themselves to groups based upon their knowledge, skills, interests, or other personal strengths. Have each team select a leader, and have the leaders or the whole class select an overall project leader. Throughout the rest of the unit, allow time for learners to work on the project. Have the teams agree on a deadline when the project will be finished. For more information see "ASAP Project" on page vi.

PREPARATION

1. Have learners read the Purpose Statement and briefly discuss what they will learn in this lesson. Use any of the Purpose Statement suggestions on page viii.

2. Use the picture cards and the large floor plan (or the floor plan on the page) to help learners review the names of places at work. Then describe routes and indicate locations to elicit the sentences in the Useful Language box. Supply any language learners need.

PRESENTATION

 1. Focus attention on the floor plan. Encourage learners to say as much as they can about it. Have them identify the rooms and state their locations. Then present the dialog.

For more information see "Presenting a Dialog" on page ix.

2. Have partners read the Partner Work instructions. Focus attention on the Useful Language box. Help learners read the expressions. If necessary, model pronunciation. Make sure learners understand that they can use the Useful Language to complete the activity. Model if necessary. Then have learners complete the activity. Have learners switch partners and repeat the activity. Have one or two pairs say their dialogs for the class.

FOLLOW-UP

Dialogs: Have pairs use the large floor plan to create dialogs in which they ask for and give directions. Have several pairs present their dialogs to the class.

♦ Have pairs write their dialogs.

WORKBOOK

Unit 2, Exercises 3A–3B

WORKFORCE SKILLS (page 18)

Give directions to places at work
Understand directions to places at work
Name places at work

★　　★　　★　　★　　★

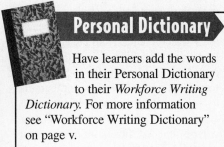

Personal Dictionary

Have learners add the words in their Personal Dictionary to their *Workforce Writing Dictionary*. For more information see "Workforce Writing Dictionary" on page v.

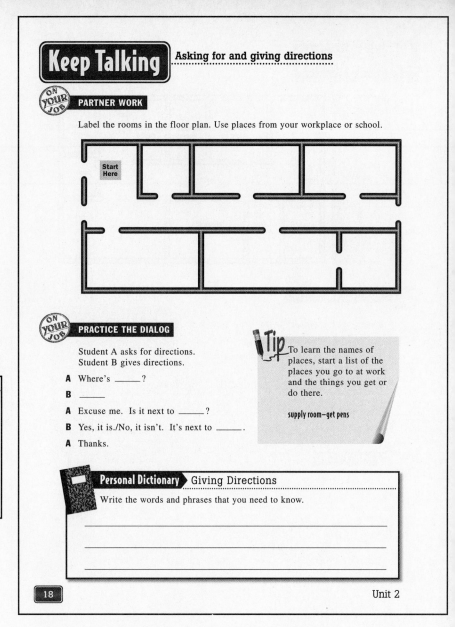

Keep Talking　Asking for and giving directions

PARTNER WORK

Label the rooms in the floor plan. Use places from your workplace or school.

Start Here

PRACTICE THE DIALOG

Student A asks for directions.
Student B gives directions.

A Where's _____?

B _____

A Excuse me. Is it next to _____?

B Yes, it is./No, it isn't. It's next to _____.

A Thanks.

Tip To learn the names of places, start a list of the places you go to at work and the things you get or do there.

supply room–get pens

Personal Dictionary　Giving Directions

Write the words and phrases that you need to know.

_____

_____

_____

18　　　　　　　　　　　　　　　　　　　　　　Unit 2

PREPARATION

Use the picture cards and the large floor plan to review the names of places at work. Have learners match the pictures with the rooms on the floor plan.

PRESENTATION

1. Have learners read the Purpose Statement and briefly discuss what they will learn in this lesson. Use any of the Purpose Statement suggestions on page viii.

2. Focus attention on the blank floor plan. Have the learners count the rooms, find the entrances and exits, and identify the hall.

 3. Have partners read the Partner Work instructions. Make sure each pair knows what to do. If necessary, model the

activity on the board. Then have pairs complete the activity. Have learners switch partners and repeat the activity. Have several pairs perform their dialogs for the class

 4. Have partners read the instructions for Practice the Dialog. Allow learners time to complete the activity. Have learners change partners and repeat. Have several pairs present their dialogs to the class.

5. Have learners read the Personal Dictionary instructions. Have learners work in teams to brainstorm vocabulary words they might put in their dictionaries. For more information see "Presenting the Personal Dictionary" on page ix.

Tip Have learners read the Tip independently. Have learners discuss how the advice will

help them. Allow learners a few minutes to start their lists. For more information see "Presenting a Tip" on page ix.

FOLLOW-UP

Workstation Floor Plans: Have learners draw simple diagrams of their immediate work areas or classroom. Have them show their drawings, indicate where they sit or stand, and identify the furniture, machines, and equipment in the diagrams.

♦ Have learners write a few sentences describing their floor plans. Have them share their sentences with the class.

WORKBOOK

Unit 2, Exercise 4

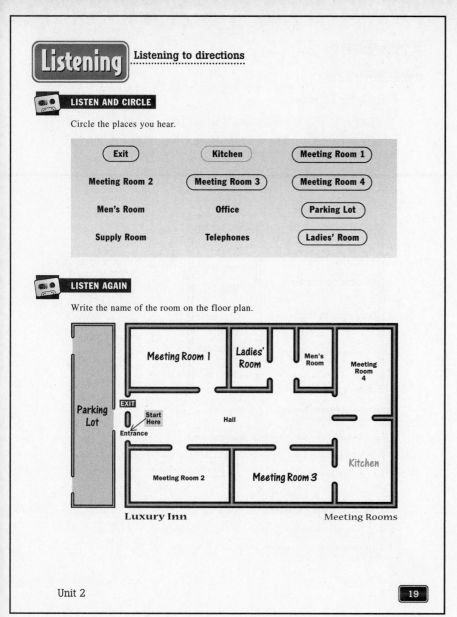

Listening   Listening to directions

LISTEN AND CIRCLE

Circle the places you hear.

Exit	Kitchen	Meeting Room 1
Meeting Room 2	Meeting Room 3	Meeting Room 4
Men's Room	Office	Parking Lot
Supply Room	Telephones	Ladies' Room

LISTEN AGAIN

Write the name of the room on the floor plan.

Meeting Room 1   Ladies' Room   Men's Room   Meeting Room 4

Parking Lot   EXIT   Start Here   Entrance   Hall   Kitchen

Meeting Room 2   Meeting Room 3

Luxury Inn   Meeting Rooms

Unit 2   19

WORKFORCE SKILLS (page 19)

Understand directions to places at work

★ ★ ★ ★ ★

PREPARATION

1. Have learners read the Purpose Statement and briefly discuss what they will learn in this lesson. Use any of the Purpose Statement suggestions on page viii.

2. Use the picture cards and the large floor plan of your learners' school or workplace to review asking for and giving directions. Give directions to a learner. Have the learner trace the directions on the floor plan for the class. Then have pairs take turns giving each other directions and tracing them on the floor plan.

PRESENTATION

 1. Have learners read the Listen and Circle instructions. Then have them read the

words in the box. Use peer teaching to clarify any unfamiliar vocabulary. Make sure that everyone understands the instructions. If necessary, model the first item. Then play the tape or read the Listening Transcript aloud two or more times as learners complete the activity. Check learners' work. See "Presenting a Listening Activity" on page ix.

 2. Have learners read the Listen Again instructions. Have learners count the rooms in the floor plan, locate the entrance and exit, and identify the rooms. Make sure that everyone understands the instructions. Follow the procedures in 1. Check learners' work.

FOLLOW-UP

More Floor Plans: Bring in floor plans for learners to examine, such as floor plans of local shopping malls, hotels, airports, or businesses. Have learners use them to ask for and give more directions.

♦ Give each team a different floor plan. Have teams write dialogs asking for and giving directions. Have them display their floor plans to the rest of the class and say their dialogs aloud.

WORKBOOK

Unit 2, Exercise 5

WORKFORCE SKILLS (pages 20–21)

Give directions to places at work

Understand directions to places at work

Name places at work

★ ★ ★ ★ ★

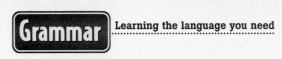

Grammar Learning the language you need

A. Study the Examples

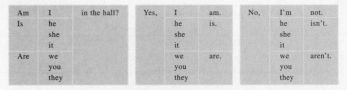

Am	I	in the hall?
Is	he	
	she	
	it	
Are	we	
	you	
	they	

Yes,	I	am.
	he	is.
	she	
	it	
	we	are.
	you	
	they	

No,	I'm	not.
	he	isn't.
	she	
	it	
	we	aren't.
	you	
	they	

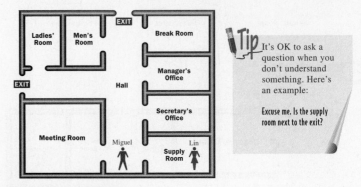

Tip It's OK to ask a question when you don't understand something. Here's an example:

Excuse me. Is the supply room next to the exit?

ANSWER THE QUESTIONS

Look at the floor plan and answer the questions.

1. Are Miguel and Lin at home? _____ No, they aren't.

2. Are they at work? _____ Yes, they are.

3. Is Lin in the break room? _____ No, she isn't.

4. Is she in the supply room? _____ Yes, she is.

5. Is Miguel in the hall? _____ Yes, he is.

6. Is the meeting room next to the break room? _____ No, it isn't.

20

Unit 2

PREPARATION

Review the language in the grammar boxes with learners before they open their books, if necessary. Follow the instructions in Preparation on pages 16 and 17.

PRESENTATION

1. Have learners read and discuss the Purpose Statement. For more information see "Purpose Statement" on page viii.

2. Have learners read the grammar boxes in A. Have learners use the language in the boxes to say as many sentences as possible. Tell learners that they can use the grammar boxes throughout the unit to review or check sentence structures.

3. Have learners read the instructions for Answer the Questions. If necessary, model the first item. Allow learners to complete the activity. Have learners check each other's work in pairs. Ask several learners to read the questions and their answers aloud while the rest of the class checks their work.

Tip Have learners read the Tip independently. Have learners discuss how the advice will help them. For more information see "Presenting a Tip" on page ix.

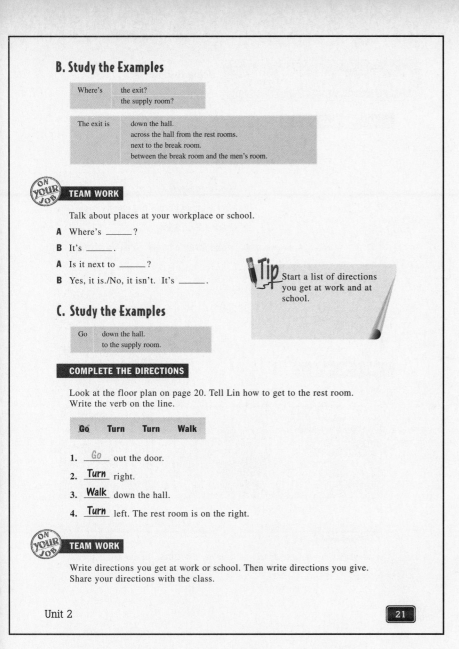

B. Study the Examples

Where's	the exit? the supply room?

The exit is	down the hall. across the hall from the rest rooms. next to the break room. between the break room and the men's room.

TEAM WORK

Talk about places at your workplace or school.

A Where's _____?

B It's _____.

A Is it next to _____?

B Yes, it is./No, it isn't. It's _____.

Tip Start a list of directions you get at work and at school.

C. Study the Examples

Go	down the hall. to the supply room.

COMPLETE THE DIRECTIONS

Look at the floor plan on page 20. Tell Lin how to get to the rest room. Write the verb on the line.

Go	Turn	Turn	Walk

1. _Go_ out the door.
2. _Turn_ right.
3. _Walk_ down the hall.
4. _Turn_ left. The rest room is on the right.

TEAM WORK

Write directions you get at work or school. Then write directions you give. Share your directions with the class.

Unit 2

21

---

4. Focus attention on the grammar boxes in B. Follow the procedures in 2.

 5. Have teams read the Team Work instructions. Make sure each team knows what to do. If necessary, model the activity. Then have teams complete the activity. Have learners switch teams and repeat the activity. Ask several teams to present their conversations to the class.

6. Focus attention on the grammar boxes in C. Follow the procedure in 2.

7. Have learners read the instructions for Complete the Directions. If necessary, model the first item. Then have learners complete the activity independently. Have a different student read each sentence aloud as the rest of the class checks their answers.

8. Have teams read the Team Work instructions. Make sure each team knows what to do. If necessary, model the activity. Then have teams complete the activity. Have team reporters share their lists with the class.

Tip Have Learners read the Tip independently. Have learners discuss how the advice will help them. For more information see "Presenting a Tip" on page ix.

FOLLOW-UP

Where Am I? Have learners use the large floor plan or the floor plan on page 17 to play this game. Demonstrate by choosing a place and giving two or three clues. For example, say *I'm across from the (place). I'm next to the (place).*

I'm between the (place) and the (place). Where am I? Divide the class into small teams and have them play the game until each student has had a chance to give clues.

♦ Have learners write two or three clues on pieces of paper for each room on the floor plan. Then have them play the game in small teams by drawing cards one at a time, reading the clues aloud, and identifying the rooms.

WORKBOOK

Unit 2, Exercises 6A–6C

BLACKLINE MASTERS

Blackline Master: Unit 2

WORKFORCE SKILLS (pages 22–23)

Use a to-do list

★　★　★　★　★

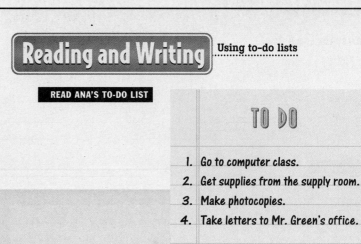

Reading and Writing — Using to-do lists

READ ANA'S TO-DO LIST

TO DO

1. Go to computer class.
2. Get supplies from the supply room.
3. Make photocopies.
4. Take letters to Mr. Green's office.

WRITE THE NUMBER

What does Ana need to do first? Second? Third? Write numbers from 1 to 3.

Discussion

Ana doesn't have time to do one thing on her list. Circle the number in the list. What does Ana tell her boss? Share your ideas with the class.

Unit 2

PREPARATION

If necessary, use picture cards to review the place names. Use pantomime to present or review the imperatives.

PRESENTATION

1. Have learners read and discuss the Purpose Statement. For more information see "Purpose Statement" on page viii.

2. Have learners preview the to-do list before they read. See "Prereading" on page x. Encourage learners to say everything they can about the list. Write their ideas on the board or restate them in acceptable English. Then have them read the list independently.

3. Have learners read the instructions for Write the Number. Make sure everyone knows what to do. Then have learners complete the activity independently. Have learners review each other's work in pairs. Ask several learners to share their answers with the class while the rest of the class checks their work.

4. Have learners read the Discussion instructions. Make sure everyone knows what to do. Then have learners work in teams to discuss ways that Ana can solve her problem. Have team reporters share their ideas with the class. Have the teams compare ideas.

English ASAP

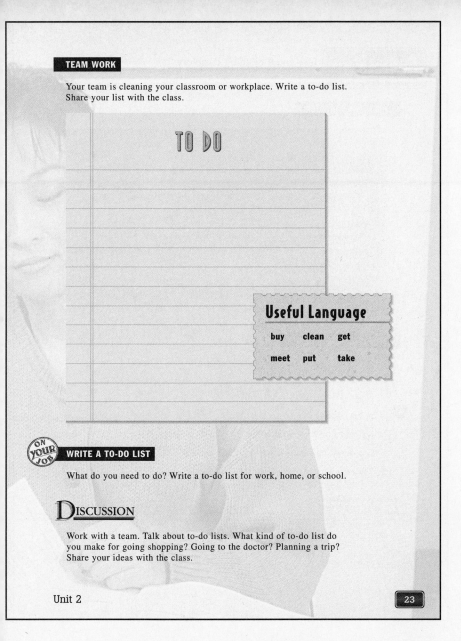

Your team is cleaning your classroom or workplace. Write a to-do list. Share your list with the class.

TO DO

Useful Language

buy	clean	get
meet	put	take

WRITE A TO-DO LIST

What do you need to do? Write a to-do list for work, home, or school.

DISCUSSION

Work with a team. Talk about to-do lists. What kind of to-do list do you make for going shopping? Going to the doctor? Planning a trip? Share your ideas with the class.

Unit 2   23

---

5. Have teams read the Team Work instructions and the Useful Language. Make sure each team knows what to do. If necessary, model the activity. Then have teams complete the activity. Have team reporters share their lists with the class. Ask teams to compare ideas.

 6. Have learners read the instructions for Write a To-Do List. Model the activity if necessary by suggesting items for your to-do list. Then have learners complete the activity independently. Have several learners share their lists with the class. Ask learners to compare lists.

7. Have learners read the Discussion instructions. Model the activity if necessary by suggesting items for one of the to-do lists mentioned. Then have learners complete the activity. Have

them discuss appropriate items for the lists mentioned in the instructions. Have team reporters share their ideas with the class. Ask the teams to compare each other's ideas.

FOLLOW-UP

Plan a Project: Have learners work in teams. Ask each team to imagine that they are their company's education committee. Ask them to think of a project they would like to plan, such as creating a computer lab or having an information fair for all employees. Ask each team to come up with a to-do list for their project and to share their projects and lists with the class.

♦ Have teams review their lists. Tell them they have to remove one item from their list because of a lack of time. Which item would they remove? Why? Have teams share their answers with the class.

WORKBOOK
Unit 2, Exercises 7A–7C

WORKFORCE SKILLS (page 24)

Give directions to places at work
Understand directions to places at work
Name places at work

★ ★ ★ ★ ★

Extension ···· Reading a building directory

READ THE DIRECTORY

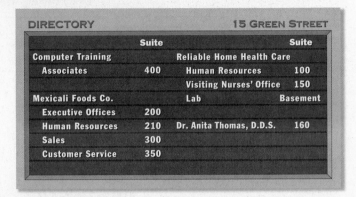

DIRECTORY		15 GREEN STREET	
	Suite		Suite
Computer Training		Reliable Home Health Care	
Associates	400	Human Resources	100
		Visiting Nurses' Office	150
Mexicali Foods Co.		Lab	Basement
Executive Offices	200		
Human Resources	210	Dr. Anita Thomas, D.D.S.	160
Sales	300		
Customer Service	350		

ANSWER THE QUESTIONS

Where do they go? Write the suite number.

1. Miguel's taking a package to the sales department of Mexicali Foods. Suite _300_

2. Alicia's taking a computer class. Suite _400_

3. Leo wants a job at Reliable Home Health Care. Suite _100_

4. Sara has an appointment with Dr. Thomas. Suite _160_

5. You want a job at Mexicali Foods. Suite _210_

Culture Notes

When you need directions at work or at school, who do you ask? Why? If you don't understand the directions, what do you do? Why?

24   Unit 2

PREPARATION

1. If your building has a directory, take the learners to look at it. Review the information provided by the directory.

2. Present or review the word **suite.** Ask learners to name places they have been that are located in suites. They may suggest doctors' offices, employment offices, etc. Help learners generalize that the first number in a suite or room number usually indicates the floor where the room is located. For example, suite 300 is located on the third floor.

PRESENTATION

1. Have learners read and discuss the Purpose Statement. For more information see "Purpose Statement" on page viii.

2. Have learners preview the items listed on the directory. Encourage them to say everything they can about them. Write their ideas on the board or restate them in acceptable English. Have learners read the directory.

3. Have learners read the instructions for Answer the Questions. If necessary, model the first item. Allow learners to complete the activity. Have learners review each others' work in pairs. Ask several learners to read their answers aloud while the rest of the class checks their work.

 4. Have learners read Culture Notes and talk over their responses in teams. Have team reporters share their ideas with the class. Ask the teams to compare each

other's ideas. For more information see "Culture Notes" on page vii.

FOLLOW-UP

The Newcomer: Make copies of a simple directory for the building where your class meets. Have learners create dialogs asking for and giving locations. Have learners use floor, room, or suite numbers and present their conversations to the class.

♦ Have learners make simple directories for their workplace or other locations they are familiar with.

WORKBOOK

Unit 2, Exercise 8

Performance Check

How well can you use the skills in this unit?
....

Complete the activities. Go over your work with a partner or your teacher.
Then complete the Performance Review on page 26.

SKILL 1 **GIVE DIRECTIONS**

Give your partner or teacher directions to the Manager's Office.

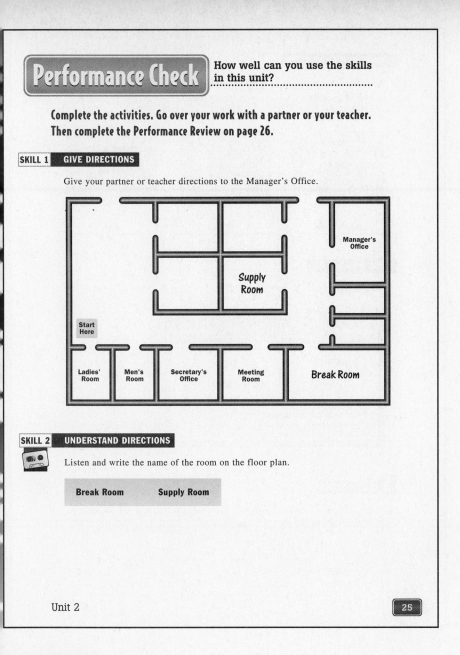

SKILL 2 **UNDERSTAND DIRECTIONS**

Listen and write the name of the room on the floor plan.

Break Room	Supply Room

Unit 2

25

PREPARATION

Use any of the procedures in "Evaluation" on page x with pages 25 and 26. Record individuals' results on the Unit 2 Individual Competency Chart. Record the class results on the Class Cumulative Competency Chart.

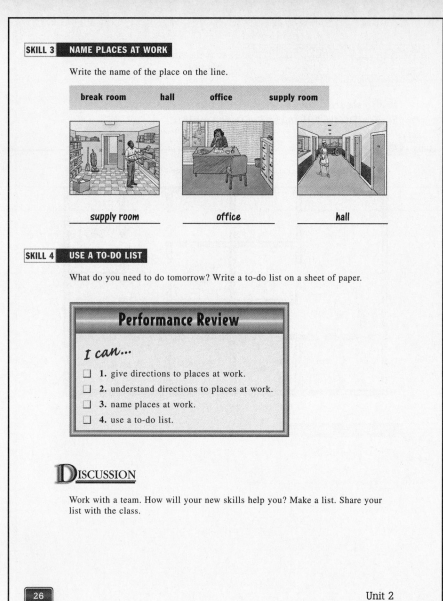

SKILL 3 **NAME PLACES AT WORK**

Write the name of the place on the line.

| break room | hall | office | supply room |

supply room   office   hall

SKILL 4 **USE A TO-DO LIST**

What do you need to do tomorrow? Write a to-do list on a sheet of paper.

Performance Review

I can...

☐ **1.** give directions to places at work.
☐ **2.** understand directions to places at work.
☐ **3.** name places at work.
☐ **4.** use a to-do list.

Discussion

Work with a team. How will your new skills help you? Make a list. Share your list with the class.

26

Unit 2

PREPARATION

Follow the instructions on page 25.

INFORMAL WORKPLACE-SPECIFIC ASSESSMENT

Ask learners to name one or two places at their workplaces that they visit regularly. How do they get from their workstations to these places? Ask for directions.

WORKBOOK

Unit 2, Exercise 9

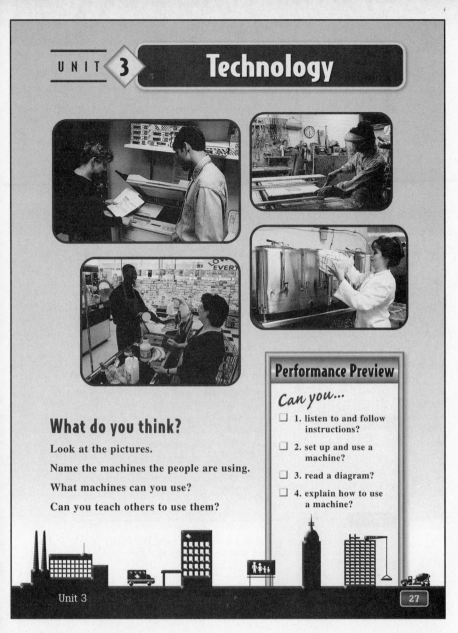

UNIT 3 — Technology

What do you think?

Look at the pictures.

Name the machines the people are using.

What machines can you use?

Can you teach others to use them?

Performance Preview

Can you...

☐ 1. listen to and follow instructions?

☐ 2. set up and use a machine?

☐ 3. read a diagram?

☐ 4. explain how to use a machine?

Unit 3

27

★ Select, apply, maintain, and troubleshoot technology

★ Teach others

★ Interpret and communicate information

Workforce Skills

● Listen to and follow instructions

● Set up and use a machine

● Read a diagram

● Explain how to use a machine

Materials

● User's manuals and diagrams for different kinds of machines

● Pictures of various kinds of office or business machinery, such as fax machine, telephone, computer

● Simple small machines, e.g., stapler, calculator, pencil sharpener

● Graph paper

Unit Warm-Up

The focus of Unit 3, "Technology," is on using machines and reading diagrams. Show learners a simple, non-electrical piece of machinery such as a stapler. Demonstrate and describe how to use the machine. Ask learners to talk about other machines they need to use.

★   ★   ★   ★   ★

WORKFORCE SKILLS (page 27)

Explain how to use a machine

★   ★   ★   ★   ★

PREPARATION

1. Show the pictures of the machines on the page. Have learners identify the machines and say their names. Encourage learners to use peer-teaching to clarify any unfamiliar vocabulary.

2. Have learners brainstorm a list of machines they use at work or at school.

PRESENTATION

1. Focus attention on the photographs. Ask learners to speculate what the unit might be about. Write their ideas on the board and/or restate them in acceptable English.

2. Have learners talk about the pictures. Have them identify the machines, name the other objects they see, and say what the people are doing with the machines. Help learners relate the machines to different workplaces: *coffee maker—restaurant.*

3. Help learners read the questions. Discuss the questions with the class.

4. You may want to use the Performance Preview to provide learners with an overview of the skills in the unit. Have learners read the list of skills and discuss what they will learn in this unit.

FOLLOW-UP

Machines in the Workplace: Have teams make lists of other workplaces that might use the machines in the photos. Have team reporters share their lists with the class.

♦ Have learners name machines they think they might find in almost any company, such as coffee makers, telephones, copiers, fax machines, and computers. Which ones do learners use? Which ones do they want to learn to use?

WORKBOOK

Unit 3, Exercises 1A–1B

Getting Started — Using machines

TEAM WORK

Anton is working in the mailroom. Work with your team. Find all the machines Anton uses. Write the names of the machines. Talk about what each machine does.

fax machine	computer
pencil sharpener	stapler
postal meter	calculator
printer	telephone

PARTNER WORK

Look at the machines Anton uses. Student A chooses a machine. Student B says what Anton can do with it.

A the computer

B Anton can write a letter on the computer.

SURVEY

As a class, make a chart with three columns: home, work, and school. Each person writes the name of a machine he or she uses at each place.

28   Unit 3

Teaching Note

Use this page to introduce the new language in the unit. Whenever possible, encourage peer teaching. Supply any language the learners need.

PREPARATION

Have learners identify as many machines as they can in the classroom and say what each machine does and how it can be used.

PRESENTATION

1. Have learners read and discuss the Purpose Statement. For more information see "Purpose Statement" on page viii.

2. Encourage learners to say as much as they can about the photograph. Write their ideas on the board and/or restate them in acceptable English.

3. Have teams read the Team Work instructions and complete the activity. If learners need help, encourage them to consult other teams. Have team reporters share their answers with the class.

4. Have partners read the Partner Work instructions and complete the activity. Have learners switch partners and repeat the activity. Have one or two pairs present their dialogs to the class.

5. Have the class read the Survey instructions. Make sure everyone knows what to do. If necessary, model the activity. Put the chart on a large sheet of paper or on the board. Have the class come up with as many machines for each category as they can. Discuss the results with learners. For more information see "Survey" on page viii.

FOLLOW-UP

Bar Graph: Help learners make a bar graph with the information from their chart. The horizontal axis shows the categories *home, work,* and *school.* The vertical axis shows the number of different machines learners named. For more information see "Survey" on page viii.

◆ Have learners look at the lists of machines they came up with for each category. Do any of them appear in more than one category?

WORKBOOK

Unit 3, Exercises 2A–2B

Talk About It — Following instructions

 PRACTICE THE DIALOG

A Do you need some help?

B Yes, I'm trying to copy this memo.

A First, open the cover and put the paper on the glass.

B Like this?

A That's right. Then, choose the number of copies you want. Next, close the cover and press the START button.

B Thanks for your help.

Useful Language

turn on	first
turn off	second
open	third
close	next
plug in	last

ON YOUR JOB **PARTNER WORK**

Make a list of machines people use at work or at home. Use the dialog and the Useful Language above to talk about how you operate these machines. What do you do if you need help?

ASAP PROJECT

As a class, choose a machine from work or home. Form three teams. One team makes a list of instructions for using the machine. Another team draws simple diagrams. The third team makes a poster of the instructions and the diagrams. Complete this project as you work through this unit.

Unit 3

29

ASAP PROJECT

Have learners read the instructions. Discuss the project and its purpose with learners. Make sure that everyone understands. Help learners assign themselves to teams based upon their knowledge, skills, interests, or other personal strengths. Have each team select a leader, and have the team leaders or the whole class select an overall project leader. Throughout the rest of the unit, allow time for learners to work on the project. Have the teams agree on a deadline when the project will be finished. For more information see "ASAP Project" on page vi.

PREPARATION

1. Present ordinal numbers **first** through **fifth** as well as other sequencing words such as **next, then,** and **last.**

2. Write ordinal numbers on the board. Mime the steps in using a simple machine you bring to class. Have learners say what you are doing. As learners say each step, write it in acceptable English next to the correct ordinal number.

3. Show a picture of a copier. Identify the cover, the glass, and the START button. Clarify as needed.

PRESENTATION

1. Have learners read and discuss the Purpose Statement. For more information see "Purpose Statement" on page viii.

 2. Focus attention on the illustration. Encourage learners to say as much as they can about it. Have them identify the machine and as many parts of it as they can. Then present the dialog. See "Presenting a Dialog" on page ix.

 3. Have partners read the Partner Work instructions. Focus attention on the Useful Language box. Help learners read the words. If necessary, model pronunciation. Then have learners complete the activity. Have one or two pairs present their lists and dialogs to the class.

FOLLOW-UP

Missing Steps: Divide the class into several teams. Show again how to use the machine you demonstrated in the

Warm-Up. Give each team a set of written instructions for using the device. Leave one step out of the instructions. Have each team write what they think the missing step is.

♦ Post learners' answers and discuss how their answers are similar and different. As a class, have learners come up with a final version of the missing step.

WORKBOOK

Unit 3, Exercise 3

WORKFORCE SKILLS (page 30)

Listen to and follow instructions

Set up and use a machine

Explain how to use a machine

★   ★   ★   ★   ★

Personal Dictionary

Have learners add the words in their Personal Dictionary to their *Workforce Writing Dictionary.* For more information see "Workforce Writing Dictionary" on page v.

Keep Talking — Showing someone how to use a machine

PARTNER WORK

Talk about what each person is doing. Choose a machine for each person.

<u>b</u> **1.** Anita is cleaning.

<u>a</u> **2.** Sumiko is ringing up a sale.

<u>d</u> **3.** Donna is building a bookcase.

<u>c</u> **4.** Luis is starting work.

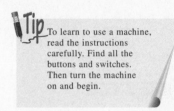

PRACTICE THE DIALOG

Choose a machine from the pictures. Tell your partner how to use the machine. Student A asks for instructions. Student B gives instructions.

A How do you use the coffee maker?

B First, put in the water. Next, put in the coffee.

A First water, then coffee?

B That's right. Now turn it on.

A Thanks for your help.

 Tip To learn to use a machine, read the instructions carefully. Find all the buttons and switches. Then turn the machine on and begin.

Personal Dictionary — Using Machines

Write the words and phrases that you need to know.

_____

_____

_____

30   Unit 3

PREPARATION

1. Use the pictures of machines or small machines you bring in to review the names of machines and the steps in using them. Have learners identify the machine and demonstrate how to use it for the rest of the class.

2. Show products or pictures of products associated with machines and have learners match them. For example, show a cup of coffee and elicit the association with a coffee maker. Continue with *time card—time clock* and *money—cash register* until you elicit all the machines on the page.

3. Use realia and pantomime to clarify **ringing up a sale** and **bookcase.**

PRESENTATION

1. Have learners read and discuss the Purpose Statement.

2. Encourage learners to say as much as they can about the illustrations. Help learners identify the machines shown and brainstorm a list of uses for each one.

3. Have partners read the Partner Work instructions and complete the activity. Ask pairs to share their answers with the class.

 4. Have partners read the Practice the Dialog instructions. Then present the dialog. See "Presenting a Dialog" on page ix.

5. Have learners read the Personal Dictionary instructions. Then use the Personal Dictionary procedures on page ix. Remind learners to continue to add words to their dictionaries throughout the unit.

Tip Have learners read the Tip independently. Have learners discuss how the advice will help them.

FOLLOW-UP

Write the Steps: Have pairs choose a picture of a machine or a machine in your classroom and write instructions for it.

♦ Have pairs exchange instructions. Have them read and peer-edit the instructions. Have partners use the feedback to produce final drafts of the instructions.

WORKBOOK

Unit 3, Exercise 4

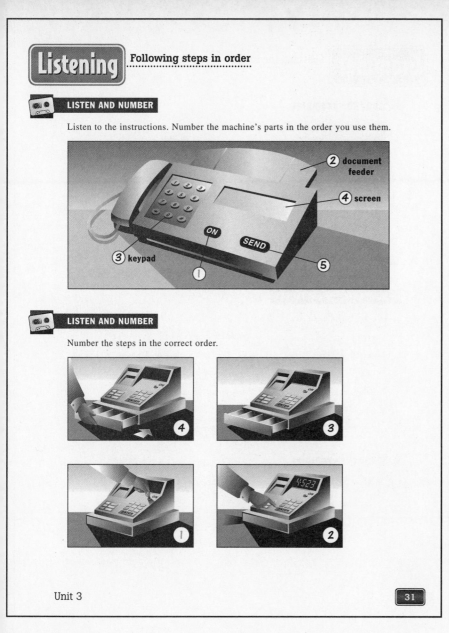

Listening — Following steps in order

LISTEN AND NUMBER

Listen to the instructions. Number the machine's parts in the order you use them.

2 document feeder
4 screen
3 keypad
5
ON
SEND

LISTEN AND NUMBER

Number the steps in the correct order.

Unit 3

`31`

Language Note

Point out to learners that ordinal numbers are used in many workplaces. They tell the locations of rooms (the first door on the right) and the names of floors in a building (the first floor).

PREPARATION

1. Review ordinal numbers and words by presenting the steps in using a machine.

2. Use pictures to introduce **fax machine** and **cash register.** Identify the **screen, keypad, document feeder,** and **SEND** button.

3. Pass out copies of a diagram of a machine. Have learners focus on how the parts of the machine are identified. Discuss what makes a diagram easy to understand.

PRESENTATION

1. Have learners read and discuss the Purpose Statement.

 2. Have learners read the Listen and Number instructions. Then have them look carefully at the diagram, identify the machine, and name the parts. Then play the tape or read the Listening Transcript aloud two or more times as learners complete the activity. Check learners' work. See "Presenting a Listening Activity" on page ix.

 3. Have learners read the Listen and Number instructions. Have them identify the machine and speculate about the order of the steps shown in the pictures. Make sure that everyone understands the instructions. Then play the tape or read the Listening Transcript aloud two or more times as learners complete the activity. Check learners' work.

FOLLOW-UP

All Mixed Up: Draw simple steps for using different machines. Each step should be drawn on a separate sheet of paper. Give a set of pictures to each team of learners, and have them arrange the pictures in the correct order. Have teams switch picture sets and repeat. Have one or two teams share their ordered pictures with the class and share their steps in using the machines.

♦ Have each team write brief descriptions of the steps on the back of the pictures in a set. Have team reporters share their descriptions with the class.

WORKBOOK

Unit 3, Exercise 5

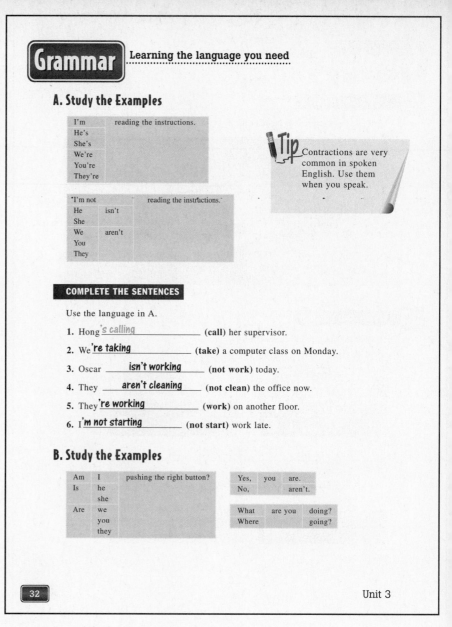

Grammar — Learning the language you need

A. Study the Examples

I'm	reading the instructions.
He's	
She's	
We're	
You're	
They're	

Tip Contractions are very common in spoken English. Use them when you speak.

I'm not		reading the instructions.
He	isn't	
She		
We	aren't	
You		
They		

COMPLETE THE SENTENCES

Use the language in A.

1. Hong 's calling _____ (call) her supervisor.

2. We 're taking _____ (take) a computer class on Monday.

3. Oscar _____ isn't working _____ (not work) today.

4. They _____ aren't cleaning _____ (not clean) the office now.

5. They 're working _____ (work) on another floor.

6. I 'm not starting _____ (not start) work late.

B. Study the Examples

Am	I	pushing the right button?
Is	he	
	she	
Are	we	
	you	
	they	

| Yes, | you | are. |
| No, | | aren't. |

| What | are you | doing? |
| Where | | going? |

32   Unit 3

PREPARATION

Review the language in the grammar boxes with learners before they open their books, if necessary.

PRESENTATION

1. Have learners read and discuss the Purpose Statement. For more information see "Purpose Statement" on page viii.

2. Have learners read the grammar boxes in A. Then have learners use the language in the boxes to say as many sentences as possible. Tell learners that they can use the grammar boxes throughout the unit to review or check sentence structures.

3. Have learners read the instructions for Complete the Sentences. If necessary, model the first item. Allow

learners to complete the activity. Have learners check each other's work in pairs. Ask several learners to read their completed sentences aloud while the rest of the class checks their work.

Tip Have learners read the tip independently. Provide any clarification needed. Ask learners to give a few examples. For more information see "Presenting a Tip" on page ix.

4. Focus attention on the grammar boxes in B. Follow the procedures in 2.

Unit 3

Nina is taking a training class at work. Use the language in A and B.

A Where _____ are _____ you _____ going _____ (go), Nina?

B I ___'m going___ (go) to the training room.

A _____ Are _____ you _____ taking _____ (take) a class?

B Yes, I _____ am _____.

A What _____ are _____ they _____ teaching _____ (teach)?

B They ___'re teaching___ (teach) me to use the new press.

PARTNER WORK

Does your company have training classes? Are you taking a training class? What are you learning?

C. Study the Examples

the mail supervisor's desk

the employees' cars

WRITE THE ANSWER

Who does it belong to? Follow the language in C.

1. the secretary—telephone
   _____the secretary's telephone_____

2. Bruno—adding machine
   _____Bruno's adding machine_____

3. the cashiers—keys
   _____the cashiers' keys_____

4. the tailor—sewing machine
   _____the tailor's sewing machine_____

Unit 3

33

---

5. Have learners read the instructions for Complete the Dialog. Make sure everyone knows what to do. If necessary, model the first item. Then have learners complete the activity independently. Have pairs of learners read exchanges from the dialog aloud while the rest of the class checks their answers.

6. Have learners read the Partner Work instructions. Ask pairs to share their answers with the class.

7. Focus attention on the new language in C. Follow the procedure in 2.

8. Have learners read the instructions for Write the Answer. If necessary, model the first item. Then have learners complete the activity independently. Have learners check each other's work

in pairs. Ask several learners to read their completed sentences aloud while the rest of the class checks their answers.

FOLLOW-UP

Charades: Write simple actions such as *ride a bicycle* or *drink coffee* on slips of paper. A learner draws a piece of paper at random and pantomimes the action for the rest of the class to figure out. Be sure learners express their answers in the present progressive tense: *He's riding a bicycle.*

♦ Have learners work in pairs on a slightly more complex charade they will present to the rest of the class. You can offer ideas or they can select their own actions. Whose charade is easiest to figure out? The most difficult?

WORKBOOK

Unit 3, Exercises 6A–6C

BLACKLINE MASTERS

Blackline Master: Unit 3

Set up and use a machine

Read a diagram

Explain how to use a machine

★   ★   ★   ★   ★

SCANS Note

Discuss with learners the different ways to use a new piece of machinery. It is always a good idea to read the instruction manual and the diagrams first. It can also be helpful to talk to someone who already uses the machine. Remind learners they should always know how to turn a machine off before they try to use it the first time.

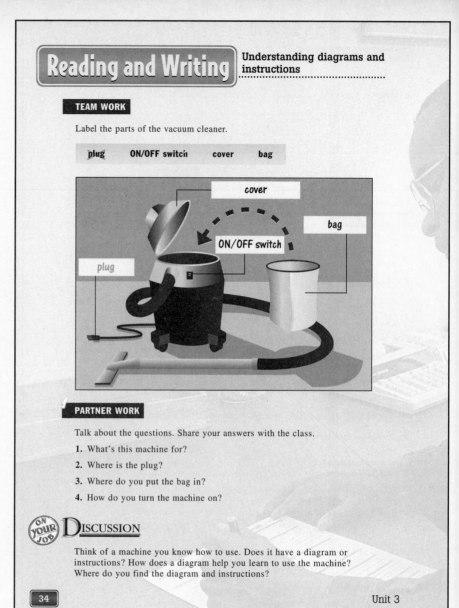

Reading and Writing   Understanding diagrams and instructions

TEAM WORK

Label the parts of the vacuum cleaner.

plug	ON/OFF switch	cover	bag

PARTNER WORK

Talk about the questions. Share your answers with the class.

1. What's this machine for?
2. Where is the plug?
3. Where do you put the bag in?
4. How do you turn the machine on?

DISCUSSION

Think of a machine you know how to use. Does it have a diagram or instructions? How does a diagram help you learn to use the machine? Where do you find the diagram and instructions?

34   Unit 3

PREPARATION

Show the sample machine diagram of a vacuum cleaner or use the one on the page. Help learners identify the **plugs, ON/OFF switches, covers,** and **bags,** if there are any on the diagrams. If these parts aren't present on the sample diagrams, draw them on the board. Pantomime vacuuming. Have learners identify what you are doing.

PRESENTATION

1. Have learners read and discuss the Purpose Statement. For more information see "Purpose Statement" on page viii.

2. Have learners look at the diagram before they begin. Encourage learners to say everything they can about the diagram. Write their ideas on the board and/or restate them in acceptable English.

3. Have learners read the instructions for Team Work. Make sure everyone knows what to do. If necessary, model the first item. Then have learners complete the activity. Have a team reporter present the answers to the rest of the class.

4. Have partners read the instructions for Partner Work. Make sure each pair knows what to do. If necessary, model the first item. Then have pairs complete the activity. Ask pairs to share their ideas with the rest of the class. Help learners notice the similarities and differences of their ideas.

 5. Have learners read the Discussion instructions. Make sure everyone knows what to

do. Then have learners work in teams to choose a machine and talk about the instructions. Have team reporters share their answers with the class.

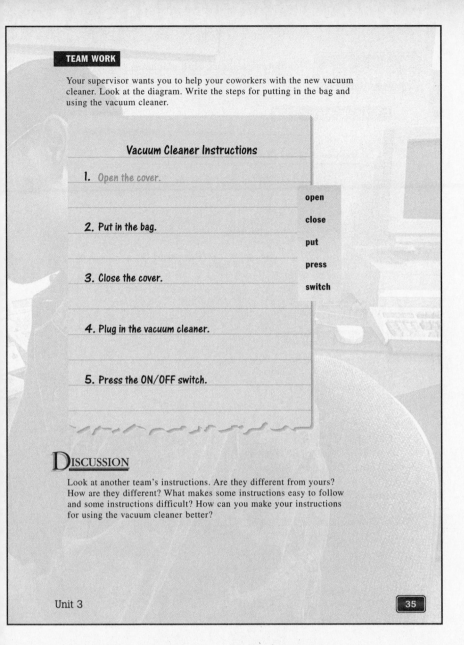

TEAM WORK

Your supervisor wants you to help your coworkers with the new vacuum cleaner. Look at the diagram. Write the steps for putting in the bag and using the vacuum cleaner.

Vacuum Cleaner Instructions

1. *Open the cover.*

2. Put in the bag.

3. Close the cover.

4. Plug in the vacuum cleaner.

5. Press the ON/OFF switch.

open
close
put
press
switch

DISCUSSION

Look at another team's instructions. Are they different from yours? How are they different? What makes some instructions easy to follow and some instructions difficult? How can you make your instructions for using the vacuum cleaner better?

Unit 3   35

---

6. Have teams read the Team Work instructions. Make sure each team knows what to do. Focus learners' attention on the word bank. Explain that these are suggested verbs and learners may choose to use other verbs. If necessary, model the first item of the activity. Then have teams complete the activity. Have team reporters share their instructions with the class. Ask teams to compare ideas.

7. Have learners read the Discussion instructions. Make sure everyone knows what to do. Then have learners work in teams to evaluate another team's instructions and make a list of suggested changes. Have team reporters share their ideas with the rest of the class.

FOLLOW-UP

Put It Together: Divide the class into teams. Assign each team a machine to write about. Have each team create a diagram with labeled parts and a set of instructions for using the machine. If your learners did the activity on page 31, you might have them use the diagrams they prepared on that page for this activity. A representative from each team should present its work to the rest of the class.

♦ Have teams exchange and peer-edit their instructions.

WORKBOOK

Unit 3, Exercises 7A–7B

WORKFORCE SKILLS (page 36)

Listen to and follow instructions

Explain how to use a machine

★   ★   ★   ★   ★

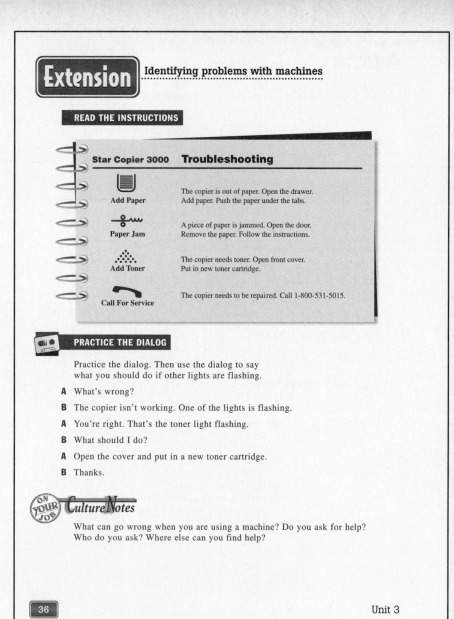

Extension — Identifying problems with machines

READ THE INSTRUCTIONS

Star Copier 3000   Troubleshooting

Add Paper
The copier is out of paper. Open the drawer.
Add paper. Push the paper under the tabs.

Paper Jam
A piece of paper is jammed. Open the door.
Remove the paper. Follow the instructions.

Add Toner
The copier needs toner. Open front cover.
Put in new toner cartridge.

Call For Service
The copier needs to be repaired. Call 1-800-531-5015.

PRACTICE THE DIALOG

Practice the dialog. Then use the dialog to say
what you should do if other lights are flashing.

A What's wrong?

B The copier isn't working. One of the lights is flashing.

A You're right. That's the toner light flashing.

B What should I do?

A Open the cover and put in a new toner cartridge.

B Thanks.

Culture Notes

What can go wrong when you are using a machine? Do you ask for help?
Who do you ask? Where else can you find help?

36   Unit 3

PREPARATION

1. Present **troubleshooting.** Choose a simple device, such as a pencil sharpener. Give a few troubleshooting tips: *Be sure the sharpener is plugged in. Empty the shavings.* Say: ***Troubleshooting*** *means figuring out what's wrong.* Show examples of trouble-shooting information from the instructional manuals you have brought in.

2. Present **toner** by explaining that toner is like ink in a copier. If you can, bring in a used toner cartridge to show the class. Clarify **jam** by saying: *Sometimes copiers have paper jams. The paper stays inside the copier. It looks like this.* Display a sheet of crumpled paper.

PRESENTATION

1. Have learners read and discuss the Purpose Statement.

2. Have learners read the instructions for using the copier. Encourage them to say everything they can about the instructions. Write their ideas on the board or restate them in acceptable English.

 3. Have partners read the Practice the Dialog instructions and complete the activity. Make sure each pair knows what to do. Have learners switch partners and repeat the activity. Have one or two partners present their dialogs to the class.

 4. Have learners read Culture Notes and talk over their responses in teams. Have team reporters share their ideas with the class. Ask the teams to compare each other's ideas. For more information see "Culture Notes" on page vii.

FOLLOW-UP

Fix the Problem: Have learners look at the diagram on page 34 or at a diagram of another machine. Help the class brainstorm a list of things that can go wrong with a vacuum cleaner and write troubleshooting instructions to solve the problems.

♦ Choose a machine in this unit. Have the class brainstorm a list of problems that can occur with the machine. Then assign one problem to each team of learners to write troubleshooting instructions for. Have learners share their instructions with the class.

WORKBOOK

Unit 3, Exercise 8

Complete the activities. Go over your work with a partner or your teacher. Then complete the Performance Review on Page 38.

SKILL 1 **FOLLOW INSTRUCTIONS**

Listen to the instructions for putting paper in the copier.
Number the steps in the correct order.

___1___ Open the top paper drawer.

___3___ Push the paper under the tabs.

___4___ Close the drawer.

___5___ Press the red button.

___2___ Put the paper in the drawer.

SKILL 2 **SET UP AND USE A MACHINE**

Read the instructions for the coffee maker.
Then write *yes* or *no*.

Is this what you do?

___no___ 1. Plug in the coffee maker first.

___no___ 2. Put water into the filter basket.

___yes___ 3. Pour water into the water tank.

___no___ 4. Press the READY button to start the machine.

___yes___ 5. After you put in the water and coffee, press the ON button.

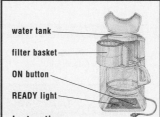

water tank
filter basket
ON button
READY light

Instructions:

1. Put coffee into the filter basket.
2. Pour water into the water tank.
3. Plug in the coffee maker.
4. Press the ON button.
5. Coffee is ready when the READY light comes on.

Unit 3

37

PRESENTATION

Use any of the procedures in "Evaluation" on page x with pages 37 and 38. Record individuals' results on the Unit 3 Individual Competency Chart. Record the class's results on the Class Cumulative Competency Chart.

Look at the diagram of a cash register. Write the letter.

___c___ 1. You keep money here.　　　　　　a. screen

___d___ 2. You use this to turn it on.　　　　b. keypad

___b___ 3. You use this to enter the prices.　c. cash drawer

___a___ 4. You see the prices here.　　　　　d. ON key

SKILL 4　EXPLAIN HOW TO USE A MACHINE

Think of a machine you know how to use. Tell your partner or your teacher how to use it.

Performance Review

I can...

☐ 1. listen to and follow instructions.
☐ 2. set up and use a machine.
☐ 3. read a diagram.
☐ 4. explain how to use a machine.

DISCUSSION

Work with a team. How will the skills help you? Make a list.
Share your list with the class.

PRESENTATION

Follow the instructions on page 37.

INFORMAL WORKPLACE-SPECIFIC ASSESSMENT

Ask each learner to name a machine at his or her workplace. Can he or she use the machine? How does one turn on the machine?

WORKBOOK

Unit 3, Exercise 9

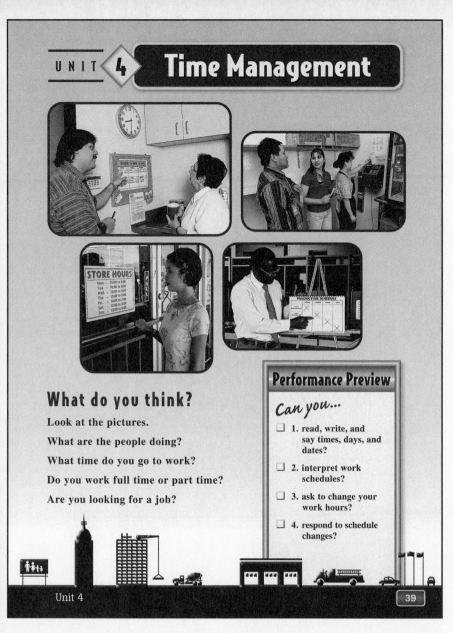

UNIT 4 — Time Management

What do you think?

Look at the pictures.

What are the people doing?

What time do you go to work?

Do you work full time or part time?

Are you looking for a job?

Performance Preview

Can you...

☐ 1. read, write, and say times, days, and dates?

☐ 2. interpret work schedules?

☐ 3. ask to change your work hours?

☐ 4. respond to schedule changes?

Unit 4

Unit 4 Overview
—SCANS Competencies—

★ Allocate time

★ Organize, interpret, communicate, and maintain information

★ Understand organizational systems

Workforce Skills

● Read, write, and say times, days, dates

● Interpret work schedules

● Ask to change your work hours

● Respond to schedule changes

Materials

● Pictures or real examples of various kinds of clocks and watches

● Teaching clock with movable hands

● Samples of blank time cards

● Samples of calendar pages of various types: wall, desk, personal

● Graph paper

Unit Warm-Up

To get learners thinking about Unit 4, "Time Management," display a large wall calendar for the current month. Help learners identify today's day and date. Use the clock in your classroom, draw a large clock on the board, or use the teaching clock. Show and say the current time. Ask learners *When do you talk about times and dates? When do you write the time or date?*

★　　★　　★　　★　　★

WORKFORCE SKILLS (page 39)

Read, write, and say times, days, dates

★　　★　　★　　★　　★

PREPARATION

1. Say the time, day, and date. Write the day and date on the board. Ask a different volunteer to write the day and the date on the board each day before class.

2. Use realia, picture cards, and/or explanation to present the words **clock, schedule, full time, part time,** and **time clock.** Have learners find the clock(s) and calendar(s) in the classroom. Ask learners if they use a time clock where they work.

PRESENTATION

1. Focus attention on the photographs. Ask learners what the unit might be about. Write their ideas on the board and/or restate them in acceptable English.

2. Have learners talk about the pictures. Have them identify the locations and say what the people are doing. Help them speculate what time they think it is in each picture and relate the time to what they normally do at that time.

3. Help learners read the questions. Discuss the questions with the class.

4. You may want to use the Performance Preview to provide learners with an overview of the skills in the unit. Have learners read the list of skills and discuss what they will learn in this unit.

FOLLOW-UP

What Are You Doing When? Have pairs talk about different times of the day and days of the week. Have them discuss their schedules and answer the question *What do you usually do at (time)?* Have pairs present their answers to the class. Compare answers. *Luis is usually at work at 8:00. Tim is taking his son to school.*

♦ Write times on slips of paper. Ask volunteers to draw a slip of paper at random and say what they usually do at that time.

WORKBOOK

Unit 4, Exercises 1A–1B

WORKFORCE SKILLS (page 40)

Read, write, and say times, days, and dates

★　　★　　★　　★　　★

Teaching Note

Use this page and the following page to introduce the new language in the unit. Whenever possible, encourage peer-teaching. Supply any language the learners need.

Culture Note

Write the date on the board using just numerals. Point out to learners that the order for writing the date in the United States is month/date/year. This format is different from that used in many countries.

Getting Started　Telling time

TEAM WORK

Look at the clocks. Say what time it is. What are you doing at these times? What are your classmates doing?

PARTNER WORK

Student A asks what time it is. Student B answers. Follow the dialog below.

A　What time is it?

B　It's 3:30.

 SURVEY

Sylvia works full time. She works 40 hours per week. Talk to your classmates. Do they work part time or full time? How many hours do they work in a week? Make a list.

Sylvia	full time	40 hours
_____	_____	_____
_____	_____	_____

40　　　　　　　　　　　　　　　　　　　　　　　　Unit 4

PREPARATION

1. Ask learners how they keep track of time. How many of them wear watches? How do the learners who don't wear watches find out the time?

2. Write the words and phrases *go to sleep*, *eat breakfast*, *go to work*, and *watch TV* on the board. Point to one of the phrases and pantomime the action. Say the time you usually do this. Have pairs of learners talk about their daily schedules.

PRESENTATION

1. Have learners read and discuss the Purpose Statement.

2. Encourage learners to say as much as they can about the illustrations. Write their ideas on the board and/or restate them in acceptable English.

3. Have teams read the Team Work instructions and complete the activity. If learners need help, encourage them to consult other teams. Have team reporters share their answers with the class.

4. Have learners read the Partner Work instructions. Make sure each pair knows what to do. If necessary, model the activity. Then have pairs complete the activity. Have learners switch partners and repeat the activity. Supply any language needed. Have one or two pairs present their dialogs to the class.

 5. Have the class read the Survey instructions. Make sure everyone knows what to do. If necessary, model the activity. Choose a secretary to record learners' answers, and then have the class complete the activity. Discuss the results. How many

work full time? Part time? Who works the most hours? For more information see "Survey" on page viii.

FOLLOW-UP

Bar Graph: Help learners use the information in the Survey chart to create a bar graph. The bars on the graph will be labeled "Full Time" and "Part Time." The vertical axis should show the number of students employed each way. Discuss the bar graph with learners.

♦ Help learners use the bar graph information to make a pie chart. Discuss the pie chart with learners.

WORKBOOK

Unit 4, Exercise 2

Talk About It — Reading times and dates

PRACTICE THE DIALOG

A What's the date next Thursday?

B Next Thursday is June 20.

A Are you sure? I'd like to take that day off.

B Why?

A I have to take my commercial driver's license test.

B You'd better talk to the manager right away.

What day would you like to take off? Talk to your partner. Use the dialog above.

PARTNER WORK

Look at Sara's calendar. Answer the questions.

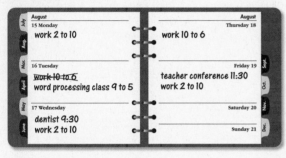

August
July
Aug.
Mar.
April
May
June

15 Monday
work 2 to 10

16 Tuesday
work 10 to 6
word processing class 9 to 5

17 Wednesday
dentist 9:30
work 2 to 10

August
Sept.
Oct.
Nov.
Dec.

Thursday 18
work 10 to 6

Friday 19
teacher conference 11:30
work 2 to 10

Saturday 20

Sunday 21

1. What month is it?

2. Does Sara work on Wednesday?

3. What days does Sara work from 2 to 10?

ASAP PROJECT

Everyone in the class works for the Copy Shop. The Copy Shop is open from 10:00 in the morning to 10:00 at night every day. Make a work schedule for everyone in the class. People can work full time or part time. Put break times on the schedule. Complete this project as you work through this unit.

Unit 4

41

WORKFORCE SKILLS (page 41)

Read, write, and say times, days, and dates

★　　★　　★　　★　　★

ASAP PROJECT

Have learners read the instructions. Discuss the project and its purpose with learners. Make sure that everyone understands. Help learners assign themselves to teams based upon their knowledge, skills, interests, or other personal strengths. Have each team select a leader, and have the team leaders or the whole class select an overall project leader. Throughout the rest of the unit, allow time for learners to work on the project. Have the teams agree on a deadline when the project will be finished. For more information see "ASAP Project" on page vi.

PREPARATION

1. Present or review the days of the week and the months of the year along with the words **date** and **calendar**. Point out months and days on the large calendar and model them. Have learners repeat. Give special attention to the pronunciation and spelling of difficult words, such as **Wednesday** and **February**.

2. Show learners additional calendars, date books, and so on. Have them find and say dates. Have them discuss the different calendar formats. Which one would be best to use for remembering personal appointments?

PRESENTATION

1. Have learners read and discuss the Purpose Statement. For more information see "Purpose Statement" on page viii.

 2. Present the dialog. See "Presenting a Dialog" on page ix.

3. Have partners read the Partner Work instructions. Focus attention on the calendar entries. Help learners read the words and expressions. If necessary, model pronunciation. Then have learners complete the activity. Have one or two pairs present their answers to the class.

FOLLOW-UP

Personal Calendar: Give learners a copy of a week-at-a-glance calendar for this week. Have them fill in personal appointments for one or two days. Have each learner say one of his or her appointments. Have learners use the appointment calendars for the week.

Ask them to say how the calendars helped them.

♦ Hand out blank calendar pages. Have learners fill in the names of the current month, the days, the dates, and the year. Have them compare their work in pairs. Have one or more learners share their calendars with the class.

WORKBOOK

Unit 4, Exercises 3A–3B

WORKFORCE SKILLS (page 42)

Read, say, and write times, days, and dates

Interpret work schedules

Ask to change your work hours

★   ★   ★   ★   ★

Personal Dictionary

Have learners add the words in their Personal Dictionary to their *Workforce Writing Dictionary*. For more information see "Workforce Writing Dictionary" on page v.

Keep Talking — Changing your schedule

PRACTICE THE DIALOG

Raymundo wants to leave early. Ms. Kelly is his supervisor.

A Ms. Kelly, can I leave early on Tuesday? I have an appointment with my son's teacher.

B What time do you want to leave?

A 2:30.

B Yes, that's fine.

A Thank you, Ms. Kelly.

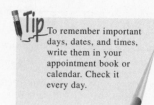

Tip To remember important days, dates, and times, write them in your appointment book or calendar. Check it every day.

PARTNER WORK

You work at Bright Cleaning Services. Look at the schedule. Take turns talking. Talk about the days and times you work. Follow the dialog below.

A Do you work on Friday?

B No, I have Friday off.

A What time do you work on Monday?

B 8:30 to 4:30.

Bright Cleaning Service

Schedule for week of 7/17 to 7/22

	Monday	Tuesday	Wednesday	Thursday	Friday	Saturday
	8:30-4:30	8:30-4:30	10:00-6:00	2:00-10:00	Off	10:00-1:00
Lunch	12:30-1:30	12:30-1:30	1:00-2:00			

Personal Dictionary ▸ Time, Calendars, Schedules

Write the words and phrases that you need to know.

_____

_____

42

Unit 4

PREPARATION

1. Use the teaching clock to review telling time. Have a learner say what time it is. Have another learner set the clock hands to that time. Continue until everyone has had a chance to say and set the time.

2. Draw a sun and a moon on the board. Write the abbreviation A.M. below the sun and P.M. below the moon. Tell learners that A.M. indicates times from midnight to noon, and P.M. indicates times from noon until midnight. You might also present the words **noon** and **midnight.** Pantomime sleeping while indicating the word **midnight.** Ask learners to brainstorm an activity they are usually doing at noon.

PRESENTATION

1. Have learners read and discuss the Purpose Statement.

2. Have partners read the Practice the Dialog instructions. Then present the dialog. See "Presenting a Dialog" on page ix. Encourage learners to substitute different days and times in the dialog for additional practice. Have several pairs present their dialogs to the class.

3. Have partners read the Partner Work instructions. Make sure each pair knows what to do. Then have pairs complete the activity. Ask pairs to share their dialogs with the class.

4. Have learners read the Personal Dictionary instructions. Then use the

Personal Dictionary procedures on page ix.

Tip Have learners read the Tip independently. Have learners discuss how the advice will help them.

FOLLOW-UP

Write a Work Schedule: Have learners work in pairs and write out their work schedules for one day. Have learners include the times they arrived at work, took breaks, had lunch, and went home. Have learners compare their schedules. Ask several learners to share details of their schedules with the class.

WORKBOOK

Unit 4, Exercise 4

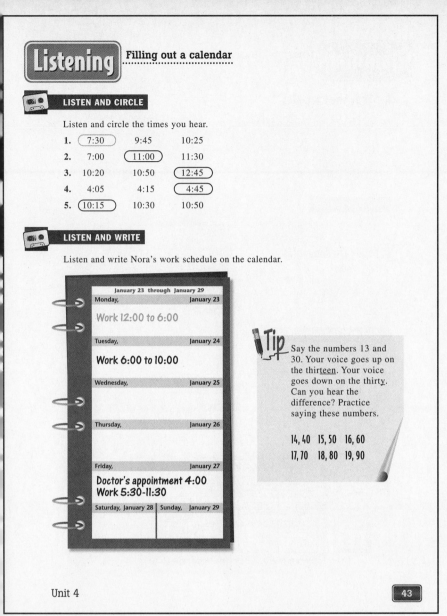

Listening — Filling out a calendar

LISTEN AND CIRCLE

Listen and circle the times you hear.

1. (7:30)   9:45   10:25
2. 7:00   (11:00)   11:30
3. 10:20   10:50   (12:45)
4. 4:05   4:15   (4:45)
5. (10:15)   10:30   10:50

LISTEN AND WRITE

Listen and write Nora's work schedule on the calendar.

January 23 through January 29

Monday,   January 23

Work 12:00 to 6:00

Tuesday,   January 24

Work 6:00 to 10:00

Wednesday,   January 25

Thursday,   January 26

Friday,   January 27

Doctor's appointment 4:00
Work 5:30-11:30

Saturday, January 28 | Sunday,   January 29

Tip
Say the numbers 13 and 30. Your voice goes up on the thir*teen*. Your voice goes down on the thir*ty*. Can you hear the difference? Practice saying these numbers.

14, 40   15, 50   16, 60
17, 70   18, 80   19, 90

Unit 4

43

WORKFORCE SKILLS (page 43)

Read, write, and say times, days, and dates

Interpret work schedules

Ask to change your work hours

Respond to schedule changes

★   ★   ★   ★   ★

SCANS Note

Allocating time and following schedules are important workplace skills and responsibilities. Ask learners to discuss their employers' policies on punctuality. Ask learners for ways to improve punctuality, such as using calendars and alarm clocks, finding reliable transportation, and so on.

PREPARATION

Present or review the word **appointment.** Say that you have a doctor's appointment tomorrow at 9:30. Ask learners to name appointments they have.

PRESENTATION

1. Have learners read and discuss the Purpose Statement. For more information see "Purpose Statement" on page viii.

 2. Have learners read the Listen and Circle instructions. Then have them look at and say the times on the page. If necessary, model the first item. Then play the tape or read the Listening Transcript aloud two or more times as learners complete the activity. Check learners' work. See "Presenting a Listening Activity" on page ix.

 3. Have learners read the Listen and Write instructions. Have them read the days and dates on the calendar. Make sure that everyone understands the instructions. Then play the tape or read the Listening Transcript aloud two or more times as learners complete the activity. Check learners' work.

Tip Have learners read the Tip independently. Have learners practice in pairs. Have them say sentences using the numbers. For more information see "Presenting a Tip" on page ix.

FOLLOW-UP

Date Dictation: Dictate five or six times and dates to learners. Have them write their answers on sheets of paper or on blank calendar forms. Check learners' work.

◆ Have learners work in small groups. Ask each learner to write a list of two or three times and dates. Then have learners take turns dictating their lists to other members of the group. Have learners compare papers and check each others' work.

WORKBOOK

Unit 4, Exercise 5

WORKFORCE SKILLS (pages 44–45)

Read, write, and say times, days, and dates

Ask to change your work hours

★　　★　　★　　★　　★

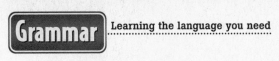

Grammar .... Learning the language you need

A. Study the Examples

Can	I	leave work early today?
	you	
	he	
	she	
	we	
	they	

Yes,	I	can.
No,	you	can't.
	he	
	she	
	we	
	they	

PARTNER WORK

Take turns asking to leave work early. Answer the request.

B. Study the Examples

What	time	is it?
	month	
	day	
	year	

It's	7:15.
	January.
	Tuesday.
	2001.

ANSWER THE QUESTIONS

Look at the picture.

1. What time is it? _____It's 3:45._____
2. What day is it? _____It's Wednesday._____
3. What month is it? _____It's March._____
4. What year is it? _____It's 2000._____

44

Unit 4

PREPARATION

Review the language in the grammar boxes with learners before they open their books, if necessary. Follow the instructions in Preparation on pages 40 and 41.

PRESENTATION

1. Have learners read and discuss the Purpose Statement. For more information see "Purpose Statement" on page viii.

2. Have learners read the grammar boxes in A. Have learners use the language in the boxes to say as many sentences as possible. Tell learners that they can use the grammar boxes throughout the unit to review or check sentence structures.

3. Have partners read the Partner Work instructions. Have learners complete the activity. Ask pairs to share their conversations with the class.

4. Focus attention on the grammar boxes in B. Follow the procedures in 2.

5. Have learners read the instructions for Answer the Questions. If necessary, model the first item. Allow learners to complete the activity. Have learners check each other's work in pairs. Ask several learners to read their answers aloud while the rest of the class checks their work.

English ASAP

C. Study the Examples

Is it	Tuesday?		Yes,	it	is.
	July 15?		No,		isn't.
	3:00?				
	Memorial Day?				

COMPLETE THE DIALOGS

Look at the calendar. Complete the sentences.

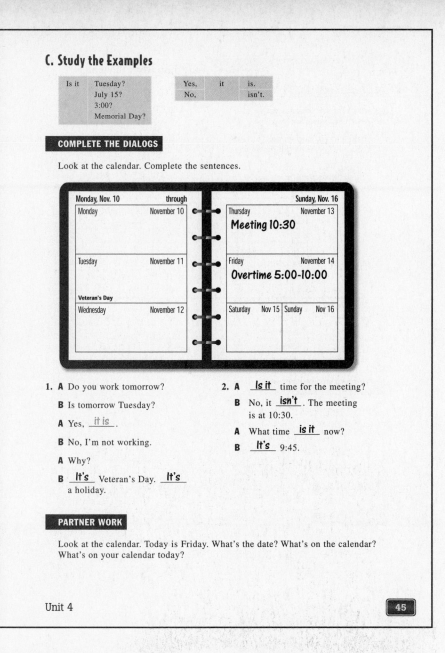

Monday, Nov. 10	through			Sunday, Nov. 16
Monday	November 10		**Thursday**	November 13
			Meeting 10:30	
Tuesday	November 11		**Friday**	November 14
			Overtime 5:00-10:00	
Veteran's Day				
Wednesday	November 12		Saturday Nov 15	Sunday Nov 16

1. **A** Do you work tomorrow?

   B Is tomorrow Tuesday?

   A Yes, _it is_ .

   B No, I'm not working.

   A Why?

   B _It's_ Veteran's Day. _It's_ a holiday.

2. **A** _Is it_ time for the meeting?

   B No, it _isn't_ . The meeting is at 10:30.

   A What time _is it_ now?

   B _It's_ 9:45.

PARTNER WORK

Look at the calendar. Today is Friday. What's the date? What's on the calendar? What's on your calendar today?

Unit 4

45

---

6. Focus attention on the grammar boxes in C. Follow the procedures in 2.

7. Have learners read the instructions for Complete the Dialogs. If necessary, model the first item. Then have learners complete the activity independently. Have a different pair of learners read each of the dialogs aloud as the rest of the class checks their answers.

8. Have partners read the Partner Work instructions. Ask pairs to share their answers with the class.

FOLLOW-UP

What Do You Know? Write different times and dates on slips of paper. Give each learner a slip. Have learners circulate and ask for one another's times and dates. Have learners write each time and date they find out. Who can find the most information?

♦ Have each learner write his or her date and time on the board. Have learners use the information on the board to check what they wrote. Who wrote all the dates and times correctly?

WORKBOOK

Unit 4, Exercises 6A–6C

BLACKLINE MASTERS

Blackline Master: Unit 4

Interpret work schedules

Ask to change your work schedule

★　　　★　　　★　　　★　　　★

Reading and Writing — Following work schedules

READ THE WORK SCHEDULE

Figure out the total number of hours each person works. Remember to include overtime. Write the numbers in the last column.

SUPERIOR TOOL & DIE

Schedule for the week of 3/13/2000

First shift 7:30-3:30		Monday 3/13	Tuesday 3/14	Wednesday 3/15	Thursday 3/16	Friday 3/17	Total Hours
J. Ramirez	Regular hours	8	8	8	8	8	40
	Overtime	5.5		3			8.5
	Total	13.5	8	11	8	8	48.5
S. Faldo	Regular hours	8	Day Off	8	8	8	32
	Overtime			2	2	3	7
	Total	8	0	10	10	11	39
Second shift 2:00-10:00							
N. Malnoff	Regular hours	8	8	8	8	Day Off	32
	Overtime	1			2		3
	Total	9	8	8	10	0	35

ANSWER THE QUESTIONS

Write *yes* or *no*.

1. It's Tuesday. Is Joe Ramirez working first shift? **yes**

2. Does Sara Faldo have Wednesday off? **no**

3. Is Thursday the 19? **no**

4. It's Thursday. Is Natalie Malnoff working overtime? **yes**

DISCUSSION

Joe Ramirez has a doctor's appointment on Tuesday at 3:00. What can he do? Who should he speak to? Who do you speak to if you need to leave early or come in late to work?

46

Unit 4

PREPARATION

Present or review the words **overtime, shift, schedule, total,** and **day off.** Have learners talk about their own schedules and days off.

PRESENTATION

1. Have learners read and discuss the Purpose Statement. For more information see "Purpose Statement" on page viii.

2. Have learners preview the schedule before they begin. Encourage learners to say everything they can about the schedule. Write their ideas on the board and/or restate them in acceptable English.

3. Have learners read the instructions for Read the Work Schedule. Make sure everyone knows what to do. If necessary, model the first item. Then have learners complete the activity independently. Have learners work in pairs to check each others' addition. Have one or two learners present their total work hours to the class.

4. Have learners read the Answer the Questions instructions. Make sure everyone knows what to do. If necessary, model the first item. Then have learners complete the activity. Ask learners to read their answers aloud.

5. Have learners read the Discussion instructions. Make sure everyone knows what to do. Then have learners work in teams to talk about the procedures for changing schedules at their workplace.

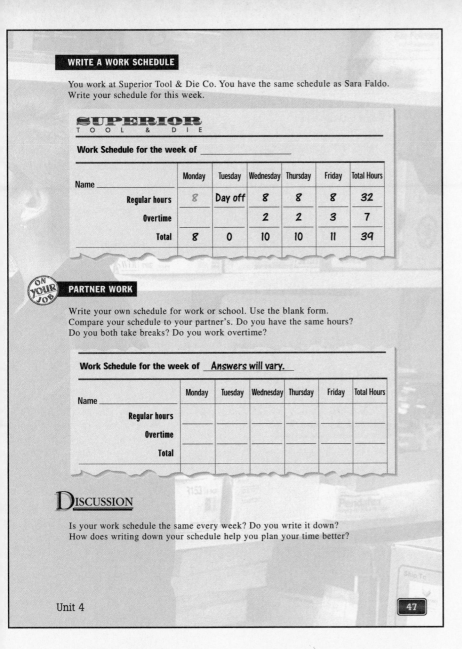

WRITE A WORK SCHEDULE

You work at Superior Tool & Die Co. You have the same schedule as Sara Faldo.
Write your schedule for this week.

SUPERIOR
T O O L & D I E

Work Schedule for the week of _____

Name _____	Monday	Tuesday	Wednesday	Thursday	Friday	Total Hours
Regular hours	8	Day off	8	8	8	32
Overtime			2	2	3	7
Total	8	0	10	10	11	39

PARTNER WORK

Write your own schedule for work or school. Use the blank form.
Compare your schedule to your partner's. Do you have the same hours?
Do you both take breaks? Do you work overtime?

Work Schedule for the week of **Answers will vary.**

Name _____	Monday	Tuesday	Wednesday	Thursday	Friday	Total Hours
Regular hours						
Overtime						
Total						

Discussion

Is your work schedule the same every week? Do you write it down?
How does writing down your schedule help you plan your time better?

Unit 4
47

---

6. Have teams read the Write a Work Schedule instructions. Make sure everyone knows what to do. If necessary, model the first item of the activity. Then have teams complete the activity. Have team reporters share their instructions with the class. Ask teams to compare ideas.

7. Have partners read the instructions for Partner Work. Make sure each pair knows what to do. If necessary, model the activity with information about your own work schedule. Then have learners complete the activity. Have volunteers present their completed schedules to the class.

8. Have learners read the Discussion instructions. Make sure everyone knows what to do. Then have learners work in pairs or small groups to complete the activity. Allow learners to present their ideas to the class. Have the class brainstorm a list of ideas for remembering schedules. Have one learner act as a secretary and record the ideas. Post the list.

FOLLOW-UP

Class Work Schedule: Divide the class into pairs or small groups. Hand out blank calendar pages for the week. Have learners create class work schedules for this week. The schedules should include the days and times of class meetings, days off from class, and time for homework. Have several pairs present their schedules to the rest of the class.

♦ Have learners talk over their schedules in pairs. Ask learners to share with the class one or two things their partners are doing.

WORKBOOK

Unit 4, Exercises 7A–7C

WORKFORCE SKILLS (page 48)

Ask to change your work hours

★   ★   ★   ★   ★

 **Asking for time off**

FILL IN THE FORM

You want to take half the day off on Friday, October 16, to go to a conference with your child's teacher. Fill in the form. Include your name and the date.

Request for Time Off Report

Name __Answers will vary._____   Date _____

Reason for absence	Dates			
☐ Vacation	From____ To____	No. of days ____	No. of hours ____
☐ Sick	From____ To____	No. of days ____	No. of hours ____
☑ Personal	From 10/16 To 10/16	No. of days 1/2	No. of hours 4
☐ Death in family	From____ To____	No. of days ____	No. of hours ____
☐ Accident on Job	From____ To____	No. of days ____	No. of hours ____
☐ Other	From____ To____	No. of days ____	No. of hours ____

Explanation (if necessary) __I want to go to a conference with my__
__child's teacher.__
_____

Supervisor's approval _____   Date _____
Please forward to Office Coordinator after Supervisor has signed.

ANSWER THE QUESTIONS

1. Who signs the form?
2. What do you think personal days are for?

 Culture Notes

Information about days off, sick days, and overtime is often in the employee handbook. Do you have an employee handbook where you work? Who do you ask if you want time off? Do you have to fill out a form?

48   Unit 4

PREPARATION

1. Present or review the words **vacation, sick, personal, accident,** and **other** (as used on a form to mean "something else not on the form").

2. Have learners talk about reasons they might need time off from work. Write their ideas on the board. Then have groups of learners rank the reasons from least to most important.

PRESENTATION

1. Have learners read and discuss the Purpose Statement. For more information see "Purpose Statement" on page viii.

2. Have learners look at the form. Encourage them to say as much as they can about it. Write their ideas on the board and/or restate them in acceptable English.

3. Have learners read the instructions for Fill in the Form. Make sure everyone knows what to do. Allow learners time to complete the activity. Have learners compare forms in pairs. Encourage partners to check each others' forms for neatness and accuracy.

4. Have learners read the Answer the Questions instructions and complete the activity. Have volunteers present their answers to the class.

5. Have learners read Culture Notes and talk over their responses in teams. Have team reporters share their ideas with the class. Ask the teams to compare each other's ideas. For more information see "Culture Notes" on page vii.

FOLLOW-UP

Responding to *No:* Have learners brainstorm ways for supervisors to deny a request for time off and ways workers should respond to the denial of a request. Then have learners work in pairs to create dialogs. One learner is the supervisor, the other is a worker. The worker requests time off for a specific reason; the supervisor says *no* for a specific reason. The first learner then responds appropriately. Have several pairs present their dialogs to the class.

♦ Have learners reverse roles: the supervisor asks a worker to make a schedule change, but the worker says *no.*

WORKBOOK

Unit 4, Exercise 8

---

48   English ASAP

Performance Check

How well can you use skills in this unit?

Complete the activities. Go over your work with a partner or your teacher. Then complete the Performance Review on page 50.

| SKILL 1 | READ, WRITE, AND SAY TIMES, DAYS, AND DATES |

Look at the clocks. Say and write what time it is.

  10:45   4:30   12:10   1:00

| SKILL 2 | INTERPRET WORK SCHEDULES |

VALDEZ CLEANING SERVICES   Schedule for the week of 2/14/2000

		Monday 2/14	Tuesday 2/15	Wednesday 2/16	Thursday 2/17	Friday 2/18	Total Hours
First shift 7:00-3:00							
S. Hernandez	Regular hours	8	8	8	off	8	32
	Overtime	7					7
	Total	15	8	8		8	39
Second shift 2:00-10:00							
V. Toshi	Regular hours	8	off	8	8	8	32
	Overtime					3	3
	Total	8		8	8	11	35

Read the schedule. Answer the questions.

1. Who works first shift? _____ S. Hernandez

2. What day does Sandra Hernandez have off? _____ Thursday

3. When did Sandra Hernandez work overtime? _____ Monday

4. How many hours did Victor Toshi work overtime? _____ 3

Unit 4   49

PRESENTATION

Use any of the procedures in "Evaluation" on page x with pages 49 and 50. Record individuals' results on the Unit 4 Individual Competency Chart. Record the class's results on the Class Cumulative Competency Chart.

SKILL 3 **ASK TO CHANGE YOUR WORK HOURS**

You work Monday through Friday from 9:00 to 5:00. Look below at your personal calendar for next week. When do you need to change your work hours? Your partner or your teacher is your supervisor. Ask to change your work hours. Remember to say why.

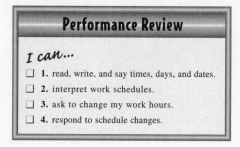

Sunday	Monday	Tuesday	Wednesday	Thursday	Friday	Saturday
4	5	6	7	8	9	10
	9-dentist			5:45 pick up Sam		party for Mom

SKILL 4 **RESPOND TO SCHEDULE CHANGES**

Look at the weekly schedule again. Your supervisor asks you to make some changes to your regular schedule. Answer *yes* or *no*. Say why you can or cannot make the changes. Follow the dialog below.

A Can you stay late on Thursday?

B No, I'm sorry. I have to pick up my son Sam at day care after work.

Performance Review

I can...

☐ **1.** read, write, and say times, days, and dates.

☐ **2.** interpret work schedules.

☐ **3.** ask to change my work hours.

☐ **4.** respond to schedule changes.

DISCUSSION

Work with a team. How will the skills help you? Make a list. Share your list with the class.

50 Unit 4

PRESENTATION

Follow the instructions on page 49.

INFORMAL WORKPLACE-SPECIFIC ASSESSMENT

Have learners say the time they go to work or school. Have them role-play asking for time off.

WORKBOOK

Unit 4, Exercise 9

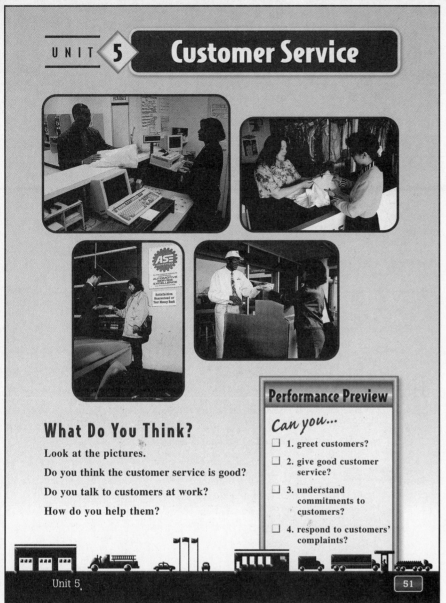

UNIT 5 — Customer Service

What Do You Think?

Look at the pictures.

Do you think the customer service is good?

Do you talk to customers at work?

How do you help them?

Performance Preview

Can you...

☐ 1. greet customers?

☐ 2. give good customer service?

☐ 3. understand commitments to customers?

☐ 4. respond to customers' complaints?

Unit 5

51

Unit 5 Overview
—SCANS Competencies—

★ Serve customers

★ Negotiate

★ Organize and maintain information

★ Understand social systems

Workforce Skills

● Greet customers

● Give good customer service

● Understand commitments to customers

● Respond to customers' complaints

Materials

● Pictures of employees and customers in various customer-oriented businesses

● Real objects or pictures of computer monitor and keyboard, envelope, light bulb, switch, plug, and extension cord

● Articles of clothing or other items to use as "returned merchandise"

● Customer comment/complaint cards

● Play money in U.S. denominations

● Sale flyers with quantity words

● Catalogs from various companies; blank order forms

● Examples of containers

Unit Warm-Up

To get learners thinking about the unit topic, ask them to share some details of good and bad customer service they have experienced.

★　　★　　★　　★　　★

WORKFORCE SKILLS (page 51)

Greet customers

★　　★　　★　　★　　★

PREPARATION

Present **customer service.** Display the pictures of employees and customers, and have learners identify the customers. Explain that customer service means "helping customers." Then have learners describe times when they have had an opportunity to give customer service. Encourage learners to use peer-teaching to clarify any unfamiliar vocabulary.

PRESENTATION

1. Focus attention on the photographs. Ask learners to speculate what the unit might be about. Write their ideas on the board and/or restate them in acceptable English.

2. Have learners talk about the pictures. Have them identify the locations and employees, and say what the customers are doing. Do they think the customers are happy? Why?

3. Help learners read the questions. Discuss the questions with the class.

4. You may want to use the Performance Preview to provide learners with an overview of the skills in the unit. Have learners read the list of skills and discuss what they will learn in this unit.

FOLLOW-UP

Role-Play: Have pairs of learners work together to create role-plays about the customer service situations in the pictures. Have several pairs present their dialogs to the class.

◆ Have pairs write their dialogs and post them for the rest of the class to read.

WORKBOOK

Unit 5, Exercises 1A–1B

WORKFORCE SKILLS (page 52)

Greet customers

★   ★   ★   ★   ★

Teaching Note

Use this page to introduce the new language in the unit. Whenever possible, encourage peer-teaching. Supply any language the learners need.

Getting Started   Greeting customers

TEAM WORK

Look at the pictures. Each employee is greeting a customer. What is each employee saying? Write the letter.

a. Thank you for calling the National Catalog Company. May I take your order?

b. Good morning. Can I get you some coffee or juice?

c. Hello. Can I help you with your bags? Where are you flying to today?

d. Welcome to Ace Electronics. Can I show you anything special?

PARTNER WORK

List different businesses and ways they greet customers. Then take turns greeting customers. Follow the example.

Welcome to Antonio's Restaurant. How many in your group?

SURVEY

What is a polite way to say hello to a new customer? Talk to your classmates. Make a list of greetings. Label one list *very polite*, the second list *polite*, and the third list *less polite*.

52   Unit 5

PREPARATION

Present the word **greet.** Greet learners as though they are entering a business. Vary the greetings: *Good morning. What can I do for you today?* and *Welcome to (business name).* Have learners figure out what type of business goes with each greeting. Write their inferences on the board.

PRESENTATION

1. Have learners read and discuss the Purpose Statement. For more information see "Purpose Statement" on page viii.

2. Focus attention on the illustrations. Encourage learners to say as much as they can about them. Write their ideas on the board and/or restate them in acceptable English.

3. Have teams read the Team Work instructions. Make sure each team knows what to do. If necessary, model the first item. Remind the teams that they are responsible for making sure that each member understands the new language. Then have teams complete the activity. If learners need help, encourage them to consult other teams. Have team reporters share their greetings with the class.

 4. Have partners read the Partner Work instructions. Make sure each pair knows what to do. If necessary, model the activity. Then have pairs complete the activity. Have learners switch partners and continue taking turns greeting customers. Supply any language needed. Have one or two pairs present their greetings to the class.

5. Have the class read the Survey instructions. Make sure everyone knows what to do. If necessary, model the activity. Choose a secretary to record learners' answers on the board, and then have the class complete the activity. For more information see "Survey" on page viii.

FOLLOW-UP

Saying Goodbye: Have teams brainstorm lists of polite ways to say goodbye to customers, such as *thanks for coming, come back again*, etc. Have learners share their lists with the class.

♦ Have teams write their lists. Post the lists around the room.

WORKBOOK

Unit 5, Exercises 2A–2B

Talk About It
Giving good customer service

PRACTICE THE DIALOG

A Good morning. May I help you?

B Yes, I'd like to return this camera. It's broken.

A No problem. Would you like a refund or an exchange?

B I'd like a refund, please.

DISCUSSION

How does the sales associate in the dialog give good customer service? Think of a time when you returned something to a store. Was the service good or bad? Why?

PARTNER WORK

Use the dialog above and the Useful Language. Practice giving good customer service in these situations:

1. You are a waiter. Some customers don't like their table. They want a different table.

2. You are an airline reservations agent. A passenger would like a different seat on the plane.

Useful Language
Hello/Hi.
How can I help you?
Of course.
Sure/Fine.

ASAP
PROJECT

As a class, prepare a list of customer service DOs and DON'Ts. Divide into two teams. One team makes the list of DOs. The other team makes the list of DON'Ts. Review the lists as a class. Complete this project as you work through this unit.

Unit 5

`53`

WORKFORCE SKILLS (page 53)

Greet customers

Give good customer service

Respond to customers' complaints

★　　★　　★　　★　　★

ASAP
PROJECT

Have learners read the instructions. Discuss the project and its purpose with learners. Make sure that everyone understands. Help learners assign themselves to teams based upon their knowledge, skills, interests, or other personal strengths. Have each team select a leader, and have the team leaders or the whole class select an overall project leader. Throughout the rest of the unit, allow time for learners to work on the project. Have the teams agree on a deadline when the project will be finished. For more information see "ASAP Project" on page vi.

PREPARATION

1. Preview the words **return, refund,** and **exchange.** Use articles of clothing or other "merchandise" and play money to demonstrate returning something to a store.

2. Write **Good Service** on the board. Give objects to be returned to several learners. Have pairs return the items and respond with good service. Have the rest of the class write the different words and phrases they hear. Decide which phrases can be used to show good customer service. Write the words and phrases on the board.

PRESENTATION

1. Have learners read and discuss the Purpose Statement. For more information see "Purpose Statement" on page viii.

2. Focus attention on the photograph. Encourage learners to say as much as they can about it. Have them identify the type of store shown. Have learners speculate about what the problem might be. Then present the dialog. See "Presenting a Dialog" on page ix.

3. Have learners read the Discussion instructions. Make sure everyone knows what to do. Then have learners talk over their answers in teams. Have team reporters share the discussions with the class.

4. Have partners read the Partner Work instructions. Help learners read the words and expressions in the Useful Language box. If necessary, model pronunciation. Then have learners complete the activity. Have one or two pairs present their situations to the class.

FOLLOW-UP

The Best Service: On slips of paper, write several scenarios similar to those in the Partner Work. Have pairs of learners create dialogs for their scenario. The dialog should demonstrate good service. Have pairs present their dialogs to each other and offer suggestions for giving even better service. Vote on the best service.

♦ Have learners write a list of general rules or guidelines for giving good customer service based on the dialogs. Post the list.

WORKBOOK

Unit 5, Exercise 3

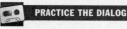

Keep Talking Apologizing to customers

PRACTICE THE DIALOG

A City Roofing. May I help you?

B Yes, this is Sara Jones. I'm having a problem with my new roof.

A I'm sorry, Ms. Jones. What's the problem?

B It's leaking again. Can you send someone out to fix it?

A Sure. I'll send someone out later today. What's your address?

B 13 Evergreen Street in Middletown. Thanks for your help.

Useful Language

I apologize.

Please accept our apology.

Can I offer you a refund/exchange/discount?

We'll take care of the problem.

PARTNER WORK

Look at the pictures. Your partner is the customer who has a problem. You try to help by giving good customer service and by apologizing. Use the dialog and the Useful Language above.

Personal Dictionary Serving Customers

Write the words and phrases that you need to know.

_____

_____

_____

54

Unit 5

Personal Dictionary

Have learners add the words in their Personal Dictionary to their *Workforce Writing Dictionary*. For more information, see "Workforce Writing Dictionary" on page v.

PREPARATION

Preteach the words **problem, sorry, discount,** and **apology.**

Role-play a situation in which you call a service person to complain about unsatisfactory work. Ask learners how they would like the service person to respond. If necessary, clarify **roof** and **leaking.**

PRESENTATION

1. Have learners read and discuss the Purpose Statement. For more information see "Purpose Statement" on page viii.

 2. Present the dialog. See "Presenting a Dialog" on page ix.

3. Focus attention on the illustrations in Partner Work. Have learners say as much as they can about them. Have learners speculate what they think the customers' complaints are. Encourage learners to talk about times when they have been dissatisfied with jobs done in their home or elsewhere.

4. Have partners read the Partner Work instructions. Help learners read the words and expressions in the Useful Language box. If necessary, model pronunciation. Then have pairs complete the activity. Ask pairs to share their dialogs with the class.

5. Have learners read the Personal Dictionary instructions. Then use the Personal Dictionary procedures on page ix. Remind learners to continue

to add words to their dictionaries throughout the unit.

FOLLOW-UP

Difficult Customers: Explain that not all customers are easy to deal with. Role-play the part of a difficult customer with a problem. Have learners respond to your complaints in front of the class. Provide any language necessary.

♦ Have learners take turns being the difficult customer. Have the class vote on who dealt most effectively with the difficult customer.

WORKBOOK

Unit 5, Exercise 4

Listening
Taking care of customers

 LISTEN AND WRITE

Listen to the orders. Write the number of items the customer says.

1. __12__ rolls of tape

2. __6__ monitors, __3__ keyboards

3. __5__ gallons of off-white paint, __15__ gallons of dark green paint

4. __6__ envelopes, __2__ boxes

 LISTEN AND WRITE

Listen to the customer place an order. Write the number of each item the customer wants.

THRIFTY
ELECTRICAL SUPPLY

Date: **5/17/99**   Order Number: **23–56783**

Name: **Georgia Bard**

Telephone: **555-6234**

Address: **17 Nobel Road**
Los Angeles, CA 90027

Qty.	Description	Price for each	Total
3	boxes light bulbs	$1.95	$ 5.85
2	switches	$7.95	$ 15.90
5	extension cords	$2.50	$ 12.50
7	plugs	$3.95	$27.65

 Tip

Double-check the information when you talk to a customer. Ask the customer to repeat each item. Then, read the information back to the customer to make sure it is exactly right.

Did you say...?
Can you repeat that, please?
Was that...?

 **LISTEN AGAIN**

Listen again and write the total cost for each item on the form.

Unit 5

55

PREPARATION

Show a sample order form. Preteach the words **quantity** and **description** and abbreviations **qty.** and **desc.** Help learners identify where to write the customer's name, the number of items, and the price of each item. Use pictures and/or real objects and containers to present **rolls of tape, monitors, keyboards, gallons, envelopes, boxes, light bulbs, switches, extension cords,** and **plugs.**

PRESENTATION

1. Have learners read and discuss the Purpose Statement.

 2. Have learners read the Listen and Write instructions. Then have them read the items

that will be ordered. Clarify as needed. Then play the tape or read the Listening Transcript aloud two or more times as learners complete the activity. Check learners' work. See "Presenting a Listening Activity" on page ix.

 3. Have learners read the Listen and Write instructions. Make sure that everyone understands the instructions. Have them identify the parts of the order form. Use peer teaching to review abbreviations and any other unfamiliar vocabulary. Follow the procedures in 2.

 4. Have learners read the Listen Again instructions. Follow the procedures in 2.

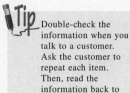 **Tip** Have learners read the Tip independently and discuss how the advice will help them.

FOLLOW-UP

Fill-Out Orders: Give learners catalogs and order forms to practice placing and taking orders. Encourage learners to use clarification strategies as they are taking the orders: *Did you say...? Was that...? Can you repeat that, please? How do you spell...? That was ..., right?* Have learners check each other's work for accuracy.

♦ Give pairs of learners catalogs and blank order forms, and have them role-play taking orders. Have learners present their role-plays to the class.

WORKBOOK

Unit 5, Exercise 5

WORKFORCE SKILLS (pages 56–57)

Give good customer service

Understand commitments to customers

★   ★   ★   ★   ★

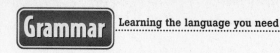

A. Study the Examples

I need	a	tube of glue.
	an	electric drill.
	some	nails and screws.

| I need | some | glue. |
| | | paint. |

COMPLETE THE DIALOG

Look at the sales flier for Jiffy Auto Supplies. Complete the dialog.
Use *a/an* or *some*.

A Do you have any oil filters?

B Yes, we have _____ some _____ oil filters on sale this week.

A Good. I'd like _____ an _____ oil filter.

B OK, do you need _____ some _____ oil, too?

A Yes. I'd also like _____ a _____ package of spark plugs.

B Is there anything else?

A Just _____ some _____ windshield washer fluid.

B Oh, I'm sorry. We don't have any windshield washer fluid left.

56

Unit 5

PREPARATION

1. Review the language in the grammar boxes with learners before they open their books, if necessary.

2. Use sale flyers and containers to review quantity words: **gallon, quart, box, case, roll,** etc. Clarify that **oil, brake pads, spark plugs,** and **windshield washer fluid** are all used for cars.

PRESENTATION

1. Have learners read and discuss the Purpose Statement. For more information see "Purpose Statement" on page viii.

2. Have learners read the grammar boxes in A. Have learners use the language in the boxes to say as many sentences as possible about the sale

flyer. Tell learners that they can use the grammar boxes throughout the unit to review or check sentence structures.

3. Have learners read the instructions for Complete the Dialog. If necessary, model the first item. Then have learners complete the activity independently. Have a pair of learners read the dialog aloud as the rest of the class checks their answers.

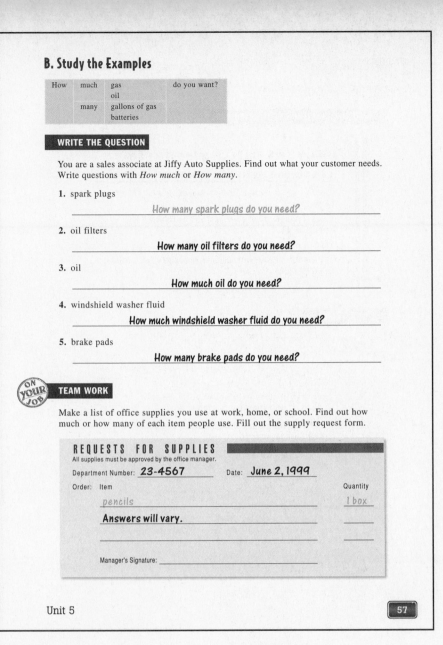

B. Study the Examples

How	much	gas	do you want?
		oil	
	many	gallons of gas	
		batteries	

WRITE THE QUESTION

You are a sales associate at Jiffy Auto Supplies. Find out what your customer needs. Write questions with *How much* or *How many*.

1. spark plugs

How many spark plugs do you need?

2. oil filters

How many oil filters do you need?

3. oil

How much oil do you need?

4. windshield washer fluid

How much windshield washer fluid do you need?

5. brake pads

How many brake pads do you need?

TEAM WORK

Make a list of office supplies you use at work, home, or school. Find out how much or how many of each item people use. Fill out the supply request form.

```
REQUESTS  FOR  SUPPLIES
All supplies must be approved by the office manager.
Department Number: 23-4567        Date: June 2, 1999
Order:  Item                               Quantity
        pencils                            1 box
        Answers will vary.
        _____   _____
        _____   _____

        Manager's Signature: _____
```

Unit 5

57

---

4. Focus attention on the grammar boxes in B. Follow the procedures in 2.

5. Have learners read the instructions for Write the Question. If necessary, model the first item. Allow learners to complete the activity. Have learners check each other's work in pairs. Ask several learners to read their questions aloud while the rest of the class checks their work.

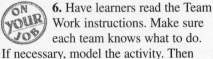

6. Have learners read the Team Work instructions. Make sure each team knows what to do. If necessary, model the activity. Then have the teams complete the activity. Have team reporters share their lists and completed order forms with the class.

FOLLOW-UP

Word Game: Divide the class into groups of three or four. Have each group make a three-column chart labeled *some, a,* and *an* on a sheet of paper or on the board. Hold up pictures of various items in the sale flyers and ask learners to write the name of each item in the appropriate column. As an example, you might hold up a picture of window washer fluid and show learners that **window washer fluid** should be written in the *some* column.

♦ Have learners make three-column charts labeled *some, a,* and *an* on sheets of paper. Have them see how many items from the flyers they can list in each column. Have volunteers read their lists to the class.

Language Note

Have learners examine the lists of nouns they created in the Follow-Up. Help them generalize that plural count nouns usually end in "s," while non-count nouns usually do not have plural forms. Encourage learners to continue adding to their lists throughout the unit.

WORKBOOK

Unit 5, Exercises 6A–6C

BLACKLINE MASTERS

Blackline Master: Unit 5

Give good customer service

Understand commitments to customers

Respond to customers' complaints

★　　★　　★　　★　　★

SCANS Note

It is important to give good customer service. To do this, employees should be aware of their company's policies regarding things such as refunds and exchanges. Do all of the learners know their company's customer service policies? If they don't know, who should they ask to find out?

Reading and Writing | Understanding commitments to customers

READ THE CUSTOMER SERVICE POLICY

Discount Office Products

CUSTOMER SERVICE POLICY

1. **Any item with a receipt can be returned for a full refund or exchange.**

2. **Items returned without a receipt can be returned for a store credit.**

3. **Telephone orders are guaranteed to arrive in 1 day.**

4. **The Customer Service Department is open 24 hours a day. Call 555-2323.**

WRITE THE NUMBER

You work at Discount Office Products. Read each situation. Write the number of the policy.

____4____ **1.** Maria's supervisor wants her to order some computer disks. It's 5:30.

____3____ **2.** Universal Trucking ordered five boxes of copier paper on July 13. It's July 16 and the paper has not arrived.

____1____ **3.** Tim bought an electric pencil sharpener. It doesn't work. He still has his receipt.

____2____ **4.** The assistant manager of Cafe America wants to return a broken stapler. She doesn't have her receipt.

ISCUSSION

Is there a customer service policy where you work? What happens if a customer is not satisfied with the service? What does your supervisor want you to do? Do customers know what the customer service policy is? How do they know?

58

Unit 5

PREPARATION

Present or review the words **receipt, return, exchange, refund, guarantee,** and **store credit.** Ask learners where they are likely to see and use such words.

PRESENTATION

1. Have learners read and discuss the Purpose Statement. For more information see "Purpose Statement" on page viii.

2. Have learners preview the customer service policy before they read. Encourage learners to say everything they can about the policy. Write their ideas on the board and/or restate them in acceptable English.

3. Have learners read the Write the Number instructions. Make sure everyone knows what to do. Then have learners complete the activity. Have several learners read their answers aloud as the rest of the class checks their work.

4. Have learners read the Discussion instructions. Make sure everyone knows what to do. Then have learners work in teams to talk about customer service policies at their jobs.

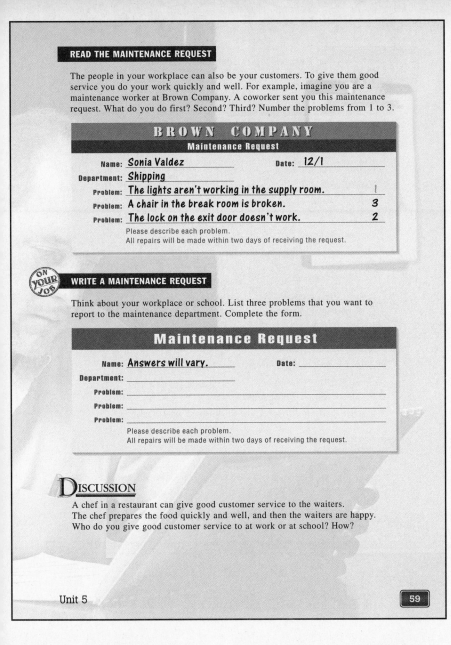

The people in your workplace can also be your customers. To give them good service you do your work quickly and well. For example, imagine you are a maintenance worker at Brown Company. A coworker sent you this maintenance request. What do you do first? Second? Third? Number the problems from 1 to 3.

BROWN COMPANY
Maintenance Request

Name: **Sonia Valdez**   Date: **12/1**

Department: **Shipping**

Problem: **The lights aren't working in the supply room.**   **1**

Problem: **A chair in the break room is broken.**   **3**

Problem: **The lock on the exit door doesn't work.**   **2**

Please describe each problem.
All repairs will be made within two days of receiving the request.

WRITE A MAINTENANCE REQUEST

Think about your workplace or school. List three problems that you want to report to the maintenance department. Complete the form.

Maintenance Request

Name: **Answers will vary.**   Date: _____

Department: _____

Problem: _____

Problem: _____

Problem: _____

Please describe each problem.
All repairs will be made within two days of receiving the request.

Discussion

A chef in a restaurant can give good customer service to the waiters. The chef prepares the food quickly and well, and then the waiters are happy. Who do you give good customer service to at work or at school? How?

Unit 5   59

SCANS Note

Learners should understand that they have both internal and external customers. Customers from within their own organization are **internal customers.** *Present a few examples: a prep cook's internal customers are the chef and waiters. Help learners understand that internal customers need good customer service, too. Have learners talk about their own jobs and who their internal customers are.*

---

5. Have teams read the Read the Maintenance Request instructions. Make sure everyone knows what to do. If necessary, model the first item of the activity. Then have learners complete the activity. Have pairs of learners compare answers. Have them discuss the way they ranked the requests.

6. Have learners read the instructions for Write a Maintenance Request. Make sure everyone knows what to do. If necessary, model the activity with information about your workplace. Then have learners complete the activity. Have one or two learners present their completed forms to the class.

7. Have learners read the Discussion instructions. Make sure everyone knows what to do. Then have learners work in pairs or small groups to complete the activity. Have groups present their ideas to the class.

FOLLOW-UP

Who Are Their Customers? Write a list of jobs on the board: cook, plumber, housekeeper, warehouse worker, etc. Have learners work in teams to come up with at least two customer groups for each job on the list. Encourage them to come up with more if they can. Have team reporters present their results to the class.

♦ Make sure learners have listed internal and external customers for each job on the list. As a class, add examples that may be missing.

WORKBOOK

Unit 5, Exercises 7A–7C

WORKFORCE SKILLS (page 60)

Understand commitments to customers

Respond to customers' complaints

★　　★　　★　　★　　★

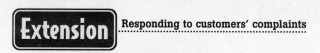

Extension | Responding to customers' complaints

READ THE CUSTOMER SERVICE CARD

Holiday Hotels

How was our service?
Please let us know how we can serve you better.

Name: **S. Aziz**　　Phone Number: **555-9070**　Date: **5/6/99**

Circle the number after each statement.

Checking in and out is fast and efficient.	1 agree	2	③	4	5 disagree
My room was neat and clean.	1 agree	2	3	④	5 disagree
The staff is friendly and helpful.	1 agree	②	3	4	5 disagree
Room service is delivered quickly.	1 agree	2	3	4	⑤ disagree

Comments: __The room was not clean when I arrived. I waited over__
__45 minutes for my food from room service.__

ANSWER THE QUESTIONS

1. Does Mr. Aziz have any complaints?

2. What are his complaints?

3. What does Mr. Aziz think of the service?

4. Do you think Mr. Aziz is a satisfied customer? Why or why not?

PARTNER WORK

You are assistant hotel managers. Make a list of things you can do to help make Mr. Aziz happy and keep him as a customer. Share your list with the class.

 *CultureNotes*

Service can be bad for many reasons. What can you do if a coworker gives poor service? Talk about ways to help employees to give better service.

60　　　　　　　　　　　　　　　　　　　　　　　　　　Unit 5

PREPARATION

Present or review the words **complaint, check in, check out, staff, room service** and **satisfied.** Show the sample customer complaint forms. Ask if their employers have such a form and if they have ever filled out a form like this. Ask how these forms can be useful.

PRESENTATION

1. Have learners read and discuss the Purpose Statement. For more information see "Purpose Statement" on page viii.

2. Have learners look at the customer service card. Encourage them to say as much as they can about it. Write their ideas on the board and/or restate them in acceptable English.

3. Have learners read Answer the Questions. Allow learners to complete the activity. Have learners check each other's work in pairs. Ask several learners to read their answers aloud while the rest of the class checks their work.

4. Have learners read the instructions for Partner Work. Make sure each pair knows what to do. Model the activity by starting a list on the board, if necessary. Then have pairs complete the activity. Have several pairs present their lists to the class.

5. Have learners read Culture Notes and talk over their responses in teams. Have team reporters share their ideas with the class. Ask the teams to compare each other's ideas. For more information see "Culture Notes" on page vii.

FOLLOW-UP

Getting Feedback: Give pairs of learners a customer service card from a local business. Have pairs imagine they have had a bad experience at the business and fill out the card. Have several pairs share their cards with the class.

♦ Tell pairs they are now managers of the business and ask them to exchange their cards and brainstorm ways to help the customer. Have several pairs share their ideas with the class.

WORKBOOK

Unit 5, Exercise 8

Performance Check

How well can you use the skills in this unit?
....

Complete the activities. Go over your work with a partner or your teacher.
Then complete the Performance Review on page 62.

SKILL 1   **GREET CUSTOMERS**

Work with a partner. Imagine a customer at this gas station or at a job you would
like to have. Greet him or her.

SKILL 2   **GIVE GOOD CUSTOMER SERVICE**

Work with your partner or teacher. He or she complains. You give good customer
service. Find out what the problem is and offer a solution.

Unit 5   61

PRESENTATION

Use any of the procedures in
"Evaluation" on page x with pages 61
and 62. Record individuals' results on
the Unit 5 Individual Competency
Chart. Record the class's results on the
Class Cumulative Competency Chart.

SKILL 3 ▐ **UNDERSTAND COMMITMENTS TO CUSTOMERS**

You work for Superior Heating and Air Conditioning. Look at its customer service policies. Then talk about the situations. What do the policies say should happen? Tell your partner or your teacher.

SUPERIOR
Heating and Air Conditioning

1. All work is guaranteed.

2. Service technicians must arrive on time. If a technician is more than 10 minutes late, there is a 15% discount.

3. We match all competitors' prices.

1. Mr. Rodriguez's air conditioner isn't working. It is 11:15. The service technician is 30 minutes late.

2. Helen Lin has a new water heater. It is leaking on the floor. She calls to complain.

SKILL 4 ▐ **RESPOND TO CUSTOMERS' COMPLAINTS**

Look at Skill 3. Apologize to the customers for the mistakes. Work with your partner or teacher.

Performance Review

I can...

☐ 1. greet customers.

☐ 2. give good customer service.

☐ 3. understand commitments to customers.

☐ 4. respond to customers' complaints.

ISCUSSION

Work with a team. How will the skills help you? Make a list. Share the list with your class.

62

Unit 5

PRESENTATION

Follow the instructions on page 61.

INFORMAL WORKPLACE-SPECIFIC ASSESSMENT

Ask each student to state a customer service problem at his or her workplace and say how to resolve it.

WORKBOOK

Unit 5, Exercise 9

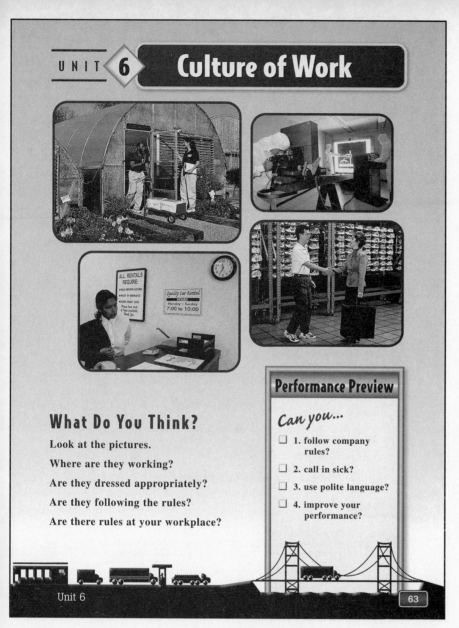

What Do You Think?

Look at the pictures.

Where are they working?

Are they dressed appropriately?

Are they following the rules?

Are there rules at your workplace?

Performance Preview

Can you...

☐ 1. follow company rules?

☐ 2. call in sick?

☐ 3. use polite language?

☐ 4. improve your performance?

Unit 6 Overview
—SCANS Competencies—

★ Understand social systems

★ Understand organizational systems

Workforce Skills

● Follow company rules

● Call in sick

● Use polite language

● Improve your performance

Materials

● Pictures of people wearing uniforms and specialized work clothing

● Examples of special work-related articles of clothing: work boots, etc.

● Paper formatted for writing memos

● Blank drawing paper; graph paper

Unit Warm-Up

To get learners thinking about the unit topic (workplace rules and appropriate behavior), tell the class you are going to enter the room a second time. Enter the room again hurriedly, as though you are late. Pretend to be a bit disorganized. Do not say hello to the class. Encourage learners to talk about how your actions make them feel.

★   ★   ★   ★   ★

WORKFORCE SKILLS (page 63)

Follow company rules

★   ★   ★   ★   ★

PREPARATION

Have learners talk about rules and appropriate behaviors they follow at work and at school. Encourage learners to discuss how such rules help make the classroom and workplace safer and more pleasant.

PRESENTATION

1. Focus attention on the photographs. Ask learners to speculate on what the unit might be about. Write their ideas on the board and/or restate them in acceptable English.

2. Have learners talk about the pictures. Have them identify the types of workplaces and the people in the photos. Ask learners to speculate about each company's rules and expected behaviors. Encourage learners to discuss why companies have rules.

3. Help learners read the questions. Discuss the questions with the class.

4. You may want to use the Performance Preview to provide learners with an overview of the skills in the unit. Have learners read the list of skills and discuss what they will learn in this unit.

FOLLOW-UP

Working Well Together: Have teams of learners make a list of three common workplace rules. Have teams share their lists with the class.

◆ Have each team compare their ideas, vote on the top five items, and then write one list and post it for the class.

WORKBOOK

Unit 6, Exercises 1A–1B

Follow company rules

Use polite language

★　　　★　　　★　　　★　　　★

Teaching Note

Use this page to introduce the new language in the unit. Whenever possible, encourage peer teaching. Supply any new language learners need.

Getting Started — Dressing for work

TEAM WORK

Read the sentences. Talk about each person's job. What do you think each person wears to work? Write the letters.

a. sweatshirt　　b. hat　　c. coveralls　　d. work boots

1. Sylvia's a welder at Quality Fabricators. _a, d_
2. Marisol's a bus driver for City Bus Line. _b_
3. Mark's a plumber at Quick Plumbing Company. _a, c, d_
4. Betty's a carpenter at Triangle Builders. _c, d_

 PRACTICE THE DIALOG

Dawn just started at Best Electric. Mr. Lynn is her supervisor.

A Dawn, welcome to the company.

B Thank you, Mr. Lynn.

A The first thing you should know is that you always need to wear your coveralls and gloves when you go into the assembly room.

B I've got them right here.

Now use the dialog to talk about what to wear at your jobs.

 SURVEY

Special clothing and equipment can be worn for many reasons. Ask your classmates about their work clothes and equipment. Make a list showing their jobs and the clothing they wear. Then write the reasons for what they wear.

64　　　　　　　　　　　　　　　　　　　　　　　Unit 6

PREPARATION

Show the pictures of people in various workplaces. Have teams of learners identify job titles and articles of special clothing for each workplace.

PRESENTATION

1. Have learners read and discuss the Purpose Statement.

2. Encourage learners to say as much as they can about the illustrations. Write their ideas on the board and/or restate them in acceptable English.

3. Have teams read the Team Work instructions. Make sure each team knows what to do. Have teams complete the activity. If learners need help, encourage them to consult other teams.

Have team reporters share their answers with the class.

 4. Have partners read the instructions for Practice the Dialog. If necessary, explain **gloves.** Then present the dialog. When learners are ready, have them read the directions under the dialog and do the activity. Have learners switch partners and repeat the activity. Have one or two partners present their dialogs to the class.

 5. Have partners read the Survey instructions and complete the activity. Have pairs share their answers with the class. For more information see "Survey" on page viii.

FOLLOW-UP

What Should I Wear? Divide the class into teams. Give each team a job title: *carpenter, food service worker, medical technician, welder, child care worker, cook.* Have each team come up with a list of appropriate clothing for the job. Have teams share their lists with the class.

♦ Have teams look again at the illustrations of clothing at the top of the page. Have the same teams brainstorm lists of jobs that use each type of clothing. Have teams share their lists with the class.

WORKBOOK

Unit 6, Exercises 2A–2B

Talk About It — Using polite language

Clocking In and Clocking Out

1. Punch time cards at the beginning and end of each shift.
2. Punch time cards when leaving and returning from lunch or dinner.
3. DO NOT punch time cards for 15-minute breaks.
4. Sign time cards every Friday.
5. Speak to your supervisor to make changes in time cards.

PRACTICE THE DIALOG

A Excuse me, Ms. Bullock?

B Yes, Ricardo?

A Do I have to punch out at lunch time?

B Yes, you punch out and back in for lunch.

A What about when we take breaks?

B No, you don't have to punch out or in for breaks.

A Thank you, Ms. Bullock.

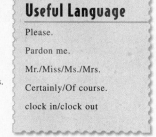

Useful Language

Please.

Pardon me.

Mr./Miss/Ms./Mrs.

Certainly/Of course.

clock in/clock out

ON YOUR JOB — PARTNER WORK

Take turns talking about rules at work. Ask your partner questions. Use polite language and correct titles. Use the dialog, the picture, and the Useful Language above.

ASAP PROJECT

Your class is writing an employee handbook. Team 1 writes rules for dressing at work. Team 2 writes rules for breaks, sick days, and vacations. Team 3 writes about other kinds of rules at work. Share information. Make suggestions for changes, and write a final version for the employee handbook. Complete this project as you work through this unit.

Unit 6

65

Use polite language

Follow company rules

★   ★   ★   ★   ★

ASAP PROJECT

Have learners read the instructions. Discuss the project and its purpose with learners. Make sure that everyone understands. Help learners assign themselves to teams based on their knowledge, skills, interests, or other personal strengths. Have each team select a leader, and have the team leaders or the whole class select an overall project leader. Throughout the rest of the unit, allow time for learners to work on the project. Have the teams agree on a deadline when the project will be finished. For more information see "ASAP Project" on page vi.

PREPARATION

Present or review **Mr., Ms., Mrs., Miss, please, thank you, pardon me,** and **excuse me.** Demonstrate the correct use of the phrases by asking for learners to hand you various classroom objects: *Ms. (name), please hand me that book. Thank you.*

PRESENTATION

1. Have learners read and discuss the Purpose Statement. For more information see "Purpose Statement" on page viii.

 2. Focus attention on the time clock. Encourage learners to say as much as they can about it. Have them say what time the clock shows. Have learners read the posted rules. Encourage them to say as much as they can about time clocks. Have learners talk about their own experiences signing in and out at work. Then present the dialog. See "Presenting a Dialog" on page ix.

 3. Have partners read the Partner Work instructions. Focus attention on the Useful Language box. Help learners read the expressions. If necessary, model pronunciation. Then have learners complete the activity. Have learners switch partners and repeat the activity. Have one or two pairs present their dialogs to the class.

FOLLOW-UP

You're the Boss: Divide the class into several teams. Have each team create rules for your classroom. These can include rules about politeness toward others, punctuality, and homework completion. Have learners compare lists. Which rules are the fairest? Which rules are the most needed?

♦ Have learners use their lists and discussion to come up with a set of agreed-upon classroom rules. Help learners write the rules on a chart. Post the chart in the classroom.

WORKBOOK

Unit 6, Exercise 3

WORKFORCE SKILLS (page 66)

Follow company rules

Call in sick

★ ★ ★ ★ ★

Personal Dictionary

Have learners add the words in their Personal Dictionary to their *Workforce Writing Dictionary*. For more information see "Workforce Writing Dictionary" on page v.

Keep Talking — Following company rules

PARTNER WORK

What are they doing wrong? What should they do to be better workers?

PRACTICE THE DIALOG

Stella is sick today. Mr. Wu is her supervisor.

A Hello, Mr. Wu? This is Stella. I have the flu. I can't come to work today.

B Thanks for calling me. Get some rest and call me if you're still sick tomorrow.

A All right, Mr. Wu. Thanks.

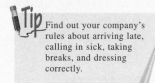
Tip Find out your company's rules about arriving late, calling in sick, taking breaks, and dressing correctly.

PARTNER WORK

Practice calling in sick. Be sure to explain what's the matter. Use the dialog above.

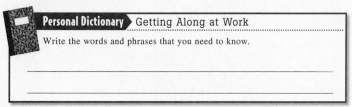
Personal Dictionary Getting Along at Work

Write the words and phrases that you need to know.

_____

_____

66   Unit 6

PREPARATION

Present or review **sick, flu,** and **call in.** Encourage learners to discuss what they do if they are sick and cannot go to work. Have them think of other reasons a person might have to call in to work.

PRESENTATION

1. Have learners read and discuss the Purpose Statement. For more information see "Purpose Statement" on page viii.

2. Focus attention on the illustrations. Have learners say as much as they can about them. Have them try to identify the workplaces and the people in them. Ask learners to talk about the behavior at their own workplace.

3. Have partners read the instructions for Partner Work. Make sure each pair knows what to do. Then have pairs complete the activity. Encourage partners to discuss how they would help a coworker they saw behaving inappropriately at work. Have pairs present their ideas to the class.

4. Present the dialog. See "Presenting a Dialog" on page ix.

5. Have partners read the instructions for Partner Work. Make sure each pair knows what to do. Then have pairs complete the activity.

6. Have learners read the Personal Dictionary instructions. Then use the Personal Dictionary procedures on page ix. Remind learners to continue to add words to their dictionaries throughout the unit.

Tip Have learners read the Tip independently. Have learners talk about who they will ask or how they will find out the rules.

FOLLOW-UP

Scenes: Divide the class into teams to role-play a scene showing inappropriate work behavior. Have each team present their scene to the class. Ask learners to spot as many things wrong as they can.

♦ Have teams present their role plays again, this time using appropriate behavior. Ask the class to say if there is anything else they could improve?

WORKBOOK

Unit 6, Exercise 4

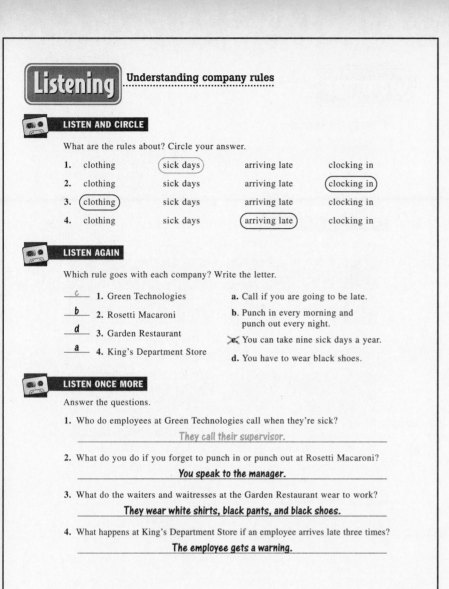

Listening · Understanding company rules

LISTEN AND CIRCLE

What are the rules about? Circle your answer.

1. clothing   (sick days)   arriving late   clocking in
2. clothing   sick days   arriving late   (clocking in)
3. (clothing)   sick days   arriving late   clocking in
4. clothing   sick days   (arriving late)   clocking in

LISTEN AGAIN

Which rule goes with each company? Write the letter.

___c___ 1. Green Technologies
___b___ 2. Rosetti Macaroni
___d___ 3. Garden Restaurant
___a___ 4. King's Department Store

a. Call if you are going to be late.
b. Punch in every morning and punch out every night.
c. You can take nine sick days a year.
d. You have to wear black shoes.

LISTEN ONCE MORE

Answer the questions.

1. Who do employees at Green Technologies call when they're sick?
   They call their supervisor.

2. What do you do if you forget to punch in or punch out at Rosetti Macaroni?
   You speak to the manager.

3. What do the waiters and waitresses at the Garden Restaurant wear to work?
   They wear white shirts, black pants, and black shoes.

4. What happens at King's Department Store if an employee arrives late three times?
   The employee gets a warning.

Unit 6   67

Follow company rules
Call in sick
Use polite language

★   ★   ★   ★   ★

PREPARATION

Use realia and pantomime to preteach or review **clothes, clothing, arriving late,** and **clocking in.** For **sick days,** explain that many companies give workers a certain number of paid sick days each year.

PRESENTATION

1. Have learners read and discuss the Purpose Statement. For more information see "Purpose Statement" on page viii.

 2. Have learners read the Listen and Circle instructions. Use peer teaching to clarify any unfamiliar vocabulary. Make sure everyone understands the instructions. Have learners read the activity. Clarify any unfamiliar vocabulary. Then play the tape or read the Listening Transcript aloud two or more times as learners complete the activity. Have learners check their work. For more information see "Presenting a Listening Activity" on page ix.

 3. Have learners read the Listen Again instructions. Make sure that everyone understands the instructions. Have learners read the answer choices before they begin. Encourage them to use peer-teaching to clarify any unfamiliar vocabulary. Then play the tape or read the Listening Transcript aloud two or more times as learners complete the activity. Have learners check their work.

 4. Have learners read the instructions for Listen Once More. Follow the procedures in 2.

FOLLOW-UP

Name the Rule: Have learners work in teams to write one company rule for each of the categories in the Listen and Circle activity. Have learners share their lists with the class.

♦ Have learners read their rules while the rest of the class writes down the category to which it belongs.

WORKBOOK

Unit 6, Exercise 5

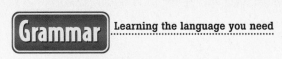

Learning the language you need

A. Study the Examples

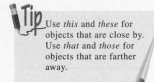

Tip Use *this* and *these* for objects that are close by. Use *that* and *those* for objects that are farther away.

COMPLETE THE SENTENCES

Circle *this*, *that*, *these*, or *those*.

Patricia, can you please take _____ (**this,** that) report to Mr. Alvarez?

Ms. Soto, _____ (this, **that**) flower order needs to go out today, please.

Hey, Alex, can you help me move _____ (these, **those**) boxes?

Can you put _____ (**these,** those) magazines on the shelves?

B. Study the Examples

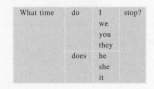

What time	do	I we you they	stop?
	does	he she it	

I We You They	stop	at 3:15.
He She It	stops	

68   Unit 6

PREPARATION

Review the language in the grammar boxes with learners before they open their books, if necessary.

PRESENTATION

1. Have learners read and discuss the Purpose Statement. For more information see "Purpose Statement" on page viii.

2. Have learners read the grammar boxes in A. Have learners use the language in the boxes to say as many sentences as possible about the objects in the classroom. Tell learners that they can use the grammar boxes throughout the unit to review or check sentence structures.

3. Have learners read the instructions for Complete the Sentences. If necessary, model the first item. Allow learners to complete the activity. Have learners check each other's work in pairs. Ask several learners to read their answers aloud while the rest of the class checks their work

4. Focus attention on the grammar boxes in B. Follow the procedures in 2.

Tip Have learners read the Tip independently. Provide any clarification needed. Ask learners to give a few examples. For more information see "Presenting a Tip" on page ix.

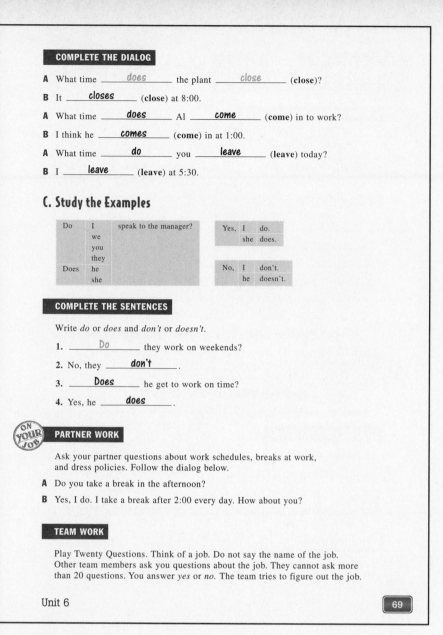

COMPLETE THE DIALOG

A What time ___does___ the plant ___close___ (**close**)?

B It ___closes___ (**close**) at 8:00.

A What time ___does___ Al ___come___ (**come**) in to work?

B I think he ___comes___ (**come**) in at 1:00.

A What time ___do___ you ___leave___ (**leave**) today?

B I ___leave___ (**leave**) at 5:30.

C. Study the Examples

Do	I	speak to the manager?
	we	
	you	
	they	
Does	he	
	she	

| Yes, | I | do. |
| | she | does. |

| No, | I | don't. |
| | he | doesn't. |

COMPLETE THE SENTENCES

Write *do* or *does* and *don't* or *doesn't*.

1. ___Do___ they work on weekends?

2. No, they ___don't___.

3. ___Does___ he get to work on time?

4. Yes, he ___does___.

PARTNER WORK

Ask your partner questions about work schedules, breaks at work, and dress policies. Follow the dialog below.

A Do you take a break in the afternoon?

B Yes, I do. I take a break after 2:00 every day. How about you?

TEAM WORK

Play Twenty Questions. Think of a job. Do not say the name of the job. Other team members ask you questions about the job. They cannot ask more than 20 questions. You answer *yes* or *no*. The team tries to figure out the job.

Unit 6

69

---

5. Have learners read the instructions for Complete the Dialog. If necessary, model the first item. Allow learners time to complete the activity. Ask pairs of learners to read their answers aloud while the rest of the class checks their work.

6. Focus attention on the grammar boxes in C. Follow the procedures in 2.

7. Have learners read the instructions for Complete the Sentences. If necessary, model the first item. Then have learners complete the activity independently. Have learners check each other's work in pairs. Ask several learners to read their answers aloud while the rest of the class checks their work.

8. Have learners read the instructions for Partner Work. If necessary, model the activity with a learner. Then have learners complete the activity independently. Have several pairs present their dialogs to the class.

9. Have teams read the Team Work instructions. Make sure each team knows what to do. If necessary, model the activity. Then have teams complete the activity.

FOLLOW-UP

Good Work Habits: Have learners work in teams to make a list of what good workers do, such as *Good workers arrive on time*. Have team reporters share their team's ideas with the class.

♦ Have the class vote on the top ten list of what good workers do. Write them down. Refer to them often.

WORKBOOK

Unit 6, Exercises 6A–6C

BLACKLINE MASTERS

Blackline Master: Unit 6

Reading and Writing
Improving your performance

READ MARTA'S JOB EVALUATION

EMPLOYEE EVALUATION

Name: **Marta Obregon**   Title: **Data Entry Clerk**   Date: **4/5/99**

Circle the number. 5 is the highest rating. 1 is the lowest.

1. The employee is punctual. She/He arrives on time and ready for work.

1	②	3	4	5
poor		satisfactory		excellent

Comments: **Marta sometimes arrives late. She is working to improve this problem.**

2. The employee is always dressed correctly.

1	2	3	4	⑤
poor		satisfactory		excellent

Comments: **Marta is always neat and professional. She is an example to others.**

3. The employee is polite and pleasant to superiors and other employees.

1	2	3	④	5
poor		satisfactory		excellent

Comments: **Marta is always polite, with a smile or a friendly word for her coworkers.**

4. The employee is flexible and willing to do different things if the supervisor or a coworker asks.

1	2	3	④	5
poor		satisfactory		excellent

Comments: **Marta is always willing to help her coworkers.**

ANSWER THE QUESTIONS

1. What is Marta's job? _____ *She's a data entry clerk.*

2. What does Marta need to improve? _____ **She sometimes arrives late.**

3. Does Marta dress well for her job? _____ **Yes, she does.**

4. What does Marta do for her coworkers? **She is always willing to help them.**

DISCUSSION

Do you think Marta is a good employee? How can Marta change to improve her work? Do you know someone who needs to improve his or her work?

70   Unit 6

Culture Note

Employee evaluations are often the basis for giving pay increases. Encourage learners to find out when, where, why, and how they are evaluated on the job.

PREPARATION

Present or review **punctual, flexible, professional,** and **polite.** Use the list of good work habits to help learners associate the words with the good work habits they have come up with. Present or review the adjectives **poor, satisfactory,** and **excellent.**

PRESENTATION

1. Have learners read and discuss the Purpose Statement. For more information see "Purpose Statement" on page viii.

2. Have learners preview the employee evaluation before they begin. Encourage learners to say everything they can about the evaluation form. Have learners identify the parts of the employee evaluation form they recognize based on other forms they have seen. Discuss why these forms are important and who fills them out. Write their ideas on the board and/or restate them in acceptable English.

3. Have learners read the form independently. Then have them complete Answer the Questions. Ask several learners to share their answers with the class while the rest of the class checks their work.

4. Have learners read the Discussion instructions. Make sure everyone knows what to do. Then have learners work in teams to talk about Marta's evaluation. Encourage learners to discuss ways Marta can improve her performance. Have team reporters share their ideas with the class. Have the teams compare ideas.

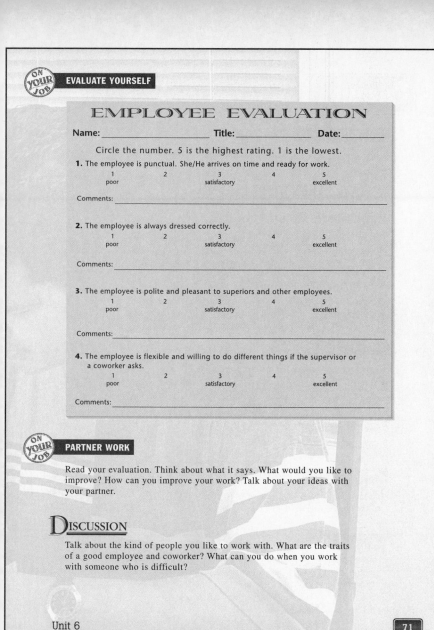

EVALUATE YOURSELF

EMPLOYEE EVALUATION

Name: _____ Title: _____ Date: _____

Circle the number. 5 is the highest rating. 1 is the lowest.

1. The employee is punctual. She/He arrives on time and ready for work.

1	2	3	4	5
poor		satisfactory		excellent

Comments: _____

2. The employee is always dressed correctly.

1	2	3	4	5
poor		satisfactory		excellent

Comments: _____

3. The employee is polite and pleasant to superiors and other employees.

1	2	3	4	5
poor		satisfactory		excellent

Comments: _____

4. The employee is flexible and willing to do different things if the supervisor or a coworker asks.

1	2	3	4	5
poor		satisfactory		excellent

Comments: _____

ON YOUR JOB

PARTNER WORK

Read your evaluation. Think about what it says. What would you like to improve? How can you improve your work? Talk about your ideas with your partner.

DISCUSSION

Talk about the kind of people you like to work with. What are the traits of a good employee and coworker? What can you do when you work with someone who is difficult?

Unit 6   71

SCANS Note

Making a list of clearly defined goals is a good way to improve one's performance on the job. Employees can make a list of goals independently or by working together with a supervisor.

5. Have learners look at Evaluate Yourself. Make sure everyone knows what to do. If necessary, model the first item with information about yourself. Then have learners complete the activity. Encourage learners to include a comment for each section of the evaluation.

6. Have learners read the instructions for Partner Work. Make sure everyone knows what to do. Encourage learners to make specific suggestions for improving their work.

7. Have learners read the Discussion instructions. Make sure everyone knows what to do. Then have learners work in pairs to complete the activity. Have groups present their ideas to the class.

FOLLOW-UP

Resolutions: Have learners use their ideas from Partner Work to write a list of resolutions for how they want to improve their work. Have them order their lists by importance and share their highest-priority item with the class.

♦ Ask learners to try to carry out their resolution. Ask them to report on their success to the class.

WORKBOOK

Unit 6, Exercises 7A–7C

WORKFORCE SKILLS (page 72)

Use polite language

★　　★　　★　　★　　★

Extension Identifying polite language

READ THE ARTICLE

Read this article from the *Newton News*.

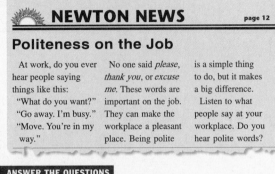

NEWTON NEWS page 12

Politeness on the Job

At work, do you ever hear people saying things like this: "What do you want?" "Go away. I'm busy." "Move. You're in my way."

No one said *please*, *thank you*, or *excuse me*. These words are important on the job. They can make the workplace a pleasant place. Being polite

is a simple thing to do, but it makes a big difference.

Listen to what people say at your workplace. Do you hear polite words?

ANSWER THE QUESTIONS

Are the people being polite? Write *yes* or *no*.

A "Give me that hammer right now."   no

B "I'm busy. I'll give it to you later."   no

A "You're blocking the door. I need to get through."   no

B "Oh, excuse me."   yes

PARTNER WORK

Which parts of the dialog above are not polite? Take turns saying them with polite language.

Culture Notes

In North America, people often say, "Hi, how are you?" Are they being polite? Are they really asking for information about you? What do you answer to be polite?

72   Unit 6

PREPARATION

Present or review **please, thank you,** and **excuse me.** Encourage learners to talk about situations in their workplace, home, or school when someone has been impolite.

PRESENTATION

1. Have learners read and discuss the Purpose Statement. For more information see "Purpose Statement" on page viii.

2. Have learners preview the article. Encourage them to say everything they can about it. Write their ideas on the board and/or restate them in acceptable English. Have learners read the article independently.

3. Have learners read the instructions for Answer the Questions. Make sure everyone knows what to do. If necessary, model the first item. Allow learners to complete the activity. Have learners review each other's work in pairs. Ask several learners to read their answers aloud while the rest of the class checks their work.

4. Have learners read the Partner Work instructions. Make sure each pair knows what to do. If necessary, model the activity by writing it on the board. Then have pairs complete the activity. Ask pairs to present their completed dialogs to the class.

5. Have learners read Culture Notes and talk over their responses in teams. Have team reporters share their ideas with the class. Ask the teams to compare each

other's ideas. For more information see "Culture Notes" on page vii.

FOLLOW-UP

Polite Requests: Have learners think of requests they hear at work or school. Have learners work in teams to create lists of polite and impolite versions of the requests. Have teams share their lists with the class.

♦ Have teams take turns acting out one or two of their polite and impolite requests. Have the rest of the class identify each request as polite or impolite.

WORKBOOK

Unit 6, Exercises 8A–8B

Performance Check

Complete the activities. Go over your work with a partner or your teacher. Then complete the Performance Review on page 74.

SKILL 1   FOLLOW COMPANY RULES

Do they follow the rules for work? What should they do? Tell your partner or teacher what each employee should do.

Dress Code for Circle Department Store: Clean shirt and pants. Name tag. No sneakers.

Late Policy for Block Technology: Any employee who arrives late must report to the supervisor immediately.

SKILL 2   CALL IN SICK

Call in sick. Your teacher or partner is your boss.

SKILL 3   USE POLITE LANGUAGE

Are the dialogs polite? How can you change what they say to be more polite? Tell a partner or your teacher.

1. **A** Hey, Marcos, help me. I want to leave early tonight.

   B All right, all right. Just wait a minute.

   A Come on, Marcos. I want to go now.

2. **A** Put these boxes on the shelves right away.

   B I can't help you right now. I'm doing something else.

   A This is more important.

Unit 6   73

PRESENTATION

Use any of the procedures in "Evaluation" on page x with pages 73 and 74. Record individuals' results on the Unit 6 Individual Competency Chart. Record the class's results on the Class Cumulative Competency Chart.

Rate yourself as an employee. If you choose *needs improvement*, say why. How can you change your work habits to meet your company's expectations?

Employee Self Evaluation

Name: _Answers will vary._

Circle the word that best describes your work.

1. **Punctuality.** Do you arrive at work on time?

   good   average   needs improvement

2. **Dress.** Is your clothing or uniform neat and complete?

   good   average   needs improvement

3. **Politeness.** Are you courteous and polite to other employees and customers?

   good   average   needs improvement

4. **Helpfulness.** Are you willing to help your coworkers?

   good   average   needs improvement

Performance Review

I can...

☐ 1. follow company rules.

☐ 2. call in sick.

☐ 3. use polite language.

☐ 4. improve my performance.

DISCUSSION

Work with a team. How will the skills help you? Make a list. Share the list with your class.

74   Unit 6

PRESENTATION

Follow the instructions on page 73.

INFORMAL WORKPLACE-SPECIFIC ASSESSMENT

Ask learners to state one or two rules from their jobs.

WORKBOOK

Unit 6, Exercise 9

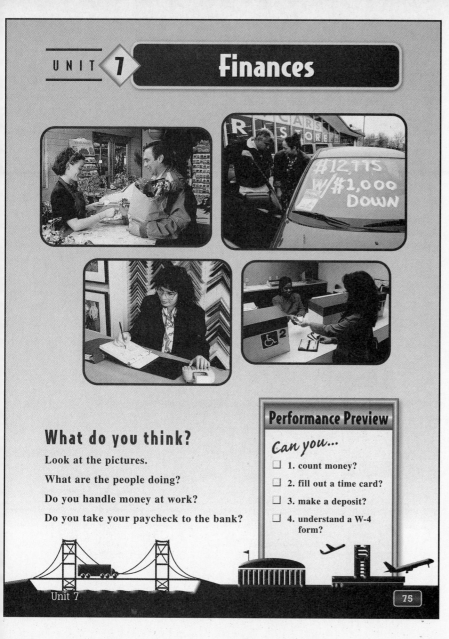

75

Unit 7 Overview
—SCANS Competencies—

★ Work on teams

★ Understand organizational systems

★ Organize and communicate information

Workforce Skills

● Count money

● Fill out a time card

● Make a deposit

● Understand a W-4 form

Materials

● Real or play money: all coins and one, five, ten, and twenty-dollar bills

● Blank sample checks, deposit and withdrawal slips, check registers, W-4 and other common tax forms

● Examples of time cards

● Price tags or stickers

Unit Warm-Up

To get learners thinking about the unit topic (money management and banking), pantomime paying for a purchase. Have learners talk about different means of payment: cash, check, credit cards. Encourage learners to talk about their experiences paying for things and using banks.

★   ★   ★   ★   ★

WORKFORCE SKILLS (page 75)

Count money

Make a deposit

★   ★   ★   ★   ★

PREPARATION

1. Show learners the pay stubs, bank forms, and money. Present or review **bank, deposit, fill out,** and **count.** Have learners identify the items by name and talk about other means of payment (money orders, credit cards, money-grams). Encourage learners to use peer teaching to clarify unfamiliar vocabulary.

2. Ask learners if they handle money as part of their work. Do they use calculators, cash registers, or computers?

PRESENTATION

1. Focus attention on the photographs. Ask learners what the unit might be about. Write their ideas on the board and/or restate them in acceptable English.

2. Have learners talk about the photographs again. Have them identify the people in the photographs and describe the different kinds of actions involving money. Help learners relate the activities shown to their own jobs or personal experiences.

3. Help learners read the questions. Discuss the questions with the class.

4. You may want to use the Performance Preview to provide learners with an overview of the skills in the unit. Have learners read the list of skills and discuss what they will learn in this unit.

FOLLOW-UP

Just Checking: Have learners talk about where they take their checks. Do they have to pay fees to cash their checks? How much? Where is the best place to take checks?

◆ Have learners make a table showing places they can cash checks and the fees charged.

WORKBOOK

Unit 7, Exercises 1A–1B

★　　　★　　　★　　　★　　　★

Teaching Note

Use this page to introduce the new language in the unit. Whenever possible, encourage peer teaching. Supply any new language the learners need.

Teaching Note

Students may be hesitant to talk about how much they make or their bank accounts. Tell them they don't have to use real information in the unit activities if they don't want to.

Getting Started
Counting money

PARTNER WORK

Talk about the coins and bills on the desk. How much is each one worth? How do you say the names of coins and bills?

penny	nickel	dime	quarter	one dollar bill
five dollar bill	ten dollar bill	twenty dollar bill		

TEAM WORK

Look at the dollar amounts. Say how many of each bill and coin you need. Make two or three different combinations of bills and coins for each amount.

1. $1.25　　**2.** $15.75　　**3.** $42.50　　**4.** $9.64　　**5.** $4.37　　**6.** $27.93

 SURVEY

Do you get paid in cash or by check at work? Do you have your pay deposited directly into your account? Ask your classmates. Make a bar graph. Label the first bar *cash*. Label the second bar *check*. Label the third bar *direct deposit*. Follow the example.

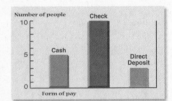

76

Unit 7

PREPARATION

Present or review **bill, money,** and **coin.** Use play or real money as examples. Ask teams to list as many names of bills and coins as they can. Write the names on the board and model correct pronunciation.

PRESENTATION

1. Have learners read and discuss the Purpose Statement. For more information see "Purpose Statement" on page viii.

2. Encourage learners to say as much as they can about the illustration. Write their ideas on the board and/or restate them in acceptable English.

3. Have partners read the Partner Work instructions and complete the activity. If learners need help, encourage them to consult other pairs. Ask several learners to name the coins and bills on the page for the rest of the class.

4. Have teams read the Team Work instructions and complete the activity. Have team reporters share their answers with the class.

 5. Have the class read the Survey instructions. Make sure everyone knows what to do. Then have learners complete the activity. For more information see "Survey" on page viii.

FOLLOW-UP

Count It Out: Have learners work in pairs. Give each pair some play money. One learner says an amount: *two dollars and fifty-six cents.* The other learner shows the amount in bills and coins.

♦ Show learners different combinations of play money. Have learners write down the total amount. Check learners' work.

WORKBOOK

Unit 7, Exercises 2A–2B

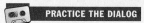

Talk About It — Understanding your pay

Bay State Telephone Company

Day	Start Time	Lunch out	Lunch in	Finish Time	Total Hours
Monday	7:30	11:30	12:30	4:30	8
Tuesday	8:00	12:30	1:30	5:00	8
Wednesday	7:45	12:00	1:00	4:45	8
Thursday	7:30	11:00	12:00	4:30	8
Friday	—	—	—	—	0

Total Hours __32__ Hourly Rate __$7.00__ Total Pay __$224.00__

Employee Signature _Maria Hernandez_ Date _12/10/99_

PRACTICE THE DIALOG

A Luis, can you help me with my time card?

B Sure. Let's take a look. How many hours did you work last week?

A 32 hours.

B You make $7.00 an hour. For 32 hours your total should be $224.00. That's what you filled in. It looks fine.

Tip People and machines can make mistakes. Check your paycheck carefully. Report mistakes to your supervisor immediately.

PARTNER WORK

Look at the pay rates and the number of hours. Figure out each person's pay. Then talk about the information. Use the dialog above.

1. 33 hours at $9 per hour 2. 39 hours at $7 per hour 3. 24 hours at $5 per hour

ASAP PROJECT

As a class, create a chart of services for two local banks. Divide into two teams. Each team finds out a bank's name, address, telephone number, hours of operation, types of accounts, interest rates, fees, minimum balances, service charges, and other services. Complete this project as you work through this unit.

Unit 7　　77

ASAP PROJECT

Have learners read the instructions. Discuss the project and its purpose with learners. Make sure that everyone understands. Help learners assign themselves to teams based upon their knowledge, skills, interests, or other personal strengths. Have each team select a leader, and have the team leaders or the whole class select an overall project leader. Throughout the rest of the unit, allow time for learners to work on the project. Have the teams agree on a deadline when the project will be finished. For more information see "ASAP Project" on page vi.

PREPARATION

Present or review **time card, total, hourly rate, per hour,** and **pay rate.** Use the sample time cards to show where each piece of information is written. Point out that **per hour** and **an hour** mean the same thing.

PRESENTATION

1. Have learners read and discuss the Purpose Statement. For more information see "Purpose Statement" on page viii.

2. Focus attention on the time card. Encourage learners to say as much as they can about it. Have them identify the name and date lines, the labels for each day of the week, and the box for the total number of hours worked. Then present the dialog. See "Presenting a Dialog" on page ix.

3. Have partners read the Partner Work instructions. Make sure everyone understands what to do. Then have learners complete the activity. Have one or two pairs present their answers to the class.

Tip Have learners read the Tip independently. Have learners discuss how the advice will help them. For more information see "Presenting a Tip" on page ix.

FOLLOW-UP

Missing Information: Give each learner a partially filled out time card. Leave the daily total hours, the weekly total hours, and the total pay lines blank. Have learners fill in the missing information.

♦ Ask pairs of learners to check each other's work. When all the information is correct, have learners sign their own time cards.

WORKBOOK

Unit 7, Exercise 3

Make a deposit

★　　★　　★　　★　　★

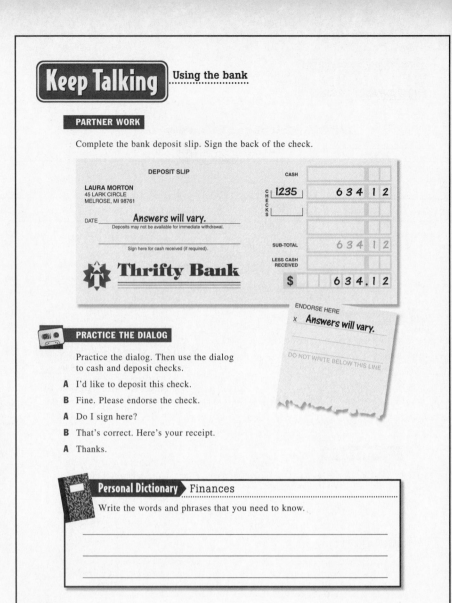

Keep Talking　Using the bank

PARTNER WORK

Complete the bank deposit slip. Sign the back of the check.

> DEPOSIT SLIP
>
> LAURA MORTON
> 45 LARK CIRCLE
> MELROSE, MI 98761
>
> DATE _____ **Answers will vary.**
> Deposits may not be available for immediate withdrawal.
>
> _____ Sign here for cash received (if required).
>
> **Thrifty Bank**
>
> CASH
> CHECKS 1235　634 12
> SUB-TOTAL　634 12
> LESS CASH RECEIVED
> $　634.12
>
> ENDORSE HERE
> x **Answers will vary.**
> DO NOT WRITE BELOW THIS LINE

PRACTICE THE DIALOG

Practice the dialog. Then use the dialog to cash and deposit checks.

A I'd like to deposit this check.

B Fine. Please endorse the check.

A Do I sign here?

B That's correct. Here's your receipt.

A Thanks.

Personal Dictionary ▸ Finances

Write the words and phrases that you need to know.

_____

_____

_____

78　　　　　　　　　　　　　　　　　　Unit 7

Teaching Note

You may want to remind learners that money orders are a safe way to send money through the mail or to make large payments. Make sure learners know to keep their receipts.

Personal Dictionary

Have learners add the words in their Personal Dictionary to their *Workforce Writing Dictionary*. For more information see "Workforce Writing Dictionary" on page v.

PREPARATION

1. Present or review **bank, receipt, endorse, deposit,** and **account.** Help learners to name other forms that require an endorsement or signature, such as time cards, insurance forms, and tax forms.

2. Use the sample deposit slips, filled out checks, play money, and a large deposit slip to model completing a deposit slip. As you write, clarify **cash, subtotal,** and **less cash received.**

PRESENTATION

1. Have learners read and discuss the Purpose Statement. For more information see "Purpose Statement" on page viii.

2. Have partners read the Partner Work instructions. Help learners identify the different parts of the deposit slip and understand what to write on each line. Make sure each pair knows what to do. Then have pairs complete the activity. Have one or two pairs share their answers with the class.

 3. Have partners read the instructions for Practice the Dialog. Allow learners time to complete the activity. Have learners change partners and repeat. Have several pairs present their dialogs to the class

4. Have learners read the Personal Dictionary instructions. Remind learners to continue to add words to their dictionaries throughout the unit.

FOLLOW-UP

Bank Teller: Have pairs of learners use the deposit slips, checks, and play money to create dialogs in which one learner deposits a check or cash. Supply any language needed. Have several pairs present their dialogs to the class.

♦ Have tellers write out receipts showing the completed transactions. Check the receipts with the class.

WORKBOOK

Unit 7, Exercises 4A–4B

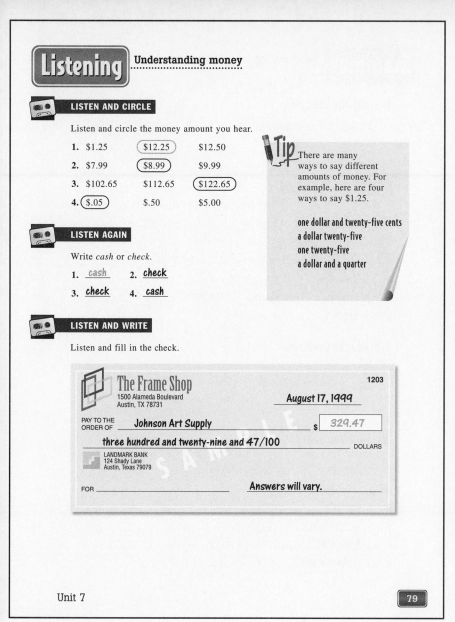

Listening — Understanding money

LISTEN AND CIRCLE

Listen and circle the money amount you hear.

1. $1.25 — ($12.25) — $12.50
2. $7.99 — ($8.99) — $9.99
3. $102.65 — $112.65 — ($122.65)
4. ($.05) — $.50 — $5.00

Tip
There are many ways to say different amounts of money. For example, here are four ways to say $1.25.

one dollar and twenty-five cents
a dollar twenty-five
one twenty-five
a dollar and a quarter

LISTEN AGAIN

Write *cash* or *check*.

1. _cash_   2. _check_
3. _check_   4. _cash_

LISTEN AND WRITE

Listen and fill in the check.

The Frame Shop
1500 Alameda Boulevard
Austin, TX 78731   1203

August 17, 1999

PAY TO THE ORDER OF   Johnson Art Supply $ 329.47

three hundred and twenty-nine and 47/100 _____ DOLLARS

LANDMARK BANK
124 Shady Lane
Austin, Texas 79079

FOR _____   Answers will vary.

Unit 7   79

SCANS Note

Accuracy when dealing with money is essential to any business. Emphasize to learners that they should carefully fill out all bank forms, proofread checks as they write them, and examine receipts for discrepancies.

PREPARATION

1. Present or review **signature** and **pay to the order of.** Draw a blank check on the board, or use an overhead transparency. Fill out each line and describe the information that goes there.

2. Use play money and a check to clarify **cash** and **check.**

PRESENTATION

1. Have learners read and discuss the Purpose Statement. For more information see "Purpose Statement" on page viii.

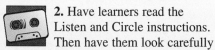 2. Have learners read the Listen and Circle instructions. Then have them look carefully at the amounts given. Have learners say the amounts shown. Then play the tape or read the Listening Transcript aloud

two or more times as learners complete the activity. Have learners check their work. See "Presenting a Listening Activity" on page ix.

3. Have learners read the instructions for Listen Again. Have learners discuss the difference between **cash** and **check.** Follow the procedures in 2.

4. Have learners read the Listen and Write instructions. Have them familiarize themselves with the check by identifying where they will write the amount, their signature, and the person who will get the money. Follow the procedures in 2.

Tip Have learners read the Tip independently. Ask learners to say amounts of money in different ways.

FOLLOW-UP

Who Do I Make It Out To? Give each pair of learners a blank check and a few classroom objects with price tags attached. One learner says the prices of the objects, gives a total, and says who to make the check out to. The other learner verifies the total and fills out a check to pay for the objects.

♦ Have learners switch partners and pay for different objects.

WORKBOOK

Unit 7, Exercise 5

Count money

Make a deposit

★　　★　　★　　★　　★

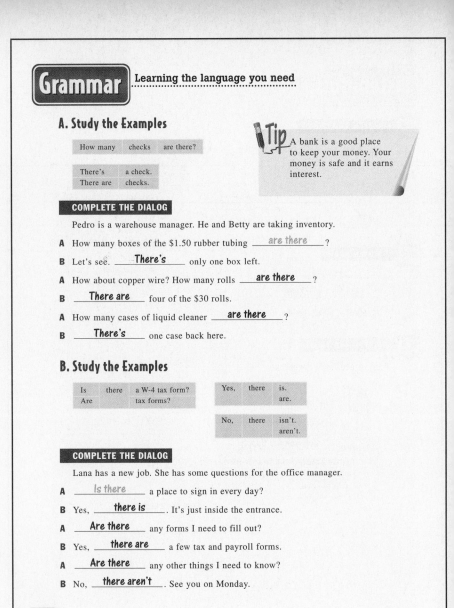

Grammar | Learning the language you need

A. Study the Examples

| How many | checks | are there? |

| There's | a check. |
| There are | checks. |

Tip A bank is a good place to keep your money. Your money is safe and it earns interest.

COMPLETE THE DIALOG

Pedro is a warehouse manager. He and Betty are taking inventory.

A How many boxes of the $1.50 rubber tubing ___are there___ ?

B Let's see. ___There's___ only one box left.

A How about copper wire? How many rolls ___are there___ ?

B ___There are___ four of the $30 rolls.

A How many cases of liquid cleaner ___are there___ ?

B ___There's___ one case back here.

B. Study the Examples

| Is | there | a W-4 tax form? |
| Are | | tax forms? |

| Yes, | there | is. |
| | | are. |

| No, | there | isn't. |
| | | aren't. |

COMPLETE THE DIALOG

Lana has a new job. She has some questions for the office manager.

A ___Is there___ a place to sign in every day?

B Yes, ___there is___ . It's just inside the entrance.

A ___Are there___ any forms I need to fill out?

B Yes, ___there are___ a few tax and payroll forms.

A ___Are there___ any other things I need to know?

B No, ___there aren't___ . See you on Monday.

80

Unit 7

PREPARATION

Review the language in the grammar boxes with learners before they open their books, if necessary.

PRESENTATION

1. Have learners read and discuss the Purpose Statement. For more information see "Purpose Statement" on page viii.

2. Have learners read the grammar boxes in A. Have learners use the language in the boxes to say as many sentences as possible. Tell learners that they can use the grammar boxes throughout the unit to review or check sentence structures.

3. Have learners read the instructions for Complete the Dialog. If necessary, model the first item. Then have learners complete the activity independently.

Ask several learners to read the dialog aloud while the rest of the class checks their answers.

4. Focus attention on the grammar boxes in B. Follow the procedures in 2.

5. Have learners read the instructions for Complete the Dialog. If necessary, model the first item. Then have learners complete the activity independently. Ask several learners to read the dialog aloud while the rest of the class checks their answers.

Tip Have learners read the Tip independently. Have learners discuss how the advice will help them. For more information, see "Presenting a Tip" on page ix.

C. Study the Examples

Which	line do I sign my name on?
	space is for checks?

ANSWER THE QUESTIONS

Look at the check register. Write questions using *which*.

Check Number	Date	Description	Amount of Payment (–)		Amount of Deposit (+)		Balance	
							1465	93
767	5/9	Warehouse Office Supply	102	35			1363	58
768	5/11	Change Computer Systems	250	00			1113	58
	5/13	Deposit			310	00	1423	58
769	5/17	Parkway Truck Repair	69	89			1353	69
770	5/18	Helpful Temporaries	391	00			962	69

1. _____ *Which check is for Helpful Temporaries?* _____
   Check number 770 is for Helpful Temporaries.

2. _____ *Which check is for $69.89?* _____
   Check number 769 is for $69.89.

PARTNER WORK

Look at the check register again. Take turns asking questions using *which*. For example, "Which check is the largest?" Then fill out the deposit slip for the deposit.

DEPOSIT SLIP

DATE **Answers will vary.**
Deposits may not be available for immediate withdrawal.

Sign here for cash received (if required).

CENTURY SAVINGS BANK
Arlington, VA

CASH

CHECKS 310 00

SUB-TOTAL 310 00

LESS CASH RECEIVED

$ 310 00

6. Focus attention on the grammar box in C. Follow the procedures in 2.

7. Have learners read the instructions for Answer the Questions. If necessary, model the first item. Allow learners to complete the activity independently. Have learners check each other's work in pairs. Ask a few learners to read the questions and their answers aloud while the rest of the class checks their work.

8. Have partners read the Partner Work instructions. Make sure everyone understands what to do. Allow learners to complete the activity. Have several pairs share their conversations with the class and show their completed deposit slips.

FOLLOW-UP

How Much Money Do You Have?
Divide the class into teams. Hand out several completed checks and a blank check register to each team. Give each team a starting amount. Have them fill in the check register and then come up with a balance. Have team reporters share their results with the class.

♦ Give learners copies of a filled-in check register in which there are one or two simple errors. Have teams see who can spot the error(s) first.

WORKBOOK
Unit 7, Exercises 6A–6C

BLACKLINE MASTERS
Blackline Master: Unit 7

WORKFORCE SKILLS (pages 82–83)

Fill out a time card

★　　★　　★　　★　　★

Culture Note

You might discuss with learners laws governing overtime pay in your area. Are learners entitled to bonus pay for working more than eight hours in a day? More than forty hours a week? What is the bonus rate?

Reading and Writing — Understanding time cards

LOOK AT THE TIME CARD

PRINT FIRMLY

SPOTLESS CLEANERS

PO BOX 9881 NEWTON, MA 02164

9/17/99
WEEK ENDING DATE

000-58-4343
SOCIAL SECURITY NUMBER

Maria Valdez
EMPLOYEE SIGNATURE

John Cho
SUPERVISOR SIGNATURE

OFFICE CODE
(Office use only)

	START TIME	LUNCH OUT / IN		FINISH TIME	DAILY HOURS WORKED
SU					
MO	10:00	12:30	1:30	7:00	8
TU	8:00	11:30	12:30	5:00	8
WE	7:30	11:00	11:30	2:00	6
TH	8:00	12:00	12:30	4:00	7½
FR	9:30	1:30	2:30	6:30	8
SA					
			TOTAL HOURS FOR WEEK		37½

ANSWER THE QUESTIONS

1. Who has to sign the time card?

 the employee and the supervisor

2. When does Maria take her lunch on Tuesday?

11:30–12:30

3. Which day does Maria work for only six hours?

Wednesday

4. What week is the time card for?

9/17/99

DISCUSSION

What other information can you find on Maria's time card? Is it easy to read and understand? Why or why not? Why do you think it says *print firmly*? Does your time card ask for similar information?

82

Unit 7

PREPARATION

1. Hand out copies of blank time cards. Help learners to identify the parts of the form: days of the week, time in and time out, signature and date lines, etc.

2. Present or review the vocabulary found on a time card. Write the day and date on the board. Have learners talk about the hours they have worked or will work today.

PRESENTATION

1. Have learners read and discuss the Purpose Statement. For more information see "Purpose Statement" on page viii.

2. Have learners look at the time card before they begin. Encourage learners to say everything they can about the time card. Write their ideas on the board

and/or restate them in acceptable English.

3. Focus attention on the Answer the Questions instructions. Then have learners complete the activity. Have pairs of learners brainstorm two or three more questions and answers about the time card.

4. Have learners read the Discussion instructions. Make sure everyone knows what to do. Then have learners work in teams to talk over their answers. Have team reporters share their ideas with the class.

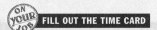

FILL OUT THE TIME CARD

You work part time at Spotless Cleaners. Fill out the time card for the hours you worked this week. Be sure to follow the instructions and fill out the time card completely.

SPOTLESS CLEANERS

PO BOX 9881 NEWTON, MA 02164

__Answers will vary.__
WEEK ENDING DATE

SOCIAL SECURITY NUMBER

EMPLOYEE SIGNATURE

SUPERVISOR SIGNATURE

OFFICE CODE
(Office use only)

PRINT FIRMLY

	START TIME	LUNCH OUT / IN	FINISH TIME	DAILY HOURS WORKED
SU				
MO				
TU				
WE				
TH				
FR				
SA				
	TOTAL HOURS FOR WEEK			

WRITE THE AMOUNT

Look at your time card. You make $9.00 per hour.

How much should your paycheck be? _____ __Answers will vary.__

Discussion

Time cards and other forms use a lot of abbreviations. Abbreviations are short forms of words. For example, on this time card *SU* stands for Sunday. Look at the time card. What are some other abbreviations? What do they stand for? Make a list.

Unit 7   83

---

5. Have teams read the Fill Out the Time Card instructions. Make sure everyone knows what to do. Model filling out the line for Sunday, if necessary. Then have learners complete the activity. Have learners exchange time cards, check each other's work, and share their time cards with the class.

6. Have learners read the Write the Amount instructions. Make sure everyone knows what to do. Have pairs of learners check each other's work. Have several learners share their totals with the class.

7. Have learners read the Discussion instructions. Make sure everyone knows what to do. Then have learners work in teams to brainstorm lists of abbreviations they know. Have team reporters share their lists with the class.

FOLLOW-UP

Supervisor Says: Give each learner a blank time card. Have learners work in teams. Have each team choose a supervisor. The supervisor will decide how many hours everyone on the team works in a week and at what pay rate. The hours and the pay rate should be the same for everyone. Then have learners complete their time cards. The supervisor checks the information and signs each card.

♦ Have learners change teams, choose new supervisors, and repeat the activity.

WORKBOOK

Unit 7, Exercises 7A–7C

Understanding a W-4 tax form

READ THE W-4 FORM

A W-4 form is a government tax form. The W-4 form tells your employer how much money to take out of your paycheck for federal taxes.

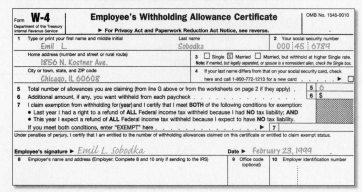

CIRCLE

What information does a W-4 form ask for?
Circle the numbers.

1. your address
2. your Social Security number
3. the names of your children
4. the date
5. your date of birth
6. whether you are single or married

Tip If you change your name when you get married, get a new Social Security card with your new name. This will make filing your tax forms much easier.

Culture Notes

How do you fill out your tax forms? Do you fill them out yourself? Do you get help from an accountant or tax preparer? Why or why not? If you need help, who do you ask? Do you call the IRS or visit an IRS office?

84

Unit 7

PREPARATION

1. Present or review the word **tax.** Ask learners what they think tax money is used for. Have learners brainstorm a list of things that are taxed besides their income.

2. Have learners look at the W-4 form you brought in or the one in the book and identify as many things as they can. Have them identify all the words they already know. They should be familiar with name, signature, date, address, and Social Security number.

PRESENTATION

1. Have learners read and discuss the Purpose Statement. For more information see "Purpose Statement" on page viii.

2. Have learners look at the W-4 form. Encourage them to say everything they can about it. Write their ideas on the board and/or restate them in acceptable English.

3. Have learners read the instructions for Circle. Make sure everyone knows what to do. Then have learners complete the activity independently. Have learners review each other's work in pairs. Ask several learners to share their answers with the class while the rest of the class checks their work.

4. Have learners read Culture Notes and talk over their responses in teams. Have team reporters share their ideas with the class. Ask the teams to compare each other's ideas. For more information, see "Culture Notes" on page vii.

Tip Have learners read the Tip independently. Have learners discuss how the advice will help them. For more information, see "Presenting a Tip" on page ix.

FOLLOW-UP

Find the Line: Hand out blank W-4 forms. Write these questions on the board: *Are you married? What's your Social Security number? Where do you live? What is your last name?* Have each learner answer the questions and write the answers in the appropriate sections of the form.

♦ Have learners work in pairs to finish filling out the forms.

WORKBOOK

Unit 7, Exercise 8

Performance Check

How well can you use the skills in this unit?

Complete the activities. Go over your work with a partner or your teacher. Then complete the Performance Review on Page 86.

SKILL 1   COUNT MONEY

Write the amount of money.

1.

2.

3.

| $4.44 | $6.12 | $28.32 |

SKILL 2   FILL OUT A TIME CARD

Complete the time card.

- You worked 8 hours on Monday.
- You worked 9 hours on Tuesday.
- You took a day off on Wednesday.
- You worked 8 hours on Thursday.
- You worked 9 hours on Friday.
- You worked 6 hours on Saturday.

XYZ Company
Employee Time Card

Name **Answers will vary.**

Week ending _____

Day	Hours worked
Monday	8
Tuesday	9
Wednesday	0
Thursday	8
Friday	9
Saturday	6
Total Hours	40

Supervisor Signature _____

Unit 7

85

PRESENTATION

Use any of the procedures in "Evaluation" on page x with pages 85 and 86. Record individuals' results on the Unit 7 Individual Competency Chart. Record the class's results on the Class Cumulative Competency Chart.

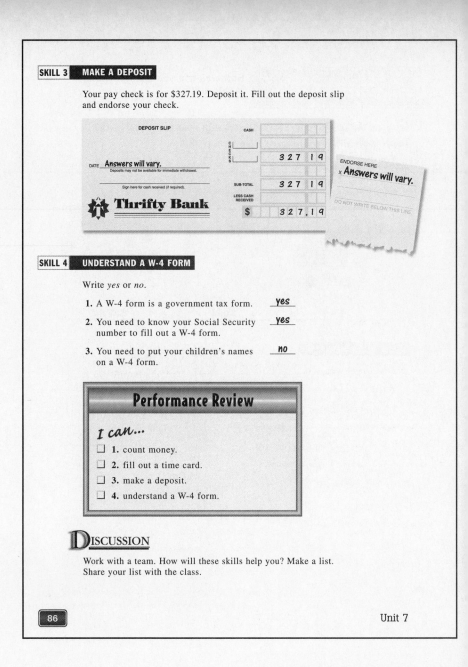

SKILL 3 **MAKE A DEPOSIT**

Your pay check is for $327.19. Deposit it. Fill out the deposit slip and endorse your check.

DEPOSIT SLIP

CASH

C H E C K S

327 19

DATE _Answers will vary._
Deposits may not be available for immediate withdrawal.

Sign here for cash received (if required).

Thrifty Bank

SUB-TOTAL   327 19

LESS CASH RECEIVED

$ 327.19

ENDORSE HERE
x _Answers will vary._
DO NOT WRITE BELOW THIS LINE

SKILL 4 **UNDERSTAND A W-4 FORM**

Write *yes* or *no*.

1. A W-4 form is a government tax form.   _yes_

2. You need to know your Social Security   _yes_
   number to fill out a W-4 form.

3. You need to put your children's names   _no_
   on a W-4 form.

Performance Review

I can...

☐ **1.** count money.
☐ **2.** fill out a time card.
☐ **3.** make a deposit.
☐ **4.** understand a W-4 form.

DISCUSSION

Work with a team. How will these skills help you? Make a list.
Share your list with the class.

86   Unit 7

PRESENTATION

Follow the instructions on page 85.

INFORMAL WORKPLACE-SPECIFIC ASSESSMENT

Have learners show you how they complete a time card from their workplace(s).

WORKBOOK

Unit 7, Exercise 9

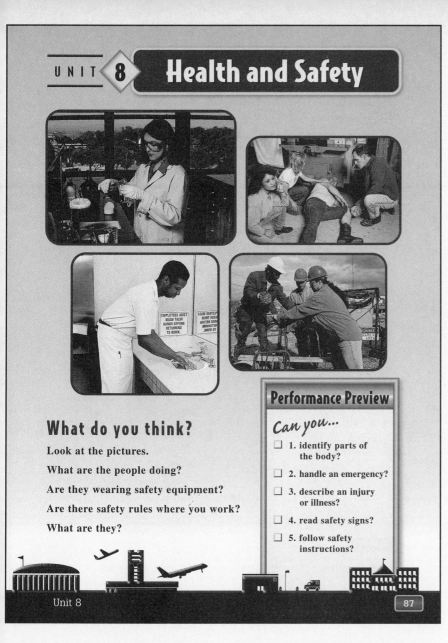

★ Interpret and communicate information

★ Understand organizational systems

Workforce Skills

- Identify parts of the body
- Handle an emergency
- Describe an injury or illness
- Read safety signs
- Follow safety instructions

Materials

- Examples of safety signs
- Large drawing of a man or woman
- Emergency numbers page from a local telephone directory
- Pictures of people with various illnesses and injuries
- Samples of safety and health rules for employees
- Graph paper

Unit Warm-Up

To get learners thinking about the unit topic (parts of the body, illness, and safety), review calling in sick. Have learners talk about their experiences calling in sick. What illness did they have? Review the names of safety equipment and clothing. Encourage learners to think of other things besides clothing that maintain health and safety on the job.

★   ★   ★   ★   ★

WORKFORCE SKILLS (page 87)

Read safety signs

Follow safety instructions

★   ★   ★   ★   ★

PREPARATION

Present or review **safety** and **emergency.** Ask learners to name different kinds of emergency situations: fire, car accident, injury at work, accidental poisoning, etc.

PRESENTATION

1. Focus attention on the photographs. Ask learners what the unit might be about. Write their ideas on the board and/or restate them in acceptable English.

2. Have learners talk about the pictures. Have them identify which picture depicts an emergency and which ones show people following safety or health precautions.

3. Help learners read the questions. Discuss the questions with the class.

4. You may want to use the Performance Preview to provide learners with an overview of the skills in the unit. Have learners read the list of skills and discuss what they will learn in this unit.

FOLLOW-UP

Safety at Work and at Home: Have pairs discuss basic safety at work and home and then come up with one basic security, safety, or accident prevention

suggestion, such as use safety belts, lock doors, check smoke detectors. Have each pair share their idea with the class.

♦ Have each pair write their suggestion on a slip of paper. Check their work. Have them write final versions of their suggestions and post them.

WORKBOOK

Unit 8, Exercises 1A–1B

Teaching Note

Use this page to introduce the new language in the unit. Whenever possible, encourage peer teaching. Supply any new language learners need.

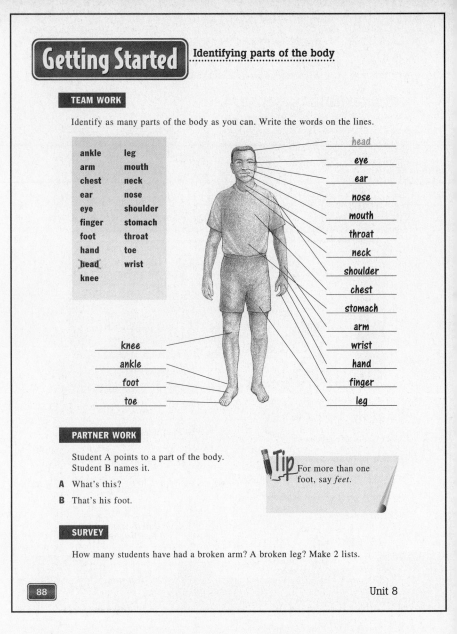

PREPARATION

Show the drawing of a person and have learners identify as many parts of the body as they can.

PRESENTATION

1. Have learners read and discuss the Purpose Statement. For more information see "Purpose Statement" on page viii.

2. Focus attention on the illustration. Encourage learners to say as much as they can about it. Write their ideas on the board and/or restate them in acceptable English.

3. Have teams read the Team Work instructions. Focus attention on the Word Bank. If necessary, model pronunciation. Then have teams complete the activity. If learners need help, encourage them to consult other teams. Have team reporters share their answers with the class.

4. Have learners read the Partner Work instructions. Then have pairs complete the activity. Have learners switch partners and repeat the activity. Supply any language needed. Have one or two partners present their dialogs to the class.

5. Have the class read the Survey instructions. Make sure everyone knows what to do. Have the class choose a learner to record the information on the board. For more information see "Survey" on page viii.

FOLLOW-UP

Sick Days: Have learners work together to create a table showing the number of days they have had to miss work this year due to illness or injury. Have learners discuss the table.

♦ Help teams use the information in the chart to create a bar graph that shows the total number of days missed due to illness and injury. One bar is labeled *injury;* the other bar is labeled *illness.* Have learners discuss the graph.

WORKBOOK

Unit 8, Exercises 2A–2B

Talk About It | Calling 911

PRACTICE THE DIALOG

A This is the 911 operator. May I have your name and phone number?

B Marta Roca. 555-9021.

A What's the emergency, Marta?

B There's a fire in the back of the building!

A What's the address?

B 765 Long Street. It's the Roca Laundry Service.

A That's 765 Long Street. I'm sending the fire department right away.

B Please hurry!

Useful Language

immediately/right away

There's a fire/an accident/ an injury.

Please send an ambulance/ the police/a fire truck.

PARTNER WORK

Look at the pictures. Take turns being the caller or the 911 operator. Call about these emergencies. Use the dialog and the Useful Language above.

ASAP PROJECT

As a class, create a set of emergency procedures for your workplace or school. Include procedures for fires and bad weather. Make a list of emergency telephone numbers. Complete this project as you work through this unit.

Unit 8

89

WORKFORCE SKILLS (page 89)

Handle an emergency

★ ★ ★ ★ ★

ASAP PROJECT

Have learners read the instructions. Discuss the project and its purpose with learners. Make sure that everyone understands. Help learners assign themselves to teams based upon their knowledge, skills, interests, or other personal strengths. Have each team select a leader, and have the team leaders or the whole class select an overall project leader. Throughout the rest of the unit, allow time for learners to work on the project. Have the teams agree on a deadline when the project will be finished. For more information see "ASAP Project" on page vi.

PREPARATION

Show learners the emergency numbers page from the phone book. Ask if they have ever had to use any of the numbers listed. Encourage learners to talk about their experiences. Ask if learners keep a list of emergency numbers at work or at home. Help learners brainstorm other numbers they might need in an emergency: spouse's work number, doctor, poison control center, baby-sitter or daycare center, etc.

PRESENTATION

1. Have learners read and discuss the Purpose Statement. For more information see "Purpose Statement" on page viii.

2. Present the dialog. See "Presenting a Dialog" on page ix.

3. Focus attention on the illustrations. Encourage learners to say as much as they can about them. Have them identify the emergency depicted in each. Focus attention on the Useful Language box. Help learners read the words and phrases. If necessary, model pronunciation. Then have learners read the Partner Work instructions and complete the activity. Have learners switch partners and repeat the activity. Have one or two pairs present their dialogs to the class.

FOLLOW-UP

Calling 911: Have teams of learners brainstorm a list of emergency situations that might occur at work or at

home. Then have learners decide which situations warrant calling 911 and which do not.

♦ Have team reporters share their ideas with the class. Have the class create a poster telling when to call 911 and the information they should be prepared to give the 911 operator.

WORKBOOK

Unit 8, Exercise 3

WORKFORCE SKILLS (page 90)

Describe injuries and illnesses

★   ★   ★   ★   ★

 **Keep Talking** ⋯ Describing an injury or illness

PARTNER WORK

What's wrong? Look at the pictures. Say what you think is wrong with each person.

  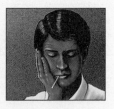

PRACTICE THE DIALOG

Galena is injured at work. She describes the injury to the company nurse.

A What's the matter?

B I cut my finger.

A Does it hurt?

B Not too much, but it's bleeding.

A Well, it doesn't look too serious. I'll put a bandage on it.

B Thanks.

Useful Language

What's wrong?

I have a broken arm/wrist/leg.

I hurt my back.

I have a fever/temperature/ burn.

I have a headache/ stomachache/toothache.

I feel sick.

It hurts.

PARTNER WORK

You are one of the people in the pictures. Tell your partner what's wrong and how you were injured or became ill. Use the dialog and the Useful Language above.

Personal Dictionary ⟩ Health and Safety ⋯

Write the words and phrases that you need to know.

_____

_____

_____

90   Unit 8

 Personal Dictionary

Have learners add the words in their Personal Dictionary to their *Workforce Writing Dictionary*. For more information see "Workforce Writing Dictionary" on page v.

PREPARATION

Have learners associate illnesses with parts of the body, such as stomach— stomachache. Use peer-teaching to clarify unfamiliar vocabulary.

PRESENTATION

1. Have learners read and discuss the Purpose Statement. For more information see "Purpose Statement" on page viii.

2. Focus attention on the pictures. Have learners say where the people are and whether they are sick or injured.

3. Have partners read the Partner Work instructions. Make sure each pair knows what to do. Have one or two pairs share their answers with the class.

 4. Present the dialog. See "Presenting a Dialog" on page ix.

5. Have partners read the instructions for Partner Work and complete the activity. Encourage learners to use the phrases in the Useful Language box to change the dialog. Have learners switch partners and repeat. Have several pairs present their dialogs to the class.

6. Have learners read the Personal Dictionary instructions. Remind learners to continue to add words to their dictionaries throughout the unit.

FOLLOW-UP

Staying Healthy: Help learners make a list of minor illnesses on the board, such as stomachache, headache, and cold.

Ask learners about ways to prevent and treat these ailments.

♦ Have learners choose one of the illnesses on the board and write two or three sentences about how to treat or prevent it. Have volunteers read their sentences to the class.

WORKBOOK

Unit 8, Exercise 4

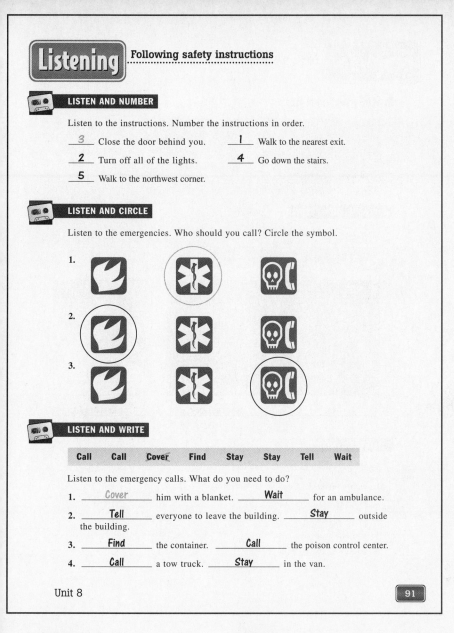

Listening — Following safety instructions

LISTEN AND NUMBER

Listen to the instructions. Number the instructions in order.

_3_ Close the door behind you. _1_ Walk to the nearest exit.

_2_ Turn off all of the lights. _4_ Go down the stairs.

_5_ Walk to the northwest corner.

LISTEN AND CIRCLE

Listen to the emergencies. Who should you call? Circle the symbol.

LISTEN AND WRITE

| Call | Call | Cover | Find | Stay | Stay | Tell | Wait |

Listen to the emergency calls. What do you need to do?

1. _Cover_ him with a blanket. _Wait_ for an ambulance.

2. _Tell_ everyone to leave the building. _Stay_ outside the building.

3. _Find_ the container. _Call_ the poison control center.

4. _Call_ a tow truck. _Stay_ in the van.

Unit 8

91

Handle an emergency

Follow safety instructions

★ ★ ★ ★ ★

SCANS Note

Workplace safety depends on the cooperation of management and employees. It is important for the safety and health of coworkers for employees to follow all safety rules and report any safety hazard or injury to a supervisor. Encourage learners to talk about how and to whom they report safety issues at work.

PREPARATION

1. Use the emergency numbers page of a local telephone book to show learners the symbols for fire department, ambulance, and poison control center. Help learners associate the kind of emergency with each symbol.

2. Review imperatives if necessary. Give an instruction to a learner such as, *Close the door and turn off the lights.* Continue this to review the imperatives **call, cover, find, stay, tell,** and **wait.**

PRESENTATION

1. Have learners read and discuss the Purpose Statement. For more information see "Purpose Statement" on page viii.

 2. Have learners read the Listen and Number instructions. Then have them read the answer choices. Have learners speculate about what kind of emergency it is. Then play the tape or read the Listening Transcript aloud two or more times as learners complete the activity. Have learners check their work. See "Presenting a Listening Activity" on page ix.

 3. Have learners read the Listen and Circle instructions. Have them identify each of the symbols. Follow the procedures in 2.

 4. Have learners read the Listen and Write instructions. Focus attention on the verbs in the Word Bank. Follow the procedures in 2.

FOLLOW-UP

Emergency Procedure: Describe an emergency situation, such as a fire or power failure. Write the emergency on the board. Divide the class into two teams. Have each team brainstorm a list of emergency procedures similar to the ones in Listen and Write. Have team reporters present their teams' ideas to the class.

♦ Have the teams work together to come up with a final set of procedures and write them on a poster. Post the procedures.

WORKBOOK

Unit 8, Exercise 5

WORKFORCE SKILLS (pages 92–93)

Describe an illness or injury

★   ★   ★   ★   ★

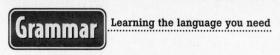

Grammar — Learning the language you need

A. Study the Examples

How	do	I we you they	feel?
	does	he she it	

I We You They	feel	fine.
He She It	feels	

HOW DO THEY FEEL?

Write how you think they feel.

sick	happy	tired	sad

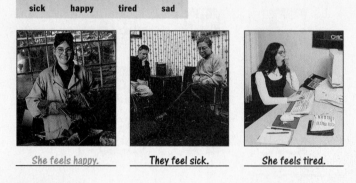

She feels happy.   They feel sick.   She feels tired.

PARTNER WORK

Read each situation. How do you feel? What do you do? Talk with your partner.

1. Your boss thanks you for your hard work.
2. You have a stomachache.
3. You are late to work in the morning.
4. You see an accident at work.
5. You are employee of the month.

afraid	nervous
angry	sick
happy	terrible

92   Unit 8

PREPARATION

1. Review the language in the grammar boxes with learners before they open their books, if necessary.

2. Present or review adjectives for feelings: *happy, nervous, tired, angry.* Pantomime each feeling and ask learners to say how you are feeling.

PRESENTATION

1. Have learners read and discuss the Purpose Statement. For more information see "Purpose Statement" on page viii.

2. Have learners read the grammar boxes in A. Have learners use the language in the boxes to say as many sentences as possible. Tell learners that they can use the grammar boxes throughout the unit to review or check sentence structures.

3. Have learners read the instructions for How Do They Feel and complete the activity. Have learners check each other's work in pairs. Ask a few learners to read their answers aloud while the rest of the class checks their work.

4. Have partners read the Partner Work instructions and complete the activity. Have several pairs share their ideas with the rest of the class.

B. Study the Examples

I	have	the flu.
We		
You		
They		
She	has	
He		

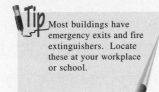

Tip Most buildings have emergency exits and fire extinguishers. Locate these at your workplace or school.

COMPLETE THE SENTENCES

Look at the pictures. Complete the sentences.

1. _____They have_____ the flu.

2. _____She has_____ a broken arm.

3. _____He has_____ a burn.

4. _____You have_____ a fever.

TEAM WORK

What do you do when you or someone in your family is sick?
What do you do when you are sick or injured at work or school?

Unit 8

93

---

5. Focus attention on the grammar box in B. Follow the procedures in 2.

6. Have learners read the instructions for Complete the Sentences. If necessary, model the first item. Then have learners complete the activity independently. Have several learners read their answers aloud as the rest of the class checks their answers.

7. Have learners read the instructions for Team Work. Make sure everyone knows what to do. Allow learners to complete the activity. Have team reporters present their teams' ideas to the rest of the class.

Tip Have learners read the Tip independently. Have learners discuss how the advice will help them. For more information, see "Presenting a Tip" on page ix.

FOLLOW-UP

Role-Play: Write a list of ailments on the board. Ask one learner, *What's the matter?* That learner chooses an illness and replies, *I have a (cold).* Ask another learner, *What's the matter?* That learner replies, *I have the (flu) and he has a (cold).* Continue until a learner can't name all of the illnesses.

♦ Have pairs or small groups of learners choose one ailment and use it to create and role-play a dialog in which one person is not feeling well and the other asks what's the matter. Have several learners present their dialogs to the class.

WORKBOOK

Unit 8, Exercises 6A–6C

BLACKLINE MASTERS

Blackline Master: Unit 8

Read safety signs

Follow safety instructions

★　　★　　★　　★　　★

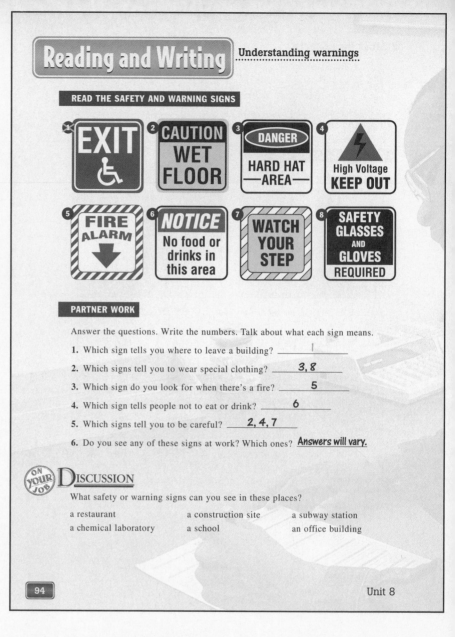

Reading and Writing Understanding warnings

READ THE SAFETY AND WARNING SIGNS

1. **EXIT** ♿
2. **CAUTION WET FLOOR**
3. **DANGER HARD HAT AREA**
4. **High Voltage KEEP OUT**
5. **FIRE ALARM** ↓
6. **NOTICE No food or drinks in this area**
7. **WATCH YOUR STEP**
8. **SAFETY GLASSES AND GLOVES REQUIRED**

PARTNER WORK

Answer the questions. Write the numbers. Talk about what each sign means.

1. Which sign tells you where to leave a building? _____1_____

2. Which signs tell you to wear special clothing? _____3, 8_____

3. Which sign do you look for when there's a fire? _____5_____

4. Which sign tells people not to eat or drink? _____6_____

5. Which signs tell you to be careful? _____2, 4, 7_____

6. Do you see any of these signs at work? Which ones? _Answers will vary._

 DISCUSSION

What safety or warning signs can you see in these places?

a restaurant	a construction site	a subway station
a chemical laboratory	a school	an office building

94　　　　　　　　　　　　　　　　　　　　　　　　　　Unit 8

PREPARATION

Draw some simple universal symbols used in safety signs: crossed-out circle meaning *no*, lightning bolt for electricity, flames for flammable, stair silhouette for stairs, etc. Help learners identify the symbols and say where they might see each sign. Supply any language needed.

PRESENTATION

1. Have learners read and discuss the Purpose Statement. For more information see "Purpose Statement" on page viii.

2. Have learners preview the safety and warning signs before they begin. Encourage learners to say everything they can about the signs. Write their ideas on the board and/or restate them in acceptable English.

3. Have learners look at the Partner Work instructions. If necessary, model the first item. Then have learners complete the activity. Have learners divide the signs into two groups: signs that warn you about dangerous situations and signs that give you general information. Have one or two pairs share their answers with the class.

4. Have learners read the Discussion instructions. Make sure everyone knows what to do. Then have learners work in teams to figure out what kinds of signs they might find in each place. Tell learners they can include other safety signs they might be familiar with but are not shown on the page. Have team reporters share their answers with the class.

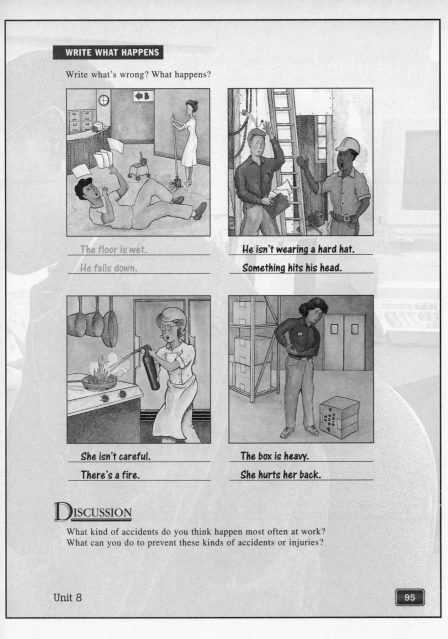

WRITE WHAT HAPPENS

Write what's wrong? What happens?

The floor is wet.
He falls down.

He isn't wearing a hard hat.
Something hits his head.

She isn't careful.
There's a fire.

The box is heavy.
She hurts her back.

DISCUSSION

What kind of accidents do you think happen most often at work?
What can you do to prevent these kinds of accidents or injuries?

Unit 8

95

Teaching Note

Learners can receive first aid and CPR training from the Red Cross or from local hospitals. Bring in a list of places and numbers learners can call if they want to learn more.

5. Have teams read the Write What Happens instructions and complete the activity. Have several groups read their answers aloud while the rest of the class checks their answers. Accept all reasonable answers. Ask learners to suggest ways the people can avoid the problems.

6. Have learners read the Discussion instructions. Make sure everyone knows what to do. Then have learners work in teams to brainstorm lists of common accidents and the best ways to prevent them. Have team reporters share their ideas with the class.

FOLLOW-UP

Scavenger Hunt: Before class compile a list of safety signs located in or near your classroom. These can include signs such as, Exit, Wet Floor, Keep Fire

Door Closed, etc. Divide the class into teams. Give each team a copy of the list. Send them out to find all the signs on the list. Be sure to tell learners the limits of the search area. Have teams check off each sign on the list as they find it. The team that completes the scavenger hunt first wins.

♦ Ask teams to make a list of safety and health signs from their workplace. Add these to the scavenger hunt list and post the class list.

WORKBOOK

Unit 8, Exercises 7A–7C

Extension ·· Reading safety instructions

READ THE FIRE SAFETY PROCEDURES

IN CASE OF FIRE

1. Pull the nearest fire alarm.
2. Use the map to find the nearest exit.
3. Exit the building quickly, but DO NOT run.
4. DO NOT use the elevators. Use the stairs.
5. Cross the street in front of the building. Meet with your supervisor.
6. DO NOT go back into the building for any reason.
7. Follow all the instructions given by your supervisor and the fire department.

ANSWER THE QUESTIONS

1. What do you do first if there is a fire? _____ *pull the fire alarm* _____
2. Can you return to the building to get your tools? _____ *no* _____
3. Do you use the elevator or the stairs during a fire? _____ *the stairs* _____
4. Where do you meet your supervisor? _____ *across the street* _____

PARTNER WORK

What other kinds of emergencies can there be? Talk about safety procedures you would follow in these situations:

1. There is a tornado or other weather emergency.
2. The electricity has gone out all over the building.

 *Culture Notes*

Do the employees where you work know first aid or CPR? Where can you get this kind of training? Do you think it is important for people to have these skills? Why?

96   Unit 8

PREPARATION

1. Present or review **stairs** and **elevator** by pantomiming climbing stairs or drawing stairs on the board. Ask learners if they know another way to go from floor to floor in a building. Present **electricity** by showing learners the Danger High Voltage sign and have them talk about the danger associated with it.

2. If there are fire safety procedures posted in or near your classroom, have learners look at them. Have they noticed them before? If there is an exit route map? Have the class practice following the route out of the building.

PRESENTATION

1. Have learners read and discuss the Purpose Statement.

2. Have learners read and discuss the Fire Safety Procedures. Write their ideas on the board or restate them in acceptable English.

3. Have learners work in pairs or small groups to complete Answer the Questions. Have several learners read their answers aloud while the rest of the class checks their answers.

4. Have pairs of learners read the instructions for Partner Work and complete the activity. Have several pairs present their ideas to the rest of the class. Have the class name other possible emergency situations at work, school, or home and state procedures for dealing with them.

 5. Have learners read Culture Notes and talk over their responses in teams. Have team reporters share their ideas with the class.

FOLLOW-UP

What Do We Do If...? Have the class brainstorm a list of emergency situations that they might face at work or at home. Divide the class into small groups. Assign each group one emergency and have them prepare a simple set of procedures to deal with it. Supply any necessary language. Have a member of each team present its procedures to the class.

◆ Have groups exchange their procedures and make suggestions for additions or changes to each other's procedures.

WORKBOOK

Unit 8, Exercise 8

Performance Check

How well can you use the skills in this unit?

Complete the activities. Go over your work with a partner or your teacher. Then complete the Performance Review on Page 98.

SKILL 1   **IDENTIFY PARTS OF THE BODY**

Write the names of the parts of the body.

arm	mouth
chest	neck
ear	nose
eye	shoulder
finger	stomach
hand	throat
head	wrist

shoulder   head

chest   eye

stomach   ear

arm   nose

wrist   mouth

hand   throat

finger   neck

SKILL 2   **HANDLE AN EMERGENCY**

Work with a partner. Call 911 to report one of these emergencies.

1. You pass a car accident on your way to work.

2. There is a fire in the kitchen where you work.

3. One of your coworkers got gasoline on her face.

SKILL 3   **DESCRIBE AN INJURY OR ILLNESS**

What's wrong with the people? Tell your partner or your teacher.

Unit 8   97

PRESENTATION

Use any of the procedures in "Evaluation" on page x with pages 97 and 98. Record individuals' results on the Unit 8 Individual Competency Chart. Record the class's results on the Class Cumulative Competency Chart.

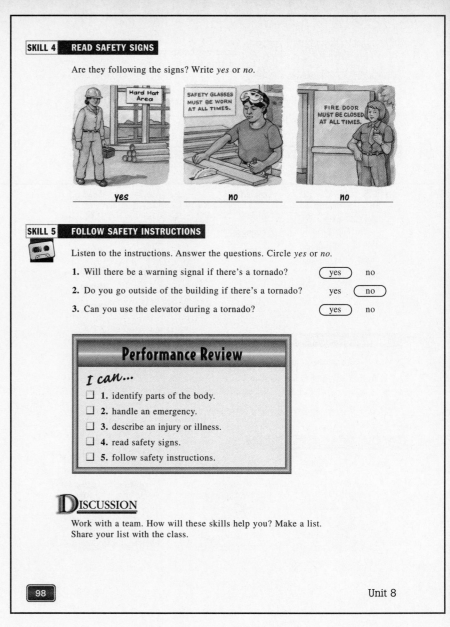

SKILL 4 | **READ SAFETY SIGNS**

Are they following the signs? Write *yes* or *no*.

yes   no   no

SKILL 5 | **FOLLOW SAFETY INSTRUCTIONS**

Listen to the instructions. Answer the questions. Circle *yes* or *no*.

1. Will there be a warning signal if there's a tornado?   (yes)   no

2. Do you go outside of the building if there's a tornado?   yes   (no)

3. Can you use the elevator during a tornado?   (yes)   no

Performance Review

I can...

☐ **1.** identify parts of the body.

☐ **2.** handle an emergency.

☐ **3.** describe an injury or illness.

☐ **4.** read safety signs.

☐ **5.** follow safety instructions.

DISCUSSION

Work with a team. How will these skills help you? Make a list. Share your list with the class.

98   Unit 8

PRESENTATION

Follow the instructions on page 97.

INFORMAL WORKPLACE-SPECIFIC ASSESSMENT

Ask learners to name one or two safety procedures from their workplaces.

WORKBOOK

Unit 8, Exercise 9

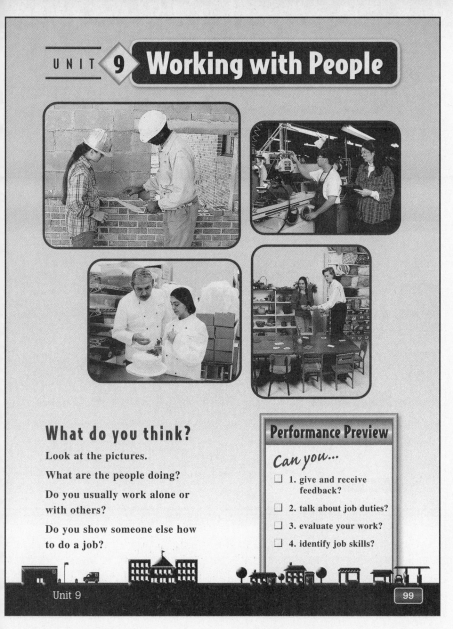

UNIT 9 Working with People

What do you think?

Look at the pictures.

What are the people doing?

Do you usually work alone or with others?

Do you show someone else how to do a job?

Performance Preview

Can you...

☐ 1. give and receive feedback?

☐ 2. talk about job duties?

☐ 3. evaluate your work?

☐ 4. identify job skills?

Unit 9   99

Unit 9 Overview
—SCANS Competencies—

★ Work on teams

★ Evaluate performance and provide feedback

★ Allocate human resources

Workforce Skills

● Give and receive feedback

● Talk about job duties

● Evaluate your work

● Identify job skills

Materials

● Pictures of people doing different jobs

● Poster paper

● Examples of employee evaluation forms

● 3 x 5 index cards

● Blank memo forms

Unit Warm-Up

To get learners thinking about the unit topic (working with people, assessing job skills and duties, and evaluating work), show the pictures of people performing different jobs. Identify the jobs and write them on the board. Ask learners about their current jobs and jobs they had before coming to the U.S.

★   ★   ★   ★   ★

WORKFORCE SKILLS (page 99)

Give and receive feedback

Talk about job duties

★   ★   ★   ★   ★

PREPARATION

1. Write **teacher** on the board and ask the class to brainstorm a list of the job duties of a teacher. Supply any language needed.

2. Have learners brainstorm a list of as many jobs as they can think of. Choose two or three and have learners speculate about what some of the duties for that job might be.

PRESENTATION

1. Focus attention on the photographs. Ask learners what the unit might be about. Write their ideas on the board and/or restate them in acceptable English.

2. Have learners identify the people and different jobs in the photographs and how the people are working together. Help learners relate the activities shown to their own jobs or personal experiences.

3. Help the learners read the questions. Discuss the questions with the class.

4. You may want to use the Performance Preview to provide learners with an overview of the skills in the unit. Have learners read the list of skills and discuss what they will learn in this unit.

FOLLOW-UP

Working Together: Have teams of learners discuss their jobs. Do they work alone or with other people? Have the teams brainstorm lists of things they do with other workers. For example, a bus-person helps a waitress by clearing the tables. Have team reporters share their ideas with the class.

♦ Have teams make lists of all the ways they help others. Post the lists.

WORKBOOK

Unit 9, Exercises 1A–1B

WORKFORCE SKILLS (page 100)

Talk about job duties

★ ★ ★ ★ ★

Teaching Note

Use this page to introduce the new language in the unit. Whenever possible, encourage peer teaching. Supply any language learners need.

Getting Started .... **Talking about job duties**

PREPARATION

Present **receptionist, security guard,** and **bellhop.** Use the pictures on the page to start a discussion about the job duties of each. Help learners associate the name of the job with the duty.

PRESENTATION

1. Have learners read and discuss the Purpose Statement. For more information see "Purpose Statement" on page viii.

2. Encourage learners to say as much as they can about the illustrations. Write their ideas on the board and/or restate them in acceptable English.

3. Have teams read the Team Work instructions and complete the activity. If learners need help, encourage them to consult other teams. Have team reporters share their answers with the class.

4. Have partners read the Partner Work instructions and complete the activity. Supply any language needed. Have one or two partners present their dialogs to the class.

 5. Have learners read the Survey instructions. Make sure everyone knows what to do. Then have learners complete the activity. For more information see "Survey" on page viii.

FOLLOW-UP

Table: Help the class use the information from the Survey to create a table showing their jobs and their job duties. Have learners divide the list into job duties they share with others and those they do alone. Have learners discuss the table.

♦ Ask learners to talk about who they work with from their departments, from outside their departments, and from other companies.

WORKBOOK

Unit 9, Exercises 2A–2B

Talk About It — Giving and receiving feedback

PRACTICE THE DIALOG

A Hi, Victor. You're doing very well your first week.

B Thanks, Dave. I still have a lot to learn.

A One of your job duties is to turn off the lights at closing time. You left some of the lights on last night.

B I'm sorry.

A Don't worry about it. I'll show you tonight.

B Thanks for the help.

A Sure. Let's get started.

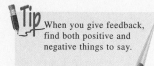
Tip When you give feedback, find both positive and negative things to say.

PARTNER WORK

You're in charge of the dishwashers at Fabulous Food Service. Your partner is a new employee. Today your partner forgot to put soap in the dishwashing machine. Talk to your partner. Use the dialog above.

ASAP PROJECT

You and your classmates work at Grand Supermarket. Choose a job at the supermarket (such as cashier, stocker, bagger). Make a chart. Team 1 writes the job duties. Team 2 writes the skills someone needs for the job. Team 3 writes the steps for training someone to do the job. Complete this project as you work through this unit.

Unit 9

`101`

WORKFORCE SKILLS (page 101)

Give and receive feedback

★   ★   ★   ★   ★

Language Note

Help learners understand that their qualifications for a job are a combination of their skills and experience, and that job duties are responsibilities they have on a job. Help learners make lists of each and discuss how skills, duties, and experience are different and how they are related.

ASAP PROJECT

Have learners read the instructions. Discuss the project and its purpose with learners. Make sure that everyone understands. Help learners assign themselves to teams based upon their knowledge, skills, interests, or other personal strengths. Have each team select a leader, and have the team leaders or the whole class select an overall project leader. Throughout the rest of the unit, allow time for learners to work on the project. Have the teams agree on a deadline when the project will be finished. For more information see "ASAP Project" on page vi.

PREPARATION

1. Present or review **feedback** by giving examples of feedback in the context of learning English: *You have good listening skills. You need to work on your pronunciation.* Associate the example of feedback at school to feedback at work. Have learners discuss feedback they have received on the job.

2. Use the pictures from the opener, or pictures you provide, to show people working together or receiving training. Name each job and talk about how the people are helping each other.

PRESENTATION

1. Have learners read and discuss the Purpose Statement. For more information see "Purpose Statement" on page viii.

2. Encourage learners to say as much as they can about the photograph. Have them identify the jobs of the people shown and speculate about their work relationship (trainer/trainee; supervisor/employee). Then present the dialog. See "Presenting a Dialog" on page ix.

3. Have partners read the Partner Work instructions and complete the activity. Have learners switch partners and repeat the activity. Have one or two pairs present their conversations to the class.

Tip Have learners read the Tip independently and discuss how the advice will help them. For more information see "Presenting a Tip" on page ix.

FOLLOW-UP

Positive and Negative: Have learners brainstorm a list of jobs and job duties. Then have them work in pairs to create dialogs similar to the one in Practice the Dialog about one of the jobs on the list. Have learners perform their dialogs for the class.

♦ Have pairs write their dialogs, circle the positive feedback, and underline the negative feedback.

WORKBOOK

Unit 9, Exercises 3A–3C

WORKFORCE SKILLS (page 102)

Talk about job duties

Identify job skills

★   ★   ★   ★   ★

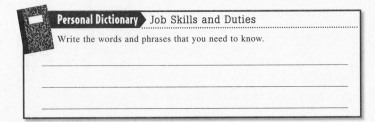

Keep Talking — Identifying job skills

PRACTICE THE DIALOG

A and B are looking for an employee to work on a new project.

A We're getting some new machines. Who's a good mechanic?

B Jean. She's really good at fixing machines.

A Great. Let's meet with Jean.

Useful Language

We're getting very busy.

We need another data entry clerk.

We need a new child care worker.

PARTNER WORK

Match the jobs to the people. Write the letter.

b   **1.** medical technician

d   **2.** auto mechanic

e   **3.** data entry clerk

c   **4.** warehouse worker

a   **5.** child care worker

a. Li enjoys working with children.

b. Marta can use X-ray equipment.

c. Ed can drive a forklift.

d. Marcos can work with tools and fix engines.

e. Sabrina knows how to use computers.

Now talk about these people and their jobs. Use the dialog and the Useful Language above.

Personal Dictionary — Job Skills and Duties

Write the words and phrases that you need to know.

_____

_____

_____

102   Unit 9

Personal Dictionary

Have learners add the words in their Personal Dictionary to their *Workforce Writing Dictionary.* For more information see "Workforce Writing Dictionary" on page v.

PREPARATION

1. Write **skills** on the board and list a few skills needed to be a good English teacher. Have learners name one or two skills needed to do their jobs.

2. Use the pictures of people in different jobs and pantomime to present or review **auto mechanic, medical technician, data entry clerk, child care worker,** and **warehouse worker.**

PRESENTATION

1. Have learners read and discuss the Purpose Statement. For more information see "Purpose Statement" on page viii.

2. Present the dialog. See "Presenting a Dialog" on page ix.

3. Have partners read the Partner Work instructions and complete the activity. Then have learners read the directions after the matching activity. Focus attention on the Useful Language box. Have pairs complete the activity and then switch partners and repeat. Have several pairs present their dialogs to the class.

4. Have learners read the Personal Dictionary instructions and complete the activity. Remind learners to continue to add words to their dictionaries throughout the unit.

FOLLOW-UP

Transferable Skills: Have learners make lists of their prior jobs and the skills needed to do each job. Then have learners work together in small groups.

Have each member of the group share their experiences and skills and the rest of the group brainstorm a short list of possible jobs the learner could do. Have volunteers share their possible jobs with the class.

♦ Have the class make a large chart showing all the skills they have come up with and the different jobs associated with each skill.

WORKBOOK

Unit 9, Exercise 4

 **Listening** Identifying strengths and weaknesses

 LISTEN AND WRITE

Listen to the dialogs. Who can do the job? Write the letter of the picture.

1. __a__ 2. __b__ 3. __c__

DELIVERY

a   b   c

 LISTEN AND CIRCLE

Circle the letter of the statement that describes each employee's performance.

1. **(a.)** Cindy gets to work on time every day.

   b. Cindy is sometimes late to work.

2. **(a.)** Enrique is usually polite to customers on the phone.

   b. Enrique is not polite to customers on the phone.

3. **a.** Hans is not a good driver.

   (b.) Hans drives safely.

4. **a.** Maria always enjoys working with other employees.

   (b.) Maria doesn't always enjoy working with other employees.

DISCUSSION

Imagine that you're giving the employees in the dialogs feedback. What do you say? How can each person do a better job? Listen to the dialogs again if you need help.

Unit 9   103

PREPARATION

1. Present or review the adverbs of frequency **sometimes, usually,** and **always** by talking about your daily activities. Choose a day of the week and have learners discuss things they usually, sometimes, and always do on that day at work or at school: *I always sweep the floors on Monday. I sometimes wash the floors on Monday.*

2. Have learners identify the jobs shown in each illustration and speculate about the skills or experience needed to do each job.

PRESENTATION

1. Have learners read and discuss the Purpose Statement. For more information see "Purpose Statement" on page viii.

 2. Have learners read the Listen and Write instructions. Make sure that everyone understands the instructions. Then play the tape or read the Listening Transcript aloud two or more times as learners complete the activity. Have learners check their work.

 3. Have learners read the Listen and Circle instructions. Then have them read the answer choices and decide which of the answer choices show positive feedback and which are things that need improvement. Then play the tape or read the Listening Transcript aloud one or more times as learners complete the activity. Have learners check their work.

4. Have learners read the Discussion instructions and then work in pairs to

practice giving feedback and making suggestions for job improvement. Have several pairs share their ideas with the class.

FOLLOW-UP

Make a Suggestion: Have the class work in pairs. Each partner should name one thing they would most like to improve about their job performance; the other partner makes a suggestion. A: *I need to improve my punctuality. I sometimes arrive a few minutes late.* B: *Set your alarm clock a half hour earlier.*

♦ Have learners change partners and repeat. Have them compare the different suggestions.

WORKBOOK

Unit 9, Exercises 5A–5B

WORKFORCE SKILLS (page 103)

Give and receive feedback
Talk about job duties
Identify job skills

★   ★   ★   ★   ★

WORKFORCE SKILLS (pages 104–105)

Talk about job duties

Evaluate your work

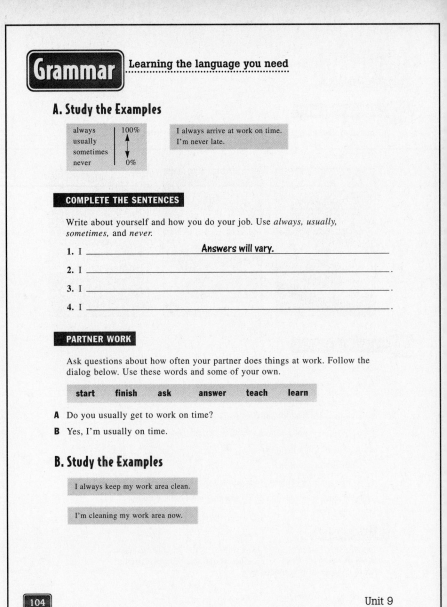

Grammar Learning the language you need

A. Study the Examples

always	100%
usually	
sometimes	
never	0%

I always arrive at work on time.
I'm never late.

COMPLETE THE SENTENCES

Write about yourself and how you do your job. Use *always, usually, sometimes,* and *never.*

1. I _____ **Answers will vary.** _____

2. I _____.

3. I _____.

4. I _____.

PARTNER WORK

Ask questions about how often your partner does things at work. Follow the dialog below. Use these words and some of your own.

start	finish	ask	answer	teach	learn

A Do you usually get to work on time?

B Yes, I'm usually on time.

B. Study the Examples

I always keep my work area clean.

I'm cleaning my work area now.

104

Unit 9

Language Note

*Use the words **now** and **every day** to help contrast the present progressive and the simple present.*

PREPARATION

Review the language in the grammar boxes with learners before they open their books, if necessary.

PRESENTATION

1. Have learners read and discuss the Purpose Statement.

2. Have learners read the grammar boxes in A. Then have learners use the language in the boxes to say as many sentences as possible.

3. Have learners read the instructions for Complete the Sentences and complete the activity independently. Have learners check each other's work in pairs. Ask several learners to share their sentences with the class.

4. Have learners read the instructions for Partner Work. Focus learners' attention on the word bank. Review the verbs and model the activity if necessary. Then have pairs complete the activity. Ask several pairs to present their dialogs to the rest of the class.

5. Focus attention on the grammar boxes in B. Follow the procedures in 2.

COMPLETE THE SENTENCES

Use the language in B.

1. I usually _____take_____ (**take**) the bus to work.

2. Right now I _'m waiting_ (**wait**) for the bus.

3. Sometimes my sister _____drives_____ (**drive**) me to work.

4. I never _____walk_____ (**walk**) to work.

5. I always _____arrive_____ (**arrive**) at work on time.

WRITE SENTENCES

Use the pairs of words to write your own sentences. Follow the language in B.

1. usually/work _____I usually work on Saturdays._____

2. work/now _____I'm working now._____

3. always/take _____I always take a break at lunch._____

4. take/now _____I'm taking a break now._____

5. sometimes/arrive _____I sometimes arrive at work early._____

6. arrive/now _____I'm arriving early now._____

PARTNER WORK

Imagine you're at work. Talk about what you usually do and what you're doing now.

---

6. Focus learners' attention on the illustration. Have learners say as much as they can about it. Write their sentences on the board and/or restate them in acceptable English.

7. Have learners read the instructions for Complete the Sentences and complete the activity independently. Have a different learner read each sentence aloud as the rest of the class checks their answers.

8. Have learners read the instructions for Write Sentences and complete the activity independently. Have learners check each other's work in pairs. Ask several learners to read their sentences aloud.

9. Have partners read the Partner Work instructions. Make sure everyone understands what to do. Allow learners to complete the activity. Have several pairs share their ideas with the class.

FOLLOW-UP

What's My Line? Write several job activities on 3 x 5 index cards (driving, vacuuming, making beds) and on the board. Have a learner come to the front of the class and select a slip at random. That learner then pantomimes the action. The rest of the class says what he or she is doing: *He's driving.*

♦ Have learners brainstorm a list of job titles associated with each action: *taxi driver, bus driver, delivery person.*

WORKBOOK

Unit 9, Exercises 6A– 6C

BLACKLINE MASTERS

Blackline Master: Unit 9

WORKFORCE SKILLS (pages 106–107)

Talk about job duties

Give and receive feedback

★　　★　　★　　★　　★

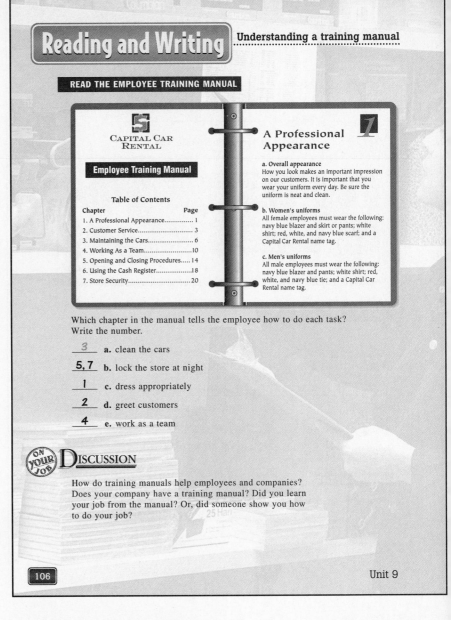

Reading and Writing · · · · · · · · · · Understanding a training manual

READ THE EMPLOYEE TRAINING MANUAL

5 CAPITAL CAR RENTAL

Employee Training Manual

Table of Contents

1 A Professional Appearance

a. Overall appearance
How you look makes an important impression on our customers. It is important that you wear your uniform every day. Be sure the uniform is neat and clean.

b. Women's uniforms
All female employees must wear the following: navy blue blazer and skirt or pants; white shirt; red, white, and navy blue scarf; and a Capital Car Rental name tag.

c. Men's uniforms
All male employees must wear the following: navy blue blazer and pants; white shirt; red, white, and navy blue tie; and a Capital Car Rental name tag.

Which chapter in the manual tells the employee how to do each task? Write the number.

   _3_   **a.** clean the cars

   _5, 7_   **b.** lock the store at night

   _1_   **c.** dress appropriately

   _2_   **d.** greet customers

   _4_   **e.** work as a team

ON YOUR JOB DISCUSSION

How do training manuals help employees and companies? Does your company have a training manual? Did you learn your job from the manual? Or, did someone show you how to do your job?

106   Unit 9

PREPARATION

1. Present or review **manual, appearance,** and **uniform.** Remind learners that they have already learned a lot about work appearance and uniforms in Unit 6. Have them recall as much as they can about appropriate dress for work.

2. Have learners look at the table of contents at the front of their books. Help them generalize the kind of information found in a table of contents, such as chapter titles, chapter numbers, and page numbers. Prompt a discussion about why it's a good idea to look at the table of contents before reading a book or manual.

PRESENTATION

1. Have learners read and discuss the Purpose Statement.

2. Have learners look at the training manual and say everything they can about it. Write their ideas on the board and/or restate them in acceptable English.

3. Have learners look at the Read the Employee Training Manual instructions and complete the activity independently. Have learners review each other's work in pairs. Ask several learners to share their answers with the class while the rest of the class checks their answers.

 4. Have learners read the Discussion instructions and work in teams to talk about how they learned to do their jobs. Have team reporters share their ideas with the class.

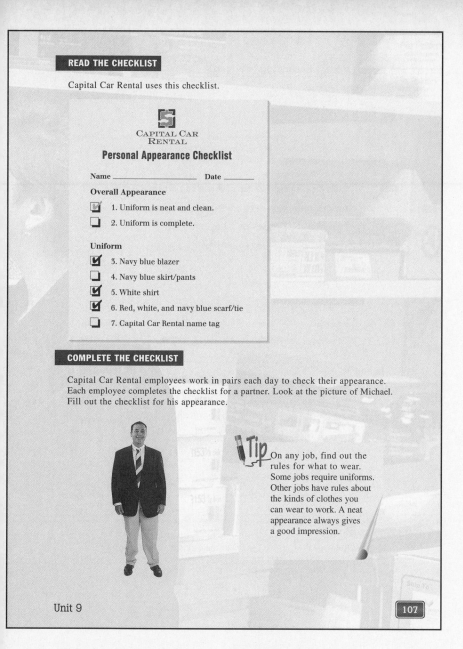

READ THE CHECKLIST

Capital Car Rental uses this checklist.

CAPITAL CAR RENTAL

Personal Appearance Checklist

Name _____ Date _____

Overall Appearance

☑ 1. Uniform is neat and clean.

☐ 2. Uniform is complete.

Uniform

☑ 3. Navy blue blazer

☐ 4. Navy blue skirt/pants

☑ 5. White shirt

☑ 6. Red, white, and navy blue scarf/tie

☐ 7. Capital Car Rental name tag

COMPLETE THE CHECKLIST

Capital Car Rental employees work in pairs each day to check their appearance. Each employee completes the checklist for a partner. Look at the picture of Michael. Fill out the checklist for his appearance.

Tip On any job, find out the rules for what to wear. Some jobs require uniforms. Other jobs have rules about the kinds of clothes you can wear to work. A neat appearance always gives a good impression.

Unit 9

107

5. Have learners look at the checklist and say everything they can about it. Write their ideas on the board and/or restate them in acceptable English.

6. Have learners read the Complete the Checklist instructions and complete the activity independently. Have learners review each other's work in pairs. Ask several learners to share their answers with the class.

Tip Have learners read the Tip independently. Have them discuss other things that make a good impression at work, such as punctuality, flexibility, and responsibility.

FOLLOW-UP

Make a Checklist: Have learners make a personal checklist for their daily personal and job routines. Have several learners present their lists to the class.

♦ Have learners work in pairs to sort their checklists. They can order them chronologically or by importance. Post learners' final checklists.

WORKBOOK

Unit 9, Exercises 7A–7C

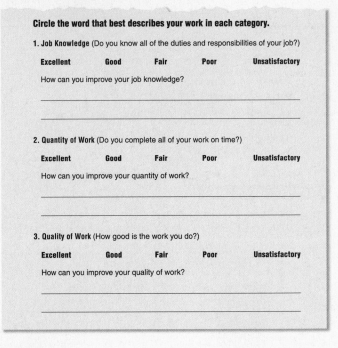

Evaluating your work

WRITE A SELF EVALUATION

Your supervisor wants you to evaluate your work. Look at the form.
Fill it out about yourself. Then talk over your evaluation with a partner.
Talk about what is good and what can be improved.

Circle the word that best describes your work in each category.

1. Job Knowledge (Do you know all of the duties and responsibilities of your job?)

Excellent　　Good　　Fair　　Poor　　Unsatisfactory

How can you improve your job knowledge?

_____

_____

2. Quantity of Work (Do you complete all of your work on time?)

Excellent　　Good　　Fair　　Poor　　Unsatisfactory

How can you improve your quantity of work?

_____

_____

3. Quality of Work (How good is the work you do?)

Excellent　　Good　　Fair　　Poor　　Unsatisfactory

How can you improve your quality of work?

_____

_____

Culture Notes

How well do you do your job? Are there some things you can improve?
What are they? Do you want more training? Can you talk to your supervisor
about ways to improve your work or to get more training?

108　　　　　　　　　　　　　　　　　　　Unit 9

SCANS Note

Learners may or may not be formally evaluated at work. However, informal evaluations are always being conducted. Have learners discuss who evaluates their work and whether they are formally or informally evaluated. Have learners discuss whether they feel comfortable talking to their supervisor about ways to improve their job performance.

PREPARATION

1. Explain the meanings of **excellent, good, fair, poor,** and **unsatisfactory.** Write the words on the board in random order. Help learners order the adjectives from positive to negative.

2. Write the three questions from the job evaluation on the board. Have learners work in pairs to ask and answer the questions. Help learners make associations between the questions and the words **knowledge, quantity,** and **quality.**

PRESENTATION

1. Have learners read and discuss the Purpose Statement. For more information see "Purpose Statement" on page viii.

2. Have learners preview the evaluation form. Encourage them to say everything

they can about it. Write their ideas on the board or restate them in acceptable English.

3. Have learners read the instructions for Write a Self Evaluation and complete the activity independently. Have learners review each other's work in pairs. Ask several learners to share their evaluations with the class. Encourage the class to make suggestions about how people can improve their job performance.

 4. Have learners read Culture Notes and talk over their responses in teams. Have team reporters share their ideas with the class. Ask the teams to compare each other's ideas. For more information see "Culture Notes" on page vii.

FOLLOW-UP

Improvement Plans: Divide the class into teams. Ask each team to imagine that they are on a work improvement committee. Each team is in charge of coming up with suggestions for improving work performance in one of the categories listed on the evaluation form: job knowledge, quality of work, quantity of work. Suggestions can include things such as consulting the training manual, taking classes, and having weekly meetings. Supply any language learners need to express their ideas.

♦ Help learners write their ideas in acceptable English. Have each team write their suggestions. Post the suggestions.

WORKBOOK

Unit 9, Exercise 8

 **Performance Check** How well can you use the skills in this unit?

Complete the activities. Go over your work with a partner or your teacher.
Then complete the Performance Review on Page 110.

SKILL 1 GIVE AND RECEIVE FEEDBACK

You are in charge of the general office clerks. Your partner is a new clerk
who typed some mailing labels. Your partner did a good job typing the labels,
but did not sort the labels by their zip codes. Give feedback about the work.

SKILL 2 TALK ABOUT JOB DUTIES

Make a list of all of the duties at your job or a job you want to have.
Explain your duties to your partner or your teacher. Which duties are
the most difficult? Which are the easiest?

SKILL 3 EVALUATE YOUR WORK

Circle the word that best describes your work at home, at school, or at your job.
Then explain your answers to your partner or teacher.

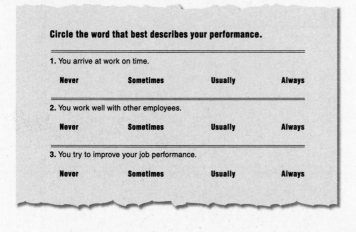

Circle the word that best describes your performance.

1. You arrive at work on time.

| Never | Sometimes | Usually | Always |

2. You work well with other employees.

| Never | Sometimes | Usually | Always |

3. You try to improve your job performance.

| Never | Sometimes | Usually | Always |

Unit 9   109

PRESENTATION

Use any of the procedures in
"Evaluation" on page x with pages 109
and 110. Record individuals' results
on the Unit 9 Individual Competency
Chart. Record the class's results on the
Class Cumulative Competency Chart.

SKILL 4   **IDENTIFY JOB SKILLS**

Match the jobs to the skills. Write the letter.

_c_   **1.** auto mechanic   **a.** likes taking care of children

_a_   **2.** day care worker   **b.** knows how to use an X-ray machine

_b_   **3.** medical technician   **c.** can fix car engines

_e_   **4.** warehouse worker   **d.** can work on a computer

_d_   **5.** data entry clerk   **e.** knows how to operate a forklift

Performance Review

I can...

☐ **1.** give and receive feedback.

☐ **2.** talk about job duties.

☐ **3.** evaluate my work.

☐ **4.** identify job skills.

DISCUSSION

Work with a team. How will your new skills help you? Make a list. Share your list with the class.

110   Unit 9

PRESENTATION

Follow the instructions on page 109.

INFORMAL WORKPLACE-SPECIFIC ASSESSMENT

Have learners comment on one job duty or skill they want to improve. Ask them how they intend to improve.

WORKBOOK

Unit 9, Exercise 9

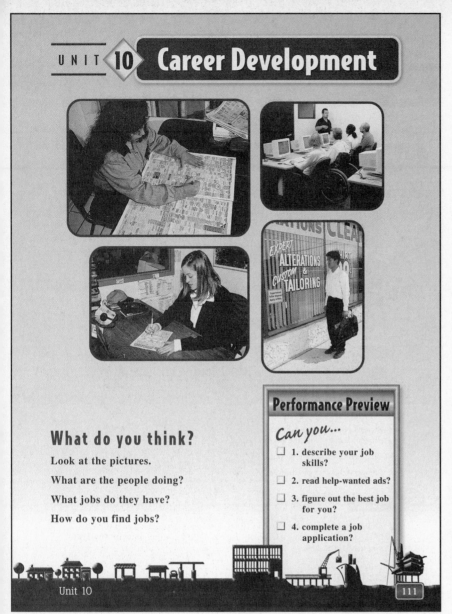

What do you think?

Look at the pictures.

What are the people doing?

What jobs do they have?

How do you find jobs?

Performance Preview

Can you...

- ☐ 1. describe your job skills?
- ☐ 2. read help-wanted ads?
- ☐ 3. figure out the best job for you?
- ☐ 4. complete a job application?

Unit 10 Overview

—SCANS Competencies—

★ Interpret and communicate information

★ Understand social systems

★ Acquire information

Workforce Skills

- Describe your job skills
- Read help-wanted ads
- Figure out the best job for you
- Complete a job application

Materials

- Pictures of people in a variety of occupations
- Samples of want ads
- Examples of help-wanted signs
- Blank job applications
- Sample catalogs or course listings for a community college or learning center

Unit Warm-Up

To get learners thinking about the unit topic (career development), show them the pictures of people in various jobs. Have them identify the jobs. Use peer teaching to clarify any unfamiliar vocabulary. Ask learners what jobs they have now. How did learners find these jobs?

★   ★   ★   ★   ★

WORKFORCE SKILLS (page 111)

Read help-wanted ads

Complete a job application

★   ★   ★   ★   ★

PREPARATION

1. Show learners the want ads and the help-wanted signs. Help them identify what they are and say where they might find each (a newspaper, the window of a store). Encourage learners to talk about other places they might look to find a job (community center job board, friends, and family).

2. Present or review **career, want ad, skills,** and **job application.** Help learners understand the relationship between job and career by talking about your own job and career.

PRESENTATION

1. Focus attention on the photographs. Ask learners what the unit might be about. Write their ideas on the board, and/or restate them in acceptable English.

2. Have learners identify what the people in the photographs are doing. Help learners relate the activities shown to their own experiences finding a job.

3. Help learners read the questions. Discuss the questions with the class.

4. You may want to use the Performance Preview to provide learners with an overview of the skills in the unit. Have learners read the list of skills and discuss what they will learn in this unit.

FOLLOW-UP

Ideal Job: Have learners work in small groups to discuss the job they would most like to have. What are the characteristics of a good job? Does the job require any special training or education? Have team reporters report to the class.

◆ Have learners work in pairs to find out about each other's jobs, asking questions to find out the name of their partner's job, the hours, the training required to do the job, and one good thing about the job. Have learners write sentences about their partner's job.

WORKBOOK

Unit 10, Exercise 1

WORKFORCE SKILLS (page 112)

Describe your job skills

★   ★   ★   ★   ★

Teaching Note

Use this page to introduce the new language in the unit. Whenever possible, encourage peer teaching. Supply any language the learners need.

Talking about your job skills

TEAM WORK

Look at the picture. What jobs do the people have? What skills do they have?

| delivery driver | construction worker | child care worker |
| grocery clerk | bus driver | police officer |

PARTNER WORK

Student A asks a question about someone in the picture.
Student B says what the person can do.

A What can a child care worker do?

B She can take care of children.

 SURVEY

Make a chart that shows everyone's jobs and skills. Write the names of all of the jobs you and your classmates have had. Next to each job write the skills you need for the job.

112   Unit 10

PREPARATION

Have learners work in groups to brainstorm a list of at least ten jobs. Have each group share their list with the rest of the class. Have a volunteer compile a master list on the board. Use the pictures of people in different occupations and peer teaching to help clarify new vocabulary.

PRESENTATION

1. Have learners read and discuss the Purpose Statement.

2. Encourage learners to say as much as they can about the illustration. Write their ideas on the board and/or restate them in acceptable English.

3. Have teams read the Team Work instructions and complete the activity. If learners need help, encourage them to consult other teams. Have team reporters share their answers with the class.

4. Have partners read the Partner Work instructions and complete the activity. Supply any language needed. Have learners switch partners and repeat the activity. Have one or two partners present their dialogs to the class.

 5. Have the class read the Survey instructions. Make sure everyone knows what to do. Then have learners complete the activity. For more information see "Survey" on page viii.

FOLLOW-UP

My Strongest Skill: Ask learners to say which of their skills is most important to them. Which skills do they want to improve?

♦ Have learners write a list of the skills they want to improve and how they hope to improve them.

WORKBOOK

Unit 10, Exercises 2A–2B

Talk About It — Describing what you want to do

PRACTICE THE DIALOG

A Hi, Bettina. How's school?

B Great, Claudette. I'm studying air conditioning repair. And you? What are you doing these days?

A I'm looking for a job. I want to be a child care worker.

B That's a good job for you. Good luck.

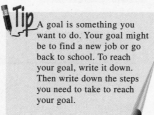

Tip A goal is something you want to do. Your goal might be to find a new job or go back to school. To reach your goal, write it down. Then write down the steps you need to take to reach your goal.

PARTNER WORK

Your partner is one of the people in the pictures. Find out what your partner is doing these days. Take turns. Follow the dialog above.

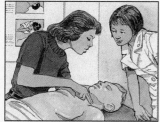
I'm studying first aid.

I'm taking truck-driving classes.

ASAP PROJECT

As a class, write a *Job Hunter's Guide*. Use the information from the Survey. Team 1 writes job titles and skills needed. Team 2 finds the names of possible employers. Team 3 organizes the information and types or writes it neatly for the guide. Complete this project as you work through this unit.

Unit 10   **113**

ASAP PROJECT

Have learners read the instructions. Discuss the project and its purpose with learners. Make sure that everyone understands. Help learners assign themselves to teams based upon their knowledge, skills, interests, or other personal strengths. Have each team select a leader, and have the team leaders or the whole class select an overall project leader. Throughout the rest of the unit, allow time for learners to work on the project. Have the teams agree on a deadline when the project will be finished. For more information see "ASAP Project" on page vi.

PREPARATION

1. Review or present the verb **want.** Ask learners to say what they want to do in the future.

PRESENTATION

1. Have learners read and discuss the Purpose Statement. For more information see "Purpose Statement" on page viii.

 2. Present the dialog. See "Presenting a Dialog" on page ix.

3. Have partners read the Partner Work instructions. Make sure everyone understands what to do. Focus attention on the illustrations. Encourage learners to say as much as they can about them. Have them identify the jobs the people might be training for. Then have learners complete the activity. Have learners switch partners and repeat the activity. Have one or two pairs present their dialogs to the class.

Tip Have learners read the Tip independently. Have learners discuss how the advice will help them. For more information see "Presenting a Tip" on page ix.

FOLLOW-UP

Choose a Class: Bring in sample catalogs or course listings from a community college or learning center. Have learners work in pairs or small groups. Each learner chooses a class he or she would like to take and thinks of one or two jobs it will help prepare him or her for. Have groups present their ideas to the class.

♦ Have pairs of learners use their course choices to create dialogs similar to the one in Practice the Dialog. Have pairs present their dialogs to the class.

WORKBOOK

Unit 10, Exercise 3

Describe your job skills

Figure out the best job for you

★   ★   ★   ★   ★

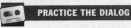
Keep Talking
Finding the best job for you

PRACTICE THE DIALOG

Student A is a career counselor. Student B is looking for a job.

A What kind of job are you looking for?

B I'd like to be carpenter.

A What job skills do you have?

B I can measure and cut wood.

A Do you have any experience?

B Yes, I was a carpenter's helper for two years.

Useful Language

drive trucks	gardener
paint houses	medical technician
bake cakes	
use X-ray machines	cook
	painter
prepare meals	baker
cut grass	delivery driver

PARTNER WORK

Ask and answer questions about jobs you would like to have. Talk about your skills. Use the dialog and the Useful Language above.

Personal Dictionary ▸ Getting the Job You Want

Write the words and phrases that you need to know.

_____

_____

_____

Unit 10

Personal Dictionary

Have learners add the words in their Personal Dictionary to their *Workforce Writing Dictionary*. For more information see "Workforce Writing Dictionary" on page v.

PREPARATION

1. Use the pictures of people in different jobs to elicit or present the occupations on the page. Have learners brainstorm as many skills associated with each job as they can.

2. Write **skill** and **experience** on the board. Ask learners about jobs they have had; write the information under the word **experience.** Have them talk again about the skills they need to do their jobs. Write their skills under the word **skills.**

PRESENTATION

1. Have learners read and discuss the Purpose Statement.

2. Have learners say as much as they can about the illustrations. Have learners speculate about the kinds of jobs the people can do.

3. Present the dialog. See "Presenting a Dialog" on page ix.

4. Have partners read the Partner Work instructions. Focus attention on the Useful Language box. Help learners read the words. If necessary, model pronunciation. Then have pairs complete the activity. Have learners change partners and repeat. Have several pairs present their dialogs to the class.

5. Have learners read the Personal Dictionary instructions and complete the activity. Remind learners to continue to add words to their dictionaries throughout the unit.

FOLLOW-UP

"I Can Do It" Challenge: Divide the class into teams to brainstorm a list of all the skills the members of the team have. Encourage learners to include a wide range of things: *Jackie can drive a truck; Manny can mow the lawn; Isabella can sew;* etc. Have teams compare their lists and cross out any items that appear on more than one list. The team with the most skills remaining wins the challenge.

♦ Have teams exchange lists, come up with one job for each skill, and write sentences: *Jackie can drive a truck. He can be a delivery person.* Post the sentences.

WORKBOOK

Unit 10, Exercise 4

English ASAP

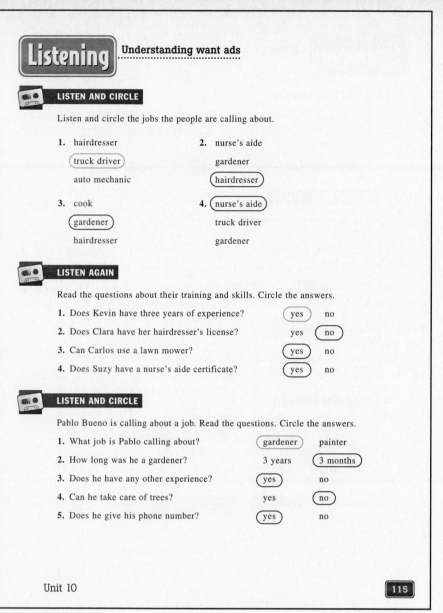

Listening — Understanding want ads

LISTEN AND CIRCLE

Listen and circle the jobs the people are calling about.

1. hairdresser
   (truck driver)
   auto mechanic

2. nurse's aide
   gardener
   (hairdresser)

3. cook
   (gardener)
   hairdresser

4. (nurse's aide)
   truck driver
   gardener

LISTEN AGAIN

Read the questions about their training and skills. Circle the answers.

1. Does Kevin have three years of experience?   (yes)   no
2. Does Clara have her hairdresser's license?   yes   (no)
3. Can Carlos use a lawn mower?   (yes)   no
4. Does Suzy have a nurse's aide certificate?   (yes)   no

LISTEN AND CIRCLE

Pablo Bueno is calling about a job. Read the questions. Circle the answers.

1. What job is Pablo calling about?   (gardener)   painter
2. How long was he a gardener?   3 years   (3 months)
3. Does he have any other experience?   (yes)   no
4. Can he take care of trees?   yes   (no)
5. Does he give his phone number?   (yes)   no

Unit 10

115

WORKFORCE SKILLS (page 115)

Describe your job skills
Figure out the best job for you

★   ★   ★   ★   ★

PREPARATION

1. Use the pictures of people in different jobs to review the names of jobs on the page and the skills associated with them.

2. Preteach **license** and **certificate** (papers from schools and government that let you do certain jobs). Review **experience, training,** and **skills.** Talk about your own job, training, educational background, and skills. Ask several learners about their jobs, training, and experience.

PRESENTATION

1. Have learners read and discuss the Purpose Statement.

 2. Have learners read the Listen and Circle instructions and the answer choices. Then play the tape or read the Listening Transcript aloud two or more times as learners complete the activity. Have learners check their work.

 3. Have learners read the instructions for Listen Again and the questions and answer choices. Follow the procedures in 2.

 4. Have learners read the instructions for Listen and Circle and the questions and answer choices. Follow the procedures in 2.

FOLLOW-UP

Find Out the Information: Have learners work in pairs. Each learner thinks of a job he or she would like to have. Then pairs role-play a telephone conversation similar to Pablo Bueno's. One learner is calling about the job; the other learner is asking about the caller's skills, experience, and training. Have several learners present their dialogs to the rest of the class.

♦ Choose one job. On several slips of paper write different levels of experience, skills, and training for that job and give the slips to learners. Have one learner conduct telephone interviews. Interviewees will answer based on the cues you have given them. Have the class decide who is best for the job based on their answers.

WORKBOOK

Unit 10, Exercise 5

Describe your job skills

★   ★   ★   ★   ★

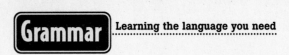

Grammar   Learning the language you need

A. Study the Examples

I	can	fix car engines.
She	can't	
He		
We		
You		
They		

Can	she	fix car engines?
	you	

Yes,	she	can.
	you	
No,		can't.

COMPLETE THE DIALOG

Keon is talking to a career counselor about her skills and experience. Write *can* or *can't*.

A I have a Class C license, so I _____*can*_____ drive a truck.

B _____*Can*_____ you drive a bulldozer or other construction equipment?

A No, I _____*can't*_____ . But I can repair cars and trucks.

B Great. I think I _____*can*_____ arrange some interviews for you.

PARTNER WORK

Talk with your partner about your job skills. Say all of the things you can do. Talk about some things you can't do.

B. Study the Examples

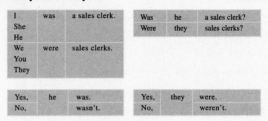

I	was	a sales clerk.
She		
He		
We	were	sales clerks.
You		
They		

Was	he	a sales clerk?
Were	they	sales clerks?

Yes,	he	was.
No,		wasn't.

Yes,	they	were.
No,		weren't.

116   Unit 10

Teaching Note

Help learners write their own work histories, including job titles, dates of employment, names and phone numbers of supervisors and business locations, experience and skills, and any references they have. Check learners' work. Tell learners to use these work histories when filling out job applications.

PREPARATION

1. Review the language in the grammar boxes with learners before they open their books, if necessary.

2. If necessary, review occupations and the language used for describing job skills and experience. Show learners pictures of people doing different jobs. Have learners name as many occupations as they can and describe the skills they think each person has.

PRESENTATION

1. Have learners read and discuss the Purpose Statement.

2. Have learners read the grammar boxes in A. Have learners use the language in the boxes to say as many sentences as possible. Tell learners that they can use the grammar boxes throughout the unit to review or check sentence structures.

3. Have learners read the instructions for Complete the Dialog and complete the activity independently. Have several pairs of learners say their dialog aloud as the rest of the class checks their work.

4. Have pairs read the instructions for Partner Work and complete the activity. Ask several pairs to present their conversations to the rest of the class.

5. Focus attention on the grammar boxes in B. Follow the procedures in 2.

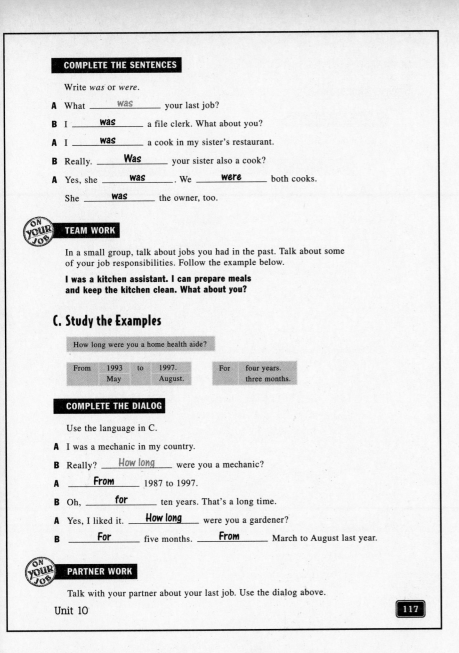

COMPLETE THE SENTENCES

Write *was* or *were*.

A What _____was_____ your last job?

B I _____was_____ a file clerk. What about you?

A I _____was_____ a cook in my sister's restaurant.

B Really. _____Was_____ your sister also a cook?

A Yes, she _____was_____. We _____were_____ both cooks.

She _____was_____ the owner, too.

ON YOUR JOB — TEAM WORK

In a small group, talk about jobs you had in the past. Talk about some of your job responsibilities. Follow the example below.

I was a kitchen assistant. I can prepare meals and keep the kitchen clean. What about you?

C. Study the Examples

How long were you a home health aide?

From	1993	to	1997.	For	four years.
	May		August.		three months.

COMPLETE THE DIALOG

Use the language in C.

A I was a mechanic in my country.

B Really? _____How long_____ were you a mechanic?

A _____From_____ 1987 to 1997.

B Oh, _____for_____ ten years. That's a long time.

A Yes, I liked it. _____How long_____ were you a gardener?

B _____For_____ five months. _____From_____ March to August last year.

ON YOUR JOB — PARTNER WORK

Talk with your partner about your last job. Use the dialog above.

Unit 10   117

---

6. Have learners read the instructions for Complete the Sentences and complete the activity independently. Have several pairs of learners read their answers aloud as the rest of the class checks their work.

7. Have teams read the Team Work instructions and complete the activity. Have team reporters share their team's ideas with the rest of the class.

8. Focus attention on the grammar boxes in C. Follow the procedures in 2.

9. Have learners read the instructions for Complete the Dialog and complete the activity independently. Have several pairs share their dialogs with the class.

10. Have partners read the Partner Work instructions and complete the activity. Have several pairs share their dialogs with the class.

FOLLOW-UP

Ask Me Questions: Write the names of different jobs on slips of paper and give a slip to each learner. Ask a learner to stand in front of the class and answer questions about the skills needed to do the job. Class members are only allowed to ask questions that can be answered with *yes* or *no:* Can you cook? Can you drive a truck? Learners try to identify the person's job. The learner who figures out the job first becomes the next to answer questions.

♦ Write a past year on the board. Have learners write sentences about what they did then and what they do now. *In 1995 I was a cook's assistant. Now I am a cook.* Have learners exchange sentences and check each other's work. Post the final sentences.

WORKBOOK

Unit 10, Exercises 6A–6C

BLACKLINE MASTERS

Blackline Master: Unit 10

WORKFORCE SKILLS (pages 118–119)

Read help-wanted ads

Figure out the best job for you

Complete a job application

★ ★ ★ ★ ★

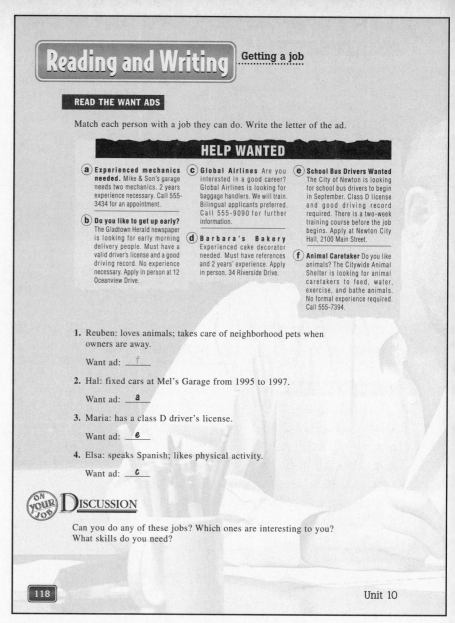

Reading and Writing ·········· Getting a job

READ THE WANT ADS

Match each person with a job they can do. Write the letter of the ad.

HELP WANTED

(a) Experienced mechanics needed. Mike & Son's garage needs two mechanics. 2 years experience necessary. Call 555-3434 for an appointment.

(b) Do you like to get up early? The Gladtown Herald newspaper is looking for early morning delivery people. Must have a valid driver's license and a good driving record. No experience necessary. Apply in person at 12 Oceanview Drive.

(c) Global Airlines Are you interested in a good career? Global Airlines is looking for baggage handlers. We will train. Bilingual applicants preferred. Call 555-9090 for further information.

(d) Barbara's Bakery Experienced cake decorator needed. Must have references and 2 years' experience. Apply in person. 34 Riverside Drive.

(e) School Bus Drivers Wanted The City of Newton is looking for school bus drivers to begin in September. Class D license and good driving record required. There is a two-week training course before the job begins. Apply at Newton City Hall, 2100 Main Street.

(f) Animal Caretaker Do you like animals? The Citywide Animal Shelter is looking for animal caretakers to feed, water, exercise, and bathe animals. No formal experience required. Call 555-7394.

1. Reuben: loves animals; takes care of neighborhood pets when owners are away.

   Want ad: ___f___

2. Hal: fixed cars at Mel's Garage from 1995 to 1997.

   Want ad: ___a___

3. Maria: has a class D driver's license.

   Want ad: ___e___

4. Elsa: speaks Spanish; likes physical activity.

   Want ad: ___c___

DISCUSSION

Can you do any of these jobs? Which ones are interesting to you? What skills do you need?

118   Unit 10

PREPARATION

1. Present or review **help-wanted ads, apply, applicant, appointment, interview, formal experience, experienced, bilingual, preferred,** and **required.** Have learners scan sample want ads for the words. What information is often included in the ads? (telephone numbers, addresses, the name of a contact person)

2. To clarify the language on a job application, show a blank job application and fill in a few of the items with information about yourself. Say, for instance: *Personal information is my name and address. Experience refers to my old jobs.*

PRESENTATION

1. Have learners read and discuss the Purpose Statement.

2. Have learners look at the want ads before they begin and say everything they can about them. Write their ideas on the board and/or restate them in acceptable English.

3. Have learners look at the Read the Want Ads instructions and complete the activity independently. Have learners review each other's work in pairs. Ask several pairs to share their answers with the class while the rest of the class checks their answers.

4. Have learners read the Discussion instructions and work in teams to talk about the skills and experience they already have. Are they qualified to do any of the jobs in the ads? Have team reporters share their ideas with the class.

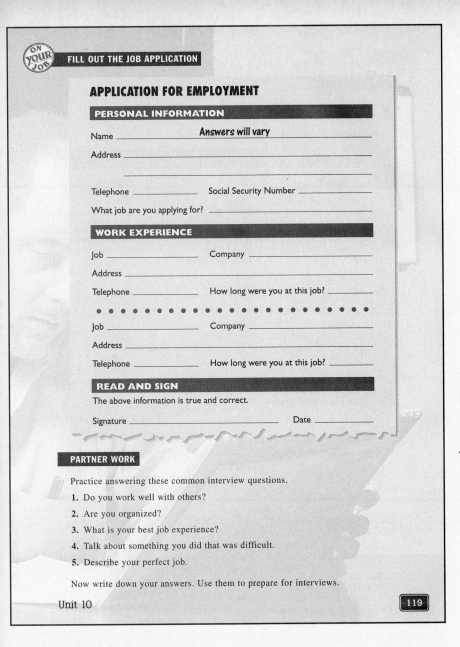

 FILL OUT THE JOB APPLICATION

APPLICATION FOR EMPLOYMENT

PERSONAL INFORMATION

Name _____ Answers will vary _____

Address _____

_____

Telephone _____ Social Security Number _____

What job are you applying for? _____

WORK EXPERIENCE

Job _____ Company _____

Address _____

Telephone _____ How long were you at this job? _____

• •

Job _____ Company _____

Address _____

Telephone _____ How long were you at this job? _____

READ AND SIGN

The above information is true and correct.

Signature _____ Date _____

PARTNER WORK

Practice answering these common interview questions.

1. Do you work well with others?

2. Are you organized?

3. What is your best job experience?

4. Talk about something you did that was difficult.

5. Describe your perfect job.

Now write down your answers. Use them to prepare for interviews.

Unit 10

`119`

SCANS Note

You might discuss effective interviewing with learners. Clarify, if necessary, that job applicants can make a good impression by demonstrating good social skills such as responsibility, politeness, cooperation, and adaptability. It is also important to have a neat and organized appearance and to be on time.

 5. Have learners look at the application and say everything they can about it. Write their ideas on the board and/or restate them in acceptable English.

6. Have learners fill out the job application independently. Have learners review each other's work in pairs. Ask several learners to share their completed applications with the class.

7. Have learners read the Partner Work instructions. Explain that an interview is a conversation between an employer and a job applicant to see if the applicant can do the job and wants the job. Then have pairs complete the activity. Have partners switch roles and repeat. Have several pairs conduct their interviews in front of the class.

FOLLOW-UP

What Can I Do? Have learners work in small groups. Hand out the want-ad sections from a local newspaper. Have learners find ads for jobs for which they might be qualified. Have learners say why they are qualified for the jobs. Have individuals present their ads to the class, say what the requirements for the job are, and tell how they fulfill them.

♦ Have learners write two or three questions they would like to ask about the jobs they chose: *What are the work hours? Does the company offer training? Is there health insurance?*

WORKBOOK

Unit 10, Exercises 7A–7D

WORKFORCE SKILLS (page 120)

Describe your job skills

Figure out the best job for you

★   ★   ★   ★   ★

COMPLETE THE SKILLS INVENTORY

Read the skills inventory. Check all the skills that you have.

WORK SKILLS — CHECK ALL THE SKILLS YOU HAVE.

Automotive
- ☐ change oil/tires
- ☐ make simple repairs
- ☐ do tune-ups
- ☐ fix flat tires
- ☐ pump gas

Clerical
- ☐ file
- ☐ keep records
- ☐ make copies
- ☐ type
- ☐ use a computer
- ☐ use a fax machine

Domestic
- ☐ cook/serve meals
- ☐ follow directions
- ☐ do housework

- ☐ shop for groceries
- ☐ wash/sort/iron clothes

Food Services
- ☐ clean tables
- ☐ cook
- ☐ serve meals
- ☐ take orders
- ☐ wash dishes

Gardening
- ☐ mow lawns
- ☐ pot/transplant plants
- ☐ water plants

Mechanical
- ☐ pack/wrap boxes
- ☐ put things together
- ☐ run machines
- ☐ work with tools

Retail
- ☐ use a cash register
- ☐ make change
- ☐ check inventory
- ☐ sell stock

Transportation
- ☐ drive a car/truck
- ☐ follow directions
- ☐ lift packages
- ☐ read maps

Other
- ☐ _____
- ☐ _____
- ☐ _____
- ☐ _____

ANSWER THE QUESTIONS

1. How many boxes did you check? _____ **Answers will vary.**

2. What job groups are they in? _____

3. How many different groups do you have skills in? _____

4. With these skills what jobs can you do? _____

_____

 Culture Notes

There are many different ways to look for a job. You can look in the want ads or look for help-wanted signs at businesses. What are some other ways to find out about jobs? How did you find the job you have now? Talk to your classmates. How did they find their jobs?

120   Unit 10

PREPARATION

Write **clerical, automotive, domestic, food services, gardening, mechanical, retail,** and **transportation** on the board and explain each one. Say, for example, *Automotive jobs have to do with cars, trucks, and buses.* Have learners name a few jobs for each category.

PRESENTATION

1. Have learners read and discuss the Purpose Statement.

2. Have learners preview the skills inventory form. Encourage them to say everything they can about it. Write their ideas on the board and/or restate them in acceptable English.

3. Have learners read the instructions for Complete the Skills Inventory and complete the activity independently. Have learners review each other's work in pairs. Ask several learners to share with the class a few of the items they checked.

4. Have learners complete Answer the Questions independently. Then have learners work in pairs to check their work. Have several pairs share their answers and ideas with the class. Encourage the class to make other job suggestions based on the skills each learner has checked off.

 **5.** Have learners read Culture Notes and talk over their responses in teams. Have team reporters share their ideas with the class.

FOLLOW-UP

Classify: Have learners work in pairs. Hand out pages of newspaper want ads. Have learners look at their partner's skills inventory checklist and find as many jobs as possible that match his or her partner's skills. Have learners cut out or circle the ads, give them to their partners, and discuss how the jobs match their skills.

♦ Have learners rank the want ads chosen for them by their partners from the job they would most like to have to the one they would least like to have. Have several learners present their rankings to the rest of the class and explain why they want the job they ranked first.

WORKBOOK

Unit 10, Exercise 8

Performance Check

How well can you use the skills in this unit?

Complete the activities. Go over your work with a partner or your teacher. Then complete the Performance Review on Page 122.

SKILL 1   DESCRIBE YOUR JOB SKILLS

Your partner or teacher is a job counselor. Tell him or her your job skills.

SKILL 2   READ A HELP-WANTED AD

Look at the want ad. Answer the questions.

> **Carpet Installer Needed**
> Must have experience. Apply in person at
> Superior Floor Coverings. 34 Tyler Street.
> Monday to Friday, 9 to 6.

1. What job is the ad for? _____ *carpet installer* _____

2. Do you need experience? _____ *yes* _____

3. Do you apply in writing? _____ *no* _____

4. Would you like a job like this one? Why or why not? __ *Answers will vary.* __

_____

SKILL 3   FIGURE OUT THE BEST JOB FOR YOU

Look at the lists. Add to them if you wish. Choose the job that is best for you. Explain your choice to your partner or your teacher.

Skills	Jobs
Drive a truck	carpenter
Work well with tools	tailor
Like to work alone	auto mechanic
Like to work with people	delivery person
Know how to use a cash register	hairdresser
Can change oil in a car	painter

Unit 10   121

PRESENTATION

Use any of the procedures in "Evaluation" on page x with pages 121 and 122. Record individuals' results on the Unit 10 Individual Competency Chart. Record the class's results on the Class Cumulative Competency Chart.

Complete the job application. Apply for a job you want.

APPLICATION FOR EMPLOYMENT

WZ Company

PERSONAL INFORMATION

Name _____ **Answers will vary.** _____

Address _____

_____

Telephone _____ Social Security Number _____

What job are you applying for? _____

WORK EXPERIENCE

Job _____ Name of Company _____

Telephone _____ Supervisor's name _____

Dates of Employment: From _____ to _____

Performance Review

I can...

☐ **1.** describe my job skills.

☐ **2.** read help-wanted ads.

☐ **3.** figure out the best job for me.

☐ **4.** complete a job application.

DISCUSSION

Work with a team. How will these skills help you? Make a list. Share your list with the class.

PRESENTATION

Follow the instructions on page 121.

INFORMAL WORKPLACE-SPECIFIC ASSESSMENT

Ask each learner to specify one or two skills he or she needs to do his or her job correctly.

WORKBOOK

Unit 10, Exercise 9

Listening Transcript

UNIT 1

Listening (page 7)

LISTEN AND CIRCLE

Complete the conversations. Circle the letter.

1.

A: Hi, my name's Yolanda. I just started working here yesterday morning. I transferred from Manufacturing.

B: It's nice to meet you, Yolanda. I'm Clark.

C: What does Yolanda say next?

2.

A: Susan, do you know what time it is? I can't find my watch.

B: Sure. It's 3:30. Time to get ready for the dinner crowd.

B: Excuse me. I need to answer the phone.

C: How does Susan answer the phone?

3.

A: Good morning, Mr. Haines.

B: Good morning, Juliette. I'd like you to meet your new partner, Pablo. He'll be working with you to process the orders that have been coming in over the last few weeks.

C: What does Juliette say?

LISTEN AND CIRCLE

Listen to the conversations. Circle the correct information for each person.

1.

A: Hi, my name's Linda Marcos. I'm the new mail clerk.

B: Hi, I'm Eric Montoya. I work across town in the warehouse. It's nice to meet you.

A: Nice to meet you, too, Eric.

2.

A: Martin, I'd like you to meet Dale, our new plumber's helper.

B: Hi, Dale. Welcome to the job.

C: Thanks, Martin. I'm glad to be here.

A: Martin is the foreman on this job. He can help you get started.

C: Sounds great. I'm ready whenever you are.

3.

A: My name is Chen Wong. I'm here to meet with a job counselor.

B: Hi, Chen. I'm Marla Smith. I'm a job counselor. What can I do to help you?

A: I'm looking for a job where I can use my skills.

B: Good. Tell me a little about yourself.

A: Well, I'm from China. I speak Chinese and English, and I'm an experienced locksmith.

B: OK. Can you tell me about your education?

4.

A: Maria, this is Elena Rios, a new employee. She's from Mexico. She speaks Spanish.

B: It's nice to meet you. My name's Maria Santos. I'm from Honduras. I speak Spanish, too.

C: I'm happy to meet you. This looks like a great place to work.

B: Oh, it is. I really like working at the clinic.

UNIT 2

Listening (page 19)

LISTEN AND CIRCLE

Circle the places you hear.

1.

A: Morning. I'm from Morrow Electric. I'm here to fix the lights in the kitchen. Can you tell me how to get there from here?

B: To the kitchen? Sure. Just walk down the hall. The kitchen is at the end of the hall on the right.

A: The end of the hall on the right. OK. Thanks.

B: No problem.

2.

A: Hey, Lew, I'm supposed to bring this coffee to Meeting Room 1. I've never been there before. Where is it?

B: Meeting Room 1?

A: Uh huh.

B: It's on the left, first door on the left.

A: First door on the left. Thanks, Lew.

3.

A: Excuse me. I think I'm lost. I'm looking for the parking lot. Can you help me?

B: The parking lot? It's right outside this door. Just go out this exit and you're there.

A: Oh, good. Now I just hope I can find my car.

B: Well, I can't help you there, but good luck.

A: Thanks. I think I'll need it.

4.

A: Excuse me. Can you tell me where the ladies' room is?

B: The ladies' room is down the hall. Turn left before Meeting Room 4. It's on the left.

A: I'm sorry. Could you repeat that?

B: Of course. Go down the hall. Then turn left before you get to Meeting Room 4. The ladies' room is on the left.

A: Thanks.

B: You're welcome.

5.

A: Phyllis, do you know where our orientation training is?

B: I know it's in Meeting Room 3. The problem is I don't know where Meeting Room 3 is.

A: Let me check the map. Hmm . . . it's down the hall on the right. It's the second door.

B: Are you sure?

A: Yes, look at the map. We walk down the hall. Meeting Room 3 is on the right. It's the second door on the right.

B: Now I see. Uh oh! Look at the time. We'd better hurry so we won't be late.

Write the name of the room on the floor plan. *(Play the tape or read the transcript of Listen and Circle aloud again.)*

Performance Check (page 25)

SKILL 2   **UNDERSTAND DIRECTIONS**

Listen and write the name of the room on the floor plan.

1.

A: Excuse me. I'm here to refill the vending machines and I need to get to the break room. Can you tell me how to get there?

B: To the break room? Sure. It's down the hall on the right. It's next to the meeting room. Don't worry. You can't miss it.

A: Down the hall on the right next to the meeting room? You're right. That sounds easy enough. Thanks.

2.

A: Hi, we're from The Paper Store and we've got a couple of cases of copier paper to deliver. We're supposed to take them to the supply room. Do you know where that is?

B: No problem. To get to the supply room, all you have to do is go down the hall and turn left. The supply room is the first door on the left.

A: Did you say it's on the left?

B: Uh huh. Go down the hall. Turn left and you'll see the supply room on the left.

A: Thanks.

U N I T ◈3◈

Listening (page 31)

LISTEN AND NUMBER

Listen to the instructions. Number the machine's parts in the order you use them.

A: Sara, can you help me fax this letter? This machine is a little different from the one I used in Production.

B: Sure. I'd be happy to. First, turn the machine on. Press the ON button.

A: OK, that makes sense. I press ON. Then what?
B: Put your letter into the document feeder.
A: Put it into the feeder like this?
B: That's right. Then, dial the fax number on the keypad.
A: Press these numbers to dial?
B: Yes, and you can check to be sure you pressed the right numbers by looking at the screen.
A: Look at the screen. That's a good idea.
B: Then, all you have to do is press SEND.
A: Press SEND and there it goes! Thanks.

LISTEN AND NUMBER

Number the steps in the correct order.

Before we begin, I'd like to thank everyone for coming in early today to learn how to use the new cash registers. The new registers were delivered and installed yesterday, so before we can open the store this morning, we need to do a little training. The new registers are not that different from the old ones. The first thing you do is put in your key. Turn the key to the ON position, like this. ON. Second, type in your employee number—mine is 4523—and press ENTER. ENTER is right here. After you press ENTER, the drawer will open. The last thing you do is close the drawer. Just push it closed. Now, as with our old cash registers...

Performance Check (page 37)

SKILL 1   **FOLLOW INSTRUCTIONS**

Listen to the instructions for putting paper in the copier. Number the steps in the correct order.

A: Can you help me with the copier?
B: Of course, Peter. What's the problem?
A: I need to add paper, but I don't know how.
B: It's easy. First open the paper drawer.
A: Which drawer? There are two.
B: Open the top drawer.
A: OK. I have it open. Now what?
B: Put some paper into the drawer.
A: About how much paper in the drawer?
B: About this much. Then push the paper under the tabs.
A: Push it down like this?

B: That's right. Now close the drawer. Make sure it's closed all the way.
A: Is that it?
B: Yes, that's right. Now press the red button. After you press the red button, it will take about thirty seconds for the copier to warm up.
A: Thanks.

Listening (page 43)

LISTEN AND CIRCLE

Listen and circle the times you hear.

1.
A: Lin, can you work until 7:30 tonight? I know it's short notice, but Harold just called in sick.
B: 7:30? No problem.
A: Thanks.

2.
A: Are you working tonight?
B: Yes, but I don't start until 11:00. I'm working the late shift.
A: That's when I'm working too. See you at 11:00.

3.
A: Tina, I'd like to take a late lunch on Friday. Around 12:45.
B: 12:45's a little late, but I think we can work around you.
A: Thanks. I appreciate it.

4.
A: Buddy wants you to turn on the lights when you leave today.
B: That will be around 4:45. Is that OK?
A: I think 4:45's OK, but I'll check with Buddy.

5.
A: Do you know when they are coming to pick up these packages?
B: I'm not sure. Let me look at the schedule. They should be here about 10:15.
A: 10:50?
B: No, 10:15.

Listen and write Nora's work schedule on the calendar.

A: Big Mart. This is Sam. How can I help you?

B: Hi, Sam, it's Nora. I called to find out about my schedule for next week.

A: Let me check. I have you working on Monday from 12:00 to 6:00 and on Tuesday from 6:00 to 10:00.

B: Monday from 12:00 to 6:00 and Tuesday from 6:00 to 10:00. Anything else?

A: Can you come in on Friday?

B: Well, I have a doctor's appointment on Friday at 4:00. But I can come in around 5:30. I could work until 11:30.

A: That'll be fine. I'll put you down for Friday from 5:30 to 11:30. Thanks for calling.

B: See you Monday. Bye.

UNIT 5

Listening (page 55)

Listen to the orders. Write the number of items the customer says.

1.

A: Good morning, Order Department. How can I help you?

B: I'd like to order some tape.

A: Extra strength?

B: No, regular.

A: And how many rolls do you need?

B: About 12.

A: That's 12 rolls of regular tape. Your name?

B: Glen Sullivan. I'll be in this afternoon to pick them up.

2.

A: Alex, can you get this order from the warehouse? I need six monitors and three keyboards.

B: Sure. Did you say three keyboards?

A: Yes, three keyboards and six monitors.

3.

A: I'm off to pick up the paint order for the Haley project. It looks like we'll need five gallons of off-white paint and 15 gallons of dark green paint.

B: 15 gallons of dark green? Are you sure?

A: Let me check. Yes, that's right. 15 gallons of dark green and five gallons of off-white.

4.

A: First Call Couriers.

B: Yes, I have some packages that need to be delivered today.

A: How many packages are there?

B: Six small envelopes and two boxes.

A: I'm sorry. Can you repeat that, please?

B: Six envelopes and two boxes.

Listen to the customer place an order. Write the number of each item the customer wants.

A: Let me see if I have this correct, Ms. Bard. You want three boxes of light bulbs.

B: Yes, three boxes.

A: OK. That'll be $5.85 for the bulbs. Can I help you with anything else today?

B: Yes, I'd also like some extension cords and some switches.

A: How many would you like?

B: I'll need two switches and, umm . . . five . . . yes, five extension cords.

A: All right. The two switches come to $15.90, and the five extension cords are $12.50. Will that be all?

B: Oh, I almost forgot. I also need seven plugs.

A: And seven plugs. That'll be $27.65. Anything else, Ms. Bard?

B: No, that's all for now. What is my total?

A: Let's see. The light bulbs are $5.85, the two switches are $15.90, the extension cords are $12.50, and the plugs are $27.65. That comes to $61.90.

Listen again and write the total cost for each item on the form. *(Play the tape or read the transcript of Listen and Write aloud again.)*

 LISTEN AND CIRCLE

What are the rules about? Circle your answer.

1.

A: Good afternoon, Uma. Welcome to Green Technologies.

B: Thank you, Mr. Robinson.

A: I need to tell you about our rules for sick days. You're entitled to nine sick days a year.

B: Nine days. Who do I call when I'm sick?

A: Call your supervisor first thing in the morning.

2.

A: Brian, here's the time clock. Everyone at Rosetti Macaroni clocks in here. You punch in when you start work every morning and punch out when you leave every night.

B: What do I do if I forget to punch in or out?

A: Speak to your manager right away. Your manager's Ms. Valdosta. She can take care of it.

3.

A: What are you doing today, Elaine?

B: Shopping for some clothes. I just started work at the Garden Restaurant.

A: That's great.

B: Yeah. I need a white shirt and black pants. Then I'm off to the shoe store. I've got to get a pair of black shoes, too.

A: You might want to go to Allman's. I bought a really comfortable pair of black shoes there last week.

4.

A: King's Department Store has a rule about arriving late. It's very simple.

B: Really? What is it?

A: Well, you have to call if you're going to be late. And, if you arrive late three times, you get a warning.

B: Three times? I won't be late that often. I don't want to get a warning.

 LISTEN AGAIN

Which rule goes with each company? Write the letter. (Play the tape or read the transcript of Listen and Circle aloud again.)

 LISTEN ONCE MORE

Answer the questions. (Play the tape or read the transcript of Listen and Circle aloud again.)

UNIT ⬥7⬥

Listening (page 79)

 LISTEN AND CIRCLE

Listen and circle the money amount you hear.

1.

A: Dora, can you look in the office supply catalog to see how much a new stapler is? Mine just broke.

B: Let me see . . . Oh, here's one like yours for $12.25. I can go out at lunch and pick one up for you if you'd like.

A: That would be great. Thanks.

B: Do you want to give me $12.25 in cash out of the register to pay for it?

A: Good idea. I'll get it for you.

2.

A: Lara just told me we have to mark down all the leather gloves. There's a sale starting tomorrow.

B: What are we marking them down to?

A: $8.99 a pair.

B: Only $8.99? I think I'll buy some for myself. Let me get my purse so I can write out a check.

3.

A: I need to talk to Gary about my paycheck.

B: Is there a problem?

A: Yes, there is. My check is for only $122.65. It looks like they forgot to include my vacation pay.

B: Let me see that . . . I don't think $122.65 is right, either. Why don't we take your check to Gary together and get this straightened out?

4.

A: Mario, we're out of small washers. Can you go to the plumbing supply store and get us some?

B: Sure, Joe.

A: Just take the money from petty cash. You shouldn't need much. The washers only cost about five cents each.

B: I'll be back in about half an hour. That was small washers, right?

A: Yes, the five-cent size.

LISTEN AGAIN

Write *cash* or *check.* (*Play the tape or read the transcript of Listen and Circle aloud again.*)

LISTEN AND WRITE

Listen and fill in the check.

A: That comes to $329.47. How would you like to pay?

B: By check. Do you take company checks?

A: We sure do.

B: Oh, good. Now how much did you say the total was?

A: $329.47.

B: Thanks. And I make the check out to...?

A: Johnson Art Supply.

B: Johnson Art Supply. J-O-H-N-S-O-N A-R-T S-U-P-P-L-Y.

A: Uh-huh.

B: Today's August 17, isn't it?

A: That's right. It's the seventeenth.

B: OK, August 17, 1999. Here's the check. Oops! I almost forgot to sign it. . . There you go.

Listening (page 91)

LISTEN AND NUMBER

Listen to the instructions. Number the instructions in order.

How do you do? My name is Alex Brace and I work with the city fire department. I'm here at March Manufacturing today to go over the procedures to follow during a fire or fire drill. In case of a fire or fire drill, you will hear an alarm. When you hear the alarm follow these instructions:
1. Walk, do not run, to the nearest exit.
2. If you are the last person to leave a room or office, turn off the lights.
3. Be sure to close the door behind you.
4. Go down the nearest stairs. Do not use the elevators.

And finally, walk out of the building and to the northwest corner of the parking lot.

LISTEN AND CIRCLE

Listen to the emergencies. Who should you call? Circle the symbol.

1.
A: Are you all right? What happened?
B: I'm fine, but there was an accident on the factory floor. Lorna cut her hand.

2.
A: Hey, I smell smoke!
B: You're right. There's smoke coming from the boiler room.

3.
A: Doug, what's the matter?
B: I was putting more dye in the drum and some splashed onto my face.
A: That stuff's dangerous. It might be poison.

LISTEN AND WRITE

Listen to the emergency calls. What do you need to do?

1.
A: 911? My name is Lisa. I work at the Park City Library. A little boy just fell off a chair. He was trying to get a book.
B: Is he hurt?
A: I think he hurt his head.
B: Cover him with a blanket. Don't let him move. Wait for an ambulance. The paramedics will be there in a few minutes.

Listening Transcript

2.

A: Fire Department.

B: I'm at the Furniture Factory on Route 3. We smell smoke in the back of the building.

A: Tell everyone to leave the building now! Stay outside the building. We'll send a fire truck right away.

3.

A: 911 operator. What's your name, please?

B: Manuel Vargas. I work at a machine shop on Laurel Street.

A: What's the emergency?

B: My partner splashed some cleaning chemicals on his skin.

A: Find the container the chemicals came in. Call the poison control center right away. Their number is 555-1212.

4.

A: Express Couriers.

B: Mr. Stephanos, this is Diego. I was returning from my last delivery when the van broke down just outside of town.

A: Is anyone with you?

B: No, I'm by myself.

A: All right. Call a tow truck. Stay in the van until the tow truck or the police get there. Then call me back and tell me what's happening.

Performance Check (page 98)

SKILL 5   **FOLLOW SAFETY INSTRUCTIONS**

Listen to the instructions. Answer the questions. Circle *yes* or *no*.

Thank you all for coming to this month's workplace safety meeting. Today's topic is what to do in case of bad weather. First on the list is tornadoes. As you know, tornadoes are very dangerous storms. If there's a tornado in the area, you will hear a very loud, sharp warning signal. If you hear this signal, don't panic. Turn off any machines you're using and walk to the nearest elevator or stairs. Go down to the basement. Do not go out of the building. You will be much safer if you stay inside. Someone will be there to tell you where to wait until the all-clear signal. The all-clear signal will tell you when it's safe to go back to work.

UNIT 9

Listening (page 103)

LISTEN AND WRITE

Listen to the dialogs. Who can do the job? Write the letter of the picture.

1.

A: We've just signed three new customers. That means starting next week, we've got three more deliveries to make every day.

B: I guess we'd better start looking for another driver.

A: I think you're right. Do you know if anyone else in the company can drive a van?

B: I don't know, but we can always advertise in the paper for a driver if we have to.

2.

A: Suni, can you put this job posting up on the bulletin board in the employee lounge?

B: Sure. What kind of job is it?

A: It's a job in the warehouse. We're looking for someone who can do some heavy lifting and knows how to work carefully and safely.

B: I'm sure you'll be able to find someone who can do that.

3.

A: Jonathan, do you know any good mechanics?

B: Why? Do you have an opening at the garage?

A: Yes, I do. Tanya just got promoted to the front office. I need someone to take her place—someone who can fix cars and who works well with people.

B: My cousin knows a lot about cars. Let me talk to him and see if he's interested.

LISTEN AND CIRCLE

Circle the letter of the statement that describes each employee's performance.

1.

A: Cindy, I've called you in to talk about your work.

B: Is everything all right?

A: Generally you're doing a good job. You get to the restaurant on time every day, and that's very important to us.

B: Is there something I should be working on?

A: Well, yes. You need to serve your customers their meals a little more quickly.

B: Thanks for telling me. I'll try to work faster.

2.

A: It's time for your three-month evaluation, Enrique. Tell me, are you enjoying the new job?

B: Yes, I am. I really like talking to the customers.

A: I've noticed that you're usually very polite to your customers on the phone. But there is a problem with your paperwork. You need to be more careful when you write out your orders. Some of your orders are hard to read. You need to write more clearly.

B: Sure. I can do that.

3.

A: Hans, I'm pleased to tell you that you have the best safety record of anyone in the company.

B: Really?

A: Yes, you always drive safely and make all your deliveries on time. We think you're doing a super job.

B: Thanks, Ms. Ford. Is there anything I can do better?

A: Well, sometimes your uniform is a little messy. We expect all of our employees to dress neatly.

B: Oh, OK. I'll dress more neatly from now on.

4.

A: Hi, Maria. How are you doing this afternoon?

B: I'm fine, Mr. Lee.

A: Maria, I wanted to talk to you because I think we have a problem. I notice that you don't always enjoy working with other employees.

B: You're right. I prefer working alone when I can.

A: I understand, but it's important for you to work more closely with your team.

B: OK. Do you have any ideas?

A: Maybe you can team up with Arthur. He's easy to work with. I think it'll be good for you.

B: All right. I'd like to do that. Thanks.

UNIT 10

Listening (page 115)

LISTEN AND CIRCLE

Listen and circle the jobs the people are calling about.

1.

A: Consolidated Fan Company. How can I help you?

B: My name's Kevin Cho. I'm calling about the ad for a delivery truck driver.

A: Yes, that job is still available. We're looking for someone with at least two years experience.

B: I've been driving a delivery truck for Acme Products for the last three years.

A: That sounds good. Would you like to come in for an interview?

2.

A: Alvarez Salon. May I help you?

B: Yes, my name is Clara Hall. I saw a sign at school that says you're looking for a hairdresser.

A: Tell me, Clara, do you have your hairdresser's license yet?

B: No, not yet. I'm going to take the exam next week.

A: I'm sorry. We can't hire anyone without a license. But call us again when you pass the test.

3.

A: Green Landscaping. Human Resources.

B: Hello, my name's Carlos Ramos. I'm calling about your ad for an experienced gardener.

A: Hello, Mr. Ramos. Have you worked as a gardener before?

B: Yes, I have. I worked for Lakeside Landscaping for five years.

A: So you know how to use a lawn mower?

B: Yes, I have experience using many kinds of lawn mowers.

A: Excellent. Would you like to come in for an interview?

4.

A: Job Hotline. This is Berta. How can I help you?

B: My name's Suzy. I just received my nurse's aide certificate from the community college, and I'm looking for a job. Are there any jobs available?

A: Yes, there are. I have several openings for nurse's aides. Would you like to come in to talk about the jobs?

LISTEN AGAIN

Read the questions about their training and skills. Circle the answers. *(Play the tape or read the transcript of Listen and Circle aloud again.)*

LISTEN AND CIRCLE

Pablo Bueno is calling about a job. Read the questions. Circle the answers.

A: Lawn and Garden Company. May I help you?

B: Yes, I'm calling about the gardener's job in the newspaper. My name is Pablo Bueno.

A: Hi. My name is Lilia Silverman. I'm going to ask you some questions, get a little information, and then have someone call you back. Is that OK?

B: Sure.

A: First, can you spell your name for me?

B: It's Pablo, P-A-B-L-O, Bueno, B-U-E-N-O.

A: Tell me a little about yourself, Mr. Bueno.

B: Well, I was a gardener for a company that manages large apartment buildings and houses.

A: Oh, for how long?

B: Three months. It was a summer job. And I have some experience working in my own garden, too.

A: That's good. Can you take care of trees?

B: I don't have any experience taking care of trees, but I'm sure I can learn.

A: Well, that's about it for now. The only other thing I need is your phone number.

B: It's 555-2133.

A: 555-2133. Thanks. Someone will call you back soon.

B: Thank you.

Vocabulary

UNIT 1

name
address
city
state
zip code
telephone number
Social Security number

hi
good-bye
good morning
good afternoon
good evening

country
language
employee

UNIT 2

break room
entrance
exit
hall
ladies' room
office
meeting room
men's room
parking lot
rest rooms
supply room

left
right
across from
between
next to

go
turn
walk

UNIT 3

cash register
coffee maker
computer
copier
document feeder
fax machine
keypad
printer
screen
vacuum cleaner

start button
stop button

close
copy
open
plug in
press
push
send
turn off
turn on

UNIT 4

part time
full time
overtime
shift
hours
holiday
day off

late
early

day
date
month
year

appointment
calendar
schedule

UNIT 5

apology
complaint
customer
order
problem
service

discount
exchange
guarantee
refund

no problem
of course
sure

UNIT 6

break
sick day
rules

flexible
pleasant
polite
punctual

late
on time

certainly
of course

clock in
clock out
punch in
punch out

Miss
Mr.
Mrs.
Ms.

excuse me
pardon me
please
thank you
thanks

UNIT 7

account
cash
check
paycheck
tax
time card
W-4 form

penny
nickel
dime
quarter
dollar

charge
deposit
endorse
sign

UNIT 8

accident
emergency
fire
fire alarm
poison control center
tornado
911

fever
flu
headache
injury
stomachache
toothache

ankle
arm
chest
ear
eye
finger
foot
hand
head
knee

leg
mouth
neck
nose
shoulder
stomach
throat
toe
wrist

burn
cut
hurt

UNIT 9

duty
feedback
responsibility
skill
task
training manual

evaluate
teach

negative
positive

UNIT 10

experience
job application
license
skills inventory
training
want ad

assistant
baggage handler
baker
bus driver
carpenter
cook
child care worker
construction worker

delivery driver
file clerk
gardener
grocery clerk
hairdresser
mechanic
medical technician
nurse's aide
painter
plumber
police officer
sales clerk
secretary
tailor
truck driver

apply
drive
fix
paint
prepare
repair

Name _____

A. Complete the sentences. Use *am, are,* or *is*.

1. You __are__ from Mexico.

2. Li _____ from China.

3. Marie and Paul _____ at work.

4. We _____ coworkers.

5. They _____ the new employees.

6. She _____ the boss.

B. Complete the sentences. Follow the example.

1. They are at work. _____They're_____ in the mail room.

2. He is from customer service. _____ the boss.

3. We are sales clerks. _____ clerks at the new store.

4. I am a hospital worker. _____ a nurse.

5. You are from Mexico City. _____ Mexican.

6. She is a restaurant worker. _____ a chef.

7. It is cool in the warehouse. _____ very cool there.

8. He is a factory worker. _____ a machine operator.

C. Complete the sentences. Use *my, your, his, her, our,* and *their.*

1. I'm sorry I'm late. _____My_____ car broke down.

2. She's a child care worker. _____ name is Berta.

3. He lives in Chicago. _____ office is downtown.

4. Jack and Bob are assistants. _____ boss is a master carpenter.

5. You have a new boss. Ms. Jones is _____ new supervisor.

6. We work in the same store. _____ store is at 23 Elm Street.

7. He has a new bicycle. _____ bicycle is green.

8. They live on First Street. _____ address is 403 First Street.

Blackline Masters

Name _____

A. Answer the questions. Follow the example.

1. Is he on time? Yes, _____*he is*_____.

2. Are the offices large? Yes, _____.

3. Is the mail room next to the supply room? No, _____.

4. Is it time to open the store? Yes, _____.

5. Are you and Sally programmers? Yes, _____.

6. Are you the new employee? No, _____.

B. Complete the questions. Follow the example.

1. _____*Is she*_____ in the break room? Yes, she is.

2. _____ hard workers? Yes, they are.

3. _____ on the third shift? No, we aren't.

4. _____ sometimes late? No, he isn't.

5. _____ in the right room? Yes, you are.

6. _____ time to take a break? No, it isn't.

7. _____ on time for the meeting? Yes, you are.

8. _____ the manager? Yes, she is.

C. Match. Follow the example.

__*b*__ 1. The room is cold.   **a.** Call a repair person.

_____ 2. There's an accident.   **b.** Turn on the heat.

_____ 3. The TV is broken.   **c.** Call 911.

_____ 4. The bread is done.   **d.** Take it out of the oven.

_____ 5. The windows are dirty.   **e.** Go home.

_____ 6. My shift is over.   **f.** Wash them.

Blackline Masters

CAR RENTAL AGENCY

A. Look at the picture. Complete the sentences. Use *carrying, completing, helping, talking, typing,* and *waiting*.

1. Bob's at the desk. He __'s talking_____ on the phone.

2. Ana is at the desk. She _____ on a computer.

3. A customer is at the desk. She _____ a form.

4. Two customers are sitting. They _____ for their cars.

5. The young man _____ car keys.

6. Bob and Ana are clerks. They _____ customers.

B. Look at the picture again. Answer the questions. Follow the example.

1. Is Bob typing? __No, he isn't_____

2. Is Ana typing? _____

3. Is the young man delivering a package? _____

4. Are two people sitting in chairs? _____

5. Are Bob and Ana selling cars? _____

6. Are the people in a car rental agency? _____

C. Complete the sentences. Follow the example.

1. Fred _____*isn't repairing*_____ a TV. He's repairing a VCR.

2. Masato _____ letters. He's copying a report.

3. The painters _____ offices. They're painting the hall.

4. We _____ on break. We're going to a meeting.

5. Miranda _____ to the boss. She's talking to a coworker.

D. Complete the questions and answers. Follow the example.

1. A _____*Is she*_____ talking on the phone?

   B Yes, she _____*is*_____ .

2. A _____ reading the instructions?

   B No, he _____ .

3. A _____ completing your daily time report?

   B Yes, I _____ .

4. A _____ looking for the employment office?

   B No, they _____ .

5. A _____ having a meeting now?

   B Yes, we _____ .

E. Complete the sentences. Follow the example.

1. The <u>carpenter</u> has a saw. The _____*carpenter's*_____ saw is big.

2. The <u>carpenters</u> have tool boxes. The _____ tool boxes are heavy.

3. The <u>supervisor</u> has an office. The _____ office is large.

4. The delivery <u>messengers</u> have bikes. The _____ bikes are strong.

5. <u>Rita</u> has a new uniform. _____ uniform is blue.

A. Complete the dialogs. Follow the example.

1. **A** I need some tape for this package. ___Can I have___ (**have**) some of your tape

   B Yes, you ___can___

2. **A** We need a place for our meeting. _____ (**use**) this room?

   B No, you _____ .

3. **A** I have a doctor's appointment. _____ (**leave**) work early?

   B Yes, you _____ .

4. **A** I think my paycheck is wrong. _____ (**go**) to Human Resources

   for a few minutes now?

   B No, you _____ . Wait until this afternoon.

B. Ask and answer the questions. Use *time, day, month,* and *year*
in the questions. Follow the example.

1. ___What time is it?___

   ___It's 1:45___

2. _____

3. _____

4. _____

   _____

5. _____

   _____

6. _____

   _____

A. Complete the sentences. Use *a* or *an*.

1. My sister works in ___a___ supermarket.

2. There's _____ exit down the hall.

3. I can't drive _____ truck, but I can drive _____ car.

4. There's _____ lounge on the first floor.

5. In _____ emergency, call 911.

B. Complete the dialog. Use **a/an** or *some*.

A We need to make _____a_____ fruit salad for today's lunch menu.

B What do we need?

A _____ grapes and _____ orange. We also

need _____ apples and _____ banana.

B OK, there's _____ small watermelon in the refrigerator.

How about that?

A Yes, use that. And add _____ cherries, too.

C. Complete the dialog. Use *how much* or *how many*.

A ___How many___ nails will we need?

B Just give me the bag over there.

A And _____ paint?

B One can of white paint and one can of black paint.

A _____ brushes?

B We'll need four brushes—two big ones and two small ones.

A What about water? _____ water do we need?

B I don't think we'll need any water.

D. Look at the picture. What's on the table? Write **a/an** or *some*.

__*some*__ forks   _____ cream   _____ big cake   _____ ice cream

_____ spoons   _____ napkins   _____ plates   _____ tablecloth

_____ ice water   _____ glasses   _____ ashtray   _____ knife

_____ tea bags   _____ hot water   _____ cups   _____ fruit juice

E. Look at the picture again. Complete the dialog. Follow the example.

A _____ *How much ice cream* _____ (**ice cream**) do we have?

B We have two gallons. I think that's enough.

A _____ (**forks**) do we have?

B We have only 6. We need more.

A _____ (**plates**) do we have?

B We have 30 plates. That's enough.

A _____ (**fruit juice**) do we have?

B We have one carton. I don't think that's enough.

A _____ (**ashtrays**) do we have?

B We have one. But that's OK. Most people don't smoke.

UNIT 6

A. Complete the sentences. Follow the example.

1. My brother _____**works**_____ (**work**) at the airport.

2. We _____ (**work**) in a restaurant on weekends.

3. I _____ (**finish**) work at 4:15.

4. She _____ (**clean**) rooms in a hotel.

5. The supermarket _____ (**close**) at 10:00.

6. Some waiters _____ (**wear**) uniforms.

7. I _____ (**drive**) a truck for the city.

8. Eddie _____ (**park**) cars at a garage.

9. That machine _____ (**count**) money.

10. Most restaurants _____ (**close**) at 11:00.

B. Complete the dialogs. Use *do, does, don't,* or *doesn't.*

1. A _____**Does**_____ the cafeteria open at 9:00?

   B No, it _____**doesn't**_____. It opens at 8:00.

2. A _____ we have a break at 10:00?

   B Yes, we _____.

3. A _____ the machine operators leave work at 4:00?

   B No, they _____. They finish at 3:00. They start work early.

4. A _____ the boss come in early?

   B Yes, she _____. And she leaves late.

5. A _____ the mail room close at 4:00?

   B No, it _____. It closes at 4:30.

6. A _____ Janet work on Monday?

   B No, she _____. She only works on weekends.

C. Complete the dialogs. Follow the example.

1. **A** What time ___*do you start*___ (**start**) work?

   B I start at 3:00 in the afternoon.

2. **A** What time _____ (**leave**) work every day?

   B She leaves at 5:00.

3. **A** What time _____ (**end**) on Wednesdays?

   B Our class ends at 9:15.

4. **A** What time _____ (**take**) your break?

   B I take my break at 2:15.

5. **A** What time _____ (**come**)?

   B The cleaners come after 6:00.

D. Complete the sentences. Use *this, that, these,* or *those.*

1. Take ___*these*___ boxes to customer service.

   Then take _____ boxes by the door to the cafeteria.

2. Pat, use _____ tape over there on the desk.

   Don't use _____ tape for the package.

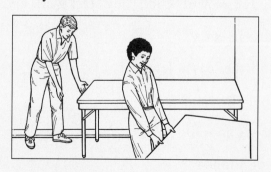

3. Can you help me move _____ table?

   Then we can move _____ table.

4. We keep old parts on _____ shelves near the window.

   We keep new parts on

   _____ shelves.

Blackline Masters

A. Look at the picture. Complete the sentences. Follow the example.

A How many boxes of envelopes _____**are there**_____ ?

B Let's see. _____**There are**_____ 5 boxes left.

A How about tape? How many rolls _____?

B _____ only 2 rolls left. We need some more.

A How many boxes of paper _____?

B _____ only one box left.

A What about computer diskettes?

B _____ one full box left. We have enough for now.

B. Look at the picture. Ask and answer questions. Follow the example.

1. _____**Is there**_____ any glue? _____**Yes, there is.**_____

2. _____ any pencils? _____

3. _____ any tape? _____

4. _____ any string? _____

5. _____ any paper clips? _____

6. _____ any pens? _____

A. Complete the dialogs. Follow the example. Use the correct form of *feel*.

1. **A** _____**How does your son feel**_____ today? (**your son**)

   B He ____**feels**____ sick. He still has the flu.

2. **A** _____ about her new job? (**Sonia**)

   B She _____ nervous. She's supervising people now.

3. **A** _____ today? (**you**)

   B I _____ great. I'm getting a raise in salary.

4. **A** _____ today? (**your friends**)

   B They _____ terrible. The factory's closing.

B. Look at the pictures. Complete the sentences. Follow the example.

1. ____**He feels**____ terrible.

   ____**He has**____ a toothache.

2. _____ happy.

   _____ a new job.

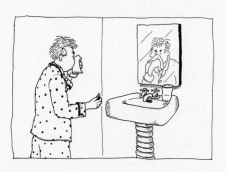

3. _____ bad.

   _____ the flu.

4. _____ nervous.

   _____ job interviews.

Blackline Masters

Name _____

A. Complete the sentences. Follow the example.

1. Nico _____ *makes* _____ (**make**) deliveries from 9:00 to 5:00.

   It's 4:00. So he __*'s making*__ deliveries now.

2. We usually _____ (**take**) a break at 10:00.

   It's 10:05. So we _____ (**take**) our break now.

3. My sister always _____ (**drive**) me to work on Mondays.

   It's Monday morning. So I _____ (**wait**) for her now.

4. My brother usually _____ (**drive**) to work.

   His car isn't working. So he _____ (**walk**) to work today.

5. Dora and Truc always _____ (**take**) the bus to work on rainy days.

   It _____ (**rain**) today. So they _____ (**take**) the bus to work.

6. Soo Ha usually _____ (**cook**) food in the restaurant.

   The busboy is sick today. So Soo Ha _____ (**clear**) tables.

7. Eva always _____ (**clean**) her desk before she goes home.

   She's ready to go. So she _____ (**put**) things away.

B. Write sentences. Write about yourself. Use the words in the box.
Use *always, usually, sometimes,* or *never.*

take the bus to work	use computers at work	work on Saturdays
work in the evening	am late for work	leave work early

1. I _____ *never take the bus to work* _____ .

2. I _____ .

3. I _____ .

4. I _____ .

5. I _____ .

6. I _____ .

Name _____

A. Complete the sentences. Use *can* or *can't*.

1. Leah and Robby are photographers.

   They ____can take____ (take) pictures, but they ____can't draw____ (draw) pictures.

2. Tuyet is a dressmaker.

   She _____ (make) dresses, but she _____ (make) suits.

3. We are bus mechanics.

   We _____ (fix) buses, but we _____ (fix) trucks.

4. Michael is a meat wrapper in the supermarket.

   He _____ (wrap) meat, but he _____ (cut) it.

5. Howard is a computer technician.

   He _____ (repair) computers, but he _____ (repair) monitors.

B. Complete the questions and answers. Follow the example.

1. **A** Sabrina is a secretary. She can type memos.

   B ____Can she____ type letters?

   A Yes, ____she can____ .

2. **A** Manuel is an electrician. He can fix wiring.

   B _____ fix cars?

   A No, _____ .

3. **A** Alice and Felix are bakers. They can bake cakes.

   B _____ decorate cakes?

   A Yes, _____ .

4. **A** I am a dancer. I can dance well.

   B _____ sing?

   A No, _____ .

Work Histories	
Casilda home care worker, 1995 child care worker, 1996–1997 student, 1998–present	**Zoltan** office cleaner, 1994–1995 taxi driver, 1996–1997 store manager, 1998–present
Evan gardener 1991–1995 electrician, 1995–1998	**Ahmed** waiter, 1992–1993 cook, 1994–present
Luis taxi driver, 1992–1995 dispatcher, 1996–present	**Lisa** sales clerk, 1995–1997 hair stylist, 1998–present

C. Read the work histories. Complete the sentences. Write *was, wasn't, were,* or *weren't.*

1. Zoltan _____**was**_____ a taxi driver. He _____**wasn't**_____ a truck driver.

2. Ahmed _____ a waiter. He _____ a busboy.

3. Luis and Zoltan _____ taxi drivers. They _____ bus drivers.

4. Casilda _____ a hospital worker. She _____ a child care worker.

D. Look at the work histories again. Complete the questions and answers. Follow the example.

1. _____**Was**_____ Evan a plumber? _____**No, he wasn't.**_____

2. _____ Luis and Zoltan drivers? _____

3. _____ Lisa a file clerk? _____

4. _____ Ahmed a waiter? _____

E. Complete the dialog. Use the work history for Casilda. Follow the example.

A What _____**was**_____ your last job, Casilda?

B I _____ a child care worker.

A Really? How long _____ you a child care worker?

B For one year. I _____ a home care worker before that.

© Steck-Vaughn Company. *English ASAP Level 1.* Permission granted to reproduce for classroom use.

U N I T 1

A. 1. are
    2. is
    3. are
    4. are
    5. are
    6. is
B. 1. They're
    2. He's
    3. We're
    4. I'm
    5. You're
    6. She's
    7. It's
    8. He's
C. 1. My
    2. Her
    3. His
    4. Their
    5. your
    6. Our
    7. His
    8. Their

U N I T 2

A. 1. he is
    2. they are
    3. it isn't
    4. it is
    5. we are
    6. I'm not
B. 1. Is she
    2. Are they
    3. Are you
    4. Is he
    5. Am I
    6. Is it
    7. Am I
    8. Is she
C. 1. b
    2. c
    3. a
    4. d
    5. f
    6. e

U N I T 3

A. 1. 's talking
    2. 's typing
    3. 's completing
    4. 're waiting
    5. 's carrying
    6. 're helping
B. 1. No, he isn't.
    2. Yes, she is.
    3. No, he isn't.
    4. Yes, they are.
    5. No, they aren't.
    6. Yes, they are.
C. 1. isn't repairing
    2. isn't copying
    3. aren't painting
    4. aren't going
    5. isn't talking
D. 1. **A** Is she, **B** is
    2. **A** Is he, **B** isn't
    3. **A** Are you, **B** am
    4. **A** Are they, **B** aren't
    5. **A** Are we, **B** are
E. 1. carpenter's
    2. carpenters'
    3. supervisor's
    4. messengers'
    5. Rita's

U N I T 4

A. 1. **A** Can I have, **B** can
    2. **A** Can we use, **B** can't
    3. **A** Can I leave, **B** can
    4. **A** Can I go, **B** can't
B. 1. What time is it? It's 1:45.
    2. What month is it? It's April.
    3. What year is it? It's 2001.
    4. What day is it? It's Thursday.
    5. What time is it? It's 11:30.
    6. What month is it? It's July.

U N I T 5

A. 1. a
    2. an
    3. a, a
    4. a
    5. an

B. **A** a
   A Some, an, some, a
   B a small watermelon
   A ~~some cherries~~
C. **A** How many
   A how much
   A How many
   A How much
D. some forks, some cream, a big cake, some
   ice cream, some spoons, some napkins, some
   plates, a tablecloth, some ice water, some
   glasses, an ashtray, a knife, some tea bags,
   some hot water, some cups, some fruit juice
E. How much ice cream, How many forks,
   How many plates, How much fruit juice,
   How many ashtrays

U N I T ◆6◆

A. 1. works
   2. work
   3. finish
   4. cleans
   5. closes
   6. wear
   7. drive
   8. parks
   9. counts
   10. close
B. 1. **A** Does, **B** doesn't
   2. **A** Do, **B** do
   3. **A** Do, **B** don't
   4. **A** Does, **B** does
   5. **A** Does, **B** doesn't
   6. **A** Does, **B** doesn't
C. 1. do you start
   2. does she leave
   3. does our class end
   4. do you take
   5. do the cleaners come
D. 1. these, those
   2. that, this
   3. this, that
   4. those, these

U N I T ◆7◆

A. **A** are there, **B** There are
   A are there, **B** There are

A are there, **B** There's
B There's
B. 1. Is there; Yes, there is.
   2. Are there; No, there aren't.
   3. Is there; Yes, there is.
   4. Is there; No, there isn't.
   5. Are there; Yes, there are.
   6. Are there; No, there aren't.

U N I T ◆8◆

A. 1. **A** How does your son feel, **B** feels
   2. **A** How does Sonia feel, **B** feels
   3. **A** How do you feel, **B** feel
   4. **A** How do your friends feel, **B** feel
B. 1. He feels, He has
   2. She feels, She has
   3. He feels, He has
   4. They feel, They have

U N I T ◆9◆

A. 1. makes, 's making
   2. take, 're taking
   3. drives, 'm waiting
   4. drives, 's walking
   5. take, 's raining, 're taking
   6. cooks, 's clearing
   7. cleans, 's putting
B. *Many answers are possible.*

U N I T ◆10◆

A. 1. can take, can't draw
   2. can make, can't make
   3. can fix, can't fix
   4. can wrap, can't cut
   5. can repair, can't repair
B. 1. **B** Can she, **A** she can
   2. **B** Can he, **A** he can't
   3. **B** Can they, **A** they can
   4. **B** Can you, **A** I can't
C. 1. was, wasn't
   2. was, wasn't
   3. were, weren't
   4   wasn't, was
D. 1. Was; No, he wasn't.
   2. Were; Yes, they were.
   3. Was; No, she wasn't.
   4. Was; Yes, he was.
E. **A** was, **B** was, **A** were, **B** was

Individual Competency Chart

Learner _____

Class _____

Teacher _____

Unit 1

	Date Presented	Date Checked	Result (✔)	Comments
1. Introduce yourself				
2. Make introductions				
3. Complete forms for work				

Unit 2

	Date Presented	Date Checked	Result (✔)	Comments
1. Give directions to places at work				
2. Understand directions to places at work				
3. Name places at work				
4. Use a to-do list				

 **Level 1**

Individual Competency Chart

Learner _____

Class _____

Teacher _____

Unit 3

	Date Presented	Date Checked	Result (✔)	Comments
1. Listen to and follow instructions				
2. Set up and use a machine				
3. Read a diagram				
4. Explain how to use a machine				

Unit 4

	Date Presented	Date Checked	Result (✔)	Comments
1. Read, write, and say times, days, and dates				
2. Interpret work schedules				
3. Ask to change your work hours				
4. Respond to schedule changes				

Individual Competency Chart

Learner _____

Class _____

Teacher _____

Unit 5

	Date Presented	Date Checked	Result (✔)	Comments
1. Greet customers				
2. Give good customer service				
3. Understand commitments to customers				
4. Respond to customers' complaints				

Unit 6

	Date Presented	Date Checked	Result (✔)	Comments
1. Follow company rules				
2. Call in sick				
3. Use polite language				
4. Improve your performance				

 **Level 1**

Individual Competency Chart

Learner _____

Class _____

Teacher _____

Unit 7

	Date Presented	Date Checked	Result (✔)	Comments
1. Count money				
2. Fill out a time card				
3. Make a deposit				
4. Understand a W-4 form				

Unit 8

	Date Presented	Date Checked	Result (✔)	Comments
1. Identify parts of the body				
2. Handle an emergency				
3. Describe symptoms, injuries, and illnesses				
4. Read safety signs				
5. Follow safety instructions				

Individual Competency Chart

Learner _____

Class _____

Teacher _____

Unit 9

	Date Presented	Date Checked	Result (✔)	Comments
1. Give and receive feedback				
2. Talk about job duties				
3. Evaluate your work				
4. Identify work skills				

Unit 10

	Date Presented	Date Checked	Result (✔)	Comments
1. Describe your job skills				
2. Read help-wanted ads				
3. Figure out the best job for you				
4. Complete a job application				

 **Level 1**

Class Cumulative Competency Chart

Unit _____ Class _____

Teacher _____

Workforce Skills

Name   **Comments**

English ASAP:
Connecting English to the Workplace
Certificate of Completion

This is to certify that

_____

has successfully completed Level 1 of
Steck-Vaughn's English ASAP series

_____
Instructor

_____
Organization or Program

_____
City and State

_____
Date

STECK-VAUGHN
C O M P A N Y
A Division of Harcourt Brace & Company